Rethinking Kant

Rethinking Kant: Volume I

Edited by

Pablo Muchnik

Rethinking Kant: Volume I, Edited by Pablo Muchnik

This book first published 2008. The present binding first published 2009.

Cambridge Scholars Publishing

12 Back Chapman Street, Newcastle upon Tyne, NE6 2XX, UK

British Library Cataloguing in Publication Data
A catalogue record for this book is available from the British Library

ISBN (10): 1-4438-1432-6, ISBN (13): 978-1-4438-1432-4

TABLE OF CONTENTS

ACKNOWLEDGEMENTS

This collection of essays bears witness to the richness and vitality of Kantian studies in North America. It contains the bulk of the papers presented at the Fourth Annual Meeting of the Eastern Study Group of the North American Kant Society (ENAKS), which took place at the University of Southern Maine in May 2007. Including pieces from the session chairs, host, and keynote speaker, it provides a sample of a whole generation of Kantian thought, ranging from doctoral students and recent Ph.Ds, to up-and-coming young scholars, to some well-established and influential players in the field. Gathering voices from philosophers at all levels of their professional development, this anthology offers a glimpse at the current state of Kantian scholarship in the US.

It was the need to pursue this type of dialogue that led Sharon Anderson-Gold to found the ENAKS in 2004. The fourth meeting was particularly auspicious: we had the good fortune of selecting a handful of papers from a large pool of first-rate submissions, and the host, Robert B. Louden, did a superb job at creating an informal and intimate atmosphere that promoted the exchange among participants. I am grateful for their vision, kindness, and support.

As the program coordinator, I had the pleasure to collaborate with Jennifer Mensch (Penn State University), Yvonne Unna (Seton Hall University), and Mark White (College of Staten Island and The Graduate Center, CUNY), who integrated the selection committee and showed fine judgment in choosing the papers for the conference. Without their "invisible hand" this anthology would not have been possible. Although I am the editor, the collection is theirs in many ways.

My student assistants at Siena College, Meredith Weinman and Samantha Montalbano, were very diligent in dealing with some of the technical difficulties of assembling the volume. Susan Kuebler, the department's secretary, offered her valuable skills with utmost generosity every time I needed her. Robert Gressis volunteered useful editing suggestions in the last stages of revision and was inexhaustible in this Sherlockean task.

With the exception of Dr. Louden's paper, all essays appear for the first time in this volume. We thank the journal *Studies in History and Philosophy of Science* and Elsevier publishers for permission to reprint Professor Louden's piece in this context.

ABBREVIATIONS

Ak *Immanuel Kants Schriften*. Ausgabe der königlich preussischen Akademie der Wissenschaten (Berlin: W. de Gruyter, 1902–)

EF *Zum ewigen Frieden: Ein philosophischer Entwurf* (1795), Ak 8
Toward Perpetual Peace: A Philosophical Project

G *Grundlegung zur Metaphysik der Sitten* (1785), Ak 4
Groundwork of the Metaphysics of Morals

I *Idee zu einer allgemeinen Geschichte in weltbürgerlicher Absicht* (1784), Ak 8
Idea toward a Universal History with a Cosmopolitan Aim

KrV *Kritik der reinen Vernunft* (1781, 1787). Cited by A/B pagination.
Critique of Pure Reason

KpV *Kritik der praktischen Vernunft* (1788), Ak 5
Critique of Practical Reason

KU *Kritik der Urteilskraft* (1790), AK 5
Critique of the Power of Judgment

MAN *Metaphysiche Anfangsgründe der Naturwissenschaft*, AK 4
Metaphysical Foundations of Natural Science

MS *Metaphysik der Sitten* (1797-1798), Ak 6
Metaphysics of Morals

O *Was heißt: Sich im Denken orientieren?* (1786), Ak 8
What does it Mean to Orient Oneself in Thinking?

P *Prolegomena zu einer jeden künftigen Metaphysik die als Wissenschaft wird auftreten können*
Prolegomena to any Future Metaphysics

R *Religion innerhalb der Grenzen der bloßen Vernunft* (1793-1794), Ak 6
Religion Within the Boundaries of Mere Reason

SF *Streit der Fakultäten* (1798), Ak 7
Conflict of the Faculties

TP *Über den Gemeinspruch: Das mag in der Theorie richtig sein, taugt aber nicht für die Praxis* (1793), Ak 8
On the Common Saying: That May Be Correct in Theory But It Is of No Use in Practice

VA *Anthropologie in Pragmatischer Hinsicht* (1798), Ak 7
Anthropology from a Pragmatic Standpoint

Vorlesungen über Anthropologie, Ak 25
Lectures on Anthropology

VE *Vorlesungen über Ethik*, Ak 27
Lectures on Ethics

VL *Vorlesungen über Logik*, Ak 9, 24
Lectures on Logic

VP *Pädagogik*, Ak 9
Lectures on Pedagogy

VpR *Vorlesungen über die philosophische Religionslehre*, Ak 28
Lectures on the Philosophical Doctrine of Religion

WA *Beantwortung der Frage: Was ist Aufklärung?* (1784), Ak 8
An Answer to the Question: What is Enlightenment?

INTRODUCTION

PABLO MUCHNIK

This collection contains essays on different aspects of Kant's philosophy, which can be grouped according to five themes:

I– Issues in Kantian Freedom

Kant did not exaggerate when he claimed that freedom "is the keystone of the whole structure of a system of pure reason." (KpV 5: 3) [1] His philosophical ingenuity was driven in great measure by a passionate defense of freedom in every domain of human interest, tempered by a sobering recognition of the limits in all that is human.

There is perhaps no topic more perplexing in this regard than Kant's endorsement of the truth of determinism and his simultaneous commitment to the freedom of the will. Kant defends the former truth in the Second Analogy of Experience, where he shows that objective succession requires that alterations follow causal laws; the reality of freedom, on the other hand, Kant establishes in the Deduction of the *Critique of Practical Reason*. His strategy to reconcile these seemingly contradictory tenets is well known: a strict division of labor preserves each truth by restricting its sphere of influence. Thus, determinism holds with respect to agents as they appear in time (i.e., *agents qua phenomena*), but not as they are in themselves (i.e., *agents qua noumena*). For, *in themselves*, agents are not as they appear in time, and hence can be thought to be free without contradiction. On the basis of this *theoretical* possibility, and resorting to the doctrine of the "fact of reason," Kant is

[1] Quotations from Kant are in accordance with the *Akademie-Edition* Vol. 1-29 of *Kants Gesammelte Schriften*, Berlin/Leipzig, 1902—. I follow the English translation in the *Cambridge Edition of the Works of Immanuel Kant*, Guyer and Wood editors (1992–), or the translations in the *Cambridge Texts in the History of Philosophy*.References to the *Critique of Pure Reason* follow the customary pagination of the first (A) and second (B) edition.

able to demonstrate the objective *practical* reality of the concept of freedom in the second *Critique*.

Although Kant is an incompatibilist when it comes to freedom, his position is unlike any other incompatibilist. For, while recognizing a fundamental conflict between determinism and free will, he simultaneously preserves the truth of determinism. The viability of this balancing act hangs on how to interpret the suggested division of labor between these concepts. In "Incompatibilism in Kant's Theory of Free Will," Ben Vilhauer argues that *only* the "ontological" interpretation, which recognizes the priority of the noumenal over the phenomenal world, can serve Kant's purposes. This view goes against the grain of the so-called "two-aspect" interpretation, usually associated with Henry Allison.[2] According to Allison's metaphysically deflationary view, phenomena and noumena refer to the same *things*. Kant's distinction, then, is meant to point to the different epistemic or semantic relationships we establish (at the meta-level of philosophical reflection) with the single ontological set of empirical objects.

Vilhauer believes that Allison's ontological evasion leads to a conceptual stalemate: unless there is a substantial reason to consider agents as noumena being more fundamentally what they *are*, "the non-determinism of agents qua noumena can do nothing to undermine the significance of phenomenal determinism…This is a view of free will which there is just as much reason to call compatibilistic as there is to call incompatibilistic." (p. 35)

Given Vilhauer's diagnosis of Allison's problem, his solution naturally follows. If we want to preserve Kant's incompatibilism, we must accept the ontological interpretation, because it is the only one equipped to tip the balance: the ontological priority of agents qua noumena ontologically undermines the significance of phenomenal determinism for agents' free will. That is, since agents qua noumena are ontologically prior to agents qua phenomena, the fact that agents qua noumena are *not* subject to determinism trumps the fact that, qua phenomena, they are. For Vilhauer, it is this metaphysical trump card that we should be concerned with in addressing issues such as free will. [3]

---

[2] See Henry Allison, *Kant's Transcendental Idealism* (New Haven: Yale University Press, 1983).

[3] Vilhauer's defense of the ontological interpretation turns on the idea that choices of maxims by agents qua noumena determine empirical causal laws, which are only instantiated by the empirical-psychological events that are the appearances of those agents' free choices.

Another puzzling feature in Kant's conception of freedom has to do with the *strictly epistemic* role one must attribute to spontaneity according to the teachings of the first *Critique*. In the Paralogisms, however, Kant betrays his best philosophical sense and makes substantial judgments about the "I" of the "I think" of the unity of apperception. Such judgments are unwarranted and lack epistemic value. Making them, Kant ignores the noumenal ignorance he has so diligently argued for in the Analytic. This is the problem Jason Fisette addresses in "The Last Beatitude of Self: Spontaneity's 'Place' in the Objectivity of the World." He describes Kant's struggle to "clean the clock of those peddling metaphysical truths about 'the soul,'" which unavoidably plague us when "we make claims about the self's noumenal freedom or spontaneity." (p. 49)

According to Fisette, Kant's metaphysical lapse is due to an impossible double bind. On the one hand, Kant needs spontaneity to explain how the knowing subject brings the world into view by unifying intuitions under concepts. In the Transcendental Deduction, Kant shows that the cognitive import of received intuitions depends on a spontaneous act of synthesis on the part of the subject, who must subsume the sensible manifold into unity under the concept of an object in general. This spontaneous activity introduces objective necessity to our representations by connecting them in judgments according to the unifying rules of the categories. However, as Kant indicates in a famous footnote (KrV B 158), one cannot possibly determine one's spontaneity as an object without unwittingly placing the free, determining self, into the realm of causally determined phenomenal objects. The paradox Kant faces, as Fisette pithily puts it, is that I lose "what I wanted to represent –my spontaneity–... in the effort to represent it." (p. 55)

This paradox explains why, on the other hand, Kant yields to the temptation of attributing spontaneity to the thinking self. Such attribution smuggles substantive commitments into the putatively logical subject of the transcendental unity of apperception. Yet, according to Kant's own critical strictures, nothing can be epistemically predicated of the thinking self without turning it into the empirical self.[4] Indeed, the goal of the Paralogisms is to warn us *not* to take the logical function of the self as if it were indicative of what it *really is* (i.e., spontaneous, simple, identical through time, etc.). But Kant flouts his own lesson of epistemic humility

---

[4] Fisette follows Robert Pippin's discussion of the problem. See Robert B. Pippin, "Kant on the Spontaneity of the Mind," *Canadian Journal of Philosophy* 17, no. 2 (June 1987), pp. 449-475.

and at moments speaks of the spontaneous self as if it were free from material causality.[5]

To escape this predicament, Fisette explores a variant of John McDowell's suggestion to introduce sociality, via language acquisition, into the atomistic Kantian subject.[6] "In being initiated into a language, a human being is introduced into something that already embodies putatively rational linkages…We can have a spontaneity that is not noumenal, and a knowledge that is not brutally causal, because there is not one order of causality, but two," (p. 64) namely, the natural and the cultural worlds. Such a move in Hegel's direction, Fisette claims, provides a way to avoid Kant's double bind while preserving his insight about an ineliminable human contribution to knowledge.

The discussion of Kantian freedom concludes with Diane Williamson's "The Merits and Deficiencies of Kant's 'Incorporation Thesis' as an Interpretation and a Revision." Williamson engages in a critical assessment of the mainstream reading of freedom in Kant's practical philosophy. This reading stems from what Henry Allison famously dubbed the "Incorporation Thesis," according to which inclinations cannot themselves be motives for action; all action must be construed, instead, as motivated by the choice of a maxim.[7] This choice is an act of freedom for which we hold the agent accountable, and without which we could not attribute rationality to her actions. Against the Humean view about the causal force of desires, Kant believes that for an inclination to be motivating the agent must first *incorporate* it into a maxim and take it as a reason—hence the name of Allison's thesis.

Kant expresses this view of motivation most clearly in the *Religion Within the Bounds of Reason Alone*.[8] The context is significant: Kant is describing here the choice of the agent's meta-maxim, i.e., the *Gesinnung* or moral disposition. According to this account, an agent's *Gesinnung* is either inherently good or inherently evil, depending on the way the agent combines the incentives of morality and happiness. Williamson's point is that the *Religion* essay does not support Allison's attempt to apply this portrayal of motivation to Kant's moral theory. For, she claims, the choice of maxims of action is clearly different from the choice of the meta-maxim

[5] See, for example, KrV A 546-7/B574-5.

[6] John McDowell, *Mind and Word* (Cambridge: Cambridge University Press, 2003).

[7] See Henry Allison, *Kant's Theory of Freedom* (Cambridge: Cambridge University Press, 1990).

[8] The passage in question is in R 6: 23-4.

(i.e., the *Gesinnung*). The latter is analogous to a religious conversion experience: it happens only once or twice in a person's life, and can be neither based on reasons (since it establishes the value reasons will subsequently have in her deliberations) nor can it be scrutinized. Allison glosses over these distinctive differences.

According to Williamson, the problem is compounded by the fact that influential contemporary interpreters of Kant accept and continue Allison's view.[9] The untoward consequence of this line of interpretation is that it downplays the difference between ordinary, heteronomous choices and autonomous, moral choices. Influenced by Allison, contemporary interpreters tend to assume that, because all choices are free in the sense of not being directly determined by inclination, they must also be free in the sense of being autonomous. Yet, Williamson complains, such an assumption conflates moral and prudential decision-making. This leads us to make Kantianism a hidden form of hedonism, at the expense of what is most valuable in Kant, i.e., his adamant defense of the absolute value of morality, independently of the desirability of consequences.

II- Dealing with Human Nature

Kant famously remarked in the *Logic* that all the fundamental questions of philosophy (What can I know? What should I do? and What may I hope for?) could be also expressed in the question: What is the human being?[10] Its answer partly depends on disentangling the complex relation between the noumenal and phenomenal dimensions of human nature.

In "Anthropology from a Kantian Point of View: Toward a Cosmopolitan Conception of Human Nature," Robert B. Louden places

---

[9] Williamson has Guyer and Korsgaard in mind. See Paul Guyer, *Kant on Freedom, Law, and Happiness* (Cambridge: Cambridge University Press, 2000), and Christine Korsgaard, *Creating the Kingdom of Ends* (Cambridge: Cambridge University Press, 1996).

[10] "The field of philosophy in the cosmopolitan sense can be brought down to the following questions:

1. What can I know?
2. What ought I to do?
3. What may I hope?
4. What is the human being?

Metaphysics answers the first question, *morals* the second, *religion* the third, and *anthropology* the fourth. Fundamentally, however, we could reckon all of this to anthropology, because the first three questions refer to the last one." (VL 9:25)

Kant's contributions to anthropology in the context of the emerging new science. At the time in which Kant started lecturing on anthropology in 1772, the study of human nature began to break loose from its traditional theological shackles. Kant was the first academic to teach regular courses in this area. His approach, self-described as "pragmatic," differs from the anthropologies advocated by other early contributors to the discipline. These were concerned with physiology and medicine, rather than with what Kant calls "the knowledge of the world," i.e., "the skill of social intercourse, the method of educating and governing human beings, hence of everything that pertains to the practical."[11] As Kant adeptly puts it in the Preface to *Anthropology from a Pragmatic Point of View*, "physiological knowledge of the human being concerns the investigation of what *nature* makes of the human being; pragmatic, the investigation of what *he* as a free-acting being makes of himself, or can and should make of himself." (VA 7: 119) The methodologically distinctive feature of the new discipline is its empirical (a posteriori) character, as opposed to the a priori and transcendental procedure Kant reserves for his "pure ethics." That is, pragmatic anthropology is a *Beobachtungslehre*, an empirical doctrine based on observation, and hence concerned with the "phenomenal effects of human freedom in the empirical world, not freedom's allegedly non-empirical origins." (p. 95)

To better understand what Kant means by "pragmatic," Louden suggests focusing on a fundamental feature that has been under-appreciated in previous discussions, namely, the particular conception of human nature anthropology leads to when properly pursued. Louden calls this conception "cosmopolitan" (*weltbürgerlich*), and interprets it as having an essentially normative function: not being tied to the idiosyncrasies of time and place, the cosmopolitan conception of human nature has an inherently critical thrust. It grasps "what human beings in all times and places share with one another" (p. 95) and hence allows us to gauge local practices in its light.[12]

There is a tension, Louden notes, between the universal and normative pretensions of Kant's cosmopolitan anthropology and its deliberately empirical character. The tension diminishes, however, once we understand

---

[11] This is extracted from a letter to Marcus Herz of 1773 (AA 10: 145). "Practical" in this context is to be understood in relation to the useful, in contrast to the merely theoretical. As Louden makes clear in the paper, Kant does not mean it in the "narrower sense of 'morally practical.'" (p. 95) "Pragmatic" has to do with prudence (*Klugheit*) and involves skill in achieving happiness and wellbeing.

[12] Kant believes that the most basic commonality is expressed in human rights, whose critical force lies in their inviolable and inalienable nature.

that "the kind of empirical knowledge [Kant] is referring to in his anthropology is one that, while experienced-based, emphasizes reflection about the chief tendencies and characteristics of the human species as a whole, rather than limited and partial observations about the behavior of particular individuals or groups." (p. 101) It is this reflective character, Louden argues, that serves as a "teleological moral map" (p. 102) to orient the human species in its historical endeavors. This has an important consequence on how to interpret Kant's anthropology: the morally neutral sense of a merely *pragmatic* "knowledge of the world" yields to an overarching moral vision of the destiny of the human species. Given the centrality of Kant's *cosmopolitan* view, there is little room for applying this knowledge to immoral purposes –a possibility that the weaker sense of "pragmatic" could not rule out. Bringing to the fore this moral dimension, Louden sheds light on the connection anthropology has with Kant's pure ethics, an issue that that has perplexed interpreters since the *Groundwork*.

In his "Understanding Kant's Claim that 'Morality cannot be without Anthropology,'" Oliver Thorndike traces the notion of *pragmatic anthropology* back to its roots in Kant's rationalist predecessor, Alexander Gottlieb Baumgarten. This alternative road, Thorndike argues, opposes those who attribute a fundamental role to anthropology in Kant's moral philosophy.[13] The genealogical approach suggests, rather, that anthropology is only "a side-project" for Kant. The key to reaching this conclusion is to realize that for Baumgarten obligation requires empirical motivating grounds. And "it is precisely because Kant dissolves the connection between empirical motivating grounds and morality … that any empirical anthropology cannot be philosophically significant for [Kant]." (p. 113) Instead, its significance is reduced to pedagogical and prudential functions, which have to do with the realization –but not the foundation– of moral ends. This justifies Kant's frequent claim that "morality cannot be without anthropology," but must not be construed as entailing any substantial *philosophical* (i.e., a priori and transcendental) contribution.

Thorndike argues that the watershed between Kant and his predecessor resides in Kant's refusal to conflate moral necessity with the psychological necessity of the most effective motivating grounds, the so-called "*causa impulsiva*." This conflation led Baumgarten to conceive the science of ethics as a unity of morality and anthropology. To obligate an agent, for Baumgarten, is to connect a motivating ground to her will. This

[13] In this list, Thorndike includes Robert B. Louden, Clemens Schwaiger and Werner Stark.

assumption sets the agenda for practical philosophy: the goal "is to make cognitions of the good effective." (p.119)

From the 1770's onward, and coinciding with the beginning of his anthropological lectures, Kant excludes all empirical conditions of volition from the metaphysical foundation of morality. Thorndike argues that this has one important implication: the dismissal of Baumgarten's empirical psychology from practical philosophy. Kant's new discipline of anthropology will welcome the outcast. Yet, the price of acceptance is to admit the *philosophical* marginality of the new body of doctrine.

III- Issues in Teleology

Whatever conclusion the reader might reach about the relation between morality and anthropology, it is clear that Kant's view of human nature is infused with an ambitious moral teleology: the realization of highest good in the world. Eoin O'Connell's "Motivation, Futility, and the Highest Good in Kant's Practical Philosophy" addresses some of the difficulties associated with the *motivational* role this idea plays in Kant's moral theory. As we have seen, Kant's foundational perspective, articulated most clearly in the Analytic of the second *Critique* and the *Groundwork*, requires a strict separation between a priori and empirical grounds for action. This leads to an apparently irreconcilable conflict between the demands of happiness and morality, whose claims are equally pressing for a will like ours –that is, a will neither totally rational nor totally sensible. The internal heterogeneity of human volition gives rise to a "natural dialectic," (G 4: 405) which Kant eventually construes in terms of an "antinomy of practical reason." (KpV 5: 113) The doctrine of the highest good is tailored to solve this antinomy by accommodating both sensible and rational demands in a single volitional object we *ought* to pursue, namely, the idea of a state of affairs in which an agent's happiness is proportional to her virtue.[14] Yet, since the order of nature and the order of freedom are incommensurably different for Kant, the attainability of such a situation involves the postulation of freedom, the immortality of the soul, and God's existence –ideas declared epistemically empty in the first *Critique*.

The introduction of happiness as part of our moral teleology, however,

[14] Kant interprets such proportionality in terms of a synthetic causal relation: in the highest good "the morality of disposition," which pertains to my existence as noumenal agent, has "a connection, and indeed a necessary connection, as cause with happiness in the sensible world, if not immediately yet mediately (by means of an intelligible author of nature)." (KpV: 5: 115)

raises important questions about Kant's conception of autonomy. The purity of virtue seems now soiled by the expectation of reward, threatening to transform the Kantian agent into a disingenuous and far-seeing egoist.[15] Traditionally, to solve this problem, sympathetic readers of Kant have appealed to the object/determining ground distinction.[16] By this means, the autonomy of the will is preserved by maintaining the purity of the motivational *ground*; the demands for happiness, on the other hand, find a place in the ultimate *object* of practical reason (the highest good), whose attainability presupposes the purity of the ground as a necessary condition.

The operating assumption in this line of defense is that for Kant human action is both motivated and purposeful, but that each of these features is analytically independent and should be kept apart. In order to preserve the purity of the will, we must separate the highest good from the motivational ground and construe it as an object (or consequent). This distinction serves to leave the purely formal conception of the moral law intact. Furthermore, against Lewis Beck's famous disparagement of the highest good as both unnecessary and unconvincing, these sympathetic readers argue that its significance lies precisely in its capacity to orient our moral endeavors and avert the sense of futility which otherwise would invade us.[17] For, as Kant notices, without an ultimate object to which we can legitimately direct our moral intentions, human beings would fall into despair and moral depression (R 6: 4-5).

O'Connell, however, is skeptical about the neatness of the proposed distinction. If we examine things from the perspective of motivation, the difference between object and ground is far more fluid than these sympathetic readers seem to admit. Lacking an object to which we can direct our moral efforts, O'Connell notices, directly affects the grounds of motivation whose purity Kant wants to preserve. For, given Kant's psychological assumptions, lacking an object is simply de-motivating. The specter of futility haunts our motivational grounds —having an end sustains our moral commitment and prevents us from falling prey to apathetic indifference. The ground, therefore, *requires* an object to be psychologically effective. Their conceptual distinction overlooks an essential feature of Kant's theory of motivation (i.e., the assumption that is

[15] This is the language of Schopenhauer, quoted by O'Connell (p. 140).

[16] See Frederick Beiser, "Moral Faith and the Highest Good" in Paul Guyer (ed.) *The Cambridge Companion to Kant and Modern Philosophy* (Cambridge: Cambridge University Press, 2006), and Allen Wood, *Kant's Moral Religion* (Ithaca: Cornell University Press, 1970).

[17] See Lewis White Beck, *A Commentary to Kant's Critique of Practical Reason* (Chicago: Chicago University Press, 1960), pp. 242 ff.

impossible to act without envisioning an end). While the distinction manages to preserve the will's autonomy, it ignores the psychological principles that make the highest good necessary in the first place. O'Connell's conclusion is that the moral motive in Kant's doctrine cannot completely dispense with the "impurity" of content. This entails that the highest good "smuggles a degree of heteronomy into the moral disposition that effectively sullies the purity of the moral will." (p. 160)

Karl Ameriks' "The End of Kant's *Critiques*: Kant's Moral 'Creationism'" approaches the question of teleology by analyzing the concluding sections of the *Critique of the Power of Judgment*. His guiding intuition is that "[a]t the end of a book devoted precisely to the topic of teleology, it is only natural to expect a significant confirmation of what Kant's whole system has been primarily aiming at all along." (p. 169) Under the "maze of terminological complications" accompanying the theoretical and moral proofs of God's existence, Ameriks finds evidence for reaching a general conclusion: "Kant's *Critiques* can be understood as confirming what I believe most of us would now call a more objectivist than subjectivist attitude toward the conclusion that persons have been created for a purpose." (p. 169) Sustaining this conclusion is Ameriks' interpretation of the attitude of *Fürwahrhalten,* a term that eschews a simple English translation. It could be rendered as "holding to be true" or "holding true," where the agent's commitments to both "holding" and "truth" are essential.

The sense we give to this terminology, Ameriks observes, carries consequences for how to interpret the status of moral belief and faith in Kantian ethics –topics that have been generally misinterpreted in the secondary literature. The crux of the problem is how to understand the "facticity" of the moral law and the standing of freedom in Kant's system. In §91, Kant distinguishes between three types of "cognizable things": matters of opinion, matters of fact, and matters of faith alone (KU 5: 467). It is tempting to assimilate them to the holding true characteristic of "opinion," "faith" (*Glaube*), and "knowing" (*Wissen*), as they appear in Kant's theoretical philosophy.[18] However, Ameriks points out, this would

[18] Ameriks refers here to KrV A822/B850 and VL 9: 65. He describes thus the different forms of holding true that accompany them: "'opinion' designates the holding true that is merely theoretical, with grounds that are subjectively as well as objectively insufficient; *Glaube* is treated at first simply as a practical attitude with grounds that are said to be subjectively sufficient but objectively insufficient; and 'knowing' is understood in a rigorous sense that requires grounds that are both

be a gross misunderstanding: such assimilation distorts the objectivity of the practical cognition (*Erkenntnis*) of the moral law and its immediate implication regarding human freedom. Their facticity refuses to be interpreted away as a *subjective* matter of faith. Yet, due perhaps to the hegemony of the model of speculative reason, Kant does not consider practical cognition as a form of knowledge (*Wissen*). Kant's reservation, unfortunately, encourages the tendency to take that cognition as if it were merely subjective. The consequence of this assimilation is to ignore that practical cognition "actually has a firmness and universal scope ... that arguably makes it even more, rather than less, objective than theoretical knowledge." (p. 178-9) That is, in Ameriks' reading, basic practical cognitions are more objective and "knowledge-like" than Kant's language often suggests.

Things look different when we consider the ideas of God, immortality and the highest good. Here the attitude of faith (*Glaube*) is appropriate, for these ideas have a different status than freedom and the moral law. The first-person character and free commitment of our holding them to be true, however, should not be taken to mean that faith in them is in some sense "idiosyncratic, private, or optional." On the contrary, Kant emphasizes their necessity for all finite rational beings. Yet, our holding them true is unlike what we experience in practical cognition. The difference, Ameriks suggests, should be interpreted in terms of whether an idea can be fundamentally understood as occurring entirely within oneself or as it extends beyond one's own will. The former is the case with freedom and the moral law; the latter obtains for the postulates of God, immortality, and the highest good.[19]

Ameriks' basic point is that Kant's distinction between these two types of holding true mirrors the difference between *intention* and *product*, which he construes in terms of basic and mediate levels of practical reason. Whereas "our freedom is so 'immediately' tied to the moral law all by itself, it is, Kant realizes, on a different level than the indirectly inferred notions of God and immortality, which have to do with reflective conditions of our realizing the ends of morality in action, and not simply intending to accept the law." (p. 182)

The organizing principle of this two-tier classification of ideas also accounts for why Kant refuses to grant happiness an unconditional value. The pursuit of happiness "makes us hostage of contingent fortune, whereas

---

subjectively and objectively sufficient and is illustrated solely by theoretical reason." (p. 178)

[19] Ameriks suggests that, in spite of the letter of Kant's writings, we interpret the highest good instead of freedom as a postulate (p. 182).

a good intention has an unconditional value because it is something that we know we can always immediately bring into being without concern for reward." (p. 183) However, since the products of our effort cannot possibly be a matter of indifference for us, we are led to find an indirect "guarantee" that the right consequences will nonetheless come about. This is the psychological root of rational faith (*Vernuftglaube*), the highest type of holding true for Kant. At the basis of this fundamental attitude, Ameriks detects an increment of the degree of "riskiness." We move from (1) the practical cognition of the moral law and the acceptance of the highest good as a necessary ideal, to (2) the recognition of the necessary conditions outside our control for its realization, to (3) the steadfast commitment to gradually actualize this transcendent ideal in the immanent world. This movement reflects also an increment of the degree of uncertainty about the results of our volitions and explains the "subjectivity" Kant attributes to moral faith. "Because the relation between … matters of faith and our original moral intention is metaphysically external rather than internal, our confidence in their existence or realization has to be highly qualified." (p. 183)

In this externality Ameriks finds the key to elucidating the complex status of faith in Kant's taxonomy of holding true: neither a matter of knowledge nor of mere opinion, faith relies on subjective grounds; yet, the subjectivity of those grounds is not private or idiosyncratic, for they are binding on all human beings and resemble the "objective." The subjectivity of faith has nothing to do, then, with its optional character; rather, it is the mark of our "distinctive and ultimately contingent need to be satisfied with something real and separate from us in this world –and therefore not to be able to know how that satisfaction will take place through any of our capacities of determinative judgment." (p. 192)

IV– The Reality of Evil

Even if we accept Ameriks' objectivist reading of moral faith, the question still remains: can anything straight come out of the crooked wood of humanity? Indeed, the most dramatic challenge to Kant's moral teleology comes from the doctrine of radical evil. In the first book of the *Religion within the Boundaries of Mere Reason*, Kant infamously claimed, "The human being (*der Mensch*) is evil by nature." Furthermore, since the "nature" in question is to be understood in moral terms, the "evil" we attribute to it must be represented as self-imposed, i.e., the result of a choice prior to any use of freedom in time. No agent is exempt from Kant's condemnation, not even the best of us. This razing anthropological indictment, therefore, casts a skeptical shadow on the feasibility of the collective pursuit of the highest good. For, Kant argues, there is no reason to exempt any human being from having inverted the ethical order of priority between the incentives of sensibility and rationality, i.e., between the demands of happiness (organized by the principle of self-love) and the demands of morality (organized by the Categorical Imperative) (R 6: 36). The radicalism of evil, therefore, threatens to break the synthetic causal connection between virtue and happiness, the cornerstone of Kant's moral teleology.

Yet, there seems to be something *prima facie* suspicious about Kant's view of evil. As Claudia Card has recently argued, Kant's description of evil as an inversion of the ethical order of priority between the incentives treats all wrongs in exactly the same way, and hence is incapable of distinguishing between their severity.[20] In Kant's view, a subway free-rider, a rapist, a murderer, a suicide bomber, etc., have all equally given priority to the pursuit of happiness over duty. Hence, the primacy of self-love in all these cases is uninformative about their respective wrongs. In order to appreciate the difference these wrongs make in our moral judgments, we must take into account the suffering involved in each of them. However, Kant refuses to gauge immorality on the basis of suffering, putting his view at odds with our moral sensibility.

In "How to Be Evil: The Moral Psychology of Immorality," Robert Gressis mounts a defense of the explanatory power of Kant's view. His strategy consists in providing a more subtle account of what is entailed in the pursuit of happiness. Essential for his reconstruction is the role of self-deception. For, given the Incorporation Thesis and the overriding authority of the moral law for Kant, people must first convince themselves that what they are doing is *not* evil if they are to engage in it. To be evil requires the agent to toy with her conscience and persuade herself of the acceptability of the action. This is due to Kant's basic motivational assumption: people act only *sub specie boni*.

There are, however, two kinds of fundamental goodness for Kant, prudential and moral, which organize the agent's *Gesinnung* depending on whether she sets happiness or duty as her ultimate end. But, if happiness is a kind of good, how is it possible for it to give rise to evil? In Gressis' reading, the answer lies in understanding that happiness has a twofold aspect for Kant: in order to judge herself happy, the agent must reflect on her whole existence and compare her lot to that of others. One's sense of

---

[20] See Claudia Card, *The Atrocity Paradigm: A Theory of Evil* (Oxford: Oxford University Press, 2002), p. 82.

happiness, therefore, contains an ineliminable comparative/competitive dimension and cannot be reduced to a mere hedonistic calculus. Our "consciousness of the agreeableness of life" (KpV, 5: 22), which at first sight seems to be based on a purely self-referential judgment, is in fact socially mediated. "Thus, to say that someone, owing to her evil *Gesinnung*, judges her happiness to be more important than morality reduces to the claim that she is willing to flout a moral obligation whenever doing so allows her to think that her life is going as well or better than others." (p. 204) This social component at the heart of self-love accounts for the great variability we see in the tolerance-thresholds for immorality among different individuals, as well as for the uncanny capacity of groups to create blind spots and obliterate the rules of moral salience.

To flesh out some of the basic mechanisms of self-deception, Gressis draws on a passage of the *Collins Lectures Notes* where Kant introduces the notion of "moral fantasies" (VE 27: 348). These fantasies are tailored to silence the qualms of consciousness by either creating the illusion of an "indulgent moral law" or, alternatively, producing the fancy that "our moral perfections … are in conformity with the moral law." Gressis calls these self-justifying stratagems "the exceptionalist" and "the adequacy" fantasies. He traces them to different variants of self-love (*philautia* and *arrogantia*), and explains how, due to the universal propensity to evil in human nature, they are used to cope with the unremitting demands of the moral law in order to preserve a semblance of self-esteem. The "adequacy fantasy" allows the agent to determine her happiness by comparing herself with the expectations of the group, and the "exceptionalist fantasy" allows her to set in motion rationalizing mechanisms that grant her moral holidays.

Gressis' taxonomy is meant to provide the largely missing psychological scaffolding supporting Kant's view of evil. With a better understanding of the multiple shapes the pursuit of happiness has in Kant, Gressis takes the sting out of Card's objection. One begins to see that the primacy of self-love is far from innocent, far more widespread and pervasive than one might have initially guessed. To say the least, this realization introduces a cautionary note in Kant's otherwise upbeat account of moral progress.

David Cummiskey provides an example of how the reality of evil can be accommodated in Kant's system. In "Justice and Revolution in Kant's Political Philosophy," Cummiskey calls to task one of the most scandalous aspects of Kant's political thought: his unflinching refusal to authorize revolt against an oppressive government, even when its authority has become unbearably abusive. Such an absolute prohibition does not mesh well with Kant's forceful defense of the principles of republican government, individual rights, freedom, equality, and political justice. Nor does it seem consistent with the inference Kant draws of a fundamental moral disposition from the enthusiasm with which contemporary spectators received the French Revolution

Kant's argument for the absolute prohibition of revolution is based on his more general justification of property rights and civil society. Indeed, the prohibition is part of a general injunction against the individual's use of coercive means to promote her ends. However, Cummiskey notes, although Kant makes a clear case for obedience to imperfect states, he does not really consider the problems raised by systematic institutional oppression and exclusion of subjects. The general prohibition against revolution does not hold in this case, because utterly despotic states break all semblance of civil society and return its members to the state of war. The thesis that one may never rebel against an imperfect civil state is defensible along Kantian lines; de facto state power, however, can sometimes be worse than the state of nature. In that case, a government loses the right to obedience that normally obtains in legitimate states – sheer might yields no right for Kant.

The gist of Cummiskey's revision, then, lies in questioning Kant's identification of a civil state with the powers that be. Only the former commands obedience; the latter, however, may give reason for revolt, for they reintroduce the antagonism that justified making the political compound in the first place. "We should not use violence to reform imperfect civil societies but awesome power alone does not transform a mafia into a legitimate government." (p. 223) In the presence of a thuggish, despotic power, and according to the very spirit of the Kantian principles of justice, the obligation of its members is *not* to obey. For, in spite of the states' monopoly on coercion, there is no semblance of sovereignty in this case, which leaves individuals in a state of nature. The consequences are clear: the reasons that led individuals to originally abandon such a state, now lead them to revolution. Indeed, they are obligated, according to the implicit logic of Kant's view of justice, to "strive to bring forth, even by violent means, a true civil society." (p. 223)

We see Cummiskey in this paper marshalling the details of Kant's political theory to investigate whether Kant's idealism is equipped to handle the undeniable presence of evil. Kant's controversial prohibition against revolution illustrates the tension we detected above, i.e., how to harmonize a pessimistic moral anthropology with Kant's utopian project of realizing the highest good in the world. I believe Cummiskey's defense of the right of revolution points us in the right direction, namely, towards the dynamics of Kant's philosophy of history. Moral progress, as Kant puts it in *Idea for Universal History*, cannot sidestep the painful effects of antagonism (wars, violence, and, we might add, revolution), which, due to the "cunning of nature" become "in the long run the cause of a law-governed social order." (I 8: 20)[21] This instrumental view of conflict reminds us of Kant's treatment of the "woeful examples" radical evil parades before us, which provide a secret spur to culture in spite of the intentions of their perpetrators (R 6: 34-5). Revolution becomes necessary when the seemingly forward move towards civil society leads us in fact backwards, i.e., returns us to the violence of the state of nature. As Cummiskey suggests, the justice of using violence against that violence resembles the reasoning Kant uses to justify coercion in the *Metaphysics of Morals*.

V– Kant in Context

The last section of this anthology places Kant's critical philosophy in the post-Kantian context. In "The Principle of Determinability and the Possibility of Synthetic *A Priori* Judgments in Kant and Maimon," Seung-Kee Lee examines the way in which Kant's immediate successors dealt with the basic question of the *Critique of Pure Reason*: How are synthetic judgments possible a priori? There is an underrated philosophical hero driving the development of German Idealism, Salomon Maimon, whose influence on Fichte, Schelling, and Hegel is as undeniable as it is often overlooked. The importance of Maimon looms large once we realize that the traditional way of understanding the distinction between synthetic and analytic judgments, i.e., whether the predicate is or is not contained in the concept of the subject, neglects a more fundamental distinction, that between the determinate and the indeterminate. As Lee sees it:

> Kant explains that there are two ways in which the same logical form of judgment can be employed in the act of judging, viz., in a determinate way (for "cognizing objects") and an indeterminate way (for relating concepts in mere "thought"). In other words, whether or not the logical form of judgment applies to an object (i.e., is used as a *category*) depends on whether or not it is *determined* which of the two concepts is given the function of the subject and which is given the function of the predicate. The logical use of the

---

[21] Allen Wood develops this line of interpretation. See Allen Wood, *Kant's Ethical Thought* (Cambridge: Cambridge University Press, 1999), particularly pp. 283 ff.

understanding leaves it *undetermined* which concept will be given which function. (p. 252)

For Kant, the determinate use of the understanding requires the provision of a schema in order to apply "the category to the appearances" (KrV A 139/B 178). Such application allows the initially indeterminate judgment to become determinate. However, Maimon finds the master at fault here: "the appeal to a schema fails to explain specifically why, for example, the hypothetical form of judgment ('if P then Q') must be applicable to certain objects." (p. 261) That is, to know that objects *in general* must be thought in certain relations for experience to be possible does not explain how *particular* objects fall precisely in that relation. Maimon's point is that Kant's schematism begs the question of the concrete application of the categories to determinate appearances. That there must be causality in nature does not explain our particular causal judgments about, say, fire and warmth. Maimon's celebrated "principle of determinability" (*Satz der Bestimmbarkeit*) is tailored to succeed where Kant fails, namely, in showing how the subject and predicate concepts in a judgment stand in a *determinate* (as opposed to merely *indeterminate*) relation. This principle thus brings Kant's philosophy to fruition, "for, to show how such a relation is possible is tantamount to showing how synthetic a priori judgments are possible." (p. 249)

In his *Versuch über die Transcendentalphilosophie* (1790), Maimon acknowledges that the principle of contradiction may well explain the *modus operandi* of analytic propositions, but has nothing to say on how representations are connected in an object and not merely in thought. The principle of determinability explains how there can be *real* thoughts, as opposed to *formal* or *arbitrary* ones. Furthermore, Lee's analysis concludes by hinting at the way that Maimon's solution, via Fichte, shapes the course of post-Kantian idealism. Without the principle of determinability, Lee believes, Fichte would not have coined his principle of reciprocal determination (*Satz der Wechselbestimmung*), nor would have Schelling been able to formulate the question driving his philosophizing, i.e., how the absolute I can step out of itself and oppose to itself the not-I. Thus, Maimon's rephrasing of the Kantian problem of the synthetic a priori allows us to understand the development of German Idealism. Such development, Lee argues, hangs on the question: "how it is possible for the logical forms of judgment to be employed determinately (as opposed to indeterminately), that is, in such a way that the predicate and the subject concepts are connected not merely in thought, but also in the object." (p. 250)

In "The Third Dogma of Rationalism," Mark Okrent discusses the Kantian roots of the view common to Davidson, Sellars, Brandom, and Korsgaard (among many others), that "only a being that is capable of self-consciousness is capable of true, real, original intentionality." (p. 271) On this position, for example, no agent could want to eat and believe that that she could eat if she killed another animal unless she was capable of recognizing that she herself had beliefs and desires. Okrent terms this position the "Third Dogma of Rationalism" –a name that involves a playful reference to Davidson's identification of "conceptual schemes" as the "third dogma of empiricism," and draws on what John Haugeland called the first two rationalist dogmas: *positivism*, the "the metaphysical view that 'reality is exhausted by facts'," and *cognitivism*, "the assumption that 'reason is to be understood in terms of cognitive operations on cognitive states'."[22]

Okrent argues that the considerations that lead so many philosophers to the conclusion that all intentionality depends upon second order intentionality derive from two central Kantian theses. The first is Kant's famous formulation: "It must be possible for the 'I think' to accompany all my representations; for otherwise something would be represented in me which could not be thought at all, and that is equivalent to saying that the representation would be impossible, or at least would be nothing to me." (KrV B 132) On Okrent's interpretation, this view amounts to the claim that only agents that are capable of self-awareness through attaching the "I think" to their representations are capable of forming discursive judgments. The second thesis is pervasive in Kant's work, but is most famously summed up in *Groundwork*: "Everything in nature works in accordance with laws. Only a rational being has the capacity to act *in accordance with the representation* of laws, that is, in accordance with principles, or has a *will*. Since *reason* is required for the derivation of actions from laws, the will is nothing other than practical reason." (G 4: 413) As Robert Brandom nicely put it, "[w]hat makes us act as we do is not the rule itself but our *acknowledgement* of it."[23]

Okrent suggests that the third dogma of rationalism is motivated by an argument that uses these two Kantian theses as premises. According to the first thesis an agent cannot formulate judgments unless she is capable of self-awareness. The second thesis embodies a particular view of the role

[22] Okrent refers to a paper by John Haugeland, "Two Dogmas of Rationalism," delivered at The Sixth Annual Meeting of the International Society for Phenomenological Studies, Pacific Grove, CA, in July 2004 (unpublished).

[23] R. Brandom, *Making It Explicit* (Cambridge, MA: Harvard University Press, 1994), p. 31.

and nature of rational inference that is motivated by the Kantian analysis of practical reason, in particular by Kant's analysis of what it is to *act for* or *because of* a reason. According to that account, an agent cannot *act for* a reason unless she is capable of formulating judgments that can serve as premises in practical reasoning. When these two premises are combined with the twentieth century assumption that only agents that are capable of acting for reasons can have intentional states, the conclusion follows that self-awareness is a necessary condition for intentionality. This is the third dogma of rationalism.

Okrent argues, however, that the Kantian analysis of acting *for* a reason is fundamentally misguided, because it renders unintelligible the way in which perceptual experience, by itself, can provide a reason for purposeful action. In light of the failure of the Kantian analysis of acting for a reason, Okrent concludes that the view that the capacity for second order intentions is a necessary condition for all intentionality is merely an unsupported dogma of a certain brand of rationalism.

The last piece of this volume, my "Competing Enlightenment Narratives: A Case Study Of Rorty's Anti-Kantianism," provides a defense of the ethical/political dimensions of Kant's liberalism by gauging the strength of the critique of one of its most acerbic contemporary critics, Richard Rorty. Rorty's dissatisfaction with Kant's position can be traced back to a narrative of the coming to age of our culture, which bears surprising similarities to Kant's account of the Enlightenment. Yet, in Rorty's version of the story Kant's philosophy is mistakenly assimilated to a form of "Platonism." This is due, I believe, to the fact that Rorty mistakes the "transcendental" for the "transcendent" in Kant: "the "a priori" structures necessary to account for the possibility of a common world of meanings, and valid only *within* that world, Rorty places in a metaphysical realm bereft of spatiotemporal contingencies." (p. 300) To set this score straight, I present a "de-Platonized" reading of Kant's 1784 Enlightenment essay, whose goal is to protect the achievements of liberalism against Rorty's poetic excesses. For, to the extent that Rorty's private irony and liberal justice "cannot be held together in a single vision,"[24] his advocacy of "private self-enlargement seems too erratic and volatile a project to secure the ethical core of liberalism." (p. 308) The desire to reduce suffering and humiliation is as ungrounded for Rorty's liberal ironist as her love for orchids or Shakespeare, and the compatibility

[24] See Richard Rorty, *Contingency, Irony, and Solidarity* (Cambridge: Cambridge University Press, 1989), p. xiv.

of these incommensurable projects is in great measure the result of good upbringing and good luck.

Kant reduces the influence of chance by placing internal communicative constraints into our private conceptions of the good. "The desires, beliefs, and values that make up our final vocabulary must have been shaped, from their very inception, by a reflection on their acceptability to others. To *claim* these fundamental meanings to be *mine,* the "I will" of morality and the "I think" of the understanding must be able to accompany them –otherwise, my final vocabulary would have meanings *I* did not set, contents of which I am not the author." (p. 312-3) Thus, Kant's identification of Enlightenment with maturity, and maturity with the use of our understanding without the guidance of another (WA 8: 35), presupposes a radical transformation of the traditional liberal boundaries of privacy: "private" does not designate for Kant the *space* where others ought not to intervene, as it does for Rorty, but a mode of thinking (*Denkungsart*) in which meanings cannot be universally shared, for they are not suited for communication.

This sense comes to focus in Kant's famous distinction between the public and private uses of reason. The latter can be hindered without jeopardizing the progress of Enlightenment, ruling out pernicious conceptions of the good before they have a chance to be expressed in the market place of opinion. Yet, pluralism and individuality are preserved in Kant's political vision: only as *Gelehrter* addressing the entire reading public do we speak on our own behalf, i.e., use our own understanding – and this use must always be free. I conclude that Kantian communicative strictures preserve a sense of "objectivity" which keeps at arm's length the metaphysical urge Rorty so eloquently denounces as being superstitious. It is undeniable that Kant's version of liberalism is more prosaic than Rorty's. This loss of poetic bloom, however, is superseded by longer-term sustainability –a competitive advantage not to be dismissed in Rorty's Darwinian world.

Works Cited

Allison, H. *Kant's Theory of Freedom* (Cambridge: Cambridge University Press, 1990).

—. *Kant's Transcendental Idealism* (New Haven: Yale University Press, 1983).

Beck, L.W. *A Commentary to Kant's Critique of Practical Reason* (Chicago: Chicago University Press, 1960).

Beiser, F. "Moral Faith and the Highest Good," in Paul Guyer (ed.) *The Cambridge Companion to Kant and Modern Philosophy* (Cambridge: Cambridge University Press, 2006).

Card, C. *The Atrocity Paradigm: A Theory of Evil* (Oxford: Oxford University Press, 2002).

Guyer, P. *Kant on Freedom, Law, and Happiness* (Cambridge: Cambridge University Press, 2000).

Haugeland, J. "Two Dogmas of Rationalism," unpublished paper delivered at The Sixth Annual Meeting of the International Society for Phenomenological Studies (Pacific Gove, CA, July 2004).

Korsgaard, C. *Creating the Kingdom of Ends* (Cambridge: Cambridge University Press, 1996).

McDowell, J. *Mind and Word* (Cambridge: Cambridge University Press, 2003).

Pippin, R.B. "Kant on the Spontaneity of the Mind," *Canadian Journal of Philosophy*, 17, 2 (June 1987).

Rorty, R. *Contingency, Irony, and Solidarity* (Cambridge: Cambridge University Press, 1989).

Wood, A. *Kant's Ethical Thought* (Cambridge: Cambridge University Press, 1999).

—. *Kant's Moral Religion* (Ithaca: Cornell University Press, 1970).

CHAPTER ONE

INCOMPATIBILISM AND ONTOLOGICAL PRIORITY IN KANT'S THEORY OF FREE WILL

BEN VILHAUER

Kant is an incompatibilist about free will and determinism. Like all incompatibilists, Kant thinks that there is a fundamental conflict between determinism and free will. But like no other incompatibilist, Kant holds both that determinism is true, and that we have free will. Kant thinks that the truth of determinism is demonstrated by the conclusion of the Second Analogy, that is, by the conclusion that the necessitation of all alterations according to causal laws is a condition for the possibility of the experience of objective succession. But he also thinks we have an immediate awareness that we are morally responsible, in a sense that implies that we have free will. This awareness is based on what he describes in the second Critique as a "fact of pure reason."

With a position like this, it is natural to wonder whether Kant would be better characterized as a compatibilist. Compatibilists think there is no fundamental conflict between determinism and free will, so it is common for them to hold that both obtain. But Kant's commitment to incompatibilism is quite clear in his texts. 5:95 in the second *Critique* provides an example:

> If I say of a human being who commits a theft that this deed is, in accordance with the natural law of causality, a necessary result of determining grounds in preceding time, then it was impossible that it could have been left undone; how then, can appraisal in accordance with the moral law make any change in it and suppose that it could have been omitted because the law says that it ought to have been omitted?[1]

Acknowledgements: This research was supported by funds from a Summer Stipend from the Research Center for the Humanities and Social Sciences at William Paterson University. Thanks to the participants in the ENAKS conference for a helpful discussion of the ideas presented here, especially Pablo Muchnik,

Kant's point here is that a thief can only be blameworthy for a theft if he could have done otherwise than commit the theft, and that he could not have done otherwise if the theft was the inevitable outcome of deterministic causation. This is a claim no compatibilist can make.

Clearly, there is some tension to be dealt with if Kant is to maintain commitments to both determinism and incompatibilistic free will. There is broad scholarly agreement that Kant thinks he can resolve the tension by means of his transcendental distinction between agents qua phenomena, and qua noumena. Kant holds that the determinism entailed by the Second Analogy constrains agents as they appear in time (i.e. agents qua phenomena), but not as they are in themselves (i.e. agents qua noumena), because they do not appear in time as they are in themselves. But there is less agreement about the nature of this distinction, and exactly how it is supposed to resolve the tension.[2]

The purpose of this paper is to argue that Kant's incompatibilism can only be accommodated if one accepts the "ontological" interpretation of this distinction, i.e. the view that agents qua noumena are ontologically prior to agents qua phenomena. The ontological interpretation allows Kant

---

Karl Ameriks, Michael Rohlf, and David Cummiskey. Thanks also to Eric Watkins, Robert Pippin, Michael Forster, and Graham Bird.

[1] References to Kant's texts will be made as follows: material from the first *Critique* (KrV) will be cited by page in A and B editions. Second *Critique* material will be cited as 'KpV', third *Critique* as 'KU', *Groundwork of the Metaphysics of Morals* as 'G', *Metaphysical Foundations of Natural Science* by 'MAN', all followed by Akademie pagination, i.e., as paginated in *Kants gesammelte Schriften*, hrsg. von der Deutschen Akademie der Wissenschaften, 29 vols. (Berlin: Walter de Gruyter, 1902-). Texts used are as follows: *Kritik der reinen Vernunt*, hrsg. von Jens Timmerman (Hamburg: Felix Meiner Verlag, 1998); *Kritik der praktischen Vernunft*, hrsg. von Karl Vörlander, (Hamburg: Felix Meiner Verlag, 1990); *Kritik der Urteilskraft*, hrsg. von Heiner F. Klemme (Hamburg: Felix Meiner Verlag, 2001). Translations are my own, in consultation with the following translations: *Critique of Pure Reason,* Norman Kemp Smith (New York: St. Martin's, 1929), and Werner Pluhar (Indianapolis: Hackett, 1996); *Critique of Practical Reason*, Lewis White Beck (New York: Macmillan, 1985), and Mary Gregor (Cambridge: Cambridge University Press, 1997); *Critique of Judgment,* Werner Pluhar (Indianapolis: Hackett, 1987), J.C. Meredith (Oxford: Clarendon, 1952), and J.H. Bernard (New York: Hafner, 1951); *Groundwork of the Metaphysics of Morals,* Mary Gregor (Cambridge: Cambridge University Press, 1998) and Lewis White Beck (Indianapolis: Bobbs-Merrill, 1959); *Metaphysical Foundations of Natural Science*, James Ellington [in *Philosophy of Material Nature* (Indianapolis: Hackett, 1985)].

[2] I also discuss this distinction in my 2004 and forthcoming papers. In some parts of the present paper I have adapted remarks from those other papers.

to be an incompatibilist because the ontological priority of agents qua noumena "ontologically undermines" the significance of phenomenal determinism for agents' free will. That is, since agents qua noumena are ontologically prior to agents qua phenomena, the fact that agents qua noumena are not subject to determinism is more fundamental than the fact that agents qua phenomena are subject to determinism, and it is the more fundamental fact that we should be concerned with in addressing metaphysical issues such as free will. It will also be argued that Kant's incompatibilism cannot be accommodated by the "two-aspect" interpretation, whose defining feature is the rejection of the ontological priority of agents qua noumena. According to the two-aspect interpretation, the transcendental distinction between agents qua noumena and qua phenomena is a semantic and epistemological distinction. Since it rejects the ontological priority of noumena, it has no way to assert that the non-determinism of agents qua noumena is more fundamental than the determinism of agents qua phenomena. For the two-aspect interpretation, the truth of determinism must remain just as fundamental as the truth of any other characterization of agents. This means that, on the two-aspect interpretation, there is no better reason to call Kant an incompatibilist than there is to call him a compatibilist.

This paper has two main parts. In the first part, the ontological interpretation will be described, and an explanation will be given of how it makes room for Kant's incompatibilism. Recent (independent) work by the present author, Eric Watkins, and Robert Hanna will be drawn on to demonstrate that the ontological interpretation can mount a better defense against some traditional objections than has often been thought.[3] In the second part, the two-aspect interpretation of Kant's theory of free will shall be described, and it will be argued that it cannot make room for Kant's incompatibilism.

I- The Ontological Interpretation

There are four sections in the first part of this paper. The first briefly describes the ontological interpretation, and explains how it makes room for both determinism and incompatibilistic free will. The second section

[3] Hanna and Moore, "Reason, Freedom and Kant: An Exchange"; Vilhauer, "The Scope of Responsibility in Kant's Theory of Free Will," and "Can We Interpret Kant as a Compatibilist about Determinism and Moral Responsibility?"; Watkins, *Kant and the Metaphysics of Causality.* Hanna and Watkins do not advance their accounts in defense of the ontological interpretation, though in my view their accounts lend themselves naturally to such a defense.

describes a line of objection that has often been thought decisive against the ontological interpretation, and then explains how some recent developments in Kant scholarship can be used to defend the ontological interpretation against this line of objection. The third section explains how transcendental idealism can block a potentially counterintuitive consequence of the ontological interpretation. The fourth section distinguishes the ontological interpretation from the "two worlds" interpretation. The overall goal of this section is not to provide a detailed defense of the ontological interpretation, but only to show that, despite its long history, the way in which it reconciles determinism and incompatibilistic free will should be of renewed interest.

I-1. Overview

According to the ontological interpretation, the ontological priority of atemporal agents qua noumena gives Kant a way to "ontologically undermine" the significance of phenomenal determinism. Though Kant's noumenal ignorance principle means that we cannot have theoretical knowledge of the existence of agents qua noumena, it is practically necessary for us to be committed to their existence if we are to accept the implications of the "fact of pure reason." The guiding idea of the ontological interpretation is that determinism is *merely* a condition for the possibility of the appearances of agents in time—it is not a condition for the possibility of the existence in themselves of the agents which are the ontological substrates of their appearances.

Agents qua noumena stand "outside" space and time, so to speak, and are therefore independent of the deterministic empirical causal series. Agents qua noumena freely shape the deterministic phenomenal causal series, in such a way as to make room for incompatibilistic alternative possibilities of action (and hence incompatibilistic free will) despite the truth of determinism. The idea is that those stretches of the empirical causal series which constitute the actions of some agent qua phenomenon would have been different if that agent qua noumenon had chosen differently, since agents qua noumena are the ontological substrates of agents qua phenomena.

Earlier proponents of the ontological interpretation include Norman Kemp Smith and Herbert Paton.[4] But many contemporary commentators have thought that the implications of this interpretation are too counterintuitive for it to be worthy of further detailed scholarly study. As

[4] See e.g. Kemp Smith, *A Commentary to Kant's Critique of Pure Reason* and Paton, *Kant's Metaphysic of Experience.*

will be argued below, however, recent work suggests that the consequences of the ontological interpretation may not be so counterintuitive after all.

I-2. An Objection to the Ontological Interpretation, and a Response

It has long been wondered how some agent qua noumenon could freely shape the part of the deterministic causal series which constitutes her actions qua phenomenon without also shaping much of the causal series prior to her own birth qua phenomenon. The problem, pointed out by Ralph Walker,[5] can be explained as follows. If determinism is true, then there is, at each instant in time prior to some agent's birth, a sufficient cause of all that agent's actions. In other words, at every instant in time prior to that agent's birth, there is a set of events which, when coupled with the laws of nature, suffices to cause all the actions that agent will take throughout her life. But it seems that an agent qua noumenon could not determine the part of the causal series constituting her actions qua phenomenon without also determining any part of the causal series that contains a sufficient cause of her actions qua phenomenon. So it seems that, if determinism is true, an agent can only determine the part of the causal series constituting her actions qua phenomenon by determining events at every instant in the past prior to her birth.

On its own, Walker's point already seems to some philosophers to constitute a *reductio ad absurdum* of Kant's theory of free will.[6] This response may be too strong. The claim that one determines events prior to one's own birth may indeed be quite counterintuitive, but it might be argued that it is not a great deal more counterintuitive than the idea that agents qua noumena are not in time. So one might think that if this strategy can in fact accommodate incompatibilistic free will, then Kant can accept the consequence that one determines events prior to one's own birth without making his theory significantly more perplexing than it already was.

Walker's basic argument against Kant can be extended further, however. The sufficient cause of any human agent's actions at some point in the past prior to his birth must inevitably include the actions of other agents. This claim is not true for all possible agents (e.g. agents which

---

[5] Walker, *Kant*, pp.148-9. Walker's point is anticipated in some ways by Kemp-Smith (Ibid., pp. 517-18).

[6] See e.g. Bennett, "Kant's Theory of Freedom."

exist necessarily or agents which come into being entirely by chance) but it is true for agents like humans whose existence is contingent upon the actions of other agents. This means that a human agent qua noumenon could only determine his own actions qua phenomenon by determining some actions of some other agents qua phenomena. If Kant's theory of free will truly entails this outcome, then we have what seems to be a clear *reductio*. Integral to Kant's incompatibilism is the view that one must noumenally determine one's phenomenal actions to be morally responsible for them. If noumenally determining one's own phenomenal actions requires one to noumenally determine the actions of some other agents, then one can only be morally responsible for one's own phenomenal actions by making it the case that other agents are not morally responsible for (at least some of) their own phenomenal actions. One agent's moral responsibility could only come at the expense of the moral responsibility of other agents.

However, recent (independent) publications by Eric Watkins, Robert Hanna, and myself demonstrate that Kant's theory of free will does not imply this outcome. The supposed *reductio* just considered makes an unwarranted assumption. It assumes a particular model of the agent qua noumenon's determination of the agent qua phenomenon. On this model, the agent qua noumenon has control over the events that constitute the actions of the agent qua phenomenon, but does not have control over the deterministic laws that render antecedent and subsequent events causally necessary. If we accept this model, then there is no way for the agent qua noumenon to determine the actions of the agent qua phenomenon without determining a swathe of events that cuts through the entire history of the world. But this model is not the only one possible. Watkins, Hanna, and I advocate a model on which the agent qua noumenon determines the actions of the agent qua phenomenon by controlling the laws of nature which necessitate the actions of the agent qua phenomenon.

Of course, if the laws of nature are structured in such a way that the laws necessitating one's own actions also necessitate indefinitely many other events that are *not* one's own actions, then this model is in little better shape than the previous one, because controlling one's own actions by means of controlling the laws necessitating them would entail controlling indefinitely many other events which were not one's own actions, potentially including the actions of other agents. Laws of nature are often assumed to have two features either of which would imply that the laws necessitating one's own actions also necessitate indefinitely many events that are not one's own actions. The first is *universal repeated instantiation* of causal laws, and the second is *complete unity* of causal laws. Universal repeated instantiation is the idea that there can only be a natural law if it is repeatedly instantiated, i.e. instantiated by more than one actual event. Complete unity is the idea that there is, at bottom, just one perfectly general law of nature from which all other laws are in principle derivable (typically this is presumed to be a law of physics). But according to Kant's account of causation, we need not assume that either of these structural features obtain.

First consider universal repeated instantiation. I argue that Kant would have to accept universal repeated instantiation if he accepted Hume's view, since according to Hume, the very concept of causal law is abstracted from observations of repeated successions of event-types. But of course Kant rejects this view: according to the Second Analogy, our knowledge that all events are causally necessitated is a condition for the possibility of the experience of objective succession, so if we had to abstract the concept of causal law from the observation of events, we could never arrive at the concept of causal law in the first place. Even a strong interpretation of the Second Analogy can allow for laws which are instantiated only once in the actual causal series. The Second Analogy entails that all events are necessitated according to causal laws, but it entails nothing about how often particular causal laws are instantiated. As will be discussed in more detail in part 2, this point is crucial for making sense of Kant's account of empirical psychology. This is because Kant holds that we can know there are laws of empirical psychology even though the absence of an enduring substrate in inner sense means that we cannot repeat experiments on it (MAN 471). If we cannot repeat experiments on it, we cannot know whether its laws are repeatedly instantiated.

Now consider complete unity. Hanna and I both point out remarks in the third *Critique* which demonstrate that Kant does not accept complete unity. In section 4 of the First Introduction Kant argues there that the unity of natural laws is a regulative idea, not a constitutive principle. We cannot develop natural science without assuming that there is a significant amount of unity of laws in nature, but unity with other laws is not a condition for the possibility of something's being a law. Hanna and I make use of this point in different ways. Hanna looks to the third *Critique*'s account of the explanation of organisms to argue that single-instance causal laws are emergent features of the organisms that embody human agents. I argue that since natural laws must be backed by forces for Kant, the supposition that irreducibly different single-instance laws are instantiated by the matter of each human body would require our theories of matter to expand indefinitely to include a vast array of fundamental forces of matter. This would conflict with Kant's view that it is inherent in the methodology of the material sciences to reduce fundamental forces of matter to the smallest possible number (as expressed in the *Metaphysical Foundations of Natural Science*). I argue that single-instance laws must be laws of empirical psychology, that is, that they must be instantiated in the phenomenal soul. It follows from Kant's empirical dualism (see e.g. KrV A379) that laws governing the phenomenal soul and its interactions with the body are not laws of matter, and this makes it possible to avoid the problem of proliferating fundamental physical forces. We must still posit forces to explain such interactions, but we can suppose that they are non-physical forces. This is just what Kant appears to do at KU 475:

> one of the forces we attribute to the soul is a *vis locomotiva*, because bodily movements do actually arise whose cause lies in the soul's representations of them, but we do this without trying to ascribe to the soul the only manner in which we know motive forces (namely, through attraction, pressure, impact, and hence motion, which always presuppose an extended being).

Though the new interpretations just discussed differ in significant ways, they share a common strategy that can be used to rebut the supposed *reductio* considered above. That is, they all make use of idea that agents qua noumena in some sense control causal laws, and this idea can be used to argue that the ontological interpretation does not have counterintuitive implications for the scope of our moral responsibility.

I-3. Transcendental Idealism and Control Over Laws of Nature

It would be natural to object that human agents cannot be supposed to control laws of nature. After all, this is a power which traditionally rests with God. If we accept the ontological interpretation of the transcendental distinction, however, it is quite natural to suppose that human agents are responsible for causal laws.

Here is an explanation of how this works. Kant is clearly committed to what scholars sometimes call the "noumenal ignorance principle," i.e. the view that that we cannot have theoretical knowledge of noumena. The noumenal ignorance principle is often taken to imply a broader proscription on knowledge about noumena than is warranted by Kant's texts, however. Theoretical knowledge is knowledge of determinations, and knowledge of determinations is synthetic knowledge that particular predicates apply to things. We can only have such knowledge about objects in space and time. But if the existence of noumena is implied by features of transcendental idealism of which we have a priori knowledge, then we can know that noumena exist without knowing any of their determinations.

According to Kant, the synthetic apriority of our knowledge of space and time implies that space and time are transcendentally ideal, i.e. that they are imposed on the empirical world by our minds. But what we thereby impose is only a formal feature of reality, that is, an empty manifold of spatiotemporal extension. The empirical objects that make up the specific content of empirical reality cannot be entirely constituted by the human mind. Their empirical content must be contributed by something that is independent of our minds: if there were nothing mind-independent to stand as the ground of the specific content of empirical reality, it would be impossible for empirical reality to amount to anything more than an empty manifold. We cannot suppose that this mind-independent ground of empirical content is the spatiotemporal object we experience. Since the spatiotemporality of those objects is the product of the human mind, this would be to suppose that mind-dependent entities were mind-independent. Instead, we must use philosophical reflection to "isolate" a non-spatiotemporal ontological substrate which is the ground of the specific content that appears in spatiotemporally extended empirical objects. This is the noumenal. As Paton puts it, noumena provide empirical content by contributing the "particularity" of the properties of empirical objects.[7] That is, noumena make it such that empirical objects instantiate the particular properties they instantiate rather than other particular properties.

It may be objected that causal laws explain why empirical objects instantiate the properties they instantiate.[8] But that explanation is only partial, because it cannot explain why *these* particular causal laws obtain, rather than some others. Noumena explain the particularity of causal laws in the same way that they explain the particularity of the properties of empirical objects. The understanding and the forms of intuition together construct the objective temporal order by imposing the form of deterministic causal necessitation on all empirical events. But this imposition only explains the formal, general fact *that there are deterministic causal laws*. It does not explain the fact that the particular causal laws that obtain are *these* laws, rather than some other laws. Instead, noumena are responsible for the fact that the particular causal laws that obtain are the laws they are.

The idea that noumena are responsible for causal laws allows us to make sense of the assumption (made practically necessary by the fact of

---

[7] See e.g. Paton, *Kant's Metaphysic of Experience,* vol. 1, p. 139.
[8] Thanks to Robert Pippin for this objection.

pure reason) that agents qua noumena freely shape the structure of the deterministic phenomenal causal series. Since human agents are noumena as well as phenomena, human agents are responsible for some of the laws of nature. We can suppose that each agent qua noumenon is responsible for the particular causal laws that govern the actions of that same agent qua phenomenon.[9]

It is important to stress that, according to the version of the ontological interpretation advocated in here, agents qua noumena only have an indirect sort of responsibility for causal laws. What we freely choose qua noumena are our maxims, that is, the principles we act upon, not causal laws. (Choosing one's maxims does not imply having theoretical knowledge of determinations of oneself qua noumenon.)[10] Our choices of maxims appear in inner sense as phenomena of empirical psychology, necessitated by the laws of empirical psychology. The practical types in terms of which we choose our maxims and the correlated theoretical a posteriori types and laws in terms of which these choices appear to us are entirely different. Because of the noumenal ignorance principle, we cannot know *why* they correlate as they do. We cannot learn anything like a function from noumenal determinations to phenomenal determinations that might be thought to undergird this correlation. But the "fact of pure reason" requires us to believe that they correlate in such a way that if our choices of maxims had been different, then the empirical-psychological events that

---

[9] This supposition does not amount to theoretical knowledge, but it is nonetheless practically necessary if reason is to maintain a belief in incompatibilistic free will along with a belief in determinism. It might be objected that the noumenal ignorance principle is enough to resolve the tension between these beliefs. That is, it might be thought that if we can know nothing about noumena, then we can suppose straightaway that, despite phenomenal determinism, our nature as noumena gives us incompatibilistic free will. It might be thought that we could end our speculations about noumenal agency there and save ourselves the additional metaphysical entanglements. There is a grain of truth in this. That is, the noumenal ignorance principle on its own suffices to make it consistent to hold beliefs in incompatibilism and determinism together. Kant clearly holds, however, that when confronted with the claim that determinism can be squared with incompatibilistic free will, reason demands more than mere consistency. Reason demands an explanation of how it can be true, and this is why Kant presents a metaphysics of free will in addition to his account of noumenal ignorance.

[10] Our maxims would seem to be properties of ourselves qua noumena in some sense, but the epistemic relation we have to our own maxims does not violate Kant's noumenal ignorance principle. Theoretical knowledge requires the spontaneous determination of something passively received, and Kant understands our relation to our maxims as entirely spontaneous.

are their appearances would have been necessitated according to different causal laws.[11]

I-4. Ontological Priority Without Two Worlds

It is not rare for contemporary Kant scholars to assume that any interpretation that makes noumena ontologically prior to phenomena must be a "two worlds" interpretation, i.e. an interpretation according to which noumena and phenomena are two sets of ontologically independent entities. Though the ontological interpretation can be explained as a two worlds interpretation, it need not be. Considerations of ontological parsimony favor rejecting two worlds versions of the ontological interpretation. According to the version advocated in the present paper, there is only one set of ontologically subsistent entities, i.e. noumena. This does not imply that phenomena are not real. It only implies that phenomena are ontologically dependent upon noumena. Phenomena can be understood as relational properties of noumena. More specifically, phenomena are (so to speak) second-order relations between noumena and human intuition. That is, they are *relations of the relations* between noumena and human intuition.

Our minds are passive with respect to first-order relations between noumena and intuition. In other words, the first-order relations are the relations through which our intuition is passively affected by noumena. They make up the purely sensible content that is transcendentally prior to the determination of intuition according to the schematized categories. Purely sensible content "fills in" various spatiotemporal locations in the empty manifold of pure intuition. It is indeterminate, however: it is what Kant calls "intuitions without concepts," and describes as "blind." We have no experience of it. Experience is only possible for the human mind through the combination of passive receptivity at the level of first-order relations, and spontaneity at the level of the second-order relations constructed through the schematization of the categories. Empirical objects and laws are spontaneously constructed second-order relations between first-order relations. In other words, empirical objects and laws are relations between the locations in space and time that are "filled in" with purely sensible content by the first-order relations. Second-order

---

[11] This account of how transcendental idealism explains responsibility for causal laws closely follows my 2004 and forthcoming papers. Watkins also discusses this issue in some similar ways in *Kant and the Metaphysics of Causality*.

relations are spontaneously constructed through the successive synthesis of the manifold, through which the schematized categories are applied to purely sensible content. The idea is that there is one spontaneous activity of the transcendental constitution of empirical reality, and the construction of the second-order relations, the construction of empirical objects and laws, and the application of the schematized categories to purely sensible content, are all different ways of talking about that one activity.

This approach explains the ontological foundations of the particular causal laws governing the free choices of agents qua phenomena as follows. As mentioned above, our choices of maxims appear in inner sense as temporally extended phenomena of empirical psychology, governed by particular laws of empirical psychology. These laws are second-order relations between agents qua noumena and the inner sense of those same agents qua phenomena. The particularity of these laws, i.e. the fact that the laws which obtain are *these* laws rather than some others, is the result of first-order relations between agents qua noumena and the inner sense of those same agents qua phenomena which "fill" the various points in time in inner sense with purely sensible content. The laws have the form of deterministic necessitation because it is imposed upon them as they are constructed according to the schematized category of causality.

This part of the paper has not been intended to provide anything like a complete defense of the ontological interpretation. It purpose has been only to explain how the ontological interpretation resolves the tension between determinism and incompatibilism, and to demonstrate that recent work shows it can mount a better defense against traditional objections than has often been thought. In the second part of the paper, it will be argued that the two-aspect interpretation's rejection of the ontological priority of noumena implies that it cannot resolve the tension between determinism and incompatibilism. Since the key difference between the ontological interpretation and the two-aspect interpretation is precisely that the former accepts the ontological priority of noumena and the latter rejects it, the second part of the paper will provide an indirect argument for the ontological interpretation.

II- The Two-Aspect Interpretation

The purpose of this part of the paper is to argue that the two-aspect interpretation's rejection of the ontological priority of agents qua noumena prevents it from accommodating Kant's incompatibilism. Since Henry Allison has presented the most detailed account of the two-aspect interpretation of the agential transcendental distinction, much of this part will proceed by way of a critique of his views.

II-1. Overview

Throughout the history of Kant scholarship, some commentators have recoiled from the idea of noumena which stand "outside" space and time. Such commentators have seen this idea as a metaphysical monstrosity, and they have thought either that Kant did not really endorse it, or that it was his greatest mistake. They have often advanced deflationary accounts of transcendental idealism that attempt to avoid a commitment to the existence of non-spatiotemporal noumena while preserving what they take to be Kant's insights. In the contemporary literature, commentators of this deflationary sensibility typically accept what is referred to as the "two-aspect" interpretation of transcendental idealism. Its central claims are that noumena and phenomena are two aspects of the same things, and that neither aspect is more ontologically fundamental than the other.

Proponents of the two-aspect interpretation face a difficult task when it comes to explaining Kant's theory of free will. As mentioned earlier, there is broad scholarly agreement that the key move in Kant's theory of free will is the idea that determinism is true for agents qua phenomena, but not for agents qua noumena. This is supposed to allow us to accept incompatibilism along with determinism and moral responsibility. On the ontological interpretation, this move works because agents qua noumena are ontologically prior to agents qua phenomena. The fact that agents qua noumena are not deterministic is more fundamental than the fact that agents qua phenomena are deterministic. But it is hard to see what good this move can do if one accepts the two-aspect interpretation. The two-aspect interpretation explains the transcendental distinction as merely a distinction between two different epistemic or semantic relationships we can stand in to things. Without some further claim to the effect that the way we represent things when we consider them as noumena is how they more fundamentally *are*, the non-determinism of agents qua noumena can do nothing to undermine the significance of phenomenal determinism. But any such further claim is ruled out by the two-aspect interpretation's rejection of the ontological priority of noumena. So proponents of the two-aspect interpretation must suppose that Kant thinks that we have free will even though determinism is just as fundamental a truth about our actions as non-determinism. But this a view of free will which one cannot in good conscience call incompatibilistic. This is a view of free will which there is just as much reason to call compatibilistic as there is to call incompatibilistic.

Henry Allison is arguably the most influential contemporary advocate of the two-aspect interpretation. He rejects "the 'noumenalistic' view that grants ontological priority to things as they are in themselves."[12] On his view, what this means is that transcendental idealism is not committed to the existence of any non-spatiotemporal things. Allison's view is that "Kant's transcendental distinction is primarily between two ways in which things (empirical objects) can be 'considered' at the metalevel of philosophical reflection."[13] In other words, the only things we can consider are empirical objects. We can consider them in abstraction from their spatiotemporality, but considering them in abstraction from their spatiotemporality does not make them any less spatiotemporal. To quote Allison again, to "consider things as they are in themselves is to reflect on them in a way which ignores or abstracts from the subjective conditions of human sensibility."[14]

Supposing that transcendental idealism is not committed to the existence of non-temporal things makes it hard to make sense of Kant's incompatibilistic theory of free will. Allison's own commitment to an incompatibilistic interpretation of Kant seems clear. He claims that

> [A]t the heart of Kant's account of freedom in all three *Critiques* and in his major writings on moral philosophy is the problematic conception of transcendental freedom, which is an explicitly…incompatibilist conception (requiring an independence of determination by all antecedent causes in the phenomenal world).[15]

If we follow Allison in rejecting the ontological priority of things in themselves, however, we cannot suppose that atemporal agents qua noumena serve as the ontological substrates of agents qua phenomena, and shape the empirical causal structure of agents qua phenomena to make room for free choices. We are left without any way to undermine phenomenal determinism. So it is not clear how we could preserve incompatibilistic free will on Allison's interpretation. If we accept Allison's account, we find ourselves with a tension between Kant's commitments to incompatibilistic free will on the one hand, and determinism on the other.[16] It looks like one of them has to be given up.

---

[12] Allison, *Idealism and Freedom*, p. 11.
[13] Ibid., p. 3.
[14] Ibid., p. 3.
[15] Allison, *Kant's Theory of Freedom*, p. 1.
[16] Karl Ameriks makes a related point about Allison's interpretation in "Kant and Hegel on Freedom: Two New Interpretations."

But Allison claims to preserve both.[17]

Allison's interpretation gives us two ways in which the tension might be resolved. First, Allison holds that his account of transcendental idealism *does* in fact make agents qua noumena independent enough from the deterministic empirical causal series to make room for incompatibilistic free will. Second, Allison argues that if we properly interpret the Second Analogy, we will see that the sort of determinism it entails is very weak, and this will show us that Kantian determinism does not pose as much of a threat to free will as some commentators have thought.[18] Allison provides additional support for his interpretation of the Second Analogy with an argument to the effect that Kant holds there are no laws of empirical psychology. In the remainder of the paper, it will be argued that these potential resolutions are unsuccessful.

II-2. Allison's Two-Aspect Interpretation of Incompatibilistic Free Will

The purpose of this section is to consider Allison's claim that the two-aspect interpretation can accommodate incompatibilist free will. Allison claims that

> by treating space, time, and the categories as epistemic rather than ontological conditions, transcendental idealism also opens up a "conceptual space" for the nonempirical thought (although not knowledge) of objects, including rational agents, as they may be apart from these conditions, that is, as they may be "in themselves"...For the most part, of course, this conceptual space remains vacant and the thought of things as they are in themselves therefore reduces to the empty thought of a merely transcendental object, a "something in general = x." In the consciousness of our rational agency, however, we are directly aware of a capacity (to act on the basis of an ought) that...we cannot regard as empirically

[17] While Allison strives to preserve Kant's incompatibilism, some commentators (e.g. Ralf Meerbote and Hud Hudson) give up incompatibilist free will, and interpret Kant as a compatibilist. (See Hudson, *Kant's Compatibilism*, and Meerbote, "Kant on the Nondeterminate Character of Human Actions.")

[18] Allison discusses the weak interpretation of the Second Analogy as what he calls a "first step" in responding to the criticism that the deterministic necessitation of empirical objects prevents us from supposing that agents qua noumena are exempt from such necessitation (Allison, *Kant's Transcendental Idealism*, p. 326) and then discusses his strategy for accommodating incompatibilism within his account of transcendental idealism as a second step. In this paper, for expository purposes, it has been necessary to discuss it second.

> conditioned...[I]nsofar as we attribute it to ourselves, we must also attribute an intelligible character, which is thought in terms of the transcendental idea of freedom. Consequently, in attributing the latter to ourselves and our agency, we do not merely prescind or abstract from the causal conditions of our actions, considered as occurrences in the phenomenal world; rather we regard these conditions as nonsufficient, that is, as "not so determining" as to exclude a "causality of our will" since we think of ourselves as initiating causal series through actions conceived as first beginnings.[19]

Allison's key claim here is that he can say more on behalf of agents qua noumena than he can on behalf of noumena in general. With respect to noumena in general, we can only consider them in a negative way, as a "something in general = x." With respect to agents qua noumena, however, we can add to this negative conception the positive idea of ourselves as initiators of causal series. We think of ourselves not just in abstraction from the causal conditions that necessitate our actions—we also think of these causal conditions as nonsufficient.

Allison's remarks here may make his interpretation sound similar to the ontological interpretation discussed above. Like the ontological interpretation, Allison's interpretation includes the idea that agents, considered as things in themselves, are independent of the deterministic causal series. But as emphasized earlier, the crucial difference is that Allison rejects "the 'noumenalistic' view that grants ontological priority to things as they are in themselves." Allison holds that Kant's transcendental distinction is between two ways in which we can think of empirical objects, and it is constitutive of anything's being an empirical object that all of its alterations have sufficient causal conditions. We can certainly "regard these conditions as nonsufficient," as Allison puts it above. But, if Allison is to maintain his account of the transcendental distinction, this inevitably involves a kind of make-believe, because we are merely regarding objects with sufficient causal conditions as if they did not have sufficient causal conditions. On Allison's account, when thinking about agents, we sometimes consider them in abstraction from their sufficient causal conditions, but this does not show that there are any agents without sufficient causal conditions.

This line of argument will surely meet the objection that this is not *mere* make-believe, on Allison's interpretation, because it is a requirement of practical reason to represent causally necessitated agents as if they did not have sufficient causal conditions. But even if this point is accepted, the problem about incompatibilism remains. Allison's basic view seems to be

---

[19] Allison, *Kant's Theory of Freedom,* pp. 44-5.

that our actions are deterministically necessitated, but we can ascribe free will to ourselves because transcendental idealism allows us to represent ourselves as if our actions were not deterministically necessitated. But this makes it no more accurate to call Kant an incompatibilist than it is to call him a compatibilist. According to Allison, phenomenal determinism is an ultimate reality. Allison cannot undermine this determinism by positing agents qua noumena as the ontological substrates of agents qua phenomena, as the ontological interpretation does, because Allison rejects the ontological priority of noumena. So, instead of undermining determinism, Allison makes free will compatible with determinism by holding that we are free because we can represent ourselves as if we were not deterministically necessitated.

In other words, according to the ontological interpretation, the idea that noumena are not deterministically necessitated is a discovery with profound implications for phenomenal determinism. It implies that phenomenal determinism is not an ultimate reality. The ontological foundations of agents are not deterministic. Agents only appear to be deterministic. On Allison's interpretation, on the other hand, the idea that noumena are not deterministically necessitated implies nothing at all about phenomenal determinism, except that reason sometimes requires us to ignore it. So, if what we have seen so far represents Allison's account of free will in its entirety, it seems fair to say that the ontological interpretation can accommodate a robust sort of incompatibilism which Allison's account cannot accommodate.

But what we have seen so far does not represent Allison's account in its entirety. Allison thinks past commentators have mistakenly interpreted Kant's phenomenal determinism as a very strong sort of determinism, when in actuality it is much weaker. Allison advances several arguments to weaken phenomenal determinism. This is important for the question of incompatibilism. Even if Allison cannot make room for incompatibilistic free will by undermining phenomenal determinism, he may be able to make room for it if he can weaken phenomenal determinism sufficiently.

The most striking manifestation of Allison's weakened interpretation of phenomenal determinism is his rejection of Kant's claim that human actions are, in principle, predictable. One example of Kant's predictability claim is at KrV A550/B578:

> [All] the actions of a human being in appearance are determined... according to the order of nature, and if we could investigate all the appearances of men's wills to their grounds, there would not be a single human action we could not predict with certainty and recognize as necessary from its antecedent conditions.

Allison claims "Kant has neither the need nor the right to assert...that, given sufficient knowledge, we could infallibly predict human actions."[20] Allison thinks this for two reasons. First, Allison holds that the Second Analogy does not imply any sort of determinism that would justify this predictability claim. Second, Allison holds that Kant is committed to an account of empirical psychology according to which there can be no psychological laws. In the next two sections, arguments will be made against both of these claims.

II-3. Allison's Interpretation of the Second Analogy

In the Second Analogy, Kant argues that if we are to represent objective successions of appearances, they must take place in accordance with "the law of the connection of cause and effect"(KrV B233). The core of Kant's argument for this claim is as follows:

> time cannot in itself be perceived, and what precedes and what follows cannot, therefore, by relation to it, be empirically determined in the object. I am conscious only that my imagination places the one state before and the other after, not that the one state precedes the other in the object. In other words, the objective relation of appearances following one another is not to be determined through perception alone. Now in order that this relation be known as determinate, the relation between the two states must be thought in such a way that it determines as necessary which must be placed before, and which after, and that they cannot be placed in the reverse relation. But a concept which carries with it a necessity of synthetic unity can only be a pure concept that resides in understanding, not in perception. In this case it is the concept of the *relation of cause and effect*...Therefore experience itself— i.e. empirical cognition of appearances— is possible only insofar as we subject the succession of appearances, and therefore all change, to the law of causality[.] (KrV B233-234)

If we consider Kant's remarks in the Second Analogy on their own, it is less than transparent what he means in claiming that we must subject the succession of appearances to the "law of causality." This is clarified in a passage at KrVA91/B94, however, when he explains that the concept of cause "makes strict demand that something, A, should be such that something else, B, follows from it *necessarily and in accordance with an absolutely universal rule*." When we add this clarification to the Second Analogy, Kant's position appears to be the following: all events are bound

[20] Allison *Kant's Transcendental Idealism,* p. 326.

to other events according to rules of causal necessitation, or, as we might instead say, according to particular causal laws.[21]

Allison rejects this account, and instead advocates a weak interpretation according to which the Second Analogy does entail that succession in the empirical causal series is necessary, but does *not* entail the existence of particular causal laws.[22] According to Allison's version of the weak interpretation,

> judgements about objective temporal succession do not presuppose that the elements of the succession are connected by empirical laws. All that is presupposed is that there is some antecedent condition (presumably roughly contemporaneous with x's being in state A at t_1) which, being given, state B necessarily ensues for *this particular x* at t_2. There are no additional assumptions regarding the *repeatability of the sequence* and its relevance to *other objects of x's type* that are either required or licensed by this presupposition.[23]

What Allison means by there being no assumption of relevance to "other objects of x's type" is that, despite there being a given case of an x in state A necessitated by some antecedent condition to enter state B, we cannot infer from this that in any other case, an x in state A with an antecedent condition of the same kind will be necessitated to enter state B. So necessity does not obtain in terms of general laws formulated at the level of types, but in terms of relations between particular states of particular objects.

A crucial part of Allison's claim that necessitation is at the level of

---

[21] It is important to emphasize that we should not interpret Kant as arguing that, if we do not know the particular causal law necessitating an alteration, we cannot experience the alteration as objective. This would be a problem, because the only way to gain knowledge of some particular causal law is by induction from repeated observations of objective alterations caused *according to* that causal law. Thus, if we had to have knowledge of the particular causal law necessitating an alteration in order to experience it as objective, we could never learn the law by induction. Learning by induction requires that we begin by not knowing the law, then make observations, and then induce the law. But if knowledge of the law is required for objective experience, then the observations required to induce the law would not be possible without already knowing the law, and that is just to say that we could not learn the law by induction. The point Kant is making in the Second Analogy is more general—we cannot experience or otherwise represent a succession of appearances as objective unless we think of it as necessitated by a causal law.

[22] Other supporters of the weak interpretation are Beck (e.g. *Essays on Kant and Hume*) and Buchdahl (e.g. *Metaphysics and the Philosophy of Science*).

[23] Allison, *Kant's Transcendental Idealism*, p. 231, my italics.

particulars is that it makes sense for us to think of sequences as causally necessitated even if they are not repeatable. If we had to understand causal necessitation in terms of repeatable sequences, we could not understand causal necessitation in terms of particulars, because particulars are not repeatable. Only the types particulars instantiate are repeatable. If Allison held that necessitated sequences had to be understood as repeatable, he would have to represent them in terms of types. But if Allison explained causal necessitation in terms of types, then he would have to accept that a sequence could only be causally necessitated if there was a causal law that covered it. The reason is as follows. Suppose that we explain something's being causally necessitated to change from A to B by saying that the thing is of a certain type, and that there was an antecedent condition of a certain type. And suppose that this is the whole explanation. If this explanation is to be genuinely explanatory, then it must be true in all cases that if a thing is of that type, with antecedent conditions of that type, the thing will change from A to B. There must, in other words, be a causal law.[24] So if Allison were forced to explain causal necessitation at the level of types, he would not be able to maintain his weak interpretation of the Second Analogy.

It is therefore crucial for Allison to maintain his position that causal sequences can be necessitated without being repeatable. But it is hard to see how he can maintain it, in view of Kant's KrV A91/B124 claim that the concept of cause involves the idea of following according to a rule. Allison attempts to incorporate this idea. He holds that Kant's explanation of causation in terms of rules expresses "merely the thought that a particular effect must be conceived to follow in every case or without exception from its cause."[25] But there is no sense in talking of a particular effect following "in every case," or "without exception," since particulars are not repeatable. If we explain what it means for a sequence to be causally necessitated in terms of the idea that the sequence is an instance of a rule, then the feature of the sequence in virtue of which it is causally necessitated has to be repeatable, because it is essential to something's being a rule that it can be repeatedly instantiated. Therefore, if we are to

---

[24] We can block this inference to a law if we say that it is only because these types are instantiated in this particular thing that it is necessitated to change in this way —that is, if we index our references to the types to their particular instantiations in this particular thing (i.e. to what analytic metaphysicians call 'tropes'). But then the structure we have individuated in this explanation is itself merely a more complicated particular, and is unrepeatable for the same reasons that other particulars are unrepeatable.

[25] Allison, *Kant's Transcendental Idealism,* p. 223.

explain causal necessitation in terms of rules, it has to be binding at the level of types, not at the level of particulars.

Said differently, to think of a rule, it must be possible to think of what it would mean for it to be broken, in order to know what is ruled out by the rule, so to speak. But a rule that cannot be repeatedly instantiated would be a rule with only one possible instance. How can we understand what it would mean for a rule with only one possible instance to be broken? It could only be broken, it seems, in a case where the only possible instance of the rule did not accord with the rule. But if we are supposing that the rule's only possible instance does not accord with the rule, then what is it that we are supposing the instance does not accord with? We can give no example that would explain the rule, because an example would imply another possible instance of the rule. This would seem to demonstrate that we can form no concept of a rule with only one possible instance. For these reasons, it seems difficult to accept the idea that the Second Analogy only entails causal necessitation at the level of particulars. Since, as argued above, causal necessitation at the level of types implies the existence of causal laws, it is equally difficult to accept Allison's claim that the Second Analogy does not imply the existence of causal laws.

Allison has a second strategy he also uses to deny that the Second Analogy entails the existence of causal laws. Allison thinks that the Second Analogy can only entail the existence of particular causal laws if it entails that the schema of causality is a condition for ordering distinct events, in addition to being a condition for ordering the successions of states that constitute events. In the following passage, he argues that it is *not* a condition for ordering distinct events:

> Kant's argument [only] attempts to prove that the concept or schema of causality is a necessary condition of the experience of the succession of the states in an object, that is, of *an event*, not that it is a condition for the ordering of distinct events. One might think this too obvious to mention, were it not for the fact that the opposite is so frequently assumed to be the case. Some Kant interpreters make this assumption because they realize that the appeal to causal laws can be used to fix the temporal location of given events or types of events vis-à-vis one another. Thus, given a causal law linking events of type A (as cause) with events of type B (as effect), we can fix the temporal location of events of these types with respect to one another. And, since time cannot be perceived, it is only by appeal to such laws that we can determine the temporal order of distinct events. By extension of this principle we arrive at the idea that the determinability of the location of all events in a time presupposes their connectibility according to causal laws. There may very well be something to this line of argument, and it is certainly Kantian in spirit. The problem is that it is not

> the argument which Kant advances in the Second Analogy. The notion of the complete or thoroughgoing determinability of the temporal position of events is, for Kant, a regulative Idea; as such, it expresses a requirement of reason, not a transcendental condition of the possibility of experience.[26]

The distinction that this criticism depends upon, between successions that constitute events on the one hand, and successions of distinct events, on the other, is not relevant to the claim made in the Second Analogy. In this passage, Allison speaks of an event as a "succession of the states in an object." But Kant makes remarks in the Second Analogy which conclusively demonstrate that events so understood are always composed of smaller such events — since every succession of states can be broken down indefinitely into shorter successions of states— so that objective successions of determinations *constituting* an event always involve objective successions *of* events. The remarks are as follows:

> Between two instants there is always a time, and between two states at those two instants there is always a difference which has a magnitude. For all parts of appearances are always themselves magnitudes in turn. Therefore all transition from one state to another occurs in a time that is contained between two instants, the first determining the state the thing leaves, and the second determining the state the thing enters. Therefore both instants are limits of the time of a change, and so of the intermediate state between the two states...Now every alteration has a cause which evinces its causality in the entire time in which the alteration takes place. This cause, therefore, does not engender the alteration suddenly, i.e. at once or in an instant, but in a time; so that, as the time increases from its initial instant a to its completion in b, the magnitude of the reality (b-a) is also generated through all the smaller degrees contained between the first and the last. Therefore all alteration is possible only through a continuous action of the causality...This is the law of the continuity of all alteration. Its basis is this: that neither time nor appearance in time consists of parts which are the smallest, and that, nonetheless, the state of a thing passes, as it alters, through all these parts...to its second state...Therefore the reality's new state arises from the first state, in which it was not, through all the infinite degrees of this reality, and the differences of the degrees from one another are all smaller than that between 0 and a. (KrV A208-9/B253-4)

Given Kant's "law of the continuity of all alteration," any alteration can be subdivided into multiple alterations extending across shorter temporal intervals. In other words, any succession of states is always a

[26] Ibid., p. 229.

succession of successions of states. Therefore, it is impossible for the Second Analogy to provide for objective succession of states *constituting* events and not for objective succession *of* events, because the objective successions constituting events are always also objective successions of events. For this reason, we cannot accept Allison's claim that Kant considered the objective orderability of events merely a regulative idea.

II-4. Allison's Interpretation of Empirical Psychology

Now let us consider Allison's interpretation of empirical psychology, which he thinks lends support to his claim that the Second Analogy does not entail the existence of causal laws. According to Allison, Kant denies that there are laws of empirical psychology. This lends support to Allison's reading of the Second Analogy because, if there is some province of the empirical world where objective succession does not require causal laws, then Kant cannot consistently argue in Second Analogy that all objective succession requires causal laws. Therefore charity in interpretation would demand that we not interpret Kant as making such a claim in the Second Analogy.

Allison claims that "If reason and its causality...exhibit an empirical character, then the study of that character must pertain to the province of empirical psychology" and on this point he is correct.[27] He is also correct when he explains that "Kant denies that empirical psychology is a science, insisting that the most it can provide is a 'natural description...but not a science of the soul' (MAN 4: 471;8)."[28] Allison errs, however, when he goes on to claim that this involves a "denial of nomological status to the empirical generalizations of psychology." (Allison 1990: 33) In the text Allison cites (MAN 4: 471), Kant directly refers to the "laws" (*Gesetze*) of "inner sense," which are part of the content of "the empirical doctrine of the soul," i.e. empirical psychology:

> the empirical doctrine of the soul must always remain still further removed than chemistry from the rank of what may be properly called natural science, since mathematics is inapplicable to the phenomena of inner sense and their laws [*Gesetze*], unless one might want to take into consideration the law of continuity in the flow of this sense's inner changes, but the extension of cognition so obtained would bear much the same relation to the doctrine of body, as the doctrine of the properties of the straight line bears to the whole of geometry. [This inapplicability is due to the fact that]

[27] Allison, *Kant's Theory of Freedom*, pp. 31-2.
[28] Ibid., p. 32.

> the pure inner intuition in which the soul's phenomena are to be constructed is time, which has only one dimension.

Kant's point in this passage is not about whether or not there are psychological laws, though he clearly implies here that there are.[29] His point is rather about how much can be known a priori about these laws. He claims that not enough can be known a priori for empirical psychology to count as a science. The context for this passage is a discussion about how, if a "body of doctrine" is to count as science, or a "pure doctrine of nature," it must be possible to have a priori knowledge of some features of the particular empirical laws it contains. Whether such a priori knowledge is possible or not depends on how much of the "body of doctrine" can be represented mathematically. All of the objects of physics appear in space and time, and mathematics is applicable to both space and time. Kant thinks this means that we can have a significant amount of a priori knowledge about the features of the particular empirical laws of physics. The objects of inner sense, by contrast, only appear in time, and given temporality alone, there is much less scope for the application of mathematics. Kant concludes that we can have little or no a priori knowledge about the features of the particular laws governing the objects of inner sense. Thus physics counts as a science, and empirical psychology does not. Kant nowhere in this passage suggests that a lack of a priori knowledge about the features of the particular laws of empirical psychology implies a lack of a priori knowledge that there *are* laws of empirical psychology.

For these reasons, Allison is wrong to read Kant as holding that there are no laws of empirical psychology. Since his interpretation of empirical psychology is the last potential source of support for his view that the Second Analogy does not entail that laws exist, his view of the Second Analogy must be rejected. This means that Allison cannot weaken phenomenal determinism in any way that might make it more hospitable to incompatibilist free will. The best Allison's interpretation can offer us is an account of why we would be justified in ignoring phenomenal determinism when we think of ourselves as agents. But a theory based on this strategy would appear to be a form of compatibilism. At the very least, it must be acknowledged that it has no better claim to be called incompatibilistic than it has to be called compatibilistic.

---

[29] Kant also makes remarks in other places in his texts that indicate equally clearly the presence of empirical psychological laws. See e.g. KU 5: 278, where Kant says that "empirical laws about mental changes…show only how we do judge; they do not give us a command about how we ought to judge."

This implies that Allison's account of Kant's theory of free will cannot satisfactorily accommodate Kant's incompatibilism. Since Allison's account fails to accommodate Kant's incompatibilism because of fundamental features of the two-aspect interpretation, it seems reasonable to suppose that the fate of the two-aspect interpretation more generally must be the same as the fate of Allison's interpretation.

Conclusion

My goal has been to argue that Kant's incompatibilism can only be accommodated by accepting the ontological priority of noumena. In the first section I argued that the ontological interpretation can accommodate Kant's incompatibilism because it accepts the ontological priority of noumena, and that recent research shows that the ontological interpretation can mount a better defense against traditional objections than has often been thought. In the second section, I argued that the two-aspect interpretation cannot accommodate Kant's incompatibilism because it rejects the ontological priority of noumena. This provides an indirect argument for the ontological interpretation. The metaphysics required by the ontological interpretation is no doubt more complicated than the metaphysics required by the two-aspect interpretation. But it has long been recognized that incompatibilistic free will comes at a high metaphysical price. So it should not be too surprising to find that an interpretation that can accommodate incompatibilistic free will is more metaphysically complicated than an interpretation that cannot. The additional metaphysical complexity of the ontological interpretation can only be taken to be an important objection to it if one thinks that incompatibilistic free will is not worth the price. Kant seems to have thought it that it was worth the price.

Works Cited

Allison, H. *Idealism and Freedom* (New York: Cambridge University Press, 1996).

—. *Kant's Theory of Freedom* (New York: Cambridge University Press, 1990).

—. *Kant's Transcendental Idealism* (New Haven: Yale University Press, 1983).

Ameriks, K. "Kant and Hegel on Freedom: Two New Interpretations," *Inquiry* 35 (1992): pp. 219-232.

Beck, L.W. *Essays on Kant and Hume* (New Haven: Yale University

Press, 1978).

Bennett, J. "Kant's Theory of Freedom," in *Self and Nature in Kant's Philosophy*, ed. A.W. Wood (Ithaca: Cornell University Press, 1984).

Buchdahl, G. *Metaphysics and the Philosophy of Science* (New York: Oxford University Press, 1969).

Friedman, M. "Causal Laws and the Foundations of Natural Science," in *The Cambridge Companion to Kant*, ed. Paul Guyer (New York: Cambridge University Press, 1992).

Hanna, R. and Moore, A. "Reason, Freedom and Kant: An Exchange," *Kantian Review* 12, no. 1 (2007): pp. 113-133.

Hudson, H. *Kant's Compatibilism* (Ithaca: Cornell University Press, 1994).

Smith, N.K. *A Commentary to Kant's Critique of Pure Reason* (Atlantic Highlands: Humanities Press International, 1992).

Langton, R. *Kantian Humility: Our Ignorance of Things In Themselves* (New York: Oxford University Press, 1998).

Meerbote, R. "Kant on the Nondeterminate Character of Human Actions," in *Kant on Causality, Freedom, and Objectivity*, ed. William Harper and Ralf Meerbote (Minneapolis: University of Minneapolis Press, 1984).

Paton, H.J. *Kant's Metaphysic of Experience* (London: George Allen & Unwin, 1936).

Pereboom, D. "Kant on Transcendental Freedom," *Philosophy and Phenomenological Research* 73, no. 3 (2006): pp. 537-567.

Vilhauer, B. "The Scope of Responsibility in Kant's Theory of Free Will," forthcoming in the *British Journal for the History of Philosophy*.

—. "Can We Interpret Kant as a Compatibilist about Determinism and Moral Responsibility?" *British Journal for the History of Philosophy* 12, no. 4 (2004): pp. 719-730.

Watkins, E. *Kant and the Metaphysics of Causality* (New York: Cambridge University Press, 2005).

Walker, R. *Kant* (Boston: Routledge & Kegan Paul, 1978).

Wood, A.W. "Kant's Compatibilism," in *Self and Nature in Kant's Philosophy*, ed. Allen Wood (Ithaca: Cornell University Press, 1984).

CHAPTER TWO

THE LAST BEATITUDE OF SELF: SPONTANEITY'S "PLACE" IN THE OBJECTIVITY OF THE WORLD

JASON R. FISETTE

The Paralogisms, in which Kant cleans the clock of those peddling metaphysical truths about "the soul," can strike readers of modern sensibilities as being among the most agreeable sections in the *Critique of Pure Reason*. Now let us suppose that, among such favorably disposed readers, there is one who is nevertheless disappointed by what she takes to be a lacuna in Kant's account; namely, a failure to address the dialectical illusions arising when we make claims about the self's noumenal freedom or spontaneity—the sorts of claims, indeed, that Kant himself occasionally lets slip. However, being an attentive reader, she has also noted those passages where Kant speculates that mental states in themselves could be causal systems; for instance, the paragraph on A359-360 that culminates with the *speculation* that, in itself, "the same thing that in one reference is called corporeal would in another reference simultaneously be a thinking being…. Thus the expression which says that only souls think (as special kinds of substances) would be dropped."[1] She is aware that such fanciful speculations have no epistemic content, but what is important to her is that Kant seems to leave open the possibility of being made consistently metaphysically neutral on this point. Sufficiently encouraged, she pens the Fifth Paralogism that she feels Kant could have been persuaded to write. Its upshot would be something like this: *Although the "I" of the "I think" must necessarily be* ***represented as*** *spontaneous, I cannot know whether I really* ***am*** *spontaneous*. And this might be quite nice, except that it is not

[1] Immanuel Kant, *Critique of Pure Reason* (KrV), trans. Werner S. Pluhar (Indianapolis: Hackett, 1996). I have taken the liberty of switching Pluhar's "presentation" to "representation" in keeping with the translation of Kemp-Smith.

at all clear that Kant can say it.

The difficulty lies in the role spontaneity plays in Kant's theory of knowledge. What I aim to do is to unpack just what that role is, and so explain why Kant is led to make a claim about the noumenal self (and we shall see that there is such a claim) that is not readily quarantined from his larger epistemological project. These two aims correspond to the two parts of my paper. In the first portion, I look at Kant's remarks about spontaneity in the Transcendental Deduction. Kant there takes himself to be demonstrating that our sensibly received intuitions only become cognitively meaningful when we make a contribution. This contribution is a spontaneous act of synthesis that subsumes a manifold of intuitions into unity under the concept of an object in general. My discussion tracks spontaneity's pivotal position in this argument by focusing on the function of the transcendental unity of apperception. I begin with Kant's elaboration of the threefold synthesis in the A-Deduction, and follow him as he re-centers the work of synthesis explicitly around judgment in the first half of the B-Deduction.[2] Particular attention is paid to Kant's insistence that the spontaneous activity of the apperceptive "I think" yields objective necessity to our representations of the world through judgment in accordance with a priori categories. Finally, in the second part of the paper, I turn to two worries about spontaneity that have recently appeared in the literature on Kant. Robert Pippin notes that Kant's claims about spontaneity unavoidably press hard against an ostensible noumenal ignorance about the self, while John McDowell argues that Kant's spontaneity is needlessly spooky and can be remedied with a Hegelian move toward sociality. My own critical remarks will come by way of reply.

I-

The great Kantian insight is that there are two irreducible sources of knowledge, not one. While the Empiricists had fixated on experience and the Rationalists on reason, Kant realized that in many cases we can only get the content we want from experience and the necessity we want from a priori forms in the mind. "Our cognition arises from two basic sources of the mind. The first is our ability to receive representations (and is our receptivity for impressions); the second is our ability to cognize an object through these representations (and is the spontaneity of concepts)." (KrV

[2] I will not take up the complications to discursivity found in the second half of the B-Deduction and beyond.

A50/B74) Or, as he puts it rather more famously just a few lines later, "thoughts without content are empty; intuitions without concepts are blind." (KrV A51/B75) The celebrated case that drove Kant to this realization has to do with the principle of causality. Hume had argued for both our mental certainty regarding causality (we cannot help but think cause and effect really do and must happen) *and* for our inability to justify this certainty. As an empiricist, Hume had been looking in experience for the principle of necessary connection between cause and effect. Since he never perceived it, finding instead mere regularity, he concluded that the principle was a purely contingent one, and that the necessity we attribute to it has no justification in reason. Kant, besides being dumbfounded by this skeptical conclusion, notices that Hume's account of causality has curiously sidestepped what it ought to have explained. For our notion of cause and effect still has a necessary feel to it, and this is something repeated association just cannot account for.[3] But if we have this certainty, and if it does not come from experience, then the question remains—how is this possible? The answer Kant lays out in the course of the Transcendental Analytic depends upon our appreciation, contra Hume and Kant's predecessors more generally, that there are two sources of knowledge. Many of our concepts are abstracted from experience, but some essential ones are not.[4] These latter concepts, which are not learned from or determined by any experience, are a priori and have their seat in the spontaneity of the understanding. And when we relate to the world, these concepts establish the objective validity of our judgments about causality, substantiality, and the like.

Kant is aware that he has just given himself a puzzle. The puzzle is to explain how a subject blends spontaneity and receptivity together to get the objectivity of the world: how the "*subjective conditions of thought* could have *objective validity*, i.e., how they could yield conditions for the possibility of all cognitions of objects." (KrV A89/B122) His answer turns on the two main actors of his representationalist theory of knowledge, intuitions and concepts. That is, Kant is committed to the view that we can know appearances only and not things-in-themselves (things as they might be beyond the limits of the human condition), and his reconciliation of the subjective and the objective hinges on his notion of how we come to represent intuited appearances as objects through the use of concepts. Here is how Kant defines intuition and concept: "An intuition refers directly to

---

[3] For a defense of Hume on this point, see Annette C. Baier's *A Progress of Sentiments: Reflections on Hume's Treatise* (Cambridge, MA: Harvard University Press, 1991), especially chapters 2 and 3.

[4] See, for instance, Kant's remarks at KrV A51/B75 and KrV A85/B117.

the object and is singular; a concept refers to the object indirectly, by means of a characteristic that may be common to several things." (KrV A320/B377) When Kant says that an intuition is singular, he means that it proleptically represents an object of indeterminate appearance.[5] But if the appearance is irreducibly singular we cannot say anything (epistemic) about it; to do that, we have to bring the intuition under a concept. Concepts are universal organizing principles that allow us to represent the object *as an object*, lifting it up out of ineffable private immediacy into a cognitive space where its characteristics can be determinatively judged. Kant's development of this problem of discursivity, or how we represent appearances through concepts, will resolve the puzzle about how we get objective validity from subjective conditions of knowing because Kant explains that there are involved in this discursive process certain a priori concepts. These a priori concepts are necessary conditions for the possibility of experience; thus, the objective validity Hume could not find in the empirical world Kant locates in the spontaneity of the understanding.

Spelling out this claim sets the task of the Transcendental Deduction. My agenda in approaching that stretch of text is relatively narrow. I shall focus on the function Kant assigns to the transcendental unity of apperception, which is to unify a manifold of intuition under the concept of an object in general. I shall introduce this function through Kant's helpful depiction of synthesis in the A-Deduction, and then move to the B-Deduction's refinement of synthesis as judgment in accordance with the a priori concepts that are the categories. In the A-Deduction, Kant presents synthesis as the activity that applies a priori concepts to intuitions and thereby renders them objects of cognition (KrV A90/B123). Synthesis is a spontaneous activity whereby the (transcendental) subject takes the manifold of intuitions delivered up by sensibility and knits it, with the thread of pure concepts, into an object: "...*receptivity* can make cognition possible only when combined with *spontaneity*. Now, this spontaneity is the basis of a threefold synthesis that necessarily occurs in all cognition..." (KrV A97) Kant's account of the threefold synthesis consists of the three analytically distinct modes of apprehension, reproduction, and

[5] I draw the description of "prolepsis" from Allison's citation of Walsh. See Henry E. Allison, *Transcendental Idealism: An Interpretation and Defense*, revised edition (New Haven: Yale University Press, 2004), p. 82. The reference is to W. H. Walsh, *Kant's Criticisms of Metaphysics* (Edinburgh: Edinburgh University Press, 1997), p. 15.

recognition in a concept.[6] With the synthesis of apprehension in intuition, Kant tries to capture the idea that we need to become aware of the manifold *as* a manifold, which is to say as a complex deliverance of content with discrete moments spatio-temporally ordered in relation to one another: "[the manifold] must first be gone through and gathered together." (KrV A99) Apprehension is in everyday practice inseparable from the synthesis of reproduction, for without the ability to hold our acknowledgement of the discrete parts of a manifold in mind as we run through it, each part would fall away as soon as it was taken up and we would never have an eye for their hanging together as a whole. Consider Kant's example of drawing a line: "…if I always lost from my thoughts the preceding representations (the first parts of the line, the preceding parts of time, or the sequentially presented units) and did not reproduce them as I proceeded to the following ones, then there could never arise a whole representation…" (KrV A102) Reproduction allows us to be aware of our experience of a manifold as occurring through time. And, to point the way to the third mode of synthesis, it enables us to steadily apprehend those bits of lead markings being drawn on the paper as something we can recognize as a line. This synthesis of recognition in a concept completes Kant's exposition of this threefold synthesis, for the "final" step that the other modes have been anticipating is recognition of the manifold *as* an object. Put another way, it is the application of a concept that ties down a complex manifold in the unity of an object.

But this notion of the "unity of an object" needs to be parsed most carefully. In the context of Kant's representationalism we have access to appearances only, not things-in-themselves, entailing that the object in question is likewise only an appearance. Kant himself reiterates this strongly before proceeding:

> …cognitions are to refer to an object, and hence in reference to this object they must also necessarily agree with one another, i.e., they must have that unity in which the concept of an object consists. We are, however, dealing only with the manifold of our representations. And since that x (the object) which corresponds to them is to be something distinct from all our representations, this object is nothing for us. Clearly, therefore, the unity that the object makes necessary can be nothing other than the formal unity

---

[6] Béatrice Longuenesse observes that with this threefold synthesis Kant effectively illustrates how each stage of a probable empiricist project could not get off the ground without any transcendental moves. For a full discussion, see her *Kant and the Capacity to Judge: Sensibility and Discursivity in the Transcendental Analytic of the Critique of Pure Reason*, trans. Charles T. Wolfe (Princeton: Princeton University Press, 1998), Ch. 2, especially pp. 35-47.

> of consciousness in the synthesis of the manifold of the representations. (KrV A104-5)

The object we recognize *as* an object is an *achievement* of the unifying act of synthesis, not a given. Synthesis is a spontaneous act of unification that gathers our representations and introduces the unity of, say, an object and its predicates. What facilitates this accomplishment is the understanding's imposition of a concept on the manifold of intuition: "When we have brought about synthetic unity in the manifold of intuition—this is when we say that we cognize the object. This unity is impossible, however, unless the intuition can be produced according to a rule through a certain function of synthesis.... All cognition requires a concept [that]..., in terms of its form, is always something that is universal and serves as a rule." (KrV A105-6) The synthetic unity of an object, then, results from the application of an a priori concept that serves as a rule for the gathering of intuitions into objective unity.

It should be implicit in what I have already stated concerning synthesis that synthetic unity is only one member of a twinned pair. There is a subtle reciprocity between synthetic unity, which presents the combination of the manifold in an object, and the analytic unity of the combining subject. The full force of Kant's argument depends on articulating that relationship more exactly, which he attempts in a series of passages devoted to the principle of the transcendental unity of apperception. Allow me to collate from the B-Deduction a few of Kant's well-known remarks on this principle:

> The *I think* must be *capable* of accompanying all my representations. For otherwise something would be represented to me that could not be thought at all—which is equivalent to saying that the representation either would be impossible, or at least would be nothing to me. (...) But this representation is an act of spontaneity.... Or, again, I call it *original apperception*; for it is the self-consciousness [that] produces the representation *I think* that must be capable of accompanying all other representations and is one and the same in all consciousness. (...) Hence only because I can combine a manifold of given representations *in one consciousness*, is it possible for me to represent the *identity itself of the consciousness in these representations*. (KrV B131-3, translator's insertions suppressed)

I shall start out by addressing the aspect of analytic unity. The issue here is, *what is this synthesizing subject like?* Preliminarily, we might say that Kant is calling our attention to the fact that when I am conscious of a representation, what I want to say is that I am conscious of it as *my* representation. If it were not *my* representation, *I* would not be thinking it; either somebody else would, or "I" would be having some sort of multiple subjectivity disorder. I need not always be consciously attending to this sense of ownership with my every thought; Kant, evidently picking up on Leibniz's idea of *la petite perception*, willingly concedes that there are some low-grade mental activities of which a subject is not going to be aware: "the *I think* must be *capable* of accompanying all my representations." Still, this begs the question of just what I am referring to when I say that it is *my* representation. The answer, as is plain from the excerpt above, is the spontaneity of the "I think."

The move is a curious one, for Kant thereby signals that analytic unity points to synthetic unity. The reason lies in a lesson learned from Hume, and consequently Kant's motivation is perhaps best exhibited negatively for a moment. Hume could not find any fixed referent for the "I think" because he was searching for an impression of it in the flow of empirical consciousness, a fruitless search that can yield only "a self as many-colored and varied as [the] representations" we are conscious of (KrV B134). C. Thomas Powell observes that Hume's project goes wrong because it reifies thinking and perceiving, meaning that Hume searches for the activity of thinking in what has been thought.[7] And Kant is quite emphatic that this is what we cannot do. As he writes in a notorious footnote to KrV B158:

> Now unless I have in addition a different self-intuition that gives, prior to the act of *determination*, the *determinative* in me (only of its spontaneity am I in fact conscious) just as *time* so gives the determinable, then I cannot determine my existence as that of a self-active being; instead, I present only the spontaneity of my thought, i.e., of the act of determination….

The moral Kant is obliquely expressing is that we cannot find the determining in the determined. If there were some way (which there is not) to determine my spontaneity *as* an object, I would be immediately floored by contradictions. Chief among them is that I would have placed my spontaneous determin*ing* self into the realm of determin*ed* phenomenal objects and thereby submitted it to the law of causality, entailing that precisely that which I wanted to represent—my spontaneity—would be lost in the effort to represent it. A variant of this wildly supposes that we could nevertheless perform such a procedure but then stumbles over a remainder, the "different self-intuition" that did the determin*ing*. This

---

[7] C. Thomas Powell, *Kant's Theory of Self-Consciousness* (New York: Oxford University Press, 1990), p. 23.

would indicate that I did not do what I took myself to have done because I would then have to determine that determin*ing*, signaling the start of a nasty *ad infinitum*. In short, Kant is keenly aware that the "I think" is not a genuine referring expression, and accordingly he changes the topic of the subject from substance to function.[8] Rather than trying to identify a determinant referent of the "I think," Kant situates his analysis of the transcendental unity of apperception at the level of the determining spontaneity that constitutes the formal condition for the possibility of synthesis (and hence experience).

So how do analytic unity, *qua* the *mine-ness* of my representations, and synthetic *unity*, *qua* the spontaneity of synthesis, come together? Kant's most lucid explanation is arguably found in two selections from the second A-Paralogism:

> For since the representations (e.g., the individual words of a verse) that are distributed among different beings never amount to a whole thought (a verse), the thought cannot inhere in something composite *as* composite. Hence a thought is possible only in *one* substance that is not an aggregate of many and hence is absolutely simple.[9] (KrV A352)

And again, a couple of paragraphs down:

> ...it is obvious that we require, in order to have any thought, the absolute unity of the subject only because otherwise we could not say *I think* (the manifold being held together in one representation). For although the whole of the thought could be divided and distributed among many subjects, still the subjective *I* cannot be divided and distributed, and... we presuppose this *I* in all thought. (KrV A353)

What Kant uncovers is that the representation of the manifold *as* a manifold requires that there be *one* thought in *one* subject.[10] If I am to be aware of the whole *as* a whole, it follows that I must be conscious of the unity of my act of synthesis. *One* act of synthesis in *one* consciousness. Synthetic unity captures the difference between having the words and having the comprehension of the verse they compose. Yet this act of synthesis demands *one* "I think," or else the verse cannot be thought *as* a

---

[8] See Jay F. Rosenberg, "'I Think': Some Reflections on Kant's Paralogisms," *Midwest Studies in Philosophy* no. X (1986):525.

[9] Needless to say, the context in which the passage occurs is bent on demonstrating how we would err in taking this "absolute simplicity" as consisting in anything more than a transcendental claim.

[10] Allison, op. cit., p. 164.

verse and it crumbles back into disconnected words. A group of people each thinking one word of the verse will not *a poem* think. Therefore, the synthetic unity of representation—"I think (M_1 and M_2)"—necessarily summons forth an awareness of the analytic unity of consciousness—"the 'I' that thinks M_1=the 'I' that thinks M_2."[11] The identity of my act of synthesis, which "subjects all synthesis of apprehension… to a transcendental unity" in the concept of an object in general, discloses my numerical identity as the single "I think" underwriting that act of representation (KrV A108). To reiterate, this numerical identity of the "I think" is a strictly transcendental unity; *qua* condition for the possibility of experience, its unity is not something we can have experience of or make substantive claims about. Function replaces substance. Hence the upshot of this discussion: the spontaneous "I think" is not in the world, but rather is my point of view on the synthesizing activity that gives me the world.

But the transcendental unity of apperception stands at a remove from the phenomenal world not so that it can flex its spontaneity any which way. Kant hones in on apperception's spontaneity because he sees it as the source of the objective validity in our experience that cannot be found in the contingent determinations of empirical consciousness:

> Only the original unity of apperception is valid objectively. The empirical unity of apperception… is only derived from the original unity under given conditions *in concreto*, [and so] has only subjective validity. One person will link the representation of a certain word with one thing, another with some other thing; and the unity of consciousness in what is empirical is not, as regards what is given, necessary and universally valid. (KrV B140)

Kant's emphatic gesture is relatively easy to follow if we recall that experience is object-awareness, and that this representation of an object *as* an object arises out of the unifying activity of the transcendental unity of apperception. Specifically, this unifying activity is the spontaneous act of synthesis whereby an intuited manifold is united in the concept of an object. Our resultant representation of an object comes with a necessary cognitive form (e.g., it is a substance with properties, it plays a role in relations of cause and effect) because what binds the manifold into its *objective* unity are a priori concepts contributed by the spontaneity of the understanding. We simply do not experience the world as dependent on the contingencies of repeated association or on the peculiarities of a subject's mental states (determinations of her inner sense). Indeed, to whatever extent we do encounter these sorts of subjective unity, we regard

---

[11] Powell, op. cit., p. 31.

them as aberrations of the way things really *are*.

Ratcheting up his argument, Kant restates the distinction between an objective and a subjective unity by proposing that we identify the former as a spontaneous act of judgment. The business of synthesis discloses itself as ultimately being about putting our representations together in an objective unity—the object *is*—whose judgmental form is underwritten by categories:

> …a judgment is nothing but a way of bringing given cognitions to the objective unity of apperception. This is what the little relational word *is* in judgments intends to indicate, in order to distinguish the objective unity of given representations from the subjective one. For this word indicates the reference of the representations to the original apperception and its *necessary unity*. (KrV B141-2)

The spontaneity of apperception is thus objective judgment about the world in accordance with a priori concepts, or categories. To pursue this notion of judgment further, I need to tack backwards to the Metaphysical Deduction. The terribly compact conclusion of §20, which marks the limit of this paper's encounter with the Transcendental Deduction, should assist in revealing why:

> …everything manifold, insofar as it is given in one empirical intuition, is *determined* in regard to one of the logical functions of judging, inasmuch as through this function it is brought to one consciousness as such. The *categories*, however, are indeed nothing but precisely these functions of judging insofar as the manifold of a given intuition is determined in regard to them. Hence, by the same token, the manifold in a given intuition is subject necessarily to the categories. (KrV B143)

Kant wants to claim that the way in which apperception's judgments form the unity of a manifold of intuition—for example, the way in which we represent objects using *logical* subject-predicate form—somehow tokens the spontaneous application of a priori concepts or categories. This seems to me obscure unless we get some sort of handle on a question that has been hovering for some time now; namely, which a priori concepts are being applied when the transcendental unity of apperception makes a judgment? Kant's reply is, just those we need to represent the objects of the world. This can sound cheap, but the deeper point behind it is not. Kant does not want to say that all our concepts are a priori categories, merely some. The categories are consequently just those indispensable for "bringing given cognitions to the objective unity of apperception" (KrV

B141), those that can provide an intuitive manifold with the objective unity that is transcendentally necessary for us to experience those representations *as* objects in the world.[12] But of course this is only the first step toward an answer, for the question still is *which concepts are these?*

Infamously, Kant claims that we need not go very far afield to find them. We can discern them through something we use everyday—the logical functions of judgment. Kant had, in fact, so identified them earlier in the Metaphysical Deduction,[13] where Kant seizes upon logic[14] as a clue "for the discovery of all pure concepts of understanding." (KrV A66/B91) We find a guide in logic because logic, like the transcendental unity of apperception, trades in concepts and their application to objects. Consider two typical logical forms of judgment: *S is P* or *if X then Y*. These judgments proceed according to rules, and a concept is just that—a rule. The important thing to notice about these rules or concepts is their function: they gather unity through "the act of arranging various representations under one common representation." (KrV A68/B93) This allows us to make some headway, because Kant tells us that there are four headings of general logic (quantity, quality, relation, modality) that perform these acts of unification. Each of these four have three corresponding operations, yielding twelve logical functions of judgment that operate as a kind of transcendental syntax. Such transcendental syntax

---

[12] Longuenesse, op. cit., 71-78.

[13] The Metaphysical and Transcendental Deductions differ in the following regard. Whereas the Metaphysical Deduction establishes that the categories are necessarily presupposed by the logical functions of judgment, what it does not show is that the categories are necessary for all epistemic representation of appearances—that is the job of the Transcendental Deduction. Hence, while the Metaphysical Deduction can only *speculate* that the categories must be necessary conditions for the possibility of experience, the Transcendental Deduction seeks to *demonstrate* that they are; Kant's transcendental "proofs" of individual categories are found in the Axioms, Anticipations, Analogies, and Postulates.

[14] Kant distinguishes between general and transcendental logic. General logic is concerned solely with the relations of thought without regard to its objects, and so countenances talk of what is logically possible but not really possible. Transcendental logic (the sort Kant is interested in doing) deals in the relation of thought to objects in an effort to say how a priori thought of really possible objects is possible: "...*transcendental logic*... deals merely with the laws of understanding and of reason; yet it does so only insofar as this logic is referred a priori to objects—unlike general logic, which is referred indiscriminately to empirical as well as pure rational cognitions." (KrV A57-8/B81-2) See also Sebastian Gardner, *Kant and the Critique of Pure Reason* (New York: Routledge, 1999), pp. 125 ff., and W. H. Walsh, op. cit., p. 63.

demands a transcendental semantics, however, because these logical functions have an objective force that is beyond the way we happen to talk. This need for semantics is met by the categories, which are those non-arbitrary concepts we make use of when we judge in accord with the logical functions of judgment. Our use of hypotheticals, for example, is only intelligible if we have a priori concepts of cause and effect. (And vice-versa; it is hard to see how we could speak of cause and effect without using something like a hypothetical.) Each logical function therefore has its corresponding category.

Consequently, the nub of the metaphysical deduction is that these twelve categories *are* the very a priori concepts we have been looking for; they are "concepts of an object in general, whereby the object's intuition is regarded as *determined* in terms of one of the *logical functions* in judging" (KrV B128). In both logical judgment and object representation we find the same unifying function at work, and what this tells us is that both activities have a shared root in one and the same understanding:

> …the same understanding—and indeed through the same acts whereby it brought about, in concepts, the logical form of judgment by means of analytic unity—also brings into its representations a transcendental content, by means of the synthetic unity of the manifold in intuition as such; and because of this, these representations are called pure concepts of understanding applying a priori to objects. (KrV A79/B105)

When the spontaneity issuing forth from the understanding then applies the categories to the intuitions delivered up by sensibility, there is introduced a transcendental content that generates what we mean by the objectivity of the world. For the world is what Kant is driving at with his notion of a category as the concept of an object *in general*. In general—something that holds generally for all subjects as the very condition of possibility for there being one world that a "mutual us" can share knowledge of and yet have particular takes on.[15] The world as we share it is not built up out of the sensible data that pool in our irreducibly singular subjective consciousnesses. On the contrary, it is only because we are able to break free from immediacy and tap into the transcendental unity of apperception's impersonal consciousness-in-general that the world and its objects come into view in the way they do.[16]

---

[15] Walsh, op. cit., p. 42.
[16] Ibid., p. 51.

II-

At this juncture I want to call attention to two linked conclusions that will serve to sharpen the balance of this paper. (1) Kant's interest is not any phenomenal self, but rather the spontaneous "I think" of the transcendental unity of apperception. From now on, my use of "self" will be in line with the latter unless noted otherwise. (2) Nothing can be epistemically predicated of this thinking self; it is simply the logical subject required for discursive cognition: "through this *I* or *he* or *it* (the thing) that thinks, nothing more is represented than a transcendental subject of thoughts=X." (A346/B404) Broadly speaking, it is armed with these two principles that Kant sails smoothly onward into the Paralogisms, setting aright troubled waters populated by the rational psychologists. Of the Paralogisms I will say only the following: their fallaciousness turns on the conflation of how we must necessarily conceive of the self as functioning with how the self really *is*. *Qua* logical subject of judgment, the self functions as a simple entity identical through time. From this arises the unavoidable illusion that these transcendentally necessary functions can be traced back to a self that *really is* so predicable. The rational psychologist, questing after the incontrovertible proofs constitutive of "spirituality" (KrV A345/B403), reads function back into substance in just this wrongheaded way.

Still, does what Kant say about spontaneity show that there lingers in him, too, this hankering after something *more*? As Robert Pippin makes abundantly clear in "Kant on the Spontaneity of Mind," there is at least preliminary reason to wonder. Perhaps the chief reason is the directness with which Kant frequently opposes the spontaneity of the transcendental unity of apperception to the causal determinations of empirical consciousness. After all, at the heart of the *Critique* lies the recognition that objects with full-blown subject-predicate form do not just drift into consciousness from the world. Our knowledge springs from an *active* faculty of thought that gathers together a passively received intuitive manifold and represents it *as* an object. Spontaneity plays an ineliminable role in Kant's story. But that spontaneity looms large in his epistemology is not in dispute; what is in dispute is that the attribution of spontaneity to the "I think" seems tantamount to making a claim about the noumenal self. And this, of course, is the very thing that the Paralogisms teach us not to do. Luckily, there is a quick counter that seemingly allows us to safely shrug off this curious problem, chalking it up instead to a hostile reading of the text. The byline of this defense is that Kant is no more claiming that the self is *in itself* spontaneous than he is that it is *in itself* simple, numerically identical, etc. These are alike in being only transcendental or formal conditions for the possibility of knowledge. If spontaneity appears any different, that may admittedly be a shortcoming of Kant's presentation, but one easily remedied by a sense for the argument as a whole.

Pippin believes that this transcendental wagon-circling cannot defend Kantian spontaneity, and squarely challenges the validity of the formalist defense. Pippin sets the stage with two theses usually credited to Kant. (1) Noumenal Ignorance: We do not know what thoughts or selves are in themselves; they might be material, immaterial, or something else entirely. (2) Metaphysical Neutrality: So long as we keep a firm grip on the distinction between the self as *logical* subject of experience and the self as *substantive* type of being, and remember that Kant will only be concerned with the former, we will not be tempted to make noumenal claims about the self.[17] I shall return to these in a moment, but first I want to nod to a number of passages where Kant evidently strays and makes claims about the self to which he was not entitled. Pippin draws our attention to an instance of this occurring at KrV A546-7/B574-5: "Only the human being, who otherwise is acquainted with all of nature solely through his senses, cognizes himself also through mere apperception—viz., in actions and inner determinations that he cannot class at all with any impressions of sense. And thus he is to himself, indeed, on the one hand phenomenon, but on the other hand—viz., in regard to certain powers—a merely intelligible object, because his action cannot be classed at all with the receptivity of sensibility."[18] Bracketing such apparent indulgences will not solve the difficulty, however. Once we go back to Pippin's two theses, we see that by these standards (which are Kant's own) even a strictly formalist interpretation of spontaneity exhibits the very symptoms it purports to cure. The reason why is that getting it off the ground obliges us to run afoul of metaphysical neutrality. Once we are committed to saying that the logical subject must be spontaneous, we have already confused the distinction between the logical and substantive selves. The requirement of spontaneity hoists a substantive commitment onto a purely logical subject (violating Metaphysical Neutrality) because if spontaneity means anything it means freedom from material causality, implying that we then know one

---

[17] Robert B. Pippin, "Kant on the Spontaneity of Mind," *Canadian Journal of Philosophy* 17, no. 2 (June 1987), p. 450. Pippin also mentions a third thesis, Empirical Dualism (or, that there is, *empirically speaking*, a dualism of mental and physical), but I have left it out because it seems not especially relevant to my focus.

[18] Ibid., p. 454.

thing about the thinking self—that it must be non-material (violating Noumenal Ignorance).[19]

Two concessions have been made to advance a pro-Kantian defense: that Kant sometimes willfully gets himself into trouble, and that spontaneity is best interpreted as a merely formal condition of apperception. Both have proven unsuccessful. However, there is another conceivable strategy, which is to concede spontaneity *tout court*. Desiring to save Kant's representationalism, and yet seeing no possibility of comfortably doing that while it houses spontaneity, some thinkers opt to essentially excise spontaneity from the theory by gutting its contentfulness. Pippin observes that Wilfrid Sellars and Patricia Kitcher have proposed variants of something like this. Without going into the details of those projects, it can be said (and only somewhat facetiously) that the idea here is to treat spontaneity as a kind of transcendental fetishism. There really is no spontaneity, but we cannot help but think we have got some. These sorts of thinkers look for inspiration in passages like the following, which I quoted at the start of this paper:

> [In itself], the same thing that in one reference is called corporeal would in another reference simultaneously be a thinking being.... Thus the expression which says that only souls think (as special kinds of substances) would be dropped. We would say, rather, as we do usually, that human beings think; i.e., that the same thing which as outer appearance is extended is intrinsically in itself a subject that is not composite but is simple and thinks. (KrV A359-360)

Such apparent "willingness to treat mental events causally"[20] goes to show that there is no insurmountable obstacle to making Kant consistently metaphysically neutral. Kant's own better instincts, so the argument might run, trump the evidence of his stubbornness. Representationalism can be translated into a kind of materialist brain functionalism without remainder, and any indeterminate feeling we have of our spontaneity can be tidily explained away as epiphenomenal. But setting aside any evaluation of neurophilosophy's independent merits, can Kant actually be reconciled with such an approach? Pippin thinks not, arguing that there lies concealed here a parting of the ways on how to define knowledge. Summing up Kant's view, he writes that, "if it turns out we really are causal systems on the noumenal level, then the states, beliefs and judgments produced by such systems *would not be* epistemic claims, even if the beliefs can be said

[19] Ibid., p. 451 and passim.
[20] Ibid., p. 466.

to correspond to both phenomenal and noumenal reality."[21] Spontaneity reflects Kant's deep commitment to the idea that knowledge is more than a procession of causally produced states. Whatever virtues a naturalistic epistemology has to offer us, what Kant means by a priori knowledge is not among them.[22] To Kant knowledge is only explicable as a product of an active intelligence. So we can junk spontaneity if we really want to, but then it is no longer clear why we would care enough about the Kantian insight to bother "saving" it.

How are we to get out of this muddle? A fresh perspective on the problem is offered by John McDowell. Coming at the issue of spontaneity from a self-identified Hegelian angle, he lays the blame directly at the feet of Kant's needlessly spooky metaphysics. Agreeing with Kant that an empiricist project of building up the world from sense-data is mistaken, and agreeing furthermore that our experience is always already conceptual, McDowell nonetheless disagrees over where the concepts that give us the objectivity of the world come from. Where Kant goes wrong, McDowell might say, is in stuffing everything needed for knowledge into a single subject. If that is all we have to work with, then to be sure we will be led into some circuitous maneuvers involving spontaneity and the categories. Luckily a single subjectivity is not all we have to work with. Each of us, presumably, is born into a community whose traditions (especially language) provide us with the normative conditions of possibility for an orientation to the world: "…human beings are born mere animals, and they are transformed into thinkers…. This transformation risks looking mysterious. But we can take it in stride if… we give pride of place to the learning of a language. In being initiated into a language, a human being is introduced into something that already embodies putatively rational linkages between concepts… before she comes on the scene."[23] We can have a spontaneity that is not noumenal, and a knowledge that is not brutally causal, because there is not one order of causality, but two. The first order is the causality of the natural world (McDowell calls this the realm of law), and it is the one from which Kant rightly withdrew when he was unable to find anything in it that could justify the necessity of our knowledge.

All the same, it does not follow that a radical break from phenomenality is needed, which is the route Kant seems to be taking with

---

[21] Ibid., p. 472.

[22] Allison, op. cit., p. 169.

[23] John McDowell, *Mind and World* (Cambridge: Harvard University Press, 2003), p. 125.

his hedging about the thinking self's noumenal spontaneity.[24] That need is obviated by the second order of causality, where spontaneity is diffused into sociality and sociality's progressive historical elaboration of what it takes to be rational standards of knowledge.[25] The Hegelian line is that we can at once be thoroughly in the world *and* preserve Kant's decisive thought that knowledge requires a human contribution to sensibility. Here I can simply tender the most minimal indications of that argument. Hegel believes that Kant is mistaken on two interlocking counts. (1) Kant, although he correctly attends to the necessary conditions for the possibility of experience, errs in supposing that these transcendental conditions are a priori concepts absolutely independent from all the contingencies of a community's historical situatedness. (2) As a direct consequence of this mistake, Kant fixates on finding a way to tap into these *independent* concepts *independently* or *spontaneously*. So, Hegel concludes, Kant's masterstroke against givenness misfires. Kant took a set of concepts that he more or less rightly identified as the necessary grounds of human experience—and then dirempted them out of their proper setting in the movement of the historical a priori and into a breathless space known only to the spontaneity of the understanding.

Continuing the trajectory of this thought would carry me well beyond the confines of this study. I shall conclude, instead, with a reflection on the image of two spheres. The first sphere comes from the Transcendental Doctrine of Method and the extended metaphor Kant treats us to in the section subtitled, "On the Impossibility of a Skeptical Satisfaction of Pure Reason as Disunited With Itself." Here we find the extraordinary image of the geographer of human reason. Like a cartographer of worlds, this surveyor of human reason also charts limits. Human reason is like the plane of the earth, promising to race before us into infinite horizons. The bad geographer sets her limits too broadly or narrowly and so wanders about lost in dogmatism or skepticism. The wise geographer, on the other hand, realizes that

> …[the dwelling-place for constant residence] can be found only in a

---

[24] Ibid., esp. pp. 99-104 and 108-126.

[25] As Pinkard frequently puts it in his excellent commentary, the progression is due to a community's seeking to assure itself that what it takes to be rational *really is* rational; when a community's standards do not prove up to the task, new standards are formed that do provide that assurance. In the *Phenomenology of Spirit*, Hegel's eye is always on folding everything that appears externally given back into relation with Spirit or sociality. See Terry Pinkard, *Hegel's Phenomenology: The Sociality of Reason* (New York: Cambridge University Press, 1996).

> complete certainty, whether certainty in the cognition of the objects themselves or certainty in the cognition of the bounds within which all our cognition of objects is enclosed. Our reason is by no means a plane spread out indeterminably far, whose limits one cognizes only in a general way. It must, rather, be compared to a sphere whose radius one can find from the curvature of the arc on its surface (i.e., from the nature of synthetic a priori propositions), from which in turn one can reliably indicate also the sphere's content and boundary. (KrV A761-2/B789-90)

This sphere is the very picture of the confident self-repose of the transcendental unity of apperception, which encircles our experience with categorical arcs spun with the spontaneity of the understanding.

The second sphere comes to us from a most remarkable setting. For it is Hegel, in an almost magical coincidence, who also presents us with a sphere at the very moment in the *Phenomenology* when he begins his push beyond Kantianism.[26] Hegel opens his chapter on "Self-Consciousness" by observing that *self-consciousness* has come to glimpse its powers of determining *consciousness*. He also describes the contrast as between self-consciousness and "life" or "the whole expanse of the sensuous world."[27] "[Life's] sphere is completely determined in the following moments. *Essence* is infinity as the *supersession* of all distinctions, the pure movement of axial rotation, its self-repose being an absolutely restless infinity; *independence* itself, in which the differences of the movement are resolved, the simple essence of Time which, in this equality with itself, has the stable shape of Space."[28] McDowell, in a different essay, calls for reading Hegel's self-consciousness as "the apperceptive I" and consciousness or life as "the empirical self."[29] If McDowell is correct, and although I cannot argue for it here I believe he is, then Hegel's image of the sphere should be read as harboring a special allusion to Kant. Hegel sees himself as breathing life back into the conditions of human cognition that Kant froze in the timelessness of spontaneity. Hegel's sphere is the infinite movement, the seemingly endless expanse of conflicts of the Kantian dialectic or the Hegelian highway of despair, from which its

---

[26] In the context of the section, it is the sphere of the living Earth.

[27] G. W. F. Hegel, *Phenomenology of Spirit*, trans. A. V. Miller (New York: Oxford University Press, 1977), pp. 105-106 (¶167-168).

[28] Ibid., 106 (¶169). The references to "Time" and "Space," the forms of human intuition, are also strong hints that Hegel is taking on Kant's transcendental epistemology.

[29] McDowell, "The apperceptive I and the empirical self: towards a heterodox reading of 'Lordship and Bondage' in Hegel's *Phenomenology*," *Bulletin of the Hegel Society of Great Britain* 47/48 (2003): pp. 1-16.

Kantian counterpart withdraws. Kantian epistemology withdraws from life in order to live in the world. The serene Kantian sphere, which recalls the perfect divine orbs of ancient philosophy, is held aloft by the strength of the conviction that there is something that can underwrite all our epistemic doubts with an absolute guarantee. Needless to say, *this* world offers no such assurances. Yet, there is a beyond—spontaneity—that does; Kant must deny the life of the community to make room for epistemological faith.

To conclude, Kant changed the question of the cognizing subject from (metaphysical) substance to (transcendental) function. But substance reappears. In a manner befitting the return of the repressed, the normative bindingness of Spirit or *Geist*—the I that is a We and the We that is an I—returns to us in spontaneity. We will remember that in his introduction to the A-Paralogisms Kant told us that the rational psychologist kept a prayer book, the sole text of which is, "I think." And perhaps, before throwing it away, Kant tore a page loose—for in spontaneity, the intersubjectively assured rationality of our concepts and our knowledge comes down to us like a blessing.

Works Cited

Allison, Henry E. *Transcendental Idealism: An Interpretation and Defense*, revised edition. New Haven: Yale University Press, 2004.

Baier, Annette C. *A Progress of Sentiments: Reflections on Hume's Treatise*. Cambridge, MA: Harvard University Press, 1991.

Gardner, Sebastian. *Kant and the Critique of Pure Reason*. New York: Routledge, 1999.

Hegel, G. W. F. *Phenomenology of Spirit*. Translated by A. V. Miller. New York: Oxford University Press, 1977.

Kant, Immanuel. *Critique of Pure Reason*. Translated by Werner S. Pluhar. Indianapolis: Hackett, 1996.

Longuenesse, Béatrice. *Kant and the Capacity to Judge: Sensibility and Discursivity in the Transcendental Analytic of the Critique of Pure Reason*. Translated by Charles T. Wolfe. Princeton: Princeton University Press, 1998.

McDowell, John. "The apperceptive I and the empirical self: towards a heterodox reading of 'Lordship and Bondage' in Hegel's *Phenomenology*." In *Bulletin of the Hegel Society of Great Britain* 47/48 (2003): 1-16.

—. *Mind and Word*. Cambridge: Harvard University Press, 2003.

Pinkard, Terry. *Hegel's Phenomenology: The Sociality of Reason*. New

York: Cambridge University Press, 1996.

Pippin, Robert B. "Kant on the Spontaneity of Mind." *Canadian Journal of Philosophy* 17, no. 2 (June 1987): 449-475

Powell, C. Thomas. *Kant's Theory of Self-Consciousness*. New York: Oxford University Press, 1990.

Rosenberg, Jay F. "'I Think': Some Reflections on Kant's Paralogisms." *Midwest Studies in Philosophy*, no. X (1986): 503-530

Walsh, W. H. *Kant's Criticisms of Metaphysics*. Edinburgh: Edinburgh University Press, 1997.

CHAPTER THREE

THE MERITS AND DEFICIENCIES OF KANT'S "INCORPORATION THESIS" AS AN INTERPRETATION AND A REVISION

DIANE WILLIAMSON

This paper evaluates a trend in recent Kant scholarship toward interpreting Kant's moral philosophy according to his so-called "Incorporation Thesis." Essentially, the Incorporation Thesis is an anti-Humean theory of rational agency, which has nothing to do with moral autonomy and noumenal agency.[1] Nevertheless, attention to the Incorporation Thesis has grown because it is thought to be the key to interpreting Kant's moral theory and his theory of freedom. Although not the first to discover it, Allison is the first to name this thesis and Guyer and Korsgaard follow his interpretation.[2] I explain Allison's presentation of the Incorporation Thesis, and I show that Korsgaard and Guyer adopt a similar strategy in their interpretations. Then I turn to an analysis of *Religion Within the Boundaries of Mere Reason*, the text that is used as the primary support for this reading, and question the soundness of using this work to mitigate or amend statements from the *Groundwork* or second *Critique*. I show that the *Religion* essay, the *Lectures on Ethics*, and the *Anthropology from a Pragmatic Viewpoint* all contain statements that both support and refute the idea that inclinations determine the will and hence undermine freedom. I argue that this inconsistency demonstrates Kant's reliance on two different notions of freedom: one conferred by our status as human beings, the other conferred by our status as moral beings.

---

[1] I am grateful to Anne Margaret Baxley for helping me to understand this point.

[2] Henry Allison, *Kant's Theory of Freedom* (Cambridge University Press, 1990); Paul Guyer, *Kant on Freedom, Law, and Happiness* (Cambridge University Press, 2000); Christine Korsgaard, *Creating the Kingdom of Ends* (Cambridge University Press, 1996).

Proponents of the Incorporation Thesis hope to downplay the importance of the latter by replacing it with the former because, as is commonly believed, Kant's notion of autonomy requires that we pit the physical, conative, and emotional aspects of the subject in opposition to her moral pursuits. Such a consequence, if it is in fact a necessary consequence of Kant's notion of autonomy, is unfortunate, if not damning. Nevertheless, none of his works gives us sufficient evidence for attributing the Incorporation Thesis to him as a means of escaping it. This paper works toward an answer to the following overarching question: Is it possible that to formulate a new understanding of Kantian freedom and morality in terms of a more general understanding of rationality and good decision-making, eschewing Kant's troublesome stance on heteronomy and the insensitivity toward all worldly concerns that seems to follow from it? While I am sympathetic to this goal, I do not think the Incorporation Thesis provides sufficient means. I also show that reliance on the Incorporation Thesis has the unintended effect of whitewashing over that which is distinct and valuable about Kantianism: its refusal to cast morality in terms of prudential reasoning.

Allison's formulation of the "Incorporation Thesis" draws from the first *Critique*. He argues that, like the *Religion* essay, the first *Critique*, when read on its own terms, offers a distinct and more defensible model of moral decision-making than do Kant's more explicitly moral works. The first *Critique* successfully supports the Incorporation Thesis as a theory of rational agency; this use of the Incorporation Thesis is relatively uncontroversial. Yet Allison, Guyer, and Korsgaard all make use of the Incorporation Thesis as an interpretation of Kant's moral philosophy. They rely exclusively on the *Religion* essay to support their specific, moral interpretation of the Incorporation Thesis because, as we shall see, the *Religion* essay is uniquely able to create a link between the Incorporation Thesis as a theory of rational agency and its use as a replacement for the formalism of Kantian autonomy.

In his book *Kant's Theory of Freedom*, Allison offers the term "Incorporation Thesis" to refer to the following quote from the *Religion* essay: "an incentive can determine the will to an action only insofar as the individual has *incorporated* it into his maxim." (R 6:24, emphasis mine)[3] An inclination cannot in itself cause the subject to act; the inclination only causes action if the subject first *freely* chooses to act on the maxim of

[3] Allison, *Kant's Theory of Freedom*, p. 40. The German text uses the verb *aufnehmen*, which is translated as "to incorporate," but could easily be translated by a verb, like "to accept," that does not imply dualism.

following inclination. As we shall see, the moral significance of this idea hangs on the meaning that is given to the term "free." The idea from the *Religion* essay is that we choose a meta-maxim for all of our behavior: either to follow inclinations even when they conflict with the moral imperative, or to always follow the moral imperative. Therefore, immoral acts are not *caused* by natural inclinations: they are caused by our choice to follow those inclinations. Allison argues that inclinations should be seen as motives, not causes, as they do not, as he puts it, "motivate by themselves… but rather [only] as being taken as reasons and incorporated into maxims."[4]

Allison elaborates on the idea of choosing a meta-maxim and assimilates it to the idea that the practical agent subsumes inclinations under practical rules or maxims just as the understanding subsumes sensibility under the categories of the understanding. Therefore, the free practical agent is an analog to the subject of the transcendental unity of apperception: "just as it must be possible for the 'I think' to accompany all my representations in order for them to be 'mine'… it must be possible for the 'I take' to accompany all my inclinations if they are to be mine qua rational agent, that is, if they are to provide motives or reasons for acting." In this way, Allison redefines "spontaneity" as "conceptual creativity" and argues that Kant believes that "spontaneity" is necessary for decision-making because "to conceive of oneself … as a rational agent is to adopt a model of deliberative rationality in terms of which choice involves both a taking as and a framing or positing." One ought to object that the spontaneity of the transcendental unity of apperception is a transcendental function and that the spontaneity of moral autonomy is a noumenal act and that neither can, on principle, be a part of phenomenal consciousness because phenomenal consciousness is subject to the categories of the understanding, specifically causality, which makes the time-series determined. To counter this likely objection, Allison gets around the phenomena/noumena dichotomy by arguing that these decision-making, mental activities can only be thought but not experienced.[5]

To support this interpretation, Allison draws from his two-aspect interpretation developed in his earlier *Kant's Transcendental Idealism*. He

---

[4] Allison, *Kant's Theory of Freedom*, p. 51. This terminology is Allison's, not Kant's: in his lectures on moral philosophy Kant distinguishes between objective and subjective motives (*motivum subjecte movens* and *motivum objecte movens*) and uses the term *Motiv* to refer generally to all kinds of grounds of action. See J. MacMurray's introduction to Immanuel Kant, *Lectures on Ethics*, trans. Louis Infield (Harper and Row, 1963).

[5] Allison, *Kant's Theory of Freedom*, pp. 38-40.

argues that Kant's notion of freedom is defensible because, given the fact that causal determinism only explains one aspect of the subject, there is no reason to think that Kant's brand of freedom requires real disconnection from the phenomenal world.[6] Allison describes the typical problem involved in accepting Kant's notion of freedom thusly: "either freedom is located in some timeless noumenal realm, in which case it may be reconciled with the causality of nature, but only at the cost of making the concept both virtually unintelligible and irrelevant to the understanding of human agency, or, alternatively, freedom is thought to make a difference in the world, in which case both the notion of its timeless, noumenal status and the unrestricted scope within nature of the causal principle must be abandoned."[7] Allison applies his two-aspect approach to Kant's theory of freedom by suggesting that we can view an action either, as scientists, from the assumption that the agent is an empirical entity and thus find causes for the action, or from the assumption that the actor is a moral agent, responsible for the action, and thereby take the agent to be its cause. We might say the latter of these two ways of viewing the agent, as it postulates an intelligible character, is merely an *idea* necessary for acting morally and holding people responsible. Although Allison does not explicitly reject such a reading, his interpretation builds more content into the idea of spontaneity, assuming that it includes the idea of the agent as a "rational deliberator."[8] The Incorporation Thesis states that all choices require freedom. Allison rightly points out that "among the major consequences of the Incorporation Thesis [...] is the recognition that even heteronomous or non-morally based actions are free for Kant in an incompatibilist sense."[9] This consequence is surprising because the opposite is often assumed: Kantian freedom is thought to apply only to autonomous acts, i.e., ones that conform to the categorical imperative. Instead, Allison argues that "*both* moral *and* pragmatic or prudential imperatives indicate a causality of reason."[10] Allison thereby uses the Incorporation Thesis to support his two-aspect defense of the Kantian notion of freedom: *every* action can be viewed from either the assumption of determinism or the assumption of freedom. Therefore, every act, when

---

[6] Henry Allison, *Kant's Transcendental Idealism: An Interpretation and Defense* (Yale University Press, 2004). See also Henry Allison, "Transcendental Idealism: The 'Two Aspect' View," in *New Essays on Kant*, ed. Bernard den Ouden and Marcia Moen (Peter Lang Publishers, 1987).

[7] Allison, *Kant's Theory of Freedom*, p. 2.

[8] Allison, *Kant's Theory of Freedom*, p. 5.

[9] Allison, *Kant's Theory of Freedom*, p. 6.

[10] Allison, *Kant's Theory of Freedom*, p. 35.

considered as free, is free. Allison then bases his interpretation of Kantian autonomy on this watered-down notion of freedom.

The move toward a more prosaic understanding of freedom is becoming popular in Kant scholarship. Many wish to downplay the idea that freedom is a special property of certain actions that can be assumed from our capacity to choose against or without incentives. Guyer and Korsgaard take up this tactic in their defenses of Kant's moral theory.

Guyer makes use of the Incorporation Thesis in his *Kant on Freedom, Law, and Happiness*, in which he argues that Kant's notion of the Highest Good ought to be seen as the goal of moral action and that Kant believes that freedom, in the general political sense, is necessary for the happiness prescribed by the notion of the Highest Good. Guyer argues that Kant assigns absolute value to freedom, understood in this familiar way, and that the value of personal freedom grounds the legitimacy of the categorical imperative. In addition to adopting the more general notion of freedom implied by the Incorporation Thesis, Guyer makes use of Allison's formulation of the Incorporation Thesis explicitly to support his idea that, for Kant, morality is meant to serve morally worthy happiness. The Incorporation Thesis is necessary for this end because it extricates Guyer from the objection that Kant believes that happiness, the object of inclination, is inimical to morality, the object of freedom. Instead, Guyer holds that inclinations are not immoral per se, just as happiness is not in conflict with morality, but that the natural goal of happiness is very much compatible with morality, especially since both require the proper use of reason for their attainment.

Korsgaard also expands the scope of freedom to include all choices. One overriding theme of her interpretation of Kant, as presented in *Creating the Kingdom of Ends*, is the idea that humans "confer value on the objects of" their "rational choice" and that this fact about the origin of value grounds the status of humans as "ends in themselves."[11] She similarly draws from the *Religion* essay to argue that all choices are free actions. Guyer and Korsgaard both hope to show that, for Kant, morality requires harmonizing inclination with moral ends, instead of totally extirpating inclination from decision-making, as some critics fear. The Incorporation Thesis helps in this regard by relieving inclination from being the cause of immorality, as the account of heteronomy suggests, and by showing that reason always adjudicates the inclinations and therefore can do so in a way that is both conducive to morality and conducive to happiness.

---

[11] Korsgaard, *Kingdom*, ix.

Now that I have shown the way that the Incorporation Thesis functions in contemporary scholarship to shift interpretive focus away from Kant's formalism and the corollary understanding of freedom in terms of autonomy toward a redefinition of freedom that allows all actions to be free, I will switch gears and turn to Kant's *Religion* essay in order to show that it does present an example of an immoral choice that is nevertheless free; but the very specific type of choice described therein is not analogous to all choices, nor analogous to choosing autonomously, and therefore cannot be used to support the Incorporation Thesis as it is formulated by Allison, Guyer, and Korsgaard.

The *Religion* essay consists of four parts. The first examines radical evil in human nature; the second, the agent's struggle between good and evil; the third, the means to a victory for the good; and the fourth, priestcraft, or the false way to the victory of the good. The title of the *Religion* essay leads one to believe that it will offer an elaboration of Kant's argument that morality leads to a very specific type of religion and a description of such a purely moral or rational religion. We are familiar with this idea from the second *Critique*, wherein Kant argues that belief in the Christian god is a necessary part of morality for two reasons: one, morality requires the goal of perfect virtue, but perfection requires infinite striving, thus infinite time and an afterlife; and two, morality requires the idea of the Highest Good, earthly happiness proportionate to virtue, and since there is no internal connection between prosperity and virtue, only a supernatural power can guarantee their concurrence—thus belief in a god is necessary for morality.[12] In a sense, then, the title of the *Religion* essay is misleading: in fact, since Kant had already described rational religion in a couple of his other works, the argument that morality requires rational religion is largely assumed and relegated to footnotes. Instead, as Kant mentions in the preface to the second edition, the goal of the work is to unify reason and scripture: Kant analyzes particular ideas from Christian

[12] For a more elaborate discussion of rational or natural religion (religion only as it is implied by morality) see lectures on moral philosophy ("On Religion" in the Collins notes), L 71-116, VE 27:299 – 27:339. Kant's discussion there is a far better place to turn for a consideration of his thoughts on religion since he offers his criticisms of religion in a way that is detached from any particular discussion of theology; in fact, he argues that most theological debates are not relevant to the practical importance of religion. One, therefore, does not need to untangle his beliefs from those under consideration. Kant argues that the most important aspect of religion is the trust that God will make up our shortcomings, and that trying our hardest will be good enough.

scripture and shows that they lead back to common sense. This explains the troubling fact that Kant begins his discussion with many religious assumptions that we do not see in his other writings, and it warns us to take the theological ideas Kant eventually reaches with a grain of salt. For example, the first section begins with the idea that humans are innately evil, but then, while keeping to the expression, Kant explains that this trait only amounts to the potential for evil, though he continues to assume that humans are in some sense born evil and must undergo a conversion. In this work Kant address many religious ideas, such as heaven and hell, the fall, a conversion experience, grace, and church participation. There is no reason to think that Kant is straightforwardly advancing any of these religious positions. In the case of a religious conversion experience, which implies, as does the choice of a meta-maxim that we shall examine shortly, that people are either all good or all bad, we know from Kant's other works that he explicitly rejects this essentialism along with the idea that the task of morality could be completed in one fell swoop, or at all.[13]

In the first section, in the context of discussing whether or not humans are innately evil, Kant argues that immoral actions are caused by the subject's free choice, "for otherwise the use or abuse of the human being's power of choice with respect to the moral law could not be imputed to him, nor could the good or evil in him be called 'moral'." (R 6:21)[14] Kant specifically states that inclinations and natural impulses cannot be seen as the ground of evil. According to this argument, evil is not caused by natural inclination; rather, evil is a result of the choice to value the satisfaction of inclination over compliance with the moral law. He explains the difference between good and evil characters with reference to the choice of a meta-maxim: the maxim either to follow the moral law in everything, or to follow inclination in everything. The main goal of this part of the essay is to show that evil is not the result of nature, nor is good or evil the result of divine dispensation, but that humans are individually responsible for their moral worth. Therefore, the proper, philosophical truth issuing from the theological idea that humans are innately evil must involve the possibility for choice of the impure maxim, so that, when we accept theological notions, we grant humans the capacity to choose the

---

[13] On the contrary, G. Felicitas Munzel accepts this account of a singular, resolute choice in his account of Kantian moral character, in G. Felicitas Munzel, *Kant's Conception of Moral Character: The "Critical" Link of Morality, Anthropology, and Reflective Judgment* (University of Chicago Press, 1999).

[14] All subsequent citations are from Allen Wood and George Di Giovanni's translation.

pure and good maxim (in a conversion experience) and thus we can hold them responsible for their moral behaviors.

The choice of a good or evil character described in the *Religion* essay is in no way analogous to normal decision-making. This choice is a meta-choice that happens once or twice in a person's life: Kant insinuates that it happens at or before birth and then during a conversion. Also, this choice is not based on reasons. It cannot be. It is a choice about the relative value of reasons, and, for that reason, Kant assumes that it cannot itself be based on reasons. Nor can we be aware of the choice: we can never know for sure whether we are of the pure or impure character type. Kant states that, although the conversion is a spontaneous revolution, the individual experiences it as a gradual change and a result of his constant striving (R 6:48).

Kant has obvious motivations for asserting each of these points. We can assume that the idea that all people are born evil is his starting point and that he is not taking responsibility for the idea in its scriptural form since he has not yet shown that it does, in fact, make sense. The sense that he makes out of it is simply to explain the content of the good and evil nature. It is important that innate evil be seen as the result of a choice or else it would not make sense to believe that we are capable of change. If people did not believe that moral change was possible, they would feel defeated and no longer strive to be good. Nevertheless, if this choice were conscious, we might think that we could simply make the choice rather than actually follow through with the demonstration of it in all of our actions. Also, if the choice were conscious, we might think that we could know which people had and had not made the choice and then persecute those that had not. This account also works to make sense of the idea of grace at the same time: we need God's help in order to change this part of our nature that is out of our conscious control. Therefore, it is clear that this account offers the most rational version of, or a rational reconstruction of, the idea of innate evil.

We can see Kant distancing himself from the original scriptural idea of innate evil with his attribution of the idea to the "rigorists." Allison's statement that Kant identifies himself as a rigorist is wrong.[15] Instead, Kant argues that one must be a rigorist when considering morality as a pure idea and one must be a "latitudinarian," or one who affirms that

[15] Allison, *Kant's Theory of Freedom*, p. 147.

humans are neither all good or all bad, when one considers morality from the point of view of human behavior (R 6:25).[16]

Kant's notion of autonomy, especially as it is advanced in the *Groundwork* and *Critique of Practical Reason*, leads us to suppose that only moral actions are free and that moral choice has the unique ability to make a human free. This argument has the unintended consequence of implying that people are not responsible for their immoral behavior. It is clear that Kant would want to fend off such a conclusion, and the fact that the Incorporation Thesis gives him a way to do so is a point in its favor. Nevertheless, even within the *Religion* essay, Kant distances himself from the idea that all actions are freely chosen. After the introduction, Kant turns to a discussion of the "original predisposition to good in human nature" and argues that we are subject to a three-fold determination: as animals, as humans, and as persons (R 6:26). Kant describes the first as determination without reason; the second requires rationality, but it is still rationality based on inclination, or prudential reasoning; and the third is determination by respect for the moral law. Kant continues to describe our inclinational or animalistic nature as a-rational. Here he does not, as the Incorporation Thesis holds, argue that inclination needs the motivating force of reason in order to cause behavior. Then, in a move that also works against the Incorporation Thesis, Kant reassigns the ability to motivate to purely moral, not broadly practical reason: in a footnote, Kant defends the separation between the second and the third form of determination (prudential and moral) by stating that "from the fact that a being has reason does not at all follow that, simply by virtue of representing its maxims as suited to universal legislation, this reason contains a faculty of determining the power of choice unconditionally, and hence to be 'practical' on its own."(R 6:26) This sentence implies that the second kind of determination uses reason but is ultimately caused by inclination and does not reach the level of autonomous moral choice, which is the only kind of cause for action that operates independently of inclination. Kant writes "Every propensity is either physical, i.e., it pertains to a human's power of choice as a natural being; or moral, i.e., it pertains to a human's power of choice as a moral being," and he goes on to explain that only the latter is free (R 6:31).

The *Religion* essay is not unique as a location for this kind of back and forth between the idea that humans are free by virtue of their humanity and

---

[16] To me this seems like a sneaky way to say that rigorism is wrong since the "pure idea" of morality does not contain reference to human nature and therefore cannot comment on whether humans are innately good or evil. Kant may agree with the idea that humans have innate *tendencies*, but not that they have an innate value.

the idea that inclination is a cause that usurps true freedom. The published versions of notes from Kant's lectures on moral philosophy, which are based on lectures given from 1775 to 1785,[17] displays this same conflict. Even in these earlier versions of Kant's thought we can see the tension between his desire to say that all human action is free and his need to argue that only those actions that express moral necessity are truly free.[18] Kant makes the same argument in the lectures as he does in the *Religion* essay: "because his will is free no man can be pathologically compelled. The human will is an *arbitrium liberum* in that it is not determined by stimuli, but the animal will is an *arbitrium brutum*, and not *liberum*, because it can be determined *per stimulus*." (L 28, VE 27:267)[19] Furthermore, "all moral evil springs from freedom; otherwise it would not be moral evil. However prone by nature we may be to evil actions, the latter have their source in our freedom."(L 67, VE 27:295) Then, only a short while later, we see Kant offer the same formulation, but this time substituting the *Groundwork*'s theory of freedom. When Kant begins, "man alone is free; his actions are not regulated by any such subjectively necessitating principle; if they were he would not be free," it looks as though he is articulating the Incorporation Thesis, but he continues: "And what then? If the freedom of man were not kept within bounds by objective rules, the result would be the completest savage disorder. There would be no certainty that man would not use his powers to destroy himself, his fellows and the whole of nature." (L 122, VE 27:344) This is not a picture of man as determined, but of man as immoral; in other words,

---

[17] This paper makes use of Louis Infield's translation of the 1924 Paul Menzer edition, which was the first published edition of these lectures. It is based largely on Theodor Friedrich Brauer's manuscript. Although they are clearly based on the same lecture or recurring lectures, they are different from the Collins notes, which are given in volume 27 of Academy edition of *Immanuel Kants Schriften*. I use the abbreviation "L" and the page numbers of the Infield translation to refer to the Brauer notes (Harper Torchbooks, 1963), but I also give the Academy edition page numbers to the corresponding, similar Collins notes for those who only have access to the Collins notes or for those who wish to examine the differences.

[18] The lecture notes are unique because they do not display the same insistence on incompatibilism that we see in the first and second *Critiques* and the *Groundwork*. Instead, Kant argues that all actions are determined, but some are determined in a way that makes us free: "in the case of a free being an action can be necessary—and necessary in the highest possible degree—and yet it need not conflict with freedom." (L 28, VE 27:267) Kant states: "every obligation is either one of duty or one of compulsion." (L 15, VE 27:256)

[19] Even this distinction is not unequivocal since, in the previous sentence, Kant states that prudential necessitation is determination *per stimulos*.

it expresses the sentiment behind the idea of heteronomy. Kant contrasts freedom understood as the absence of lawfulness, which he describes above as the height of immorality and determination, with the understanding of freedom as lawfulness. He advances an early version of the categorical imperative that expresses this identification: "Let thy procedure be such that in all thine actions regularity prevails. What does this restraint imply when applied to the individual? That he should not follow his inclinations." To follow one's inclinations is not only immoral but determined: "he who subjects his person to his inclinations, acts contrary to the ends of humanity, for as a free being he must not be subjected to inclinations, but ought to determine them in the exercise of his freedom." (L 122, VE 27:345)

Even without recognizing this seeming self-contradiction, is clear that freedom in the sense of the *arbitrium liberum* is not the most important notion of freedom for Kant. In some ways this understanding of freedom is totally devoid of content and seems to be freedom in name only, as it is conferred based on our status as humans and cannot be contravened. This sense of freedom does not allow for the possibility of compulsion in any sense. Kant argues: "However much, for instance, we may try by torture to force a man to action we cannot compel him to do it if he does not will it; if he so will he can withstand every torment and not yield. In a relative sense he can be compelled, but not in an absolute sense." (L 28, VE 27:267) Nevertheless, without denying that humans are always free in this abstract sense, Kant remarks that they are often too weak to withstand compulsion. In his lectures on moral philosophy Kant either treats the *arbitrium liberum* as an empty notion or he subtly remakes it into the moral notion of freedom. An example of the latter tendency can be seen when Kant states: "a high degree of freedom is requisite for moral compulsion, for then the arbitrium liberum is more powerful, and in its freedom from *stimuli* it can submit to the compulsion of rational grounds of action. The freer man is from stimuli, the more he can be compelled morally, and the degree of his freedom grows with the degree of his morality." (L 29, VE 27:268) Kant even argues that responsibility is diminished in the case of determination by animal appetites (L 63, VE 27:292), implying that non-human animals are not the only ones with an *arbitrium brutum*. At the very least, we can see that many of Kant's remarks from his lectures on moral philosophy contradict the conclusion of the Incorporation Thesis, as does the further discussion of freedom in the *Religion* essay. It is clear that, in at least one sense, humans can be and are determined by their inclinations, and this determination yields both immorality and the lack of the freedom. In the terminology of the lectures, sensibility can and does overpower the understanding (L 45, VE 27:1429), and the more a man is compelled pathologically the less he is free (L 29, VE 27:268).

Kant's *Anthropology from a Pragmatic Point of View*, which was published after the *Religion* essay, contains a similar discussion of innate evil. There Kant argues that humans are innately good insofar as they have a natural sense of the moral law, but innately evil as they naturally desire to choose the satisfaction of their selfish inclinations above following the moral law. He writes:

> Here the question is whether man is good by nature or bad by nature, or whether by nature he is equally susceptible to one or the other, depending upon which guiding hand he happens to fall into (*cereus in vitium flecti etc.)*; in this last instance the species itself would have no character. But this last instance is contradictory in itself because a being endowed with the faculty of practical reason and with consciousness of free-will (a person) sees himself in this consciousness, even in the midst of the darkest imaginings, subject to a moral law and to the feeling (which is then called moral feeling) that he is treated justly or unjustly and that he is treating others justly or unjustly. This is the intelligible character of humanity as such, and thus far man is good (by nature) according to his inborn gift. But experience also shows that in man there is an inclination to desire actively what is unlawful. This is the inclination to evil which arises unavoidably and as soon as man begins to make use of his freedom. Consequently the inclination to evil can be regarded as innate. Hence, according to his sensible character, man must be judged as being evil (by nature). This is not contradictory when we are talking about the character of the species because it can be assumed that the species' natural destiny consists in continual progress toward the better (A 7:324).[20]

Kant goes on to write that man is destined to overcome his animalistic selfishness so that the species can achieve universalism: "no matter how great his animalistic inclination may be to abandon himself passively to the enticements of ease and comfort, which he calls happiness, he is still destined to make himself worthy of humanity by actively struggling with the obstacles that cling to him because of the crudity of his nature." (A 7:325) As with many of Kant's works, the *Anthropology* gives us evidence in support of the Incorporation Thesis, as when Kant remarks that the experience of pleasure always involves the simultaneous evaluation of that pleasure (A 7:237), and evidence to deny it, as when Kant writes, in direct contradiction to the *Religion* essay's account of choosing a meta-maxim,

[20] Victor Lyle Dowdell's translation.

that "man never sanctions the evil in himself, and so there is actually no evil coming from principles, but only from the forsaking of them." (A 7:293)

I believe that Kant's inconsistency regarding the topic of the Incorporation Thesis shows us two things. One, Kant's texts do not unequivocally support the conclusion that Kantian moral theory allows inclination to be compatible with morality and freedom. Two, Kant appears to be contradicting himself on this issue because he is employing two distinct meanings for the term "freedom," yet he does not always keep them distinct. The best way to characterize these two meanings is with a parallel to Kant's distinction between prudential and moral reasoning. Prudential reasoning is free because it is reasoning: it is based on the subject's conscious and relatively uncoerced decision-making process. Still, it is not free to the same extent that moral reasoning is free because it is tied to the subject's selfish ends. It is not pure because it does not rely only on the subject qua rationality; instead it is linked to her subjective physical needs and desires. Moral reasoning is free, and the highest expression of freedom, because it expresses our essence as rational beings, through which we are unified into a group with all people.

It has become clear that there are at least two meanings of freedom at work in Kant's philosophy: the ability to do otherwise and the ability to conform one's actions to the moral law. The Incorporation Thesis conflates the two. We would all agree that the former is the most normal understanding of agential freedom. The former makes the free/determined distinction through Allison's first-person/third-person distinction, or the theoretical/practical distinction. As we have seen, Allison argues that when we consider a behavior empirically, or from the third person perspective, we assume that it is determined and can study the factors that determined it; but when we consider the action from the point of view of the agent and her feeling of freedom, we know that she could have acted otherwise. According to this understanding of freedom, simply being able to act otherwise suffices to make an action free, and therefore, we can safely reason that all human actions that were chosen are actions that are free.[21] The second notion of freedom, the more exclusive one, makes the freedom/determinism distinction by means of the autonomy/heteronomy distinction. Clearly heteronomous choices are still choices, as we see affirmed in the *Religion* essay and elsewhere (and so Kant's strategy there is to explain evil by way of conflating these two senses of freedom), but

[21] We should note that this understanding of freedom does not fully resolve the problem of our responsibility for evil acts; since we can view all actions either as free or as determined, it casts the net for responsibility too widely.

they are choices based on inclinations, not the pure thought of lawfulness. Thus they do not follow the categorical imperative and are not examples of a good and free will. In terms of Kant's theory of causal determination by efficient and teleological influences, heteronomous actions are not free.

Muchnik has suggested that the *Religion* essay is not necessary to ground the Incorporation Thesis as a theory of rational agency, since it is not likely that the noumenal choice of essential moral character portrayed therein is meant to establish a model of normal decision-making. Instead it is the other way around: In the *Religion* essay Kant describes maxim choice, and not inclination, as the motivating force behind action because this is his general theory of action, implied by the *Wille*/*Willkür* distinction.[22] Many believe that Kant introduced this distinction late in his writings, with the *Religion* essay and the *Metaphysics of Morals*, specifically to account for the freedom of evil action.[23] As we have just seen, however, Kant was aware of this problem from his first professional engagement with ethics. Kant uses the term *Willkür* to refer to the capacity of the subject for free choice, in the more normal everyday sense of freedom (*willkürlich* can be translated as "arbitrary" and so the *Willkür*, or free will, is analogous to the *arbitrium liberum*). *Wille* denotes freedom in the robust, noumenal sense.[24] *Willkür* is often referred to as "practical freedom" by commentators, but this may be confusing because it is not the freedom of *pure* practical reason, rather freedom in a prosaic, practical sense, as opposed to a metaphysical or noumenal sense. When Kant describes the choice of a meta-maxim in the *Religion* essay he usually uses the term *Wille*, but he occasionally refers to *Willkür*, for example in the statement: "a propensity to evil can only attach to the moral faculty of choice (*Willkür*)." (R 6:31) Kant must refer to *Willkür* here because he describes moral choice with an analogy to normal decision-making in order to account for its freedom. This overlap demonstrates exactly the reason that *Religion* essay is used by those who wish to highlight to role of *Willkür* in Kant's moral philosophy and downplay the role of the *Wille*. If

[22] Pablo Muchnik, personal communication.

[23] Allison discusses this mode of interpretation and rejects it. He does not need to take this route of deflating the importance of autonomy for Kantian philosophy because he has already defined autonomy as "self-determination" in the more general sense entailed by the Incorporation Thesis; *Kant's Theory of Freedom*, pp. 95-96.

[24] George Di Giovanni addresses the issue of the relationship between the two notions in terms of the response of German Idealism to Kantianism in his "The First Twenty Years of Critique: The Spinoza Connection," in *The Cambridge Companion to Kant*, ed. Paul Guyer (Cambridge University Press, 1992).

we limit the discussion of the Incorporation Thesis to its place as a theory of rational agency, as the assertion that prudential reasoning expresses a non-moral kind of freedom, there is little at stake in taking up a distinction between *Wille* and *Willkür*. This distinction is helpful as long as we keep one thing in mind. The noumenal choice of moral character presented in the *Religion* essay is different from normal maxim choice even though it is ascribed to the *Willkür*. It is the choice of a meta-maxim, and for that reason cannot be based on reasons; furthermore, because it determines our underlying moral character, it cannot be conscious. Therefore the Incorporation Thesis as theory of rational agency ought to be seen as unrelated to the Religion essay's portrait of the choice of meta-maxim. As a matter of fact, as we have seen, the *Religion* essay gives us less support for believing that Kant accepts the Incorporation Thesis as a general theory of rational agency than does the first *Critique*. In the Religion essay Kant suggests that in being determined as animals we do not exercise choice or rationality at all. The contrary, if it is really implied by the Incorporation Thesis, would be strange anyway: surely we do not choose to be hungry or get tired, or any behavior that belongs to us in virtue of the nature we share with all animals.

Nevertheless, as I have already made clear, my disagreement is not with the Incorporation Thesis as an anti-Humean theory of rational agency, since I think Kant generally supports it as such; it is with the Incorporation Thesis as a theory of freedom meant to trump Kant's notion of autonomy. As is commonly known, the second *Critique* and the *Groundwork* describe moral choice in terms of autonomy. Autonomy is the ability to give the law to oneself, in opposition to heteronomy, which is the determination from outside influences: "If the will seeks the law which is to determine it elsewhere than in the fitness of its maxims to be given as universal law, and thus it goes outside and seeks the law in the property of any of its objects, heteronomy always results. For then the will does not give itself the law, but the object through its relation to the will gives the law to it." (G 411)[25] It bears reminding my reader that the autonomy formulation of the categorical imperative is interwoven with the "kingdom of ends" formulation. As autonomy is defined in opposition to heteronomy, the kingdom of ends is defined in opposition to the kingdom of nature: "a realm of ends is thus possible only by analogy with a realm of nature. The former is possible only by maxims (i.e., self-imposed rules), while the latter is possible by laws of efficient causes and things externally necessitated." (G 438) Hence, we have the connection between moral

[25] Lewis White Beck's translation (Prentice Hall, 1997).

action and free action: "As a will is a kind of causality of living beings so far as they are rational, freedom would be that property of this causality by which it can be effective independent of foreign causes determining it, just as natural necessity is the property of the causality of all irrational beings by which they are determined to activity by the influence of foreign causes." (G 446)[26] The mutual implication of free and moral action is what many commentators call Kant's reciprocity thesis: "a free will and a will under moral laws are identical." (G 447) As we see, autonomy entails formalism, or the idea that moral choice must be made with reference only to the form of the judgment (it ought to be a universal judgment) and not with reference to the content of the choice or the likely outcomes of the choice.

The Incorporation Thesis implies that the extra step of using autonomy to define metaphysical freedom is unnecessary, since we can already state that all of our actions are free on separate grounds, by virtue of being caused by prudential reason and not directly by inclination. Kant says as much in the *Groundwork*: "[Man] does not even hold himself responsible for these inclinations and impulses and attribute them to his proper self (i.e., his will), though he does impute to his will the indulgence which he may grant them when he permits them to influence his maxims to the detriment of the rational laws of the will." (G 457-458) Nevertheless, we can see from Kant's discussion of autonomy that he uses the notion of freedom in a special sense, as a tribute to moral action. Whether or not all actions are free independently of their moral worth, autonomy is a higher notion of freedom meant to exalt moral action. Obviously, not all actions are moral actions and therefore the moral value of freedom as autonomy cannot transfer to all choices.

One might object that only Korsgaard and Guyer accept this watered-down notion of freedom in place of the more strictly Kantian notion of autonomy and that Allison is only interested in the Incorporation Thesis as a theory of rational agency. Unfortunately, this is not the case. Allison distinguishes between rational and moral agency but argues that Kant believes that the former suffices for moral action: "freedom for Kant is just the capacity for self-conscious rational activity." In clarifying his position from Meerbote's, Allison writes: "Although my interpretation denies that the claim that reason has causal power can be taken literally without

[26] Note that the text implies that acting by one's will, and even rationally, does not imply freedom. Freedom here refers to a more restrictive instance of action determined by will. We see this fact again when Kant explains that volition normally acts by the law of nature (G 444).

leading to absurdity (the timeless agency problem), it also leaves room for the notion that such power can be attributed instead to the will (*Willkür*) of a rational agent, with the latter being itself noncausally determined (governed) by reason."[27]

I have shown that the Incorporation Thesis is often used to highlight the importance of the more prosaic understanding of freedom in Kant's philosophy as opposed to freedom understood as autonomy. This elision has the effect of downplaying the importance of the categorical imperative for Kantian morality. In his attempt to show that the *Groundwork* demonstrates the Incorporation Thesis's notion of practical agency, Allison agrees with Singer and Sidgewick's interpretation of universalizability as a test for rationality. Allison then identifies the idea of a universal law with the idea of a practical law, and finally he conjoins the notion of the categorical imperative with the idea of a practical law in general.[28] This conclusion is clearly unacceptable, but it is required if we want to show that Kant's argument for the categorical imperative makes use of the idea that freedom is defined by rational agency, as Allison does, i.e., if we want to substitute rational agency for moral agency. Allison appears to recognize the distinction between rationality and morality, but he then collapses it again by defining transcendental freedom as the capacity to choose based on a higher-level maxim, per the *Religion* essay's discussion, not *the* higher-level *moral* maxim.[29]

The desire to use the Incorporation Thesis to save Kantian freedom from the troublesome consequences of the notion of autonomy explains the necessity of using the *Religion* essay specifically to ground the Incorporation Thesis, since only there does Kant merge the idea of normal rational decision-making with an account of moral choice. Only in the *Religion* essay does normal rational choice become an example of moral choice because Kant is there trying to show that non-moral choice is free in some sense, since it is obviously not free in the sense of being autonomous. Everywhere else, Kant consistently distinguishes between prudential and moral reasoning and prudential and moral imperatives. Of course, he also makes this distinction in the *Religion* essay, only not during his argument that humans are free to choose evil.

Even if it is possible to base an interpretation of Kantian freedom on this argument in the *Religion* essay, this text does not help us to address the problem that transcendental freedom, as it is a part of the noumenal realm, must be prescinded from the phenomenal realm, or the sphere of

---

[27] Allison, *Kant's Theory of Freedom*,pp. 79-80.
[28] Allison, *Kant's Theory of Freedom*, p. 212.
[29] Allison, *Kant's Theory of Freedom*, p. 208.

consciousness. Even if an action can be free and determined at the same time, depending on the way that we regard it, a free action, in so far as it is free, must be, or be able to be regarded as, free from the sequence of causality, since Kant worries that determination in this sequence undermines freedom. If freedom is construed as a process of rational decision-making, we are left with the problematic consequence that rational decision-making, since it must escape the determinism of the phenomenal realm, must be something of which we are unaware. It is clear from the *Religion* essay that we could not possibly be aware of the maxim selection involved in forming a good or evil character. Allison recognizes this and presents the theory such that we can, on the model of apperception, be aware of free rational thought, but not as an "inner experience," since that would make it subject to the categories.[30] Even if awareness without experience is not a contradiction, it is not likely that the kind of awareness involved in the "I think" of the transcendental unity of apperception can expand to fit all that is required by rational decision-making. Surely, we must be able to experience our decision-making processes, or else we could not be self-critical and hence we could not be rational.

If it is the case that we cannot find sufficient textual evidence to attribute the Incorporation Thesis to Kant, we might want to adapt it into a modified Kantian theory. It offers some obvious benefits in addition to the one already mentioned, viz., it helps Kant explain the reason that we ought to be held responsible for immoral acts. As we see from Guyer's interpretation, it helps us mold Kantianism into a moral theory more compatible with the recognition of the moral importance of happiness. The Incorporation Thesis points to a partial willingness on Kant's part to do exactly what the name describes: to incorporate inclination with rationality by hypothesizing a unified decision-maker who must experience all parts of the self. Nevertheless, if we were to do so, we would need to first clarify the role we are going to leave to Kant's theory of freedom as it is normally understood. Allison, Guyer, and Korsgaard all reserve a special connection between rational decision-making and moral action, attempting to privilege the latter as the most rational type of decision. While it might be possible to argue that moral action is more rational than immoral action, it is difficult to prove that moral decision-making requires that one use more of her rational capacity than does pragmatic decision-making, unless one follows the normal understanding of Kantian autonomy.

---

30 Allison, *Kant's Theory of Freedom*, p. 37.

One might protest that Allison's interpretation helps bring the idea of the categorical imperative down to earth, drawing parallels between it and everyday decision-making. There is no doubt that the equation between morality and rationality is a key element of Kantianism. Nevertheless, in suggesting that all choices are free and then collapsing the distinction between autonomy and heteronomy, the Incorporation Thesis leaves us with very little moral direction on the path towards morality: the most "rational" decisions become the right decisions. The fact is that Kantian moral theory is based on the distinction between pragmatic and moral concerns; it captures the intuition that sometimes an action is unacceptable for no other reason than that it is morally wrong. If we subordinate the concept of morality to the concept of rationality, rather than privileging morality and giving it the ability to define a pure form of rationality, the meaning of rationality changes. This watered-down notion of rationality may be both the attraction of and the problem with the Incorporation Thesis.

Nevertheless, it is possible to use the Incorporation Thesis merely as a theory of rational agency and retain, rather than collapse, the two ideas of freedom in Kant's work. Doing so would salvage Kant's theory of responsibility, but it is not clear that it would make it easier to incorporate pragmatic concerns into moral reasoning. If we assume that choice cannot be determined by inclination, the notion of heteronomy loses its sting and we overcome the idea that inclinations must be *mastered* by moral reasoning. We will then need to talk about free choice instead of about the opposition between desire and respect for the moral law. Still, if someone chooses individual advantage over following the moral law, she will be choosing heteronomously, however rational her decision-making process. There is a great deal to be gained by overcoming Kant's opposition between reason and desire (or overcoming our tendency to represent Kant in this way). Nevertheless, there is reason to think that opposition is a deep structure of Kant's thought. Zinkin demonstrates that Kant's preoccupation with opposition is with him from his early "Negative Magnitudes" through the three *Critiques*.[31] Still, we are not required to use Kant's work only as he did or would have; there always remains the option to take some aspects of Kant's theory as stimulus for a better, Kantian-inspired moral theory and leave others that we find problematic. The Incorporation Thesis as a theory of rational agency helps us move Kant's thought past his obsession with opposition, and, as it is more psychologically accurate, it

---

[31] Melissa Zinkin, *Degree, Intensity, and Force: Kant's Theory of Value* (unpublished manuscript).

helps us make room for a more plausible moral psychology within his work. Still, it is unlikely that the full effects of this innovation will help us to integrate the moral end and the end of personal happiness; happiness, for Kant, is always a separate topic. More work is needed in order to develop this restrained version of the Incorporation Thesis. Whichever route we take, our work would benefit from accepting that the statements in *Religion within the Boundaries of Mere Reason* were not intended to ground a theory of rational agency and were not intended to trump Kant's notion of autonomy.

Works Cited

Allison, H. *Kant's Theory of Freedom* (Cambridge University Press, 1990).

—. *Kant's Transcendental Idealism* (Yale University Press, 1983).

—. "Transcendental Idealism: The 'Two Aspect' View," in *New Essays on Kant*, ed. Bernard den Ouden and Marcia Moen (Peter Lang Publishers, 1987).

Di Giovanni, G. "The First Twenty Years of Critique: The Spinoza Connection," in *The Cambridge*

Companion to Kant, ed. Paul Guyer (Cambridge University Press, 1992).

Guyer, P. *Kant on Freedom, Law, and Happiness* (Cambridge University Press, 2000).

Korsgaard, C. *Creating the Kingdom of Ends* (Cambridge University Press, 1996).

MacMurray, J. "Introduction" in Immanuel Kant, *Lectures on Ethics*, trans. Louis Infield (Harper and Row, 1963).

Munzel, G.F. *Kant's Conception of Moral Character: The "Critical" Link of Morality, Anthropology, and Reflective Judgment* (University of Chicago Press, 1999).

Singer, M. *Generalization in Ethics*. (Alfred A. Knopf, 1961).

Zinkin, Melissa. *Degree, Intensity, and Force: Kant's Theory of Value* (unpublished manuscript).

Chapter Four

Anthropology from a Kantian Point of View: Toward a Cosmopolitan Conception of Human Nature

Robert B. Louden

A New Discipline

Anthropology was a new field of study when Kant first began offering lectures on it at Königsberg University in the winter semester of 1772 – a product of the larger Enlightenment effort to emancipate the study of human nature from theologically-based inquiries, best captured in Alexander Pope's famous remark:

> Know then thyself, presume not God to scan;
> The proper study of Mankind is Man.
> (*An Essay on Man*, 1733-34. Epistle II)

Kant himself was a leader in the development of anthropology as an academic discipline; indeed, he was the first academic to offer regular university lectures on the topic. For instance, in a frequently cited letter to his former student Marcus Herz written toward the end of 1773, he states:

> This winter for the second time I am offering a *collegium privatum* on anthropology, a subject that I now intend to make into a proper academic discipline. But my plan is quite different (*ganz anders*).[1] The intention that I have is to disclose through it the sources of all the sciences that are concerned with ethics, with the skill of social intercourse, of the method of

[1] Quite different, that is, from Platner (2000/1772), which Herz had already reviewed in Herz (1773), and to which Kant refers earlier in this same letter. I discuss the key differences between Platner and Kant's approaches to anthropology below.

> educating and governing human beings, hence of everything that pertains to the practical. I seek then more phenomena and their laws rather than the first grounds of the possibility of modifying human nature in general. Hence the subtle and in my eyes eternally futile investigation concerning how bodily organs stand in connection with thoughts is left out entirely. I include so many observations of ordinary life that my listeners have constant occasion to compare their ordinary experience with my remarks and thus, from beginning to end, find the lectures always entertaining and never dry. In the meanwhile I am working on a preliminary exercise for students from this (in my opinion) very pleasant empirical study (*Beobachtungslehre*) of skill, prudence, and even wisdom that, along with physical geography[2] and distinct from all other instruction, can be called knowledge of the world (*Kenntnis der Welt*). (10: 145-46)

Kant's own interests in anthropology actually began much earlier than 1772, and can be traced back at least as far as the summer of 1756, when he first began lecturing on physical geography. For example, in his *Sketch and Announcement of a Lecture Course on Physical Geography* (1757), he notes that his lectures will include a discussion "of the inclinations of human beings which flow from the climate in which they live, the variety of their prejudices and ways of thinking, in so far as this can all serve to make the human being more known to himself, [as well as] a short sketch of their arts, business, and science." (2: 9)[3]

A second source for Kant's anthropology was the material on empirical psychology included in his metaphysics lectures, which date from the 1760s. For instance, in the *Announcement of the Organization of His Lectures in the Winter Semester 1765/66*, Kant states: "after a brief introduction I shall begin with *empirical psychology*, which is actually the metaphysical science of *the human being* based on experience (*metaphysische Erfahrungswissenschaft vom Menschen*)." (2: 309)

---

[2] Physical geography and anthropology for Kant comprise the two kinds of knowledge of the world or "world-cognitions" (*Welterkenntnisse*). For instance, in his *Lectures on Physical Geography*, he states: "Experience (*Erfahrungen*) of nature and of the human being together constitute the world cognitions (*Welterkenntnisse*). Knowledge (*Kenntniß*) of the human being teaches us *anthropology*, and to knowledge of nature we owe *physical geography*." (9: 157) Kant lectured on physical geography in the summer semesters; anthropology, in the winter. For general discussion of Kant's university teaching, see Kuehn (2001).

[3] For further discussion of Kant's physical geography and its relation to his anthropology, see Adickes (1911), May (1970), and Elden and Mendieta (forthcoming).

However, empirical psychology itself constitutes only a part of the new experience-based science of man that would eventually be named anthropology. Other important components include the character of the sexes as well as of the different peoples and nations. In Sections III and IV of his 1764 book, *Observations on the Feeling of the Beautiful and the Sublime*,[4] Kant offered some reflections on these two topics which he later revised and expanded when he began lecturing on anthropology in 1772.

Anthropology and the Philosophical Physicians

Before turning to Kant's own anthropology, it is important to get a sense of one prominent non-Kantian anthropology. As we have already seen from Kant's earlier-cited letter to Herz in 1773 (see esp. n. 1), he developed his own approach to anthropology in explicit opposition to the medical or physiological conceptions of human nature that were gaining popularity in the late eighteenth century.[5] His most frequent sparring partner in this regard was the German physician Ernst Platner (1744-1818), whose book *Anthropologie für Ärzte und Weltweise* (Anthropology for Physicians and Philosophers) was published in 1772 – the same year that Kant inaugurated his own anthropology course. In his letter to Herz Kant criticizes what he calls Platner's "eternally futile investigations concerning how bodily organs stand in connection with thoughts," adding that "my plan is quite different." (10: 145)

Twenty-five years later, in the Preface to *Anthropology from a Pragmatic Point of View*, Kant again contrasts his own distinct approach to anthropology – which he now calls 'pragmatic' – to the physiological approach championed by Platner and others:

> A doctrine of the knowledge of human being, systematically formulated (anthropology), can exist either in a physiological or in a pragmatic point of view. – Physiological knowledge of the human being concerns the investigation of what *nature* makes of the human being; pragmatic, the

[4] A new translation of this work, prepared by Paul Guyer, is included in Zöller and Louden, eds. (2007). In his Translator's Introduction to the text, Guyer notes that "the work contains little by way of detailed aesthetic theory … Instead, the *Observations* is really a work in what Kant would later call "anthropology from a pragmatic point of view." (p. 19)

[5] For further discussion of the philosophical physicians, see Zammito (2002), pp. 221-53 and Cohen (Forthcoming). For discussion of Herz and the vocation of medicine, see Davis (1995), pp. 72-144.

> investigation of what *he* as a free-acting being makes of himself, or can and should make of himself. (7: 119)[6]

In the earlier *Menschenkunde* transcription[7] of his anthropology course (1781-82), Kant also bluntly criticizes Platner for having merely "written a scholastic anthropology" (25: 856) –an anthropology, that is, that produces "science for the school," but which is of "no utility to the human being" and from which "one could not obtain any enlightenment for common life." (25: 853)

Platner, however, was by no means the only physician championing a physiological approach to the study of human nature, or even the most prominent one. The most famous example from this genre is probably Julien Offray la Mettrie's book, *L'Homme machine* (*Man a Machine* – 1748), in which he declares confidently that in studying human nature we should be

> guided by experience and observation alone. They abound in the annals of physicians who were philosophers, but not in those of philosophers who were not physicians. Physician-philosophers probe and illuminate the labyrinth that is man. They alone have revealed man's springs hidden under coverings that obscure so many other marvels.[8]

In addition to La Mettrie, other prominent authors associated with the physiological or medical approach to the study of human nature include Charles Bonnet, Albrecht von Haller, and Georges-Louis Leclerc de Buffon.

Here too, Kant's interests in these Enlightenment medical approaches to human nature began early in his career, long before he began teaching his anthropology course in 1772. And he was by no means entirely dismissive of them. For instance, in his *Essay on the Maladies of the Head* (1764),[9] he goes as far as to say that "I see nothing better for me than to imitate the method of the physicians" (2: 260). And in his *Review of Moscati's Work Of the Corporeal Essential Differences Between the*

---

[6] I have recently prepared a new English translation of this text, which appears in both Louden (2006b), and Zöller and Louden, eds. (2007).

[7] Louden and Wood, eds. (forthcoming).

[8] La Mettrie (1994), p. 29. For further discussion, see Gay (1967), pp. 375-86; and Schings (1977), pp. 11-40.

[9] An English translation of this text, prepared by Holly Wilson, appears in Zöller and Louden, eds. (2007).

Structure of Animals and Humans (1771),[10] he congratulates the "astute anatomist" for his insights into early human life – insights that "*Rousseau* as a philosopher did not succeed" in reaching (2: 423). Other publications of Kant's that are relevant to physiological approaches to the study of human nature include *A Note to Physicians* (1782), *On the Philosophers' Medicine of the Body* (1786), and *From Soemmerring's On the Organ of the Soul* (1796),[11] as well as the third essay in *The Conflict of the Faculties* (*The Conflict of the Philosophy Faculty with the Faculty of Medicine* – 1796).

Broadly speaking, the physiological anthropology promoted by Platner and other philosophical physicians of the Enlightenment is the predecessor to physical anthropology, whereas Kant's pragmatic anthropology, with its emphasis on free human action, is the progenitor of various philosophical and existentialist anthropologies. For instance, Max Scheler, an important voice in this latter tradition who also influenced Martin Heidegger, holds that the human being is not only an animal being but also "a 'spiritual' being (*ein 'geistiges' Wesen*)" that is "no longer tied to its drives and environments, but rather 'free from the environment' (*'umweltfrei'*), or, as we shall say, 'open to the world' (*'weltoffen'*)."[12]

Kant's Pragmatic Anthropology

Kant's most famous marker for his own approach to anthropology is of course 'pragmatic' – a term that he did not yet stress when he first began teaching his anthropology course in 1772, but which is featured prominently in the title of his 1798 book, *Anthropology from a Pragmatic Point of View*. Described modestly as "the present manual for my anthropology course" in a footnote at the end of Preface, *Anthropology from a Pragmatic Point of View* is essentially Kant's last set of lecture notes for the course that he taught annually for twenty-four years until his retirement from university lecturing in 1796.

But what exactly does he mean in calling his anthropology *pragmatic*? The term 'pragmatic', as Kant uses it, is intentionally broad and incorporates a variety of interrelated but different meanings –not all of

---

[10] An English translation of this text, prepared by Günter Zöller, appears in Zöller and Louden, eds. (2007).

[11] English translations of these three texts are also available in Zöller and Louden, eds. (2007).

[12] Scheler (1989), p. 51. Heidegger's *Kant and the Problem of Metaphysics* is "dedicated to the memory of Max Scheler." See Heidegger (1962), pp. iv, xxiii, 216-217.

which fit readily under current mainstream uses of 'pragmatic'. We have already touched on two of these meanings in the previous section. First, pragmatic anthropology is conceived in opposition to the physiological anthropology of Platner and the philosophical physicians. The latter anthropology concerns "the investigation of what *nature* makes of the human being," while the former involves "the investigation of what *he* as a free-acting being makes of himself, or can and should make of himself." (*VA* 7: 119) However, the pragmatic investigation of the human being as a free-acting being is to be conducted empirically, not transcendentally. For Kantian anthropology, as we saw earlier in the letter to Herz, is also conceived of as a *Beobachtungslehre*, an empirical doctrine based on observation. (Whether Kant himself always manages to adhere to this self-imposed constraint is an issue that I will return to later.) As concerns freedom, what this means in effect is that pragmatic anthropology studies the phenomenal effects of human freedom in the empirical world, not freedom's allegedly non-empirical origins.

Secondly, Kantian pragmatic anthropology is also distinguished from Platner's "scholastic anthropology." (*Menschenkunde* 25: 856) Scholastic anthropology is a "science for the school" that is developed "in accordance with the standards of the school and of the professions," but unfortunately we are unable to "obtain any enlightenment for common life from it" –it is of "no utility to the human being." (*Menschenkunde* 25: 853) Here Kant is invoking a more conventional meaning of 'pragmatic', one that had been present in German philosophy at least since 1720, when Christian Wolff employed the term in this manner in one of his works.[13] Pragmatic anthropology is anthropology that is useful and practical for human beings. However, 'practical' here is to be understood in opposition to what is merely theoretical or speculative: we are not yet talking about 'practical' in Kant's narrower sense of "morally practical." As he remarks in the Introduction to the *Critique of the Power of Judgment*, this latter sense of 'practical' is restricted to principles "which are grounded entirely on the concept of freedom to the complete exclusion of the determining grounds of the will from nature." (5: 173) To call pragmatic anthropology 'practical' in this second, narrower sense would entail giving up the requirement that anthropology be a *Beobachtungslehre*. Kantian pragmatic anthropology can certainly be applied to moral purposes, and it is clear that Kant hoped people would choose to make moral use of his pragmatic anthropology.[14] But strictly speaking, the knowledge of human nature that

---

[13] For discussion and references, see Louden (2000), pp. 68-69.

[14] For discussion, see Louden (2006a), esp. pp. 354-55.

one gains from the study of pragmatic anthropology can be useful for many purposes –moral, non-moral, and even immoral.

A third core feature of pragmatic anthropology in Kant's sense involves a specific kind of usefulness. Pragmatic anthropology is useful in the sense that the knowledge of human nature we obtain from it enables us to more effectively use others for our own purposes (whatever these purposes may be). As he remarks toward the end of *Anthropology from a Pragmatic Point of View*, pragmatic anthropology teaches a person how "to use other human beings skillfully for one's purposes." (7: 322) In showing us "how we can use people for our own ends," (*Busolt* 25: 1436)[15] pragmatic anthropology holds out the promise of a kind of usefulness (viz., skill in human relations) not to be found in either physiological or scholastic anthropology. Again though, pragmatic anthropology implicitly contains multiple application possibilities. If people's chosen ends are moral ones, then they can apply anthropology as a means toward this goal. But if their ends are non-moral, anthropological knowledge of human beings can also be of service here.

Finally, a fourth core dimension of Kantian pragmatic anthropology concerns the acquisition of prudence. Pragmatic anthropology is also a *Klugheitslehre*, a doctrine of prudence. Near the beginning of the *Friedländer* anthropology lectures (1775-76),[16] Kant states: "all pragmatic doctrines are doctrines of prudence, where for all our skills we also have the means to make a proper use of everything; for we study human beings in order to become more prudent, which prudence becomes a science." (25: 471) Admittedly, the prudence aspect of pragmatic anthropology overlaps somewhat with the "using others for one's own purposes" aspect discussed above. For instance, at one point in *Anthropology from a Pragmatic Point of View* Kant glosses the term 'prudence' simply as "using other human beings for one's purposes" (7: 201); and later in this same text he refers to "technically practical reason" or "the maxim of prudence," which includes the ability to get "other human beings' inclinations into one's power, so that one can direct and determine them according to one's intentions." (7: 271)

But prudence in Kant's sense also involves more than merely the ability to use other people for one's own purposes, and points ultimately to an understanding of human well-being and happiness. As he writes in the *Groundwork of the Metaphysics of Morals*: "skill in the choice of one's own greatest well-being (*Wohlsein*) can be called *prudence*." (4: 416) And

[15] Louden and Wood, eds. (forthcoming).
[16] Louden and Wood, eds. (forthcoming).

in the earlier *Parow* anthropology lectures from 1772-73[17] he states: "The capacity to choose the best means to happiness (*Glückseligkeit*) is prudence. Happiness consists in the satisfaction of all inclinations, and therefore to be able to choose happiness, one must be free." (25: 413) In this broader sense of prudence, Kantian pragmatic anthropology holds out a promise, to those who have successfully learned its lessons, that anthropology can show people what they need to learn about human nature in order to achieve a greater level of well-being and happiness. And in making a contribution to greater human well-being and happiness, Kantian pragmatic anthropology also makes good on its claim of obtaining "enlightenment for common life."

Toward a Cosmopolitan Conception of Human Nature

However, there remains an additional central feature of Kantian anthropology, one that is still under-explored and not at all evident when one focuses on the well-established meanings of his 'pragmatic' anthropology discussed above. In my view this additional component constitutes the single most important dimension of Kant's distinctive approach to anthropology, but it is also one that stands in occasional tension with other core features of his anthropological project.

This additional component concerns the particular conception of human nature that Kant believes a proper anthropological investigation points to, and it is a markedly cosmopolitan conception of human nature. In other words, Kant believes that in studying anthropology in the manner he proposes the student will eventually arrive at a cosmopolitan conception of human nature. Additionally, he holds that the most important reason to study anthropology is to obtain this specific conception of human nature.

Although Kant himself does not consistently employ a uniform term for this cosmopolitan conception of human nature in his anthropology lectures, he does explicitly articulate it in a number of places. Perhaps the most prominent and direct articulation occurs in the Preface to *Anthropology from a Pragmatic Point of View*, where he announces that anthropology is only properly called *pragmatic* "when it contains knowledge of the human being as a *citizen of the world* (*Erkenntnis des Menschen als Weltbürgers*) (7: 120). Here the cosmopolitan conception of human nature is described as a necessary condition for any anthropology's being called *pragmatic*: the only anthropology that should count as

[17] Louden and Wood, eds. (forthcoming).

pragmatic is an anthropology that contains knowledge of the human being as a *Weltbürger*. However, there is nothing in either the conventional usage of the term *pragmatic* or in Kant's better-known pronouncements about *pragmatic* that suggests that this cosmopolitan component needs to be regarded as a necessary part of the definition of *pragmatic*. The centrality of this wider, normative conception of human nature to Kant's approach to anthropology is further underscored when he adds later on the same page of the Preface that

> *general* knowledge always precedes *local* knowledge here, if the latter is to be ordered and directed through philosophy: in the absence of which all acquired knowledge can yield nothing more than fragmentary groping around and no science (*fragmentarisches Herumtappen und keine Wissenschaft*). (*VA* 7: 120)

In other words, Kantian anthropology begins with a general conception of human nature (albeit one that is arrived at empirically –more on this later), and then uses this general conception to assess more particular conceptions of particular subgroups of human beings. An anthropology that fails to do this yields nothing more than a fragmentary groping around.

A second key text asserting the centrality of a cosmopolitan conception of human nature occurs in the Preamble to the *Friedländer* anthropology lectures, where Kant states that

> anthropology is not however a local (*locale*) but rather a general (*generale*) anthropology. In it one comes to know not the state of human beings but rather the nature of humanity, for the local properties of human beings always change, but the nature of humanity does not. Anthropology is thus a pragmatic knowledge of what results from our nature, but it is not a physical or geographical knowledge, for that is tied to time and place, and is not constant… Anthropology is not a description of human beings, but of human nature. (25: 471)

In this text the term *Weltbürger* does not occur, but the triple emphases on "the nature of humanity," "human nature," and "general anthropology" – each of which is contrasted with a more provincial, transitory, and less global project – clearly point in the same direction. And here also he maintains that anthropology is only properly designated *pragmatic* when it begins with reflection on a general conception of human nature.

A third key text occurs in the Prolegomena to the *Pillau* anthropology lectures (1777-78),[18] where Kant praises anthropological knowledge above all other kinds of knowledge: "There is no greater and more important investigation for the human being than knowledge of the human being" (25: 733). When knowledge of the human being "is treated pragmatically," Kant adds, "then it is a knowledge of the world and forms a man of the world (*bildet einen Weltmann*)." (25: 733) However, there are two distinct types of knowledge of the world:

> 1) A local (*local*) knowledge of the world, which merchants (*Kaufleute*) have, which is also called empirical. 2) A general (*general*) knowledge of the world, which the man of the world has, and which is not empirical but cosmological. Local knowledge of the world is tied to place and time, and also gives no rules to a person to act in common life. He who becomes acquainted with the world through travel has only this knowledge of it, which, however, also lasts only for a while, for when the behavior in the place where he has been changes, then his knowledge of it also ceases. (25: 734)

In each of these three texts Kant explicitly links his use of the term *pragmatic* to a cosmopolitan conception of human nature, a conception that is not tied to time and place. Anthropologies that study only the behavior and characteristics of human beings as they are found in particular times and places are merely 'local' anthropologies, but what Kant advocates is 'general' anthropology; an anthropology that is concerned with what human beings in all times and places share with one another.[19] And this wider knowledge of what human beings share in common with one another "is not empirical but cosmological;" that is, it is concerned with the totality of human beings as a species throughout space and time, not with features or aspects that only some human beings in some times and places have. As he states in the Introduction to his *Physical Geography* lectures, in summarizing the second part of *Weltkenntniß*, knowledge of the human being: "From anthropology one gets to know what is pragmatic in the human being and not speculative. The human being is considered here not physiologically, so that one distinguishes the sources of phenomena, but cosmologically." (9: 157) The intentionally wide scope of Kantian anthropology results in a knowledge that is pragmatic rather than merely speculative in the straightforward sense of being useful. For, once we acquire this knowledge, it never

[18] Louden and Wood, eds. (forthcoming).

[19] For related discussion, see Wood (2003), esp. pp. 39-41.

becomes obsolete. On the other hand, the more usual kind of inductively-acquired knowledge of particular human beings as they exist in particular times and places becomes obsolete as soon as styles and habits change.

Finally, it is also worth noting that Kant's concern to locate a cosmopolitan conception of human nature not tied to time and place is plainly evident even in some of his pre-critical writings, long before he first began teaching anthropology in 1772. For instance, in the *Announcement of the Organization of his Lectures for the Winter Semester 1765-66*, he emphasizes the centrality of "the study of man" in his ethics lectures, adding: "And by *man* here I do not only mean *man* as he is distorted by the mutable form which is conferred upon him by the contingencies of his condition… I rather mean the *nature* of man, which always remains [*die immer bleibt*], and his distinctive position within the creation." (2: 311)[20]

Ambiguities and Tensions

Thus far I have tried to achieve two interrelated goals: 1) articulating what Kant means by a "cosmopolitan conception of human nature," and 2) establishing the central role of this conception within Kant's own distinctive approach to anthropology. In the present section, I wish to address briefly three basic ambiguities and tensions engendered by Kant's cosmopolitan conception of human nature, and to do what I can to disambiguate and resolve these problems.

Cosmological/Empirical. Kant's commitment to an anthropology that provides general as opposed to local knowledge of human beings "and which is not empirical (*nicht empirisch*) but cosmological" (*Pillau* 25: 734) appears to contradict his claim that anthropology as he conceives it is a *Beobachtungslehre* – an empirical study or observation-based doctrine (letter to Herz toward the end of 1773, 10: 146). For instance, in *Collins*, one of the earliest surviving anthropology transcriptions (1772-73),[21] Kant begins by stating that in "the science of man (anthropologia)… the grounds of cognition are taken from observation and experience (*Beobachtung und Erfahrung*)." (25: 7) And the empirical credentials of Kantian anthropology are also touted later in the Preface to the

[20] For discussion, see Thorndike (2007), who argues that Kant's claims regarding the connection between anthropology and morality are deeply influenced by the scholastic conception of practical philosophy that Kant encountered in Alexander Gottlieb Baumgarten's texts –texts which he used for his own ethics and metaphysics courses.

[21] Louden and Wood, eds. (forthcoming).

Groundwork, when Kant states that "practical anthropology"[22] constitutes "the empirical part" (*der empirische Teil*) of moral philosophy (4: 388; cf. 387). But how can anthropology be both *empirisch* and *nicht empirisch*?

Kant's choice of language here is unfortunate: strictly speaking, he has contradicted himself. However, I believe his considered view is that the knowledge of human nature and of humanity that he emphasizes in his anthropology is a type of empirical knowledge, albeit one that aims at a high degree of generality and stresses reflection on common features and tendencies shared by all individual members of the species rather than distinguishing marks that set off individuals and/or groups from each other. Kant is certainly not claiming that the kind of knowledge of humanity stressed in his anthropology is an example of what (in the first *Critique*) he calls an "*a priori* cognition" –a cognition that occurs "*absolutely* independently of all experience." (*KrV* B 3) Rather, knowledge of the nature of humanity is an empirical cognition, which has its source "*a posteriori*, namely in experience." (KrV B 2) But the kind of empirical knowledge he is referring to in his anthropology is one that, while experience-based, emphasizes reflection about the chief tendencies and characteristics of the human species as a whole rather than limited and partial observations about the behavior of particular individuals or groups within the species in particular times and places. This point is evident in the concluding section of *Anthropology from a Pragmatic Point of View*, where Kant discusses the character and vocation of the human species at some length (7: 322-33), and several earlier transcriptions of his anthropology lectures contain similar discussions (see *Friedländer* 25: 675-97, *Menschenkunde* 25: 1194-1203, *Mrongovius* 25: 1415-29).[23] A key statement in this discussion is the following: "The character of the species, as it is known from the experience of all ages and by all peoples (*so wie er aus der Erfahrung aller Zeiten und unter allen Völkern kundbar wird*), is this..." (*VA* 7: 331) Here the experiential basis of the knowledge is clearly asserted, but so too is its wide temporal and spatial scope.

This emphasis on wide reflection about human nature and humanity is one key reason why Kant repeatedly includes "plays and novels" among the mot important aids (*Hilfsmittel*) for acquiring anthropological knowledge (*VA* 7: 121; cf. *Pillau* 25: 734, *Menschenkunde* 25: 857-58, *Mrongovius* 25: 1213). Novelists and playwrights frequently provide us

---

[22] Again though, the scope of pragmatic anthropology is broader than that of practical anthropology. The former concerns *all* uses to which we may put our knowledge of human nature; the latter, only moral ones.

[23] Louden and Wood, eds. (forthcoming).

with deeper and more enduring insights into the human condition than do social scientists, for the latter typically are only concerned with specific subgroups within the species as they exist in specific times and places.

Empirical/Normative. A second tension implicit in Kant's concept of a cosmopolitan conception of human nature is that between the *empirical* and the *normative*. I have discussed the empirical dimension of the concept already (see *Cosmological/Empirical*, above), and in my conclusion (see *Moral Motives*, below) I draw attention to its important moral dimension. Briefly, the primary function that Kant assigns to the cosmological conception of human nature is that of a teleological moral map: a tool by means of which we are to orient ourselves toward the present as well as the future. But here it is the tension between these two dimensions to which I wish to draw attention. How can something be both empirical and morally normative – especially for a non-naturalist such as Kant, who holds that moral oughts are in no way derivable from nature? In the first *Critique*, for instance, he writes:

> *Ought* expresses a kind of necessity and connection with grounds which is not found anywhere else in the whole of nature. In nature the understanding can cognize only *what exists*, or has been, or will be. It is impossible that something in it *ought to be* other than what, in all these time-relations, it in fact is; indeed, the *ought*, if one has merely the course of nature before one's eyes, has no meaning whatsoever (KrV A 547/B 575).[24]

Is there any viable way to defuse this tension? One possibility might be to argue that the oughts entailed by the cosmopolitan conception of human nature are merely hypothetical rather than categorical –that (e. g.) when Kant points to a future world in which human beings are "cosmopolitically united," (*VA* 7: 333) and when he argues that it is humanity's duty to pursue this goal (cf. *KpV* 5: 114), he is calling attention merely to a future possibility that is contingent on our own inclinations. But Kant's texts simply do not support such a reading. "We are determined *a priori* by reason to promote with all of our powers the best for the world (*das Weltbeste*)." (*KU* 5: 453; cf. *TP* 8: 309-10) The relevant oughts to which he refers are categorical, not hypothetical.

A second strategy, which I have defended in more detail elsewhere,[25] is to argue that a moral (categorical) imperative lies behind the acquisition of knowledge of our own nature. We have a moral duty to learn how nature

---

[24] For related discussion, see Louden (2000), pp. 16-19; Louden (2003), pp. 75-79.
[25] See Louden (2003), pp. 78-79.

(particularly our own nature) works in order to put into effect a system of freedom in the world of nature –that is, to bring about a moral world within the natural world in which we live.This strategy, I continue to believe, is viable and coherent. And it enables Kant to hold onto the claim that his anthropology is a *Beobachtungslehre* while still maintaining that there is a distinctively *moral* anthropology within it, which forms the second part of morals (cf. *Moral Mrongovious II* 29: 599). However, it is unfortunate that Kant's own discussion of this strategy is episodic and not systematically developed.

Cosmological/Cosmopolitan. The terms "cosmological" and "cosmopolitan" both feature prominently in Kant's discussions of human nature, and they overlap with each other in virtue of their shared Greek prefix κόσμος (order, world, universe). Again, however, Kant's use of the term 'cosmological' in his discussions of anthropology and physical geography does not signal a non-empirical study of the world or universe, as is often the case, say, in the Dialectic of the *Critique of Pure Reason*. When he emphasizes the need for a cosmological approach to the study of humanity in his anthropology, Kant is not dogmatically succumbing to the errors of "an alleged pure (rational) cosmology" (KrV B 435); rather, he is simply stressing the need to focus on the whole rather than the parts. And the relevant whole in this case is the entire human species, conceived teleologically with a view to its long-term political, legal, and moral vocation.

Another key text where this specifically anthropological sense of the term 'cosmological' is invoked occurs in an important concluding note to the essay, *Of the Different Races of Human Beings* (1775),[26] where Kant in effect advertises his physical geography and anthropology courses for the forthcoming year. Both courses aim "to procure the *pragmatic* element for all otherwise acquired sciences and skills, by means of which they become useful not merely for *school* but rather for *life*, and through which the accomplished student is introduced to the stage of his destiny (*Bestimmung*), namely, the *world*." (2: 443) Additionally, both physical geography and anthropology "must be considered *cosmologically*, namely, not with respect to the noteworthy details that their objects contain (physics and empirical psychology), but with respect to what we can note of the relation as a whole in which they stand and in which everyone takes his place." (2: 443) It is the relation of each individual to the species as a whole, where this whole is conceived both spatially and temporally (the

[26] A translation of this essay, prepared by Holly Wilson and Günter Zöller, is included in Zöller and Louden (2007).

latter in terms of the vocation or destiny of the species –its *Bestimmung*), that ultimately receives pride of place within Kantian anthropology.

The Greek suffix πολίτης (citizen) is crucial to the term "cosmopolitan," and here is where the terms "cosmological" and "cosmopolitan" part ways. There are distinct political, legal, and moral overtones in Kant's anthropological use of the term 'cosmopolitan' that are absent in the term "cosmological."

The legal dimension involves a strong commitment to international law and global as opposed to merely national jurisdiction; a global civil society where all individuals possess the same basic human rights and are judged by one internationally agreed-upon set of legal principles. In *Idea for a Universal History with a Cosmopolitan Aim* (1784),[27] Kant states that attaining such a society is humanity's most momentous task: "*The greatest problem for the human species, whose solution nature compels it to seek, is the achievement of a* ***civil society*** *that administers justice universally… This problem is at the same time the most difficult and the last to be solved by the human species*." (8: 22-23). In the conclusion to *Anthropology from a Pragmatic Point of View* he stresses that while "human beings feel destined (*bestimmt*) by nature to [develop] . . . into a *cosmopolitan* (*weltbürgerliche*) *society* (*cosmopolitismus*)," (7: 331) we are to regard this goal as "only a regulative principle" rather than a constitutive one. In effect, we are to treat it as an idea that strongly influences our practical orientation toward the world, but not as one that contributes directly to our knowledge of it. We are to regard the present warring nation-states *as if* they are headed in the direction of a viable, peaceful, cosmopolitan condition, but we have no reliable knowledge that they are *in fact* doing so. And Kant also holds that all individuals have a moral duty to work toward the achievement of the goal: we are commanded "to pursue this diligently as the vocation (*Bestimmung*) of the human race, not without grounded expectation (*gegründete Vermutung*) of a natural tendency toward it." (7: 331)

However, Kant is exasperatingly vague about the political makeup of this hoped-for cosmopolitan society. At times he appears to favor the strong universalism of a world-state. For instance, in *Toward Perpetual Peace* (1795) he contrasts "the positive idea *of a world republic*" to "the *negative* surrogate of a *league*" (*Bund*) of sovereign states (8: 357); and at the end of the *Theory and Practice* essay (1793) he states that he puts his "trust in theory, which proceeds from the principle of right," and which

[27] A new translation of this essay, prepared by Allen Wood, appears in Zöller and Louden (2007).

supports the establishment of "a universal state of peoples" (*ein allgemeiner Völkerstaat*) (8: 313; cf. 311). But his considered view appears to favor the initial establishment of a small, voluntary league of nations without coercive powers ("this league does not aim to acquire any power of the state" –8: 356), which will then expand gradually into a stronger world-wide federation of all states with at least some coercive authority at the federal level –presumably, the authority to enforce peace between nations as well as to prosecute fundamental human rights violations within states.[28] The stronger alternative of a universal "state of peoples" (*Völkerstaat*), while "correct *in thesi*," (8: 357) is neither a realistic nor a morally desirable option. Sovereign nations "are not to be fused into a single state," (8: 354) for a world-state is likely to result only in "a soulless despotism." (8: 367) However, while Kant prudently declines to speculate about the precise political contours of humanity's future cosmopolitan condition, it is clear that a political dimension forms a necessary part of his cosmopolitan conception of human nature. For instance, in the final sentence of *Anthropology from a Pragmatic Point of View* he urges readers to work for the "progressive organization of the citizens of the earth (*Erdbürger*) into and toward the species as a system that is cosmopolitically united (*kosmopolitsch verbunden*)." (7: 333)

Moral Motives

Finally, the moral dimension of Kant's cosmopolitan conception of human nature, a dimension which, to the best of my knowledge, has been overlooked, indeed denied, by other scholars who have discussed it.[29]

[28] For a good recent analysis of Kant's position, see Kleingeld (2006). See also Louden (2007), pp. 94-106.

[29] Gregor (1974), for instance, toward the end of her "Translator's Introduction," argues that Kant's pragmatic anthropology works under the guidance of the philosophy of history, and suggests that Kant views history "as the account of what nature does to prepare the human race for its final end." (p. XXII) But she also holds (following her teacher H. J. Paton) that Kant's moral anthropology is simply a misnomer – it is "not ethics but rather a sort of psychology" [Gregor (1963), p. 8; cf. Gregor (1974), p. XIII]. Similarly, Brandt (2003), in his discussion of the vocation of the human being and its central role in Kant's anthropology, rightly stresses its strong species orientation, as I have also done in the present essay. But Brandt too denies that we find a moral anthropology in any of Kant's lectures on anthropology: "in none of its phases of development is pragmatic anthropology identical with the anthropology that Kant repeatedly envisions as the complement to his moral theory after 1770" [Brandt and Stark (1997), p. XLVI; cf. Brandt

Here as elsewhere,[30] we see clear signs of a moral agenda within Kant's anthropology. By means of his cosmopolitan conception of human nature, Kant intends to provide readers with a conceptual orientation and delineation of where humanity as a species is headed, as well as to indicate what human beings need to do in order to reach their destination. The cosmopolitan conception of human nature is in effect a teleological moral map, a practical guide by means of which human beings are to orient themselves in both the present and future.

A second moral motive behind the cosmopolitan conception is simply to stress what all members of the human species share in common with one another, rather than to dwell on what sets them apart from one another. In this role, it serves as an anthropological reminder that *all* human beings have rights simply in virtue of their shared humanity, and that these rights "must be held sacred, however great a sacrifice this may cost the ruling power." (*EF* 8: 380) All citizens of the earth (*Erdbürger*), regardless of their different national affiliations, possess the same basic human rights, and all human beings have a duty to promote the effective legal enforcement of these rights.

Thirdly, the *Bestimmung* (vocation, destiny, determination – each of these meanings is present in Kant's use of the term) of humanity in a cosmopolitan condition is something that only the species as a whole can achieve. And in this respect, human beings differ markedly from other animals: "with the animal species each individual reaches its *Bestimmung*, but in the human race a single individual can never do this, rather only the whole species can reach its *Bestimmung*, despite the fact that the human being is equipped by nature like an animal." (*Menschenkunde* 25: 1196; cf. *Mrongovius* 25: 1417, *VA* 7: 324) Here Kant indicates that the empirical and comparative study of different terrestrial beings supports the case for human exceptionalism. Human beings *are* different from other animals: we have a collective cultural, political, and moral vocation that they lack.

It is true that Kant's anthropology, like other anthropologies past and present, is infected by multiple ethnic, racial, religious, and sexist prejudices that continually threaten to undermine its core progressive principles. But it is also important not to lose sight of the core progressive principles, and the cosmopolitan conception of human nature is ultimately what anchors them. In placing what the members of the human species

(2003), p. 92]. Both Gregor and Brandt deny that Kant's anthropology should be viewed as the second part of morals, the empirical counterpart to pure moral philosophy. For responses, see Louden (2000, 2003, 2006a).

[30] See Louden (2000, 2003, 2006a).

share in common with one another at the center of his anthropology, and in trying to show "that there is a cosmopolitical predisposition (*cosmopolitische Anlage*) in the human species," one which, "even with all the wars… gradually wins the upper hand over the selfish predispositions of peoples in the course of political affairs," (*VA* 7: 412)[31] Kant gives readers rational grounds both for adopting a stance whereby "a violation of rights in *one* place of the earth is felt in *all*" as well as for believing that "the idea of a cosmopolitan right is no fantastic and exaggerated way of representing right." (*EF* 8: 360) At the same time, anthropology from a Kantian point of view stresses that whether human beings ever will in fact become "cosmopolitically united" (*VA* 7: 333) and enter into a condition where "a universal peace rules the world" (*Mrongovius* 25: 1429) depends ultimately on what they choose to do. Peace is by no means guaranteed. But this too is eminently appropriate for a project that sets out to investigate what human beings as free-acting beings make of themselves, or can and should make of themselves (cf. *VA* 7: 119).[32]

Works Cited

Adickes, E. (1911). *Untersuchungen zu Kants physisicher Geographie.* Tübungen: J. C. B. Mohr.

Brandt, R. (2003). The Guiding Idea of Kant's Anthropology and the Vocation of the Human Being. In B. Jacobs and P. Kain (Eds.), *Essays on Kant's Anthropology* (pp. 85-104). Cambridge: Cambridge University Press.

---

[31] This passage is one of many that appear in the margins of the *Handschrift* for *Anthropology from a Pragmatic Point of View* –Kant's own hand-written manuscript that formed the basis for the book published in 1798. The *Handschrift* often differs from the two editions of the *Anthropology* that were printed during Kant's lifetime, and it is not known how many of the changes between the *Handschrift* and the printed editions were approved by Kant himself. Many scholars believe that the *Handschrift* in fact gives us a closer indication of Kant's own position. In Louden (2006b), supplementary texts from the *Handschrift* are printed as footnotes –e.g., the passage cited is n. 11 on p. 231. For further discussion, see the "Note on the text and translation" in Louden (2006b).

[32] An earlier version of this essay was presented as an invited lecture to the Philosophy Department at Marquette University in February, 2007. I would like to thank the members of the audience for raising a number of issues that eventually led to improvements in my argument. Thanks also to two anonymous referees of the essay, for drawing my attention to several points that I had overlooked.

Brandt, R. and Stark, W. (1997). Einleitung. In I. Kant, *Kant's gesammelte Schriften*, vol. 25.1 (pp. VII-CLI). Berlin: Walter de Gruyter.

Cohen, A. (Forthcoming). Physiological vs. Pragmatic Anthropology: A Response to Schleiermacher's Objection to Kant's 'Anthropology'. *Proceedings of the Tenth International Kant Congress*. Berlin: Walter de Gruyter.

Davis, M. L. (1995). *Identity of History? Marcus Herz and the End of Enlightenment*. Detroit: Wayne State University Press.

Elden, S. and Mendieta, E. (Eds.) (Forthcoming). *Reading Kant's Geography*. Albany: State University of New York Press.

Gay, P. (1967). The Enlightenment as Medicine and as Cure. In W. H. Barber et al. (Eds.), *The Age of Enlightenment. Studies Presented to Theodore Besterman* (pp. 375-86). Edinburgh: Oliver and Boyd.

Gregor, M. J. (1963). *Laws of Freedom: A Study of Kant's Method of Applying the Categorical Imperative in the "Metaphysik der Sitten."* Oxford: Basil Blackwell.

—. (1974). Translator's Introduction. In Immanuel Kant, *Anthropology from a Pragmatic Point of View* (pp. IX-XXV). The Hague: Martinus Nijhoff.

Guyer, P. (2007). Translator's Introduction to *Observations on the Feeling of the Beautiful and the Sublime*. In G. Zöller and R. B. Louden (Eds.) *Anthropology, History, and Education. The Cambridge Edition of the Works of Immanuel Kant* (pp. 71-80). Cambridge: Cambridge University Press

Guyer, P. & Wood, A. W. (1992 –) (General Eds.) *The Cambridge Edition of the Works of Immanuel Kant*. 14 volumes to date. Cambridge: Cambridge University Press.

Heidegger, M. (1962). *Kant and the Problem of Metaphysics*, tr. James Churchill. Bloomington: Indiana University Press. (Original work published in 1929.)

Herz, M. (1773). D. Ernst Platner, der Arzneykunst Professors in Leipzig, *Anthropologie für Ärzte und Weltweise*. Erster Theil. Leipzig, in der Dyckischen Buchhandlung, 1772. 8. 292 Seiten. *Allgemeine deutsche Bibliothek, vol. 20*, 25-51.

Kant, I. (1900 –). *Gesammelte Schriften*. Ed. by the Royal Prussian (later German) Academy of Sciences. 29 volumes to date. Berlin: Georg Reimer, later Walter de Gruyter.

Kim, Soo Bae (1994). *Die Entstehung der Kantischen Anthropologie und ihre Beziehung zur empirischen Psychologie der Wolffschen Schule*. Frankfurt: Peter Lang.

Kleingeld, P. (2006). Kant's Theory of Peace. In P. Guyer (Ed.), *The Cambridge Companion to Kant and Modern Philosophy* (pp. 477-504). Cambridge: Cambridge University Press.

Kuehn, M. (2001). *Kant: A Biography*. Cambridge: Cambridge University Press.

La Mettrie, J. O. de (1994). *Man a Machine and Man a Plant*, tr. R. A. Watson and M. Rybalka. Indianapolis: Hackett. (Original work published in 1747.)

Louden, R. B. (2000). *Kant's Impure Ethics: From Rational Beings to Human Beings*. New York, Oxford: Oxford University Press.

—. (2003). The Second Part of Morals. In B. Jacobs and P. Kain (Eds.), *Essays on Kant's Anthropology* (pp. 60-84). Cambridge: Cambridge University Press.

—. (2006a). Applying Kant's Ethics: The Role of Anthropology. In G. Bird (Ed.), *A Companion to Kant* (pp. 350-63). Oxford: Blackwell Publishing.

—. (Tr. & Ed.). (2006b). *Anthropology from a Pragmatic Point of View*. Cambridge: Cambridge University Press.

—. (2007). *The World We Want: How and Why the Ideals of the Enlightenment Still Elude Us*. New York, Oxford: Oxford University Press.

Louden, R. B. & Wood, A. W. (Eds.). (forthcoming). *Lectures on Anthropology. The Cambridge Edition of the Works of Immanuel Kant.* Cambridge: Cambridge University Press.

Makkreel, R. A. (2001). Kant on the Scientific Status of Psychology, Anthropology, and History. In E. Watkins (Ed.), *Kant and the Sciences* (pp. 185-203). New York: Oxford University Press.

May, J. A. (1970). *Kant's Concept of Geography and its Relation to Recent Geographical Thought*. Toronoto: University of Toronto Press.

Platner, E. (2000). *Anthropologie für Ärzte und Weltweise*. Hildesheim: Olms. (Original work published in 1772.)

Scheler, M. (1989). Die Stellung des Menschen im Kosmos. In Hans Dierkes (Ed.), *Arbeitstexte für den Unterricht: Philosophische Anthropologie* (pp. 49-53). Stuttgart: Reclam. (Original work published in 1928.)

Schings, H.-J. (1977). Der philosophische Arzt. Anthropologie, Melancholie und Literatur im 18.Jahrhundert. In *Melancholie und Aufklärung* (pp. 11-40). Stuttgart: J. B. Metzler.

Sturm, T (2001). Kant on Empirical Psychology: How Not to Investigate the Human Mind. In E. Watkins (Ed.), *Kant and the Sciences* (pp. 163-84). New York: Oxford University Press.

Thorndike, O. (2007). On the Original Connection between Anthropology and Morality. Paper presented at the Annual Meeting of the Eastern Study Group of the North American Kant Society, University of Southern Maine, May 2007.

Wood, A. W. (2003). Kant and the Problem of Human Nature. In B. Jacobs and P. Kain (Eds.), *Essays on Kant's Anthropology* (pp. 38-59). Cambridge: Cambridge University Press.

Zammito, J. H. (2002). *Kant, Herder, and the Birth of Anthropology*. Chicago: University of Chicago Press

Zöller, G. & Louden, R. B. (Eds.). (2007). *Anthropology, History, and Education. The Cambridge Edition of the Works of Immanuel Kant*. Cambridge: Cambridge University Press.

CHAPTER FIVE

UNDERSTANDING KANT'S CLAIM THAT 'MORALITY CANNOT BE WITHOUT ANTHROPOLOGY'

OLIVER THORNDIKE

I- Introduction

1. Kant's frequently repeated claim that '*morality cannot be without anthropology*' has prompted various Kant scholars to argue for a fundamental or supplemental function of anthropology for Kant's moral philosophy.[1] These authors typically refer to passages such as the following:

> [M]orality cannot exist without anthropology, for one must first know of the agent whether he is also in a position to accomplish what it is required from him that he should do. One can, indeed, certainly consider practical philosophy even without anthropology, or without knowledge of the agent,

[1] Louden, Robert B. (2003), *The Second Part of Morals*, in: Jacobs, Brian / Kain, Patrick (eds.) (2003), *Essays on Kant's Anthropology*, Cambridge University Press, Cambridge, pp.60-84. See also his *Applying Kant's Ethics: The Role of Anthropology*, in: Graham, Bird (ed.) (2006), *A Companion to Kant*, Blackwell Publishing, pp.350-363; and his *Anthropology from a Kantian Point of View: Toward a Cosmopolitan Conception of Human Nature*, 2008, this volume.

Schmidt, Claudia M. (2007), *Kant's Transcendental, Empirical, Pragmatic, and Moral Anthropology*, in: Kant-Studien 98, 2007, pp.156-182, pp.165-166.

Stark, Werner (2003), *Historical Notes and Interpretive Questions about Kant's Lectures on Anthropology*, in: Jacobs, Brian / Kain, Patrick (eds.) (2003), pp.15-37.

Wood, Allen (1999), *Kant's Ethical Thought*, Cambridge University Press, pp. 193-225. See also his *Practical Anthropology*, in: Gerhardt, Volker et al. (eds.), *Kant und die Berliner Aufklärung. Akten des IX. Internationalen Kant-Kongresses*. Walter de Gruyter, Berlin, New York, 2001, Vol.4, pp.458-475.

> only then it is merely speculative, or an Idea; so man must at least be studied accordingly… Considerations of rules is useless if one cannot make man ready to follow them, so these two sciences are closely connected. (27:244$_{20\text{-}37}$)[2]

Passages like the one just cited seem to indicate that Kant regarded the empirical study of human nature as (in a sense that needs to be determined) necessary for morality. In this paper, I take up two questions, on which even the two editors of Kant's anthropology lectures in the Academy Edition could not agree.[3] (1) In what sense does Kant think that morality and anthropology are 'closely connected?' (2) What kind of significance does this connection allow us to attribute to anthropology for Kant's moral philosophy?

I will address these questions in two steps. First, I try to reconstruct the historical origin of Kant's anthropology. Kant used Alexander Gottlieb Baumgarten's (1714-1763) *Ethica* and later also his *Initia* as a foil for his lectures on ethics.[4] Kant's course in anthropology, which was first taught

---

[2] All quotations in German/Latin are in accordance with the *Akademie-Edition* (=AA) Vol. 1-29 of *Kant's Gesammelte Schriften*, Berlin/Leipzig, 1902—. All translations from Latin are mine. Quotations in English are taken from *The Cambridge Edition of the Works of Immanuel Kant*, unless I indicate that translations are mine. Hereafter, I do not follow the convention – adopted by some of the editors of the Cambridge Edition – of using bold face to emphasize italics in the German original editions of Kant's respective works. As is customary, citations from Kant's *Critique of Pure Reason* are located by the pagination of the first edition of 1781 (A) and/or the second edition of 1787 (B).

For other passages making identical or similar claims see: *Lectures on Ethics Herder* 27:12$_{35\text{-}36}$; *Anthropology Collins* 25:9$_{14\text{-}16}$; *Moral Philosophy Kaehler* pp.5-6; *Moral Philosophy Collins* 27:244$_{11}$-245$_{31}$; *Anthropology Friedländer* 25:471$_{33}$-472$_{8}$; *Moral Mrongovius II* 29:598$_{21}$-599$_{22}$; *Menschenkunde* 25:858$_{9\text{-}22}$; *Anthropology Mrongovius* 25:1211$_{30\text{-}33}$; 2:311; A15/B29 ; 4:388, 412; 5:8; 6:217.

[3] Brandt and Stark are the two editors of the lectures on anthropology (vol. 25 of the Academy Edition). I thus assign the positions proposed in their introduction to this volume to both authors. However, this is not unproblematic in so far as Stark (2003:21) writes: "For years now, the two editors of volume 25 of the Academy edition have disagreed about the role and relevance of the anthropology. In contrast to Reinhard Brandt, I am of the opinion that an internal, positive relationship exists between Kant's lectures on anthropology and his moral philosophy… The positive and critical content of the anthropology, in my opinion, cannot be reduced to a mere doctrine of prudence."

[4] Baumgarten, Alexander Gottlieb, *Ethica philosophica*, Halle ^{1}1740 (^{2}1751, ^{3}1763). The second edition is reprinted in AA 27:733-869; the third edition is reprinted in AA 27:871-1015. The *Ethica* will be abbreviated by 'E,' then follow

in 1772 and then published as a book in 1798 under the title "Anthropology from a Pragmatic Point of View,"[5] is based on Baumgarten's *Psychologia Empirica*, which is a part of Baumgarten's *Metaphysica.* I will show that Baumgarten's *theory of action*, which evolves around the notion of empirical 'motivating grounds,' lies at the basis of his *theory of obligation.* It is precisely because Kant dissolves the connection between empirical motivating grounds and morality by basing moral philosophy on an entirely formal (intellectual) principle that any empirical anthropology cannot be philosophically significant for Kant. For Kant, anthropology is a side-project.

After discussing the origin of Kant's anthropology, I will then, in the second part of this essay, distinguish four tasks of Kant's anthropology:

> (1) *A general didactical function*, which does not denote a specifically *moral* anthropology because it aims to provide a general orientation for Kant's students' future engagement with the world.
> (2) *A function of determining ethical duties*, which is of fundamental importance to Kant's moral philosophy, but which is not contained in the *Anthropology.*
> (3) *A pedagogical function*, which considers the subjective conditions that hinder or further the fulfillment of the laws of a metaphysics of morals.
> (4) A role regarding the *instantiation of an ethical principle* through an action under specific circumstances.

I will argue that the third and the fourth aspects of anthropology justify Kant's claim that morality cannot be without anthropology. But they do

---

paragraph number and reference to the Academy Edition. Baumgarten, Alexander Gottlieb, *Initia philosphiae practicae primae*, Halle 1760; reprinted in AA 19:7-91. The *Initia* will be abbreviated by 'I,' then follow paragraph number and reference to the Academy Edition. For his lectures on metaphysics Kant mainly used Baumgarten's *Metaphysica.* Baumgarten, Alexander Gottlieb, *Metaphysica*, Halle, [1]1739 ([4]1757); reprinted in AA 17:5-226 and AA 15:5-45. References to the *Metaphysica* will be abbreviated by 'M,' followed by paragraph number, and followed by a reference to the (not always accurate) German translation by: Meier, G.F., *Metaphysik* (neue vermehrte Auflage von Johann August Eberhard), Halle, [1]1766 ([2]1783), Dietrich Scheglmann Reprints, Norderstedt, 2004.

[5] Kant, Immanuel, *Anthropology from a Pragmatic Point of View* (=*Anthropology*). Edited by Robert B. Louden. With an introduction by Manfred Kuehn. Cambridge Texts in the History of Philosophy. Cambridge University Press, 2006.

not allow us to attribute a philosophical significance to Kant's anthropology course. Kant's *Anthropology* does neither reinforce nor supplement his transcendental account of morality.

II- Pragmatic and Theoretic Motivating Grounds in Baumgarten's Theory of Obligation

II.1

It is my thesis that a study of Baumgarten's work is pivotal for a proper understanding of Kant's practical philosophy, because Baumgarten's textbooks provide the motivation to reflect on and clarify the moral concepts Kant found therein. Through his compendia, Baumgarten was Kant's constant interlocutor in his lecture courses for more than thirty years. Erich Adickes, the editor of much of Kant's work in the Academy Edition, has attributed a significant influence of Baumgarten's compendia for the development of Kant's thought (14:L). Nevertheless, Baumgarten has received relatively little attention in Kant scholarship.

Joseph Schmucker's study of the early sources of Kant's ethical thought is a rare exception.[6] Roughly a quarter of Schmucker's monograph interprets the extensive notes Kant inserted into his copy of the *Initia*. Dieter Henrich claims that a study of Baumgarten is helpful in better understanding the dynamic of Kant's development,[7] although he rarely puts this thesis to work. Recently, Clemens Schwaiger has focused on Baumgarten's influence on Kant.[8] Werner Stark deserves full credit for

---

[6] Schmucker, Josef, *Die Ursprünge der Ethik Kants in seinen vorkritischen Schriften und Reflektionen*, Meisenheim, 1961.

[7] Henrich, Dieter, *Über Kants früheste Ethik. Versuch einer Rekonstruktion*, in: Kant-Studien 54 (1963), pp.404-431, p.422.

[8] Schwaiger, Clemens, *Kategorische und Andere Imperative. Zur Entwicklung von Kants praktischer Philosophie bis 1785*, Stuttgart-Bad Cannstatt, 1999. See also his *Die Anfänge des Projekts einer Metaphysik der Sitten. Zu den wolffianischen Wurzeln einer kantischen Schlüsselidee*, in: Kant und die Berliner Aufklärung. Akten des IX. Internationalen Kant-Kongresses, Walter de Gruyter, 2001, Vol. II, pp.52-58. Further his *Ein "missing link" auf dem Weg der Ethik von Wolff zu Kant. Zur Quellen- und Wirkungsgeschichte der praktischen Philosophie von Alexander Gottlieb Baumgarten*; in: Jahrbuch für Recht und Ethik, Vol.8 (2000). Further, his *Vollkommenheit als Moralprinzip bei Wolff, Baumgarten and Kant*, in: Oberhausen, Michael (ed.), Vernunftkritik und Aufklärung. Studien zur Philosophie Kants und seines Jahrhunderts. Stuttgart-Bad Cannstatt, Friedrich Frommann Verlag, Günther Holzboog, 2001, pp.317-328. Also his yet unpublished

editing the *Kaehler-Lecture*[9] on practical philosophy in such a way that the connections to Baumgarten's textbooks are immediately apparent.

To be sure, one must not over-interpret the significance of Baumgarten's influence. Henrich's judgment that Kant was a 'genius of combination'[10] is certainly correct. Baumgarten is by far not the only influence on the young Kant. Moreover, most of the time Kant disagrees with Baumgarten. Nevertheless, Baumgarten sets the framework that shapes Kant's investigations. A sizable part of Baumgarten's terminology and thematic vocabulary informs Kant's thought. In discussing the origin of Kant's anthropology, I hope to show that it is worthwhile attending to the Baumgartian background of Kant's thought.[11]

II.2

Baumgarten tries to understand the concept of obligation via a theory of action, at the center of which stand empirical motivating grounds which propel an agent towards realizing what she perceives as good. Baumgarten's theory of action states, very roughly, that we cannot pursue an end or abstain from pursuing it unless we desire to do so.[12] Accordingly, Baumgarten defines the "law of the appetitive faculty" as the intention to realize what induces pleasure.[13] That which moves us, is called the *causa impulsiva* (motivating ground)[14] or the *elateres animi* (incentives of the mind).[15] These are the representations in virtue of which

---

essay: *Zur Theorie der Verbindlichkeit, bei Wolff, Baumgarten und dem frühen Kant*.

[9] Kant, Immanuel, *Vorlesung zur Moralphilosophie*. Stark, Werner (ed.). Mit einer Einleitung von Manfred Kuehn, Berlin, De Gruyter, 2004.

[10] Henrich, Dieter, *Über Kant's Entwicklungsgeschichte*, in: Philosophische Rundschau 13 (1965), pp. 252-263, p.254.

[11] Since Baumgarten's terminology stands in the tradition of natural law theories, I will occasionally (for the purpose of elucidation) provide references to Christian Wolff (1679-1754), who is arguably the most famous predecessor of Baumgarten, and Georg Friedrich Meier (1718-1777), who, as a student of Baumgarten is perhaps the most important successor. Kant discusses both of these latter figures in his lectures and notes. However, I will focus on the specifically Baumgartian influence on Kant's practical philosophy.

[12] Baumgarten, A.G., *Metaphysica*, M §726 (§534).

[13] Baumgarten, A.G., *Metaphysica*, M §665 (§491).

[14] Baumgarten, A.G., *Metaphysica*, M §342 (§243); cf. *Initia*, I §§12-26 (19:12_{33}-16_{32}).

[15] Baumgarten, A.G., *Metaphysica*, M §669 (§493) and M §671 (§495).

(or: because of which) we intend or avoid something.[16] For Baumgarten, the divers motivating grounds of agents are the most immediate building blocks of action. Desires, beliefs, affects, values, reasons, feelings, rewards and punishments are all inner representations that are understood as making up the set of motivations leading to x (x being an action).[17] Baumgarten's theory of action is developed in his empirical psychology (*psychologia empirica*) and focuses on empirical motivating grounds. Proceeding from his empirical conception of choice, Baumgarten *defines* obligation in terms of *moving causes* and the science of ethics in terms of obligation.[18] 'Motivating grounds' take center stage in Baumgarten's account of moral obligation.

The philosophically interesting question is whether it is possible to get from such a theory of action (that is based on motivating grounds) to a theory of obligation. Baumgarten tries to understand the ground of obligation from the concept of inner motivation. This is also plausible from his perspective, because the ground on which we intend an object is the motivating ground.[19] When we say "A ought to do x," it is reasonable to assume that unless A has some representational ground for pursuing x, it has not been explained why "A ought to do x" should be valid for A. In other words, "A ought to do x" is only true if we can connect a motivating ground to A's will. This might sound strange at first. For, even if we cannot make comprehensible to A why she ought to do x, there might be good reasons (albeit independently of A's individual insight) to claim 'A ought to do x.' Of course, it is here that a theory of obligation would have to enter the debate, i.e., a theory that makes comprehensible the ground, on which 'A ought to do x' is valid.

For Baumgarten, practical philosophy is the science that demonstrates the validity of normative propositions of the form "A ought to do x" by showing that A, qua being a human being, always already has a motivating ground to do x – she just does not know it. Baumgarten's science of ethics is meant to demonstrate why agents ought to make the transition from 'not being motivated to x' to 'being motivated to x' given their actual human

---

[16] Baumgarten, A.G., *Metaphysica*, M §342 (§243).

[17] Cf. Schmucker, Josef (1961:37). Cf. *Metaphysics Herder* (28:96$_{28\text{-}29}$, 98$_{30\text{-}31}$). More recently, Bernard Williams used the notion of a 'motivational set' to describe this internalist perspective on human action. Cf. Williams, Bernard, *Moral Luck*, Cambridge University Press, 1981, pp.101-113.

[18] Baumgarten, A.G., *Initia*, I §12 (19:12$_{33}$-13$_{25}$), I §15 (19:13$_{35\text{-}37}$), I §§4-5; Baumgarten, A.G., *Ethica*, E §1 (27:378$_{3\text{-}5}$). Cf. Schwaiger, Clemens (1999:51, 160-161).

[19] Baumgarten, A.G., *Metaphysica*, M §342 (§243).

nature. This is to say, if a human agent does not perceive the good as good, it is the task of the science of ethics to appeal to something in the agent's motivational make-up, so that the agent comes to see things "aright."[20] This transition is brought about by showing that there is something in the motivational set of every human agent (qua human nature), which only needs to be correctly recognized (distinctly perceived) in order to motivate to x. Baumgarten's science of ethics is a science that aims to demonstrate that x is an action that a human agent wants to do if she only comes to view things correctly. Baumgarten holds that to oblige someone is nothing but to connect a motivating ground with his will. To put it in a nutshell, obligation is motivation.[21] Baumgarten's theory of obligation is derived from his theory of action.

There is, of course, one important missing link in the identity of motivation and obligation. For, how is it possible to conceive of obligation (or: moral necessity) as the psychological necessity of the most effective motivating grounds,[22] and still hold that there is an objective standard of obligation? Isn't the subjective motivational set of an agent the strict opposite of an inter-subjectively valid (i.e., objective) standard of obligation? The trick, if I may so call it, consists in the assumption that, by nature, the more strongly motivating causes are directed towards the good.[23] This is to say, there is a subjective (what we perceive as good) and an objective side (what is good by nature) to Baumgarten's explanation of the concept of obligation. Beginning from the subjective side, we may say the following: Obligation is grounded in correct deliberation, which, in turn, is brought to light in terms of reasons *internal* to the human motivational set. Beginning from the objective side, Baumgarten says that the good is good because of its good consequences in reality.[24] Human nature is constituted in such a way that "a man is obliged to committing good."[25] What Baumgarten here means is that there are *natural* obligations or *natural* duties, which (by nature) motivate us to pursue the good in virtue of their good consequences. Coming to see things 'aright' simply means to recognize that obligations are the indispensable means to realize good consequences, i.e., to attain happiness. Thus, by nature, human beings

---

[20] I am here using John McDowell's language. Cf. McDowell, John, *Mind, Value, and Reality*, Harvard University Press, 1998, pp.95-111.

[21] Cf. Schwaiger, Clemens (1999:160-164); Schmucker, Josef (1961:280-284).

[22] Baumgarten, A.G., *Initia*, I §§15 (19:13$_{35\text{-}37}$).

[23] Baumgarten, A.G., *Initia*, I §§39 (19:23$_{21\text{-}33}$).

[24] Baumgarten, A.G., *Initia*, I §33 (19:20$_{16\text{-}22}$).

[25] Baumgarten, A.G., *Initia*, I §39 (19:23$_{21\text{-}33}$).

"are obliged to pursue happiness."[26] Since by nature the stronger motivating grounds propel us towards the good (objective side), all that a philosophical ethics needs to do is to guide reason to think correctly (subjective side).

In this context, the anthropological dimension of Baumgarten's theory of obligation is most prevalent. Since by nature the stronger motivating grounds propel us towards the good, Baumgarten's philosophical ethics must aim at the effectiveness of its application. In the context of guiding reason to think correctly, and thus in the context of considering the transition from 'not being motivated to x' (i.e., not seeing things correctly) to 'being motivated to x,' Baumgarten distinguishes between effective and ineffective motivating grounds. Baumgarten says that incentives of the mind that make us desire or avoid something are either *pragmatic* (*pragmatica*, *practica*), which means that they are effective, empirically real and actually move to action (*movens*, *efficientes*, *causa efficiens*),[27] or they don't move to action (*iners*, *inefficientes*), in which case the incentives are called *theoretica* or *speculativa*. Baumgarten's insertion after *theoretica* in German: *ein untaugliches Hirngebäude*, i.e., an impotent figment of the brain, further elucidates the distinction between pragmatic and inefficient motivating grounds. A motive lacking sufficient moving force (*causae impulsivae*, *vis movendi*) is called inefficient or *theoretica et mortua latius* (i.e., theoretical and dead in a wider sense).[28]

---

[26] Baumgarten, A.G., *Ethica*, E §13 (27:875$_{27}$). Baumgarten's principle of obligation is thus at bottom a principle of utility or eudemonism. Strictly speaking, this eudemonism is already contained in the very definition of the appetitive faculty, i.e., the intention to realize what induces pleasure. Cf. Wolff, Christian, *Vernünfftige Gedancken von der Menschen Thun und Lassen, zu Beförderung ihrer Glückseeligkeit*, Halle [1]1720 (Frankfurt am Main / Leipzig [4]1733). Reprinted in: Wolff, Christian, Gesammelte Werke, École, Jean et.al. (Ed.), Abt.1, Bd.4, Georg Olms Verlag, Hildesheim, New York, 1976, §139. Cf. Schmucker, Josef (1961:28-51); Henrich, Dieter (1963:428-429).

[27] Latin expressions are quotations and thus not grammatically revised.

[28] Baumgarten, A.G., *Metaphysica*, M §669 (§493), M §671 (§495). This does not mean that an insufficient moving cause cannot be supplemented by *causa auxiliaries* (M §§319-321) (§§225-226)) so that it does become efficient. Most prominently, Kant conceives of God's distributive justice as such *causa auxiliaries* moving to moral action because without the assumption of a "wise author and regent" moral laws would be without effect and thus "figments of the brain" (A811/B839). The distinction between 'speculative' and 'moving' also occurs numerous times in Kant's lectures and figures prominently in his letter to Marcus Herz dated toward the end of 1773 (10:145$_{7\text{-}17}$). Cf. Kant, Immanuel (2004:193-194).

In the *Initia*, we find the same pairs of oppositions: a representation can be either moving and pragmatic (*movens et pragmatica*) or inert and empty (*iners et vana*).[29] It is precisely because "deeds cannot exist without the effectual appetite of the person who is obligated to them"[30] that the task of ethics is to provide "its cognitions with life [*Leben*], [i.e.,] presenting the will with sufficient motivating grounds to do what is good and to omit what is evil."[31] The most important *practical* task of practical philosophy (for Baumgarten) is to make cognitions of the good *effective*.[32]

Notably, all three parts of the soul, which Baumgarten traditionally divides into the intellectual faculty, the feeling of pleasure and displeasure and the appetitive faculty, are relevant for making ethics effective. In *Ethics Herder*, Kant reports on this threefold division:

> Introduction into practical philosophy. Foundation in psychology. Three main concepts within the soul. 1) Cognition. To hold phenomena for true or false: theoretical philosophy. 2) Feeling: presupposes cognition, phenomena [are] pleasure and displeasure … 3) Desire presupposes both: a) representation b) reference to pleasure and displeasure.[33]

As has been pointed out in the literature, Baumgarten's practical philosophy is a typical example of the so-called Wolffian *Schulphilosophie*,[34] which divides the soul into the intellectual faculty, the feeling of pleasure and displeasure and the appetitive faculty.[35] Practical philosophy (for Baumgarten) is grounded in psychology, which comprises (1) cognition of the good, which induces (2) pleasure and displeasure,

---

[29] Baumgarten, A.G., *Initia*, I §§15-16 (19:13_{33}-14_{5}), §137 (19:65_{38}).
[30] Baumgarten, A.G., *Initia*, §141 (19:$67_{17\text{-}18}$).
[31] Baumgarten, A.G., *Philosophische Briefe von Aletheophilus*, Frankfurt/Leipzig, 1741, p.12. Cf. Baumgarten, A.G., *Initia*, §4 (19:10_{21}).
[32] Cf. Baumgarten, A.G., *Initia*, §3 (19:$9_{27\text{-}28}$). Cf. Meier, Georg Friedrich, *Allgemeine Practische Weltweisheit*, Halle, 1764. Reprinted in: Wolff, Christian, Gesammelte Werke, École, Jean et.al. (Ed.), Abt.3, Bd.107, Georg Olms Verlag, Hildesheim, Zürich, New York, 2006, §§10, 13, 18, 21.
[33] Lectures on Ethics Herder (27:$12_{3\text{-}15}$, my translation); cf. Metaphysics Herder (28:$73_{16\text{-}18}$, $74_{1\text{-}2}$). Cf. 29:$45_{3\text{-}11}$.
[34] Here I use the German phrase '*Schulphilosophie*' because its translation 'scholastic philosophy' has a different meaning in the English literature.
[35] Cf. Brandt, Reinhard / Stark, Werner in AA 25:xxv-xxvi. See also Hinske, Norbert, *Kants Idee der Anthropologie*, in: Rombach, Heinrich (ed.), *Die Frage nach dem Menschen. Aufriss einer Philosophischen Anthropologie*. Verlag Karl Alber, Freiburg, München, 1966, pp. 410-427, p.416.

which in turn provides (3) the motivating ground for action.[36] Moral action can *fail* with respect to each of these three cognitive faculties. For example, (*ad* 1) we do not *cognize* that an action possible through our will contributes to our true perfection (happiness); (*ad* 2) we are indifferent to certain motivating grounds, because they do not induce *pleasure or displeasure* (e.g., anticipating the social recognition associated with hard study does not induce pleasure); or (*ad* 3) the *motivating grounds* flowing from a distinct cognition are outweighed by other motivating grounds (e.g., the work predictably required by my desire to study diligently makes me reluctant to pursue it).[37]

Given these potential sources of moral failure, the topic of the *life of cognitions*, which provides the motivating ground for action, continuously re-occurs in Baumgarten's textbooks. The more vividly, the more lively we comprehend the good or bad consequences of our conduct, the more likely it is that we end up doing the right thing. In order to attain the greatest degree of distinctness about our deeds, i.e., their effects on our condition, Baumgarten urges us "to collect as many observations and experiments" as we can. Then he adds:

> The more a science is conjoined with definite knowledge of yourself the more it is *anthropological* [*anthropologica*]... and the more moral certainty it gives.[38]

According to Baumgarten, the specific judgment of something as good is bound to a vivid understanding of the good consequences of our conduct. These consequences are brought to 'life' through examples taken from books, plays, history, and observations of oneself and others.[39] Only in this way, Baumgarten emphasizes, can cognition of the good become alive (*lebendig*) and thus become an incentive qua being intuitively (*anschaulich*) convincing.[40] Baumgarten demands that ethics be not

---

[36] Cf. Baumgarten, A.G., *Metaphysica*, M §947 (§705), M §§669-671 (§§493-495).
[37] Cf. Baumgarten, A.G. (1741:19). See also his *De Vi et Efficacia Ethices Philosophicae*, which deals with the question of how a philosophical ethics can be effective. Printed by Martin Hübner, Frankfurt an der Oder 1741. Edited by Armin Emmel: http ://www.ruhr-uni-bochum.de/aesth/Emmel/Spalding.pdf.
[38] Baumgarten, A. G., *Ethica*, E §185 ($27{:}918_{31\text{-}38}$), my emphasis.
[39] In his anthropology, Kant frequently refers to novels, biographies, plays and history as pedagogical aids to "produce an enlivening of the will" (7:253-254) to act on the laws of pure practical reason. See 7:121; $25{:}734_{24\text{-}25}$; $25{:}857_{33}$-858_{22}; $25{:}1213_{17}$-1214_{31}, cf. 5:151-154 and Louden, Robert (2006:358).
[40] Cf. Pimpinella, Pietro, *Cognitio intuitiva bei Wolff und Baumgarten*, in: Oberhausen, Michael (ed.), *Vernunftkritik und Aufklärung. Studien zur Philosophie*

merely *theoretical* but *pragmatic*, i.e., it has to provide a real influence on the will. In this way, both justification and application of practical philosophy, as understood by Kant's predecessor Baumgarten, are thoroughly intertwined with an empirical study of human nature. We can now understand in principle why one would claim that morality cannot be without anthropology. For Kant's predecessor *Baumgarten*, this claim is correct and essential to his theory obligation. The question is whether this is also the kind of connection *Kant* sees between anthropology and morality.

II.3

When Kant begins to teach on anthropology in 1772, it is already clear to him that the foundation of moral obligation lies in an intellectual idea, separated from all sensible conditions of volition. The *Inaugural Dissertation* of 1770 had just drawn this philosophical distinction.

> *Moral philosophy*, therefore, in so far as it furnishes the first principles of judgment [*principia diiudicandi*], is only cognized by the pure understanding and itself belongs to pure philosophy. (2:396$_{4\text{-}7}$)

Kant's strict (as opposed to gradual) separation of the senses (*mundus sensibilis*) and the intellect (*mundus intelligibilis*) cuts feelings of pleasure and displeasure, and all other anthropological conditions of volition, entirely off from the foundations of morality. What motivated this strict distinction in practical philosophy?

The problem with Baumgarten's account of obligation in terms of inner motivation consists in the fact that it understands the necessity of ends as *conditioned* on motivating grounds. However, explaining the immediate necessity of ends would be the task of a theory of obligation. Kant holds that the essence of the concept of obligation is the demand that "I ought *immediately* to do something." (2:298$_{8\text{-}17}$) As long as this 'immediate' necessity is unaccounted for, the "first concept of obligation" will not have been accounted for (2:298$_{4\text{-}8}$). In order to understand the notion of obligation correctly, Kant brackets all questions regarding the motivation to act morally and focuses on the question on which ground ends can be *thought* as necessary. Accordingly, Kant says that by not

---

Kants und seines Jahrhunderts, Friedrich Frommann Verlag / Günther Holzboog, Stuttgart-Bad Cannstatt, 2001, pp.265-294.

distinguishing between the ground of obligation and the motivating ground "everything was false in morality."[41]

Thus if one accepts Kant's claim that the notion of 'obligation' can only be explained through an *immediate* necessitation, and I think one must accept this point in order to distinguish between prudence and moral obligation, then the deep problem with Baumgarten's motivational internalism is that it cannot make comprehensible such an immediate necessitation. With Baumgarten and Wolff in view, Kant says in retrospect:

> Baumgarten and Wolff say that duty is the necessity of an action according to the greatest and most important grounds of motivation. Now to them it is all one, whether these grounds are from inclinations or from reason. (29:598$_{6\text{-}9}$)

If we understand *moral* as the immediate necessity of ends, we cannot capture this necessity through the psychological determinism of motivating grounds. Kant's point in the above quotation is that the only way to understand the concept of obligation is by grounding it on *reason*. Only an unconditional ground can function as the *supreme* principle of obligation. It can never be *derived* from some other principle and must thus be *indemonstrable* (2:299$_{1\text{-}2}$). Kant separates the various dimensions of ethical action, isolating the problem of a supreme principle. Since all members of a motivational set are empirically conditioned, they cannot explain the immediate necessity of ends. For this reason, Kant claims that only a formal, intellectual principle can function as a supreme principle of morality. Precisely this insight is reflected in the passage cited from Kant's *Inaugural dissertation* at the beginning of this section.

What is perhaps not so well known is the fact that besides the *critical* separation of sensible from intellectual cognitions,[42] Kant also wants to secure a *dogmatic* use of pure principles in the *Inaugural Dissertation*.[43]

---

[41] *Kaehler*, p.56. Cf. 19:199$_{30\text{-}31}$, 112$_{13\text{-}17}$, 220$_{20}$-221$_{5}$. Cf. *Ethics Herder*: "The ethics of our author [Baumgarten] is coaxing, since he always wrongly presupposes the broad concept of obligation, to which he attributes motivating grounds of utility, merely, in an improper sense of the term 'ethics.' For only he performs a morally good action, who does it from principles, not as a means, but as an end." (27:14$_{14\text{-}18}$).

[42] 2:395 (§§8, 9).

[43] "The second end is dogmatic, and in accordance with it the general principles of the pure understanding, such as are displayed in ontology or in rational psychology, lead to some paradigm, which can only be conceived by the pure

More precisely, Kant knows two paradigms of *noumenal* perfection: an *ens summum* (God) for theoretical reason (ontology), and moral perfection (freedom) for practical reason (rational psychology). These paradigms of perfection cannot be given in reality and their content is derived by mere conceptual analysis. It is for this reason that Kant calls these concepts *dogmatic*. A proof of their objective reality is neither intended nor provided. Kant's reflections on the supreme standard of moral perfection take place in the context of rational psychology and its concept of (*noumenal*) freedom. It is in virtue of this paradigm of rational psychology, which cannot be experienced, that "moral philosophy in so far as it furnishes the first principles of judgment [*principia diiudicandi*], is only cognized by the pure understanding and itself belongs to pure philosophy."[44]

For the purpose of this essay, the crucial implication of Kant's expelling all sensible conditions of cognition and volition from philosophy proper is that Baumgarten's empirical psychology can neither form a proper part of theoretical metaphysics nor of practical philosophy. Kant frequently repeats this claim.[45] Once Baumgarten's *Psychologia Empirica* is detached from theoretical and practical metaphysics, it evolves into an eclectic discipline, which deals with all kinds of empirical observations. Kant's new discipline of anthropology, which evolves out of Baumgarten's empirical psychology, becomes an eclectic venture that is open to *everything* that is practical.[46] The simultaneous birth of critical

---

understanding and which is a common measure for all other things in so far as they are realities. This paradigm is NOUMENAL PERFECTION." (2:395-396 (§9))

[44] 2:396 (§9). The supreme standard of moral perfection, just like the *ens summum*, is an *ideal*, derived from mere conceptual analysis. The 'object' of pure morality is a self-produced paradigm of perfection, and nothing is further for Kant than arguing for the objective reality of it. The mere concept of *noumenal* freedom contains dogmatically, i.e., through analysis of mere concepts and independent of any experience, the idea of the formal lawfulness of human volition. Only this thought, which is not (yet) part of any critical enterprise, belongs to metaphysics proper. Many reflections and lecture notes of the same time confirm this contrast between critical and dogmatic metaphysics (the former referring to objects of cognition, the latter to objects of the will). Cf. 17:552$_{16}$-553$_{11}$; 18:89$_{16\text{-}10}$; 24:481$_{9\text{-}12}$; 28:173$_{29\text{-}34}$. With respect to the merely intellectual, *a priori* character of Kant's conception of a metaphysics of morals, see his letter to Lambert (September 2nd, 1770; 10:97$_{14}$-98$_{36}$). With respect to Kant's conception of the *mundus intelligibilis* and its law as a moral law, compare 17:483$_{14}$-484$_{14}$; 515$_{29}$-516$_{14}$, 520$_{6\text{-}9}$; 19:120$_{10\text{-}13}$. Cf. Schmucker, Joseph (1961:389-391).

[45] Cf. 10:145-6; 28:223$_{2}$-224$_{6}$; cf. 25:7$_{16}$-8$_{8}$, 243$_{3}$-244$_{17}$; A848-849/B876-877.

[46] 10:145$_{23}$-146$_{9}$.

philosophy and anthropology does thus not witness a necessary supplementation of moral philosophy by anthropology, or any other positive relation between these two disciplines. What is more, Kant's anthropology increasingly loses its 'moral' Baumgartian inheritance. Kant's anthropology originates in a *residuum* of the Baumgartian conception of practical philosophy after the *Inaugural Dissertation* has separated the a priori foundation of ethics from all sensible conditions.[47] For Kant, anthropology is a side-project but not philosophically interesting.

III- The Four Tasks of Anthropology: General Education, Determination of Ethical Duties, Moral Pedagogy, and Ethical Action

III.1

As I have argued, both the tripartite structure of the soul and the observation of outer phenomena bind anthropology to moral action in the Baumgartian science of ethics. The underlying unity of Kant's *Anthropology form a Pragmatic Point of View*, in its most fundamental twofold division, closely follows the same pattern. Its first part examines the three faculties of the soul, i.e., the intellectual faculty, the feeling of pleasure and displeasure, and the appetitive faculty. Its second part, the "anthropological characteristic" (7:285), considers outer phenomena insofar as they *characterize* specific differences of "what belongs to a human being's faculty of desire (what is practical)." (Ibid.) Accordingly (and here I just mean to mention two representative examples taken from each of the two parts of the *Anthropology*), Kant discusses the diverse inner *psychological* motivating grounds of suicide (which he explicitly

---

[47] "Moral concepts are not entirely pure concepts of reason, because they are grounded on something empirical (pleasure or displeasure). But in regard to the principle through which reason places limits on a freedom which is in itself lawless, they can nevertheless serve quite well (if one attends merely to their form) as examples of pure concepts of reason. Virtue, and with it human wisdom in its entire purity, are ideas." (A569/B597) "The supreme principles *diuidicationis moralis* are only rational, but only *principia formalia*. They determine no end but only the moral form of all ends." ($19{:}120_{10\text{-}12}$) "In the metaphysics of morals we must abstract from all human conditions, the application and its hindrances *in concreto*. We only look for the canon, which is a pure and universally valid idea." ($19{:}172_{26\text{-}29}$)

contrasts with a *moral* discussion of the subject),[48] and aims to *derive from outer* observations the specific difference of the *incentives* of man and woman.[49]

That anthropology has to do with the inner motivating grounds is thus not refuted by arguing that anthropology aims to depict *the entire human being*.[50] Both the psychological phenomena of inner sense (tripartite structure of the soul) and the observation of the external behavior of others, from which, as Kant says, one infers by analogy to the inner sense,[51] have a common point of reference in Baumgarten's theory of obligation and its central notion of motivating grounds. This becomes immediately clear when Kant points to methodological difficulties of conducting anthropology. In the *Menschenkunde* lecture we read:

> What are the sources of anthropology? When the incentives [*Triebfedern*] of man are at work we don't observe these incentives. For example, when man is in affect he cannot observe himself in the play of his incentives. However, when he observes himself then all incentives are at rest and he has nothing to observe [*nichts zu beobachten*].[52]

I think we have to take Kant's remark seriously that in the absence of the phenomena of human incentives we have *nothing* to observe in anthropology. Kant repeats this point frequently in both his published works and lectures.[53] He considers "the human being solely by *observing*, and, as happens in anthropology, by trying to investigate the moving causes of his actions physiologically."[54] That anthropology is the physiology of the *inner sense* is thus preserved in the two parts of the published *Anthropology*.

From its Baumgartian pragmatic roots, which make the overall setup comprehensible, Kant's anthropology quickly evolves into an eclectic discipline, which becomes a 'hodgepodge,' as it were, of all kinds of empirical observations. For this reason, the bulk of Kant's anthropology is

---

[48] 7:258-259=first part of *Anthropology*.

[49] 7:307=second part of *Anthropology*.

[50] For a different view see Brandt, Reinhard / Stark, Werner in AA 25:xi. See also Stark, Werner (2003:26-30) for an elaboration on the twofold structure of the anthropology course. Cf. Brandt, Reinhard (2003), *The Vocation of the Human Being*, in: Jacobs/Kain (eds.), pp. 86-89.

[51] $28{:}224_{13\text{-}21}$, $29{:}44_{24\text{-}28}$.

[52] $25{:}857_{5\text{-}9}$, my translation; cf. $25{:}1214_{18\text{-}26}$.

[53] 7:121, 4:471, $15{:}801_{1\text{-}4}$.

[54] A550/B578.

not at all concerned with ethical action. For example, in the first book of the *Anthropology*, which deals with the faculty of cognition, Kant elucidates the synthesis of apprehension of 'the doctrine of the threefold synthesis'[55] through an observation of the behavior of an infant who is several weeks old. The infant, Kant says, "begins to follow with his eyes shining objects held before him, and this is the crude beginning of the progress of perception (apprehension of the ideas of sense)."[56] Kant continues, a little further on, that this does not produce experience but merely "scattered perceptions not yet united under the concept of an object." Here, Kant uses an observation in order to elucidate what the *First Critique* states abstractly. Kant gives an example of what it means that experience is essentially conceptual and dependent on the activity of the understanding. This example of *inner psychology* nicely illustrates the use to which Kant puts his new science of anthropology after the *psychologia empirica* is detached from theoretical and practical metaphysics.[57]

III.2

Robert Louden is perhaps the most important proponent of those Kant scholars who argue for a systematic connection between morality and anthropology. He claims that "we do find a distinctively moral anthropology within Kant's anthropology lectures," which is supposed to be of "fundamental importance" for "his [Kant's] philosophical project."[58] In order to support this strong thesis, which "has been overlooked, indeed denied, by other scholars who have discussed it,"[59] Louden presents a list of "moral messages" contained in the anthropology lectures. These messages are taken to support the view that Kant's "specifically *moral*

---

[55] Cf. A95-114.

[56] 7:127-128.

[57] This reading is also endorsed by Reinhard Brandt, who is of the opinion that Kant's anthropology is an "encyclopedia of Kant's philosophy on an empirical level" that provides examples for the doctrines developed in the three Critiques. Brandt, Reinhard (1999), *Kritischer Kommentar zu Kants Anthropologie in pragmatischer Hinsicht (1798)*, Felix Meiner Verlag, Hamburg, pp.8, 17.

[58] Louden, Robert (2003:66-67, 79).

[59] Louden, Robert (2008) is referring to Gregor, Mary J. (1963), *Laws of Freedom. A Study of Kant's Method of Applying the Categorical Imperative in the Metaphysik der Sitten.* New York, Barnes and Noble, Inc., Basil Blackwell; and Brandt, Reinhard (2003), and Brandt/Stark in editor's introduction to AA 25.

anthropology" is "'the other member of the division of practical philosophy as a whole'."[60]

This is to say, in order to argue for the significance of Kant's anthropology for Kant's moral philosophy, Louden first singles out "moral messages" (2003) or "moral motives" (2008) contained in Kant's anthropology, and subsequently interprets these as part of what Kant calls in the *Metaphysics of Morals* 'the counterpart to pure morality' or 'the other member of the division of practical philosophy as a whole' (6:217). There are thus two claims. First, Kant's anthropology is a specifically *moral* anthropology. This claim is supported by listing moral messages contained in Kant's anthropology lectures. Second, these moral messages are of fundamental philosophical importance, so that we are justified to view Kant's anthropology course as the counterpart to pure philosophy. But is it really the case that Kant's anthropology is a specifically *moral* anthropology, and that Kant's anthropology, which we find under this name, is of fundamental importance?

III.3 General Education

In the introduction to volume 25 of the Academy Edition, Reinhard Brandt and Werner Stark emphasize the *didactical aspect* of Kant's lectures on anthropology, which consists in conveying knowledge of the world (*Weltkenntnis*).[61] Kant describes the *phenomena* of human action in order to derive "rules of conduct" (7:189) from them that are "immediately" [*auf der Stelle*] applicable to ordinary life.[62] Pragmatic knowledge is prudential knowledge in a *variety* of senses: *technical* knowledge [*Kunstausübung*] to master the world,[63] knowledge to master one's own passions and to unite one's goals to one's lasting advantage,[64] and knowledge of how to deal with people in the world.[65] Prudence is thus knowledge of how to achieve our goals in communal life very broadly conceived.[66] Robert Louden has spelled out the *manifold features* of pragmatic anthropology, which he rightly (in my view) interprets in the

[60] Louden, Robert (2003:79, 66-67).

[61] 25:9$_{9-12}$, 472$_{23-24}$.

[62] 25:472$_{21-24}$, 25:856$_{7-9}$; 7:119.

[63] 7:176; 25:854$_{23-24}$.

[64] 25:1123$_{17}$-1124$_{22}$.

[65] 7:322, 4:416n; 25:854$_{13-17}$.

[66] 25:854$_{28-37}$, 1210$_{10-18}$, 4:416n.

sense that anthropology contributes to achieving a greater level of well-being and happiness.[67]

As we saw, this kind of 'pragmatic-prudential-technical' knowledge is relevant for Baumgarten's moral theory, which focuses on calculating the consequences of one's conduct. Kant preserves this 'consequentialism' of his predecessor in the form of a *didactical* point of view. He begins his lectures with an empirical description of man because he aims to convey some practical knowledge to his students.[68] Anthropology is taught in a *popular* fashion, i.e., by proceeding by means of examples, and thereby conveying rudiments of prudence of commerce and wisdom in morals: "*all* that is practical."[69] Anthropology is a discipline conceived of in opposition to mere *speculative* learnedness and instead emphasizes the fruitful *application* of one's knowledge in everyday life.[70] This *didactical* aspect of anthropology, which aims to provide a *general orientation* for Kant's students' future engagement with the world, is not concerned with specifically *moral* action. Rather, Kant intends to provide a mixture of 'pragmatic-prudential-technical' knowledge that is immediately applicable to the world. This kind of knowledge does thus not denote a specifically *moral* anthropology. This does not seem to be the close connection between morality and anthropology that Kant has in mind in the passage, which I cited at the beginning of this paper.

III.4 Determination of Ethical Duties

In the *Preface* to the *Groundwork*, Kant distinguishes between an *a priori* part of morality called *metaphysics of morals* and its empirical counterpart called *anthropology*, which determines laws for the human will insofar as it is affected by nature. Kant says:

> In this way, there arises the idea of a twofold metaphysics, a *metaphysics of nature* and a *metaphysics of morals*. Physics will therefore have its empirical part but it will also have a rational part; so too will ethics, though here the empirical part might be given the special name *practical*

[67] Cf. Louden, Robert (2006:352-354) and (2008).
[68] 2:309-310.
[69] 10:145, my emphasis. Cf. Kuehn, Manfred (2006:viii). Also: Stark, Werner (2003:22).
[70] Cf. 15:799$_{5}$-800$_{18}$; 25:733$_{21\text{-}24}$, 25:1210$_{34\text{-}35}$; 29:12$_{21\text{-}29}$. Cf. Brandt, Reinhard, in his introduction to: Immanuel Kant, *Anthropologie in pragmatischer Hinsicht*, Reinhard Brand (ed.), Philosophische Bibliothek Band 40, Felix Meiner Verlag, Hamburg, 2000, XIV.

> *anthropology*, while the rational part might properly be called *morals*. … I ask only whether the nature of science does not require that the empirical part always be carefully separated from the rational part, and that a metaphysics of nature be put before physics proper (empirical physics) and a metaphysics of morals before practical anthropology.[71]

In his lecture on ethics of the same time Kant underscores this distinction:

> The metaphysics of morals, or *metaphysica pura*, is only the first part of morality; the second part is *philosophia moralis applicata*, moral anthropology, to which empirical principles belong. Just as there is metaphysics and physics, so the same applies here … Moral anthropology is morality applied to men. *Moralia pura* is based upon necessary laws, and hence it cannot be founded upon the particular constitution of man. The particular constitution of man, and the laws based upon it, come to the fore in moral anthropology under the name of ethics.[72]

According to these passages, Kant intends the metaphysics of morals to ground and precede moral anthropology in the same way as the metaphysics of nature grounds and precedes empirical physics.[73] We thus have here the idea of a *foundational perspective*. From the vantage point of this foundational perspective, physical and ethical duties have to be founded on *a priori* principles.

With respect to Kant´s foundational perspective, it seems to be essential to distinguish between the ground and the content of ethical duties. The *ground* of duty is autonomy or the *homo noumenon*. The *content* of duty can only be determined with respect to the *homo phenomenon*, i.e., the empirical human being. *If* the *homo phenomenon* were empirically described in Kant's anthropology lectures with the intent to determine specific human duties, this second function of anthropology would certainly be of fundamental importance to Kant's moral philosophy. However, as Brandt / Stark rightly claim with respect to this second aspect of anthropology, "at no point of its development" is Kant's anthropology "identical with the anthropology Kant repeatedly envisions as the complement to his moral theory after 1770."[74] Rather, the determination of human duties is attempted in the *Doctrine of Virtue* of the *Metaphysics of Morals* but not in Kant's anthropology lectures. There is no indication that

---

[71] 4:388, cf. 4:387, 410n; A15/B29.

[72] 29:599$_{6\text{-}22}$, my translation.

[73] Kant uses *practical* and *moral* anthropology synonymously in the above quotations.

[74] 25:XLVI, my translation.

Kant's anthropology intends to present the system of ethics, i.e., the application of pure morality to the human being. Kant's anthropology lectures do not contain the *philosophia moralis applicata*, which Kant already in the 1770s conceives of as "practical anthropology, i.e., ethics or doctrine of virtue, which relates to objects *in concreto*, and which deals with the good use of freedom with respect to the human being."[75]

III.5 Pedagogical Implementation of Morals

Kant frequently talks in his writings about the *cultural and moral improvement* of his students.[76] In the *Anthropology*, Kant says:

> The human being is destined by his reason to live in a society with human beings and in it to *cultivate* himself, to *civilize* himself, and to *moralize* himself by means of the arts and sciences ... The human being must therefore be *educated* to the good.[77]

This same pedagogical function of anthropology is picked up in the *Metaphysics of Morals*, where Kant says that the

> counterpart of a metaphysics of morals, the other member of the division of practical philosophy as a whole, would be moral anthropology, which, however, would deal only with the subjective conditions in human nature that hinder people or help them in *fulfilling* the laws of a metaphysics of morals. It would deal with the development, spreading and strengthening of moral principles (in education in schools and in popular instruction), and with other similar teachings and precepts based on experience. (6:217)

Attending to the subjective conditions in human nature in order to devise *means* to carry out the laws of a metaphysics of morals can be subsumed, broadly speaking, under the problem of how to make ethics *effective*. In this sense, educational institutions such as the Basedowian institutes that aim to educate children in a cosmopolitan manner *contribute* to the acquisition of a good character and thus help to pedagogically implement ethics and to render it effective.[78]

However, the question of how to make *ethics* effective, Kant says in the *Critique of Pure Reason*, roughly compares to the question of how to apply the *pure laws of general logic* "under the contingent conditions of

---

[75] $29:12_{10\text{-}20}$, my translation.
[76] This point has been emphasized by Robert Louden (2006:358-359).
[77] 7:324-325; cf. 9:449-450.
[78] Cf. 9:448; $8:288_4\text{-}289_5$.

the subject, which can hinder or promote this use."[79] Whereas *pure morality* "contains merely the necessary moral laws of a free will in general," it is a further problem to assess "these laws under the hindrances of the feelings, inclinations, and passions to which human beings are more or less subject."[80] For example, knowing how to make students focus their attention is important for applying the general laws of logic. However, just as showing how to deal with attention deficit disorder does not make pure logic more human, Kant's pedagogical aspect of anthropology does not make the laws of pure morality more human. Anthropology does not render Kant's morality impure or supplements it in any way. This is why Kant explicitly states that this pedagogical aspect of anthropology is a part of practical philosophy but does not belong to *moral philosophy*.[81]

III.6 Ethical Action

Throughout his career, Kant strictly distinguishes between the ethical *maxim*, which holds unconditionally, and the *action* based on that maxim. As Wood puts it, "I fulfill my duty to make my own perfection an end [=ethical *maxim*] if I take up weight-lifting, learn to play the violin, study quantum physics, or learn how to interpret the poetry of Wallace Stevens [=*actions* based on that maxim]."[82] Any end we adopt must be realized in action, and for this reason our *actions* require empirical knowledge.[83] This means that the formulation of ethical principles cannot lead to action without empirical knowledge of oneself and the world, i.e., without anthropology. All ethical *action* is thus indeed closely connected to anthropology because there is a gap between 'the adoption of an end into one's maxim' and 'the determination of an action instantiating this maxim under specific conditions.' But note that because Kant strictly distinguishes between the 'level of principle' and 'the level of action,' the systematic role of anthropological knowledge for ethical action is *irrelevant* for

---

79 A53/B77, A55/B79.

80 A54-55/B79.

81 Cf. passage cited above (6:217). See also 8:288$_{30}$-289$_{5}$. Cf. Louden, Robert (2003:70-71).

82 Wood, Allen (1999:328-329); see on this point also Denis, Lara (2006), *Kant's conception of virtue*, in: The Cambridge Companion to Kant and Modern Philosophy. Guyer, Paul (ed.), Cambridge University Press, Cambridge, 2006, pp.505-537, p.521.

83 Cf. Sullivan, Roger J., *The Positive Role of Prudence in the Virtuous Life*, in: Jahrbuch für Recht und Ethik / Annual Review of Law and Ethics, Band 5, pp.461-470, pp.465-466.

Kant's moral philosophy.[84] Indeed, Kant warns us against the conflation of these two levels of reflection. For example, Kant emphasizes that

> one who complies with the basic principles of virtue can, it is true, commit a *fault* (*peccatum*) in putting these principles into practice, by doing more or less than prudence prescribes. But insofar as he adheres strictly to these basic principles he cannot practice a *vice* (*vitium*). (6:433n)

What counts, *morally* speaking, is that we adhere to the principles by adopting them into our maxims. But, it is not required that we can always realize these principles perfectly. The failure to *exercise* the commands of reason due to lack of virtue (strength of the will) or prudence (anthropological knowledge) is perfectly compatible with the notion of an ethical *principle* because it is always *possible* to act on what the principle prescribes.[85]

The 'systematic' role of empirical knowledge (provided by anthropology) for 'morality' is thus a systematic role for ethical *action*, but it is *not* a systematic role for moral philosophy. Anthropological knowledge only takes us from principle to action. But this connection between moral principle and ethical action is not philosophically problematic (for Kant). Kant distinguishes very carefully between morality and its empirical conditions of applicability. This is to say, neither pedagogical nor any other empirical means for the realization of ethical duties are of 'fundamental importance' for Kant's *moral philosophy* itself. Nevertheless, anthropology and morality are indeed 'closely connected' in the sense that only empirical knowledge of oneself and the world leads from the adoption of ethical maxims to ethical action.

IV- Conclusion

I have argued that Kant's notion of *pragmatic* anthropology can be traced back to Baumgarten's *theory of morality*, at the center of which stand pragmatic motivating grounds. I have then shown that Kant brackets all empirical considerations from the *a priori* justification of morality. A theory of moral obligation that explains the necessity of ends through the mediation of empirical motivating grounds cannot make the immediate necessity of ends comprehensible. Kant's new discipline of anthropology, which evolves out of Baumgarten's empirical psychology, becomes an

---

[84] Cf. $27{:}613_{19\text{-}20}$.

[85] $27{:}611_{23}$-613_{29}; cf. 6:433-434; cf. Lehmann, Gerhard (1980), *Kants Tugenden. Neue Beiträge zur Geschichte und Interpretation der Philosophie Kants*, Walter de Gruyter & Co., Berlin/New York, p. 80.

eclectic venture that is open to *everything* that is practical. The simultaneous birth of critical philosophy and anthropology does thus not witness a necessary supplementation of moral philosophy by anthropology. Kant's anthropology originates in a *residuum* of the Baumgartian conception of practical philosophy after the *Inaugural Dissertation* has separated the a priori foundation of ethics from all sensible conditions. For Kant, anthropology is a side-project but not philosophically interesting.

Subsequently, I pointed to four different aspects or functions of Kant's anthropology:

(1) *The general didactical function*, which does not denote a specifically *moral* anthropology.
(2) *The function of determining ethical duties*, which is of fundamental importance to Kant's moral philosophy, but which is neither contained in the *Anthropology* nor in the anthropology lectures.
(3) *The pedagogical function*, which considers the subjective conditions that hinder or further the fulfillment of the laws of a metaphysics of morals.
(4) *The function* regarding the *instantiation of ethical duties* through *action* under specific circumstances, which has a systematic role for ethical *action* but not for moral philosophy.

The third and the fourth aspects of anthropology justify Kant's claim that morality cannot be without anthropology. But this does not allow us to attribute a philosophical significance, i.e., any significance with respect to the *a priori* justification of moral obligation, to Kant's anthropology course.

Louden addresses "the vital question of how his [Kant's] projects in anthropology and ethical theory link up with one another" through "multiple moral messages" contained in Kant's anthropology lectures (2003:75). However, multiple moral messages are neither sufficient to establish the strong claim of a *fundamental* role of anthropology for Kant's critical practical philosophy, nor are multiple moral messages sufficient to establish the weaker claim that Kant's anthropology is the systematic counterpart to the metaphysics of morals. On my reading, we need to distinguish between two entirely different kinds of 'counterpart-claims' that Kant makes. The first 'counterpart-claim' regards anthropology in its *pedagogical function*, which considers the subjective conditions that hinder or further the fulfillment of the laws of a metaphysics of morals.

As I understand it, Louden's cosmopolitan interpretation of human nature can be subsumed under this aspect of anthropology. The second 'counterpart-claim' regards anthropology in its *function to determine ethical duties*. Kant does not always *conceptually* distinguish clearly enough between these two different counterpart-claims. This conceptual inaccuracy opens the room for misinterpreting the third (pedagogical) function of anthropology in terms of the fundamental importance of the second conception of anthropology (the function of determining ethical duties).[86] The problem of how "to put into effect a system of freedom in the world of nature,"[87] as important as it is for a *philosophia moralis applicata*, is neither specific to Kant's course in anthropology nor of *critical* interest to Kant. A close reading of Baumgarten and of Kant's departure from him gives further ground to believe this is true.[88]

Works Cited

Baumgarten, Alexander Gottlieb (1741a): *Philosophische Briefe von Aletheophilus*, Frankfurt/Leipzig, 1741.

—. (1741b): *De Vi et Efficacia Ethices Philosophicae*, Printed by Martin Hübner, Frankfurt an der Oder 1741. Edited by Armin Emmel: http ://www.ruhr-uni-bochum.de/aesth/Emmel/Spalding.pdf.

—. (1757): *Metaphysica* (1757), Halle ^{1}1739 (^{4}1757). Reprinted in AA 17:5-226 and AA 15:5-45.

—. (1760): *Initia philosphiae practicae primae*, Halle 1760. Reprinted in AA 19:7-91.

—. (1763): *Ethica philosophica*, Halle ^{1}1740 (^{2}1751, ^{3}1763). Reprinted in AA 27:871-1015.

—. (1783): *Metaphysik* (tr. Meier, Georg Friedrich, ed. Eberhard, Johann August), Halle, ^{1}1766, ^{2}1783, Dietrich Scheglmann Reprints, Norderstedt, 2004.

Brandt, Reinhard (1999): *Kritischer Kommentar zu Kants Anthropologie in pragmatischer Hinsicht (1798)*, Felix Meiner Verlag, Hamburg, 1999.

—. (2003): *The Vocation of the Human Being*, in: Jacobs, Brian / Kain, Patrick (eds.) (2003:85-104).

---

[86] Cf. Louden, Robert (2003:79-80), (2006:361-362).

[87] Louden, Robert (2008).

[88] I would like to thank Hilary Bok, Michael Hicks, Dean Moyar, Marius Stan, Allen Wood and all participants of the ENAKS Meeting for helpful comments on earlier versions of this paper.

Denis, Lara (2006): *Kant's conception of virtue*, in: The Cambridge Companion to Kant and Modern Philosophy. Guyer, Paul (ed.), Cambridge University Press, Cambridge, 2006, pp.505-537.

Gregor, Mary J. (1963): *Laws of Freedom. A Study of Kant's Method of Applying the Categorical Imperative in the Metaphysik der Sitten*. New York, Barnes and Noble, Inc., Basil Blackwell.

Henrich, Dieter (1963): *Über Kants früheste Ethik. Versuch einer Rekonstruktion*, in: Kant-Studien 54 (1963), pp.404-431.

—. (1965): *Über Kant's Entwicklungsgeschichte*, in: Philosophische Rundschau 13 (1965), pp. 252-263.

Hinske, Norbert (1966): *Kants Idee der Anthropologie*, in: Rombach, Heinrich (ed.), *Die Frage nach dem Menschen. Aufriss einer Philosophischen Anthropologie*. Verlag Karl Alber, Freiburg, München, 1966, pp. 410-427.

Jacobs, Brian / Kain, Patrick (eds.) (2003): *Essays on Kant's Anthropology*, Cambridge University Press, Cambridge.

Kant, Immanuel (1902—.): *Kant's Gesammelte Schriften*, hrsg. von der Königlich Preussischen Akademie der Wissenschaften, Bd. 1-29, Berlin/Leipzig, 1902—.

—. (2000): *Anthropologie in pragmatischer Hinsicht*, Reinhard Brand (ed.), Philosophische Bibliothek Band 40, Felix Meiner Verlag, Hamburg, 2000.

—. (2004): *Vorlesung zur Moralphilosphie*. Stark, Werner (ed.). Mit einer Einleitung von Manfred Kuehn, Berlin, De Gruyter, 2004.

—. (2006): *Anthropology from a Pragmatic Point of View*, Edited by Robert B. Louden. With an introduction by Manfred Kuehn. Cambridge Texts in the History of Philosophy. Cambridge University Press, 2006.

Lehmann, Gerhard (1980): *Kants Tugenden. Neue Beiträge zur Geschichte und Interpretation der Philosophie Kants*, Walter de Gruyter & Co., Berlin/New York.

Louden, Robert B. (2003): *The Second Part of Morals*, in: Jacobs, Brian / Kain, Patrick (eds.) (2003:60-84).

—. (2006): *Applying Kant's Ethics: The Role of Anthropology*, in: Graham, Bird (ed.) (2006), *A Companion to Kant*, Blackwell Publishing, pp.350-363.

—. (2007): *Anthropology from a Kantian Point of View: Toward a Cosmopolitan Conception of Human Nature*, 2007, this volume.

Meier, Georg Friedrich (1764): *Allgemeine Practische Weltweisheit*, Halle, 1764. Reprinted in: Wolff, Christian, Gesammelte Werke, École, Jean et.al. (ed.), Abt.3, Bd.107, Georg Olms Verlag, Hildesheim, Zürich, New York, 2006.

McDowell, John (1998): *Mind, Value, and Reality,* Harvard University Press, 1998.

Schmidt, Claudia M. (2007): *Kant's Transcendental, Empirical, Pragmatic, and Moral Anthropology*, in: Kant-Studien 98, 2007, pp.156-182.

Pimpinella, Pietro (2001): *Cognitio intuitiva bei Wolff und Baumgarten*, in: Oberhausen, Michael (ed.), *Vernunftkritik und Aufklärung. Studien zur Philosophie Kants und seines Jahrhunderts*, Friedrich Frommann Verlag / Günther Holzboog, Stuttgart-Bad Cannstatt, 2001, pp.265-294.

Schmucker, Josef (1961): *Die Ursprünge der Ethik Kants in seinen vorkritischen Schriften und Reflektionen*, Meisenheim, 1961.

Schwaiger, Clemens (1999): *Kategorische und Andere Imperative. Zur Entwicklung von Kants praktischer Philosophie bis 1785*, Stuttgart-Bad Cannstatt, 1999.

—. (2000): *Ein "missing link" auf dem Weg der Ethik von Wolff zu Kant. Zur Quellen- und Wirkungsgeschichte der praktischen Philosophie von Alexander Gottlieb Baumgarten*; in: Jahrbuch für Recht und Ethik, Vol.8 (2000).

—. (2001a): *Die Anfänge des Projekts einer Metaphysik der Sitten. Zu den wolffianischen Wurzeln einer kantischen Schlüsselidee*, in: Kant und die Berliner Aufklärung. Akten des IX. Internationalen Kant-Kongresses, Walter de Gruyter, 2001, Vol. II, pp.52-58.

—. (2001b): *Vollkommenheit als Moralprinzip bei Wolff, Baumgarten and Kant*, in: Oberhausen, Michael (ed.), Vernunftkritik und Aufklärung. Studien zur Philosophie Kants und seines Jahrhunderts. Stuttgart-Bad Cannstatt, Friedrich Frommann Verlag, Günther Holzboog, 2001, pp.317-328.

—. (unpublished manuscript), *Zur Theorie der Verbindlichkeit, bei Wolff, Baumgarten und dem frühen Kant*.

Stark, Werner (2003): *Historical Notes and Interpretive Questions about Kant's Lectures on Anthropology*, in: Jacobs, Brian / Kain, Patrick (eds.) (2003:15-37).

Sullivan, Roger J., *The Positive Role of Prudence in the Virtuous Life*, in: Jahrbuch für Recht und Ethik / Annual Review of Law and Ethics, Band 5, pp.461-470.

Williams, Bernard (1981): *Moral Luck*, Cambridge University Press, 1981.

Wolff, Christian (1733): *Vernünfftige Gedancken von der Menschen Thun und Lassen, zu Beförderung ihrer Glückseeligkeit*, Halle [1]1720 (Frankfurt am Main / Leipzig [4]1733). Reprinted in: Wolff, Christian, Gesammelte Werke, École, Jean et.al. (Ed.), Abt.1, Bd.4, Georg Olms Verlag, Hildesheim, New York, 1976.

Wood, Allen (1999), *Kant's Ethical Thought*, Cambridge University Press.

—. (2001): *Practical Anthropology*, in: Gerhardt, Volker et al. (eds.), *Kant und die Berliner Aufklärung. Akten des IX. Internationalen Kant-Kongresses*. Walter de Gruyter, Berlin, New York, 2001, Vol.4, pp.458-475.

CHAPTER SIX

MOTIVATION, FUTILITY AND THE HIGHEST GOOD IN KANT'S PRACTICAL PHILOSOPHY

EOIN O'CONNELL

Introduction

Kant's doctrine of the highest good has been variously interpreted as part of his philosophy of history, his philosophy of religion, an expression of his Pietist Christian upbringing, an attempt to add content to an otherwise inadequately formal conception of ethics, and an attempt to force an architectonic parallel between his conceptions of theoretical and practical reason.[1] This list is no doubt incomplete. In this paper I will argue that the idea of the highest good is best understood and most defensible as part of Kant's conception of moral motivation. It is not possible in the confines of a single paper to address all these various interpretations, in particular, I will not address religious or historical issues; however, I believe that the interpretation offered here allows this doctrine to speak to a philosophical audience that does not presuppose religious belief or a distinct faith tradition. The argument that I will be concerned to address is that of Lewis White Beck, who presents a widely held belief that this entire aspect of Kant's philosophy is an unnecessary and unconvincing adjunct to his wider theory, born from an unphilosophical concern with the architectonic integrity of his system.

The highest good is, according to Kant, the idea of a situation where the possession of happiness is proportionate with virtue. In the "Dialectic" of the *Critique of Practical Reason*, Kant argues that the realization of the highest good is the a priori object of the moral will. But the reintroduction of a teleological and eudaimonistic concept has struck many commentators

[1] See Yovel (1980), Wood (1970), Beiser (2006), Silber (1959, 1963), Beck (1960).

as inconsistent with Kant's basic moral premises. Schopenhauer, whose comments are somewhat typical, writes:

> [W]e do not find Kant's doctrine of virtue so pure…[it] has in fact lapsed into inconsistency…Now supreme happiness in the highest good should not really be the motive for virtue; yet it is there like a secret article, the presence of which makes all the rest a mere sham contract. It is not really the reward for virtue, but yet is a voluntary gift for which virtue, after work has been done, stealthily holds its hand open…all virtue in any way practiced for the sake of a reward is based on a prudent, methodical, far-seeing egoism. (Schopenhauer 1959 [1844], 524)

In a similar vein, Lewis White Beck expresses the opinion that

> Kant simply cannot have it both ways. He cannot say that the highest good is a motive for the pure will, and then say that it is so only under the human limitation that man must have an object that is not exclusively moral…The theory of the Analytic requires him to deny that the highest good provides an autonomous motive. While the hope for the highest good may in fact be a necessary incentive to do that which the conduct of duty would not move man, it is clear that to admit the latter human–all too human–fact into the determination of conduct in accord with moral norms is to surrender autonomy. (Beck 1960, 244)

T.H. Greene adds to this chorus of disapproval in his introduction to *Religion Within the Limits of Reason Alone*, where he maintains that the doctrine of the highest good is "inconsistent with [Kant's] own principles and highly detrimental to them" (Greene 1960, lxii). Similar criticisms of the highest good abound in the literature, and in each case the charge is one of inconsistency.[2]

More recent commentators such as Allen Wood (1970) and Frederick Beiser (2006) have dissented from this negative judgment. Wood notes that the precise nature of this notorious inconsistency "is seldom stated with the clarity one would wish" and that this aspect of Kant's philosophy "is more often treated with indignant rejection than with reasoned refutation" (Wood 1970, 39). More positively, Wood and Beiser point to Kant's distinction between the "determining ground" and "object" of the will, as the key to saving Kant from what would otherwise be an embarrassing lapse of philosophical judgment. Moreover, as Wood points out, Kant stresses this distinction precisely to foreclose the kind of misunderstanding that is on display among his critics in this regard.

---

[2] Allan Wood provides an overview of Kant's early critics who have found fault with this idea. See Wood (1970), 39.

Kant writes that the “highest good may be the whole *object* of a pure practical reason…it is not on that account to be taken as its determining ground” (KpV 5: 109, 91). According to Wood, the determining ground of an action is its motivation and the object its purpose. Together they are the formal components of willing. Kant, Wood tells us, is making the relatively innocuous observation that actions are both motivated and purposeful. To say that something is one’s purpose in acting is not the same as saying that it is the motivation for the action, thus when Kant says that the highest good is the object of the moral will, it does not mean that it is the determining grounds of the will. This distinction can be read into Kant’s argument in the *Groundwork* that we can adopt a course of action purely from the motive of duty without concern for consequences. Kant then famously argues that the purity of moral willing is sullied when it is motivated by something, such as a purpose, other than simply doing one’s duty. This argument motivates the interpretation that Kant’s moral philosophy should be understood as anti-teleological. In any case, designating the highest good as the object of the moral will, so the defense goes, distinguishes it from the will’s motivations; therefore, the doctrine is not necessarily inconsistent with the idea of a pure moral will.

The determining ground/object distinction has come to play a pivotal role in the defense of Kant’s practical philosophy by his recent apologists. There are two elements to this defense: (i) an argument establishing that the highest good is an essential aspect of Kant’s practical philosophy; and (ii) the use of the determining ground/object distinction to defend Kant from the inconsistency charge. I shall defend the first thesis and criticize the second. The criticism offered here does not vindicate the idea that Kant is inconsistent; I shall argue that a successful defense of the first thesis vouchsafes his consistency. But it does weaken Kant’s moral position overall, and in particular his claim that pure reason is practical. The principle reason for this is that the determining ground/object distinction fails to maintain a distinction between motivation and purpose, and for this reason, the defense mounted by Kant’s apologists is ultimately unsuccessful. I shall argue that if Kant is justified in saying that it is necessary to believe in the possibility of attaining the highest good to enable moral willing, then he cannot maintain that the highest good plays no role in moral motivation. However, I will also argue that this does not establish that the will is always motivated by the thought of the possibility of happiness, or that Kant effectively surrenders his commitment to autonomy, rather that it establishes the weaker conclusion that it remains an open question whether or not a pure moral will is a possibility for finite rational beings.

The argument is organized as follows: section 1 defends the necessity of the doctrine of the highest good in Kant's philosophy against some criticisms made by Lewis White Beck; section 2 argues that the object/determining ground distinction cannot be maintained, and that this undermines any argument Kant might have for a distinctively moral motive. In the conclusion I argue that this does not mean that Kant's philosophy collapses into a form of heteronomy.

I- The Necessity of the Highest Good

Wood is right to criticize those critics who precipitously dismiss the idea of the highest good as inconsistent with the rest of Kant's practical philosophy; however, Lewis White Beck does go to some lengths to provide a reasoned refutation of this doctrine. Beck is also a Kantian apologist, and much of his interpretative strategy aims at trying to "save" Kant's moral theory from the supposed inconsistency. Beck argues that the doctrine of the highest good adds nothing to Kant's conception of duty and may safely be ignored. He writes:

> [S]uppose I do all in my power…to promote the highest good, what am I to do? Simply act out of respect for the law, which I already knew…The truth of the matter is that the concept of the highest good is not a practical concept at all, but a dialectical Ideal of reason. It is not important in Kant's practical philosophy for any consequences it might have, for it has none… (Beck 1960, 244-245)

We can see from this passage that Beck criticizes the doctrine because it does not answer the question "What ought I to do?" Beck's argument is that because the concept in question is an essentially empty "dialectical ideal of reason," it does not provide the will with any particular objective. He further conjectures that the "Dialectic" section of the second *Critique* was included by Kant on the purely architectonic grounds of wanting to see an organization parallel between the first two *Critiques*. It is, in his final analysis, an otiose and philosophically unconvincing appendix to Kant's practical philosophy.

Beck's negative assessment of the highest good was first attacked in a series of articles by John Silber (1959, 1963). Despite that fact that it was not the issue concerning Kant when developing the highest good thesis, the terms of the Beck-Silber debate arise from the old formalism charge against Kant's moral philosophy. This is particularly true of Silber's discussion, where he tries to show, contra Beck, that the highest good does in fact add "content" to the otherwise merely formal moral law.

Silber states that the "[t]he concept of the highest good is proposed by Kant as the necessary material object of moral volition" (Silber 1959, 469). The concept of a "material object" makes Silber's intentions immediately clear: the highest good is meant to tell us what it is, in particular, we are to do when we are being moral. It is meant to fill out Kant's formal moral theory by providing distinct and concrete moral tasks. Silber writes:

> This concept–whose analysis, deduction, and elaboration constitutes the central problem of the *Critique of Practical Reason*–gives concrete significance to moral obligation. No longer obligated to strive for the abstraction of good-willing itself as its object, the will is now guided by means of the idea of the highest good to seek its own moral perfection and the happiness of others as its categorically obligated ends. The idea of the highest good thereby provides the answer to the second of Kant's three basic questions: What can I know? What ought I to do? What may I hope? (Silber 1959, 469)

There are a number of problems with this line of reasoning. The content that Silber thinks the highest good provides–the duties to perfect ourselves and promote the happiness of others–are the two "imperfect" duties discussed by Kant in the *Groundwork*. Although they are only meant as illustrations of the application of the categorical imperative in that text, they are introduced without any reference to the highest good. However, they turn out to be central to his overall moral theory, and it is odd therefore that they are introduced without any mention of the highest good; and when the highest good is mentioned the duties in question are never raised.[3]

With regard to the first injunction that is a corollary to our striving to bring about the highest good, Silber writes:

> Kant suggests: "It can be nothing other than the cultivation of one's own power (or natural capacity) and also of one's will (moral disposition) to satisfy the requirement of duty in general." The last part of this explanation merely repeats that the object of the will is its own moral perfection; it is, therefore, of no help in adding material significance to the object of pure practical reason. The first part seems more promising. Kant suggests that, in the cultivation of his powers, man has a duty to educate and refine himself to the fullest extent possible. (Silber 1963, 187)

---

[3] In the *Metaphysics of Morals,* Kant argues that "one's own perfection and the happiness of others" are ends that are also duties (MS 6: 385, 517).

It surely does nothing to support Silber's argument to note that the text he is quoting from here is the *Metaphysics of Morals* rather than the *Critique of Practical Reason.* In the former, Kant does indeed discuss specific moral issues, but he does not suggest that this "content" is due to the doctrine of the highest good, in fact the highest good plays no role in this work. In the *Critique of Practical Reason*, where Kant is concerned to talk about the highest good, he never mentions any of the issues that Silber brings forward. In the short final section of that work on methodology, Kant does speak of moral education, and in particular he mentions how immature dispositions should be exposed to stories that speak to autonomy; but this is not the content that Silber is after, in fact this is really just a kind of moral indoctrination that Kant thinks will ultimately make the young more amenable to taking up their duty when they arrive at the age of majority. It is only then that the question of content becomes an issue. There is simply no evidence in either text to support Silber's contention that this is what the doctrine of the highest good enjoins. Silber may well be correct in the contention that students of morality should be doing the kinds of things he mentions, but as we shall see more clearly, this not what Kant is getting at through the idea of the highest good. Even in regard to the *Metaphysics of Morals*, Silber goes beyond the scope of the text in "deducing" a duty to educate and refine oneself from the duty to perfect oneself. What the text actually says is that "[man] has a duty to raise himself out of the crudity of his nature, out of his animality more and more to humanity" (MS 6: 387, 518). This may indeed involve education of some kind, but the only thing specified by Kant in this passage is that in raising oneself from animality to humanity, one becomes more aware of one's duty. Moreover, in the light of what Kant says in the famous opening paragraph of the *Groundwork*, it is doubtful that he would argue that those who are more educated are more likely to be morally upright. Indeed the Rousseauian overtones here suggest something quite the opposite.

At a more general level, it appears that in his eagerness to show that the highest good provides content to the moral will, Silber ends up loosing sight of the formalist thrust of Kant's ethics. We only have an instance of the self-legislation of reason if an individual decides what to do in a particular situation without specific guidance; if the content of moral principles are determined a priori we return to a position of heteronomy. Kant is able to delve into material content in writing a metaphysics of morals, but a formal analysis of practical reason abstracts from material considerations, except when it is necessary to discuss the place of material in the formal structure of willing.

Beck agrees with Silber that the practical purpose of the doctrine of the highest good is to provide formal maxims with content; his criticism is that it fails in this regard. He remarks with some degree of incredulity that in comparison with the highest good, "[n]one of the formulations of the categorical imperative have had this content…" (Beck, 1960, 244) This is, of course, true because the categorical imperative is the form of a maxim that commands an action with the sense of intrinsic and unconditional obligation. Beck's remark is strange, however, because all he has said in regard to the highest good is that we are commanded to promote it, and that it involves a synthesis between happiness and virtue. This hardly amounts to much in the way of content. This raises again the issue of what is meant by "content." There is an ambiguity between content meant in a formal sense, as in the form/content distinction, and the particular content a given maxim might have. Silber is presumably getting at this distinction when he talks of the "material object" of the will, as opposed to the formal object. However, despite this, both have remarkably little to say about what "content" is. Beck seems to be saying that, because happiness is a necessary element of the highest good, then the idea of the highest good involves content; yet Kant also speaks of "happiness" as little more than a placeholder for the sum total of ends an agent has. Beck goes on to say:

> [S]uppose I do all in my power…to promote the highest good, what am I to do? Simply act out of respect for the law, which I already knew. I can do absolutely nothing else toward apportioning happiness in accordance with desert–that is the task of the moral governor of the universe, not of a laborer in the vineyard…it is seriously misleading to say that there is a command to seek the highest good which is different from the command to fulfill the requirements of duty." (Beck, 1960, 244-245)

The contradiction between attributing content to the highest good and then criticizing the doctrine for lacking in any content points to the problem arising out of the unresolved ambiguity of the meaning of the word. It is also noteworthy that, as we have already seen, Beck rejects the idea due to its failure to answer the question "What ought I to do?" and yet, as Beck himself points out, the doctrine is meant to answer the question "For what may I hope?" (Beck 1960, 241)

Beck is right to argue that the highest good does not provide distinct content to maxims, but it is questionable that this is what it was designed to do. Indeed it is questionable whether the formalism charge is in fact an effective criticism of Kant's ethics in the first place. It is usually leveled by virtue of a neglect of the anything but the first formulation of the categorical imperative, and in addition it could be argued that the level of formality achieved in Kant's ethics is in fact one of its strengths. Beck's criticisms, however, are not limited to this question. He also develops a more subtle critique around Kant's presentation of the antinomy of practical reason, which he argues, is a "devised and artificial" opposition not in need of the kind of "critical resolution" undertaken, making the postulation of the highest good unnecessary. His most important argument in support of this contention is based on the imperfect parallel he detects between it and the antinomies of theoretical reason. An attempt to answer Beck's objection in this regard allows us to see what is the purpose of this doctrine in Kant's practical philosophy.

Antinomies

In the *Critique of Pure Reason*, Kant puts forward the thesis that the activity of reasoning–the kinds of questions asked and answers sought by the faculty of reason–tends to leads us into a particular kind of illusion he refers to as "reason's dialectic." In particular, when speculating on cosmological questions, reason's dialectical tendency produces "antinomies." Antinomies are philosophically justified and seemingly irreconcilable oppositions. This is problematic because if pure reason necessarily produces equally justified but contradictory propositions, then the very coherence of reason itself is threatened.

First, as to the source of reason's dialectic, Kant writes:

> Pure reason always has its dialectic…for it requires the absolute totality of conditions for a given conditioned…Since…the unconditioned can never be found, an unavoidable illusion arises…which would never be noticed as deceptive if it were not revealed by a conflict of reason with itself… (KpV 5: 107, 90)

There are three issues to be considered here: (i) why pure reason requires the totality of conditions for a given conditioned; (ii) the basis and significance of the fact that the unconditioned can never be found; and (iii) the nature of the conflict of reason with itself. Consideration of the third issue will be postponed until the next section for reasons that shall be made clear.

(1) Why pure reason requires the totality of conditions for a given conditioned

The basic operation of reasoning is to ask questions, the purpose of which is to seek a sufficient explanation for the object of questioning. A sufficient explanation might be the cause of a certain effect, the motivation for an action, and so forth. As all of these explanations are kinds of reason, the faculty of reason is the ability to give reasons.

Reasoning is a ubiquitous human activity, but the distinctively philosophical use of reason seeks ultimate reasons, or in Kant's terminology, unconditioned conditions. To see how this leads to a dialectical *impasse*, consider the standard operation of causal explanation. When we wish to comprehend the existence of some physical phenomenon, *A*, we seek its cause in some prior state, *B*, that caused *A* to come into being. *B* causes *A*. This might be sufficient explanation for certain purposes, but beyond the remit of those purposes we may also question what accounts for the existence of *B*, namely *C*. In this manner we begin to trace back a regress of causes that we can follow until we reach the point where a sufficient explanation is found. But at what point do we reach a sufficient explanation? What constitutes a sufficient explanation? Very often quotidian contingencies determine the point at which questioning comes to an end; philosophy, however, does not limit the remit of its questioning in this regard. Rather, Kant takes it that the trajectory of philosophical thinking is to synthesize knowledge, and discover some form of unity among multiplicity. In Kant's terminology, this unity is the unconditioned condition for any and all conditions.

The unconditioned condition is an a priori object of reason because it is due in the first place to the maxims of reasoning. This object can be conceived in one of two ways: either as the first beginning of a sequence, like the unit that is the first in a numerical sequence, or as the totality of any collection of elements taken together. Broadly speaking, tracing the regress of reasons back to a unitary beginning is the move that distinguishes rationalist metaphysics, whereas rejecting the idea of a first principle and instead positing an infinite regress is typical of empiricism. However, both schools make the assumption that there is a reality that corresponds to this object. Both positions wrongly assume that "if the conditioned is given…the complete series of conditions, a series which is itself therefore unconditioned, is also given" (KrV A 308/B 364). In the case of rationalism it is the idea of some unitary object that is the unconditioned condition, however it might be conceptualized (god, the unmoved mover, the *ens causa sui*, etc.); for empiricism it is the infinite totality.

(2) The basis and significance of the fact that the unconditioned can never be found

According to Kant's transcendental idealism our experience is always conditioned by the forms of experience: space, time and the categories of the understanding. These forms necessarily condition any possible experience. In addition, Kant also argues that for anything to be an object of knowledge, it must first be given in experience. Since this implies that objects of knowledge are always conditioned, the unconditioned is not an object of knowledge. However, this does not mean that the idea of the unconditioned condition should cease to play a role in thinking. On the contrary, Kant thinks that the faculty of reason cannot operate without the idea of the unconditioned condition as a projected end-point for which we strive when engaging in reasoning. In Kant's terminology it is a regulative principle; the mistake, made by both rationalism and empiricism, is to take it that this principle is constitutive of reality. Kant thinks that regulative principles are "indispensably necessary if we are to direct the understanding beyond every given experience." (KrV A 645/B 673) However, even ideals are able to contradict each other and merely relegating the use of the idea of the unconditioned to a regulative role does not remove the antinomies or avoid the paradoxical suggestion that reason contradicts itself. Kant must, therefore, find a mechanism whereby the idea of the unconditioned can be maintained while avoiding the semblance of contradiction. The doctrine of transcendental idealism once again proves fruitful, for it provides a basis to distinguish between things as they appear and things as they are in themselves. As this distinction establishes that our knowledge is limited to what appears to us, it means that we cannot make any claims, positive or negative, about things in themselves. This distinction is then used by Kant to reconcile the antinomies, essentially by saying that each side of the opposition is pertinent either to appearances or to things in themselves. As different antinomies are resolved in different ways, it is necessary for our purposes to examine the specifics of reason's dialectic as it arises in practical considerations.[4]

The Highest Good

Kant's conception of practical reason is in part a standard teleological account of the motivation for, and evaluation of, action (KpV 5: 57-63,

---

[4] For a further discussion of the issues surrounding the ways different antinomies are resolved see Allison (1990, 22-25).

186-190; TP 8: 278-280, 282-283). The basic assumption is that there are always possible reason-giving explanations for actions that involve some conception of ends, goals, or purposes. If something is an end, goal or purpose then it can be characterized as good. Moral disagreements can, however, drive a wedge between the evaluative and motivational meanings of "good." There may not be agreement that a given purpose is truly good but, from a motivational perspective, it must at least be an apparent good for the agent for whom it is a purpose. Anything that is in fact an end, goal or purpose must be characterizable as good in some sense otherwise it could not count as a motivation. But to qualify a good as apparent implies a negative evaluation.

The ambiguity can be seen in the contrast between saying, for example, "I got a good look at that person" and "It is good to be honest." The former is evaluative but provides no motive; whereas, the latter relies on considerations that have actual or intended motivational heft. When Aristotle says that the good is that at which all things aim, he is making a universal statement about motivation; we are motivated to do things by "the good", whatever that turns out to be. This distinction is also at work in Kant's distinction between theoretical and practical reason. Our primary interest in statements of theoretical reason involves the criterion of truth; we are concerned with their truth value based on a correspondence model. The theoretical interest is not primarily focused on whether statements have motivational implications, although they might also have motivational implication.

Statements of practical reason are primarily of motivational importance. If someone were to question "Why is honesty such a good thing?" the answer will be a theory that explains why one should be honest. While there can be a purely evaluative sense of goodness with no relationship to action, the motivational conception of goodness must be either a possible or actual reason for acting. The teleological conception of practical reason unifies both the evaluative and motivational significations, and therefore, the "good" of practical reason must incorporate both evaluative and motivational elements. As the evaluative sense of "good" may be true or false, it implicitly claims some kind of objectivity.

Now, the purposes that are actual reasons for acting may be incorporated in longer-term purposes; actions may be good as a means to some further end. But any regressive series of practical reasons must find some terminus. This may be located in some pragmatic consideration, but as we have seen, Kant not only thinks that it is a basic tendency of reason to seek the unconditioned condition–in this case the highest good –but also that reason cannot do without this idea. The importance of the idea of an unconditioned condition for practical reason can be seen when we consider the experience of futility. If there is no unconditioned condition for action then there is an infinite regress of reasons for action. An infinite regress in practical reason means (i) that there is no ultimate reason why anything is good, and (ii) that the pursuit of ends is an exercise in futility. To vouchsafe the rationality of action, the teleologist posits a highest good which is good in itself, and for the sake of which we desire other things. As it makes no sense to ask why anyone would want to be happy (one wants to be happy simply because one wants to be happy, whereas one wants other things, such as money, because one wants to be happy), happiness is a typical candidate for the highest good. It is eminently defensible to say that everyone wants to be happy, and that the totality of their actions are intelligible in this light. Even the suicidally depressed, the suicide bomber or the politically inspired hunger-striker are motivated by their unhappiness with the present situation, and act for the sake of something better.

It is possible to speak of things other than happiness as ends in themselves, but the special significance of the concept of happiness is partly due to its functioning as a whole made up of parts. For example, it is not uncommon to hear the idea that (political) freedom is the most important thing to have in life, that without freedom, life is not worth living; however, it is still possible to incorporate the good of freedom into a totalizing conception of happiness. The champion of freedom will accept that freedom is a necessary condition of happiness; that there can be no happiness where there is no freedom. Freedom, among other things, can be said to be good in itself and for the sake of happiness. The expansive nature of the concept of happiness means that it is always possible to incorporate all goods, including goods that are ends in themselves, into an overall good that is simply good in itself and cannot be good for anything other than itself.

The highest good is the unconditioned condition of practical reason posited as an object for practical reason. We saw that the unconditioned condition in theoretical reasoning can be conceived as either a unity or a totality. The same pattern is evident in how we may conceive of the highest good. It can be conceptualized as either the supreme good (*bonum supremum*) or the complete good (*bonum consummatum*). The supreme good occupies the same logical space as the typically rationalist conception of a unitary object to which all other objects in a sequence are subordinate; in Kant's words it is "that condition which is itself unconditioned." The complete good is the idea of all the objects of practical reason taken together as a totality; it is "that whole which is not part of a still greater whole of the same kind." (KpV 5: 110, 92) In practical reasoning, the supreme good is a perfectly virtuous or unconditionally good will. It is a morally evaluative conception of the highest good, a measure against which any particular virtuous disposition or practical maxim may be judged. The complete good is happiness. This is a motivational concept.

We have already noted that a teleological account of practical reason incorporates both motivational and evaluative considerations in its conception of the highest good. Both these moments must be present in practical reasoning, but they are also distinct. The fallacy evident in practical reason's dialectic turns on how the two are brought together. As in theoretical reason, the fallacy generates two opposing schools of thought, so it does in practical reason. The antinomical positions are occupied by stoicism and Epicureanism. The mistake made in both instances, according to Kant, is that both try to find an "identity" between "extremely heterogeneous concepts." (Ibid.) The Epicureans believe that virtue is identical with the wise pursuit of happiness and the stoics believe that the practice of virtue necessarily leads to happiness. Both of these moral philosophies think the relationship between virtue and happiness is analytic; Kant's argument in the *Groundwork* and the "Analytic" of the second *Critique* concludes, however, that they are essentially distinct.

Stoicism and Epicureanism

Kant takes it that his moral philosophy agrees on many points with the stoic conception of virtue, at least on his interpretation of stoicism. The stoics, he writes,

> …derived their universal moral principle from the dignity of human nature, from its freedom (as an independence from the power of inclinations)…they then drew the moral laws directly from reason…and so was everything quite correctly apportioned–objectively as regards the rule, and also subjectively, with respect to the incentive. (R 6: 58, 77)

We see here key elements of Kant's moral vision: universal moral principles, the will's negative freedom over the influence of the inclinations, the dignity of human nature, etc. But Stoicism errs, according to Kant, in believing that "to be conscious of one's virtue is happiness" (KpV 5: 111, 93). Rather than unite virtue and happiness, the stoics, on Kant's account, essentially give up on the attainment of happiness and instead declare that happiness is the state of being virtuous. He writes:

> [A]ccording to the stoic…the feeling of happiness was already contained in consciousness of one's virtue. What is contained in another concept, however, is indeed identical with a part of the concept containing it but not identical with the whole. (KrV 5: 112, 94)

We can illustrate the problem that Kant is gesturing towards if we consider Job. We can say that Job is good because he is virtuous, but we cannot say that Job's life is good in the light of what he suffers; we cannot maintain that virtue alone is tantamount to the complete good. Happiness is, at least in part, a matter of *feeling* happy. While the stoics have an admirable conception of the nobility of human nature, Kant thinks that their version of happiness is entirely unrealistic, and because of this they have an unrealistic conception of motivation. The stoic ideal of the sage bears little relationship to the reality of a being of finite rational and motivational resources. Indeed the ideal of the sage seems so far removed from human possibilities that it could even demoralize one's ethical resolve. The stoic conception of the highest good, as Kant understands it–in its focus on a purely morally evaluative conception of virtue–looses sight of motivational considerations. It ceases to be a conception of the good that can operate effectively in practical reasoning. The extirpation of the emotions cannot lead us to happiness, but it can undermine our ability to be motivated at all. Kant thinks that stoicism ends up being a philosophy of apathetic stasis that lends itself to the development of a fatalistic disposition.

Epicureanism incorporates a more realistic conception of what it is possible for human beings to achieve based on a psychological appraisal of the nature and limits of human motivation. Rather than starting with an ideal that is meant to draw us towards it by a sort of magnetic attraction, the focus is on the forces that actually push human beings to act, namely our passions, inclinations and desires. In keeping with other teleological conceptions of desire, Epicureanism holds "that happiness is the *whole highest good*, and virtue only the form of the maxim for seeking to obtain it, namely, the rational use of means to it." (KrV 5: 112, 94)

Kant recognizes that Epicureanism, properly understood, is not a crudely hedonistic pursuit of pleasure, rather, the Epicurean conception of pleasure really means "contentment." He characterizes this as "the most disinterested practice of the good among the ways of enjoying the most intimate delight." The disinterestedness is rooted in temperance; Epicurus "included in his scheme of pleasure (by which he meant a constantly cheerful heart) such moderation and control of the inclinations as the strictest moral philosopher might require." (KrV 5: 115, 97) However, Kant also thinks that Epicureanism involves a certain fallacy that makes it impossible to actually achieve true happiness. This argument turns on the idea of "worthiness to be happy."

In the *Lectures on Ethics*, Kant asks invites his students to imagine a world where everyone is happy, and then points out that this world could be further improved if everyone there was not only happy but deservedly so. The highest good for any possible world is where people are happy in proportion to their virtue and the wicked are punished in proportion to their viciousness. This conception of virtue introduces a notion of desert, and the related notion of justice into the highest good. The existence of injustice is, on Kant's view, an impediment to attaining happiness:

> …an impartial rational spectator can take no delight in seeing the uninterrupted prosperity of a being graced with no feature of a pure and good will, so that a good will seems to constitute the indispensable condition of even worthiness too be happy. (G 4: 393, 7)

Furthermore, he argues that we cannot be happy unless we are also conscious of our own virtue: "Man can only hope to be happy insofar as he makes himself worthy of it, for that is the condition of happiness demanded by reason itself." (VE 27: 247, 44) This thesis presupposes the success of the arguments Kant makes in *Groundwork* and the "Analytic" section of the *Critique of Practical Reason* establishing that finite rational beings are necessarily under moral obligations that impinge in principle on the pursuit of happiness. According to Kant, finite rational beings are knowingly and necessarily under unconditional moral obligations, and this introduces a moral condition for the enjoyment of happiness, for we are, as it were, always subject to the sting of conscience.

There are two importantly distinct senses in which Kant talks about happiness. According to the better known account, found in the *Groundwork* and the "Analytic" of the second *Critique*, happiness is the satisfaction of sensible inclinations. The second kind of happiness appears in the "Dialectic" of the second and third *Critiques*, and incorporates the moral conception of "worthiness." Kant refers to this kind of happiness as "contentment with oneself." He distinguishes it from the Epicurean conception of the fulfillment of physical needs and desires, and a stoic sounding notion of beatitude, which is only possible based on complete independence from needs and desires.

Despite the positive things he has to say about Epicurus, Kant thinks of Epicureanism as a form of reductive materialism committed to the idea that all motives are sourced in the body's receptivity to sense impressions. Kant thinks that there are also intellectual incentives that are not objects of sensation, such as the respect we have for the idea of the moral law. The distinction between intellectual and sensible incentives is paralleled by a distinction Kant makes between pleasure and satisfaction. The expectation of the former motivates us to seek the fulfillment of our desires; the latter is an affect of freedom derived from the determination of the will. Kant thinks, however, that we cannot have this kind of satisfaction unless we determine our will autonomously; therefore, the kind of happiness of which it is a part, is not possible unless we act independently of inclinations. Now, we could ask: what if we act for the sake of satisfaction and the happiness it buys, is this not mere heteronomy? Kant's reply is that we cannot make this kind of satisfaction a purpose, for we can only experience this kind of satisfaction as a beneficial "secondary quality" of acting on the basis of the moral law. To attempt to make this idea into a motive would destroy the possibility of actually experiencing this kind of contentment. The problem of self-righteousness is somewhat analogous. The self-righteous fail to achieve moral virtue precisely because the motivation for the adoption of moral principles is the prospect of enjoying the sense of being moral. It is only when we act out of respect for the moral law that we act in way that makes us deserving of happiness and capable of achieving contentment with oneself. But it is the respect not the contentment that must be the motivating factor; we must be conscious of the fact that we are primarily motivated by respect for the moral law if we are to enjoy the good fortune to be happy. Anything less subjects us to the reproach of conscience. This is the basis for Kant's remark that Epicurus "fell into the error of presupposing the virtuous *disposition* in the persons for whom he wanted first of all to provide the incentive to virtue." (KrV 5:116, 97)

On the basis of these reflections, Kant thinks that the Epicurean conception of happiness is ultimately lacking. Epicureanism is capable of providing a descriptively realistic portrayal of what virtue looks like, and Kant clearly holds Epicurus in high moral regard, but it prescriptively insufficient to meet the moral demands of a conception of the highest good adequate to practical reason. Kant's criticism of the Epicurean conception of the highest good is that the morally evaluative side of the good drops out. Epicurus, he writes, "accommodated virtue to human weakness"; his philosophy succeeds in giving virtue "motives and no value." (VE 27: 250, 46) It is notable that this criticism of Epicureanism is different to and separate from the more usual Kantian charge of heteronomy. Both stoicism and Epicureanism are ultimately heteronomous on Kant's view because both are grounded on hypothetical imperatives to achieve to happiness. Based on that moral criticism, Kant then is able to argue that it is precisely because Epicureanism is based on the pursuit of happiness that it cannot achieve what it sets out to do.[5] The heteronomy of stoicism, however, is closer to the Kantian moral ideal because the happiness they make their end is really virtue and not happiness.

Kant's argument is that the attempt to treat the relationship between the evaluative and motivational sides of the highest good as an identity by stoicism and Epicureanism, ends up effacing either one determination of the concept or the other. In this way both are "false." The stoic thinks that we will become happy if we become virtuous, whereas the Epicurean thinks that virtue is the wise pursuit of happiness. Stoicism is strongly normative but weakly motivational; it is a moral but unrealistic doctrine. Epicureanism, on the other hand, is strongly motivational but weakly normative; it is a descriptively realistic philosophy of prudence, but because of this it fails to rise to the level of true morality. Even though stoicism is strongly normative, it is not truly a moral doctrine because it remains heteronomous. Even though Epicureanism is motivationally realistic, it ultimately fails to provide a true prescription for happiness as it misses the necessary moral condition for happiness. In eliding the distinction between the motivational and evaluative senses of "good", both philosophies are indicted by Kant for a double failure.

Resolving the antinomies and Beck's criticism

As with dialectic in general, Kant looks to his doctrine of transcendental idealism to resolve the practical antinomy. He describes the "critical resolution of the antinomy of practical reason" as follows:

> [T]hat the endeavor after happiness produces a ground for a virtuous disposition, is *absolutely false*; but…that a virtuous disposition necessarily produces happiness, is false *not absolutely* but only insofar as this disposition is regarded as the form of causality in the sensible world, and consequently false only if I assume existence in the sensible world to be the one and only kind of existence of a rational being; it is thus only *conditionally false*. (KpV 5: 114, 96)

---

[5] There is an alternative possibility, which is to abandon the moral ideal of being worthy of happiness, and instead embrace the hedonistic ideal of the unimpeded pursuit of pleasure. Although, as mentioned, Kant does not attribute this position to Epicurus, he does regard it as a possibility implicit in Epicureanism, in its prioritization of sensuous gratification. However, once again this disposition is inadequate for its own ends because the pursuit of the fulfillment of desire is not only futile, but it only increases the number and intensity of our desires. Like Epicureanism, hedonism is irrational because it is a pursuit of happiness that is always condemned to fail.

Beck points out that there is a greater justification for the stoic side of the supposed antinomy whereas Epicureanism "is not vindicated at all." If the highest good of stoicism—virtue–is only "conditionally false," while the Epicurean conception of same doctrine is "absolutely false," then there is no need to present the relationship between the two as an antinomy. Based on the imperfect parallel between the antinomies of theoretical and practical reason, Beck argues that we are presented in the second *Critique*, not with a real antinomy, but a "devised and artificial" opposition. The opposition is not in need of the kind of "critical resolution" undertaken, and therefore it is unnecessary to argue that the highest good is a necessary postulate of practical reason.

The first step to answering Beck's criticism is to refer back to a point, previously broached, that while "transcendental idealism is the key to resolution of the entire antinomical conflict…this idealism yields different resolutions to the different antinomies." (Allison 1990, 22) Allison's argument suggests that the nature of an antinomy will be in some regard specific to the kind of philosophical question at hand, and given the difference between theoretical and practical questions, we may then expect there to be some difference between the theoretical and practical antinomies.

Beck suggests that Kant's discussion of practical reason implies a coherence theory of truth (Beck 1960, 263). Although he does not develop this point, the suggestion turns out to be useful in regard to seeing the difference between the theoretical and practical antinomies. The philosophical question for the antinomical practical philosophies, stoicism and Epicureanism, is the rationale for disposition formation. This is not a matter of truth on Kant's strictly correspondence conception of truth, but it may be characterized as a matter of validity. In both the theoretical and practical spheres of Kant's philosophy there is reference to an object. In the former the object is given; in the latter it is willed. The willing in question is that of a finite rational being. Finite rational beings are driven by the desire to be happy, but are also subject to a moral demand placed upon them by reason. A coherent disposition must be able to reconcile these sometimes competing demands. The question of validity in regards to a theory of a practical disposition is a factor of how coherent it is, how well it "holds together" given the terms of reference of practice. One that is "false" fails to do this.

Epicureanism has a solid motivational foundation in the desire to achieve happiness, but it fails to adequately respond to the moral demand placed on rational beings. Epicureanism is based on the false belief that the wise pursuit of happiness renders an agent virtuous. Stoicism in part fulfills the formal conception of moral philosophy but its posture of indifference to the demands of happiness is entirely unrealistic. Stoicism fails to properly take in to account the finitude of human beings; it is a moral philosophy that has no solid basis in motivation. Kant's argument proceeds as it does in the first *Critique*: reason inevitably presents us with a pair of incompatible general positions with regard to some issue, both of which have a certain degree of justification, and which can be accommodated if we can make the distinction between appearances and things in themselves. The question is how does the distinction between the sensible and intelligible make stoicism only "conditionally false."

Stoicism is false only when it takes appearances to be things in themselves, the kind of stoicism that Kant saw in the philosophy of Spinoza. Frederick Beiser refers to a passage in the *Critique of Judgment*, where Kant expounds upon the roots and attendant dangers of a pessimistic or fatalistic moral outlook. It is due in the first place to atheism. The well-intentioned atheist, "like Spinoza", has no reason to think that the highest good is possible, so when such a person reflects upon their life overall, the question of "what is the point of any of it?" is left dangerously open to a nihilistic answer. Kant writes:

> How would he judge his own inner purposive determination by the moral law, which he actively honors? He does not demand any advantage for himself from his conformity to this law, whether in this or in another world; rather, he would merely unselfishly establish the good to which that holy law directs all his powers. But his effort is limited; and from nature he can to be sure, expect some contingent assistance here and there, but never a law-like agreement in accordance with constant rules (like his internal maxims are and must be) with the ends to act in behalf of which he still finds himself bound and impelled. Deceit, violence and envy will always surround him, even though he is himself honest, peaceable and benevolent; and the righteous ones besides himself that he will still encounter will, in spite of all their worthiness to be happy, nevertheless be subject by nature, which pays no attention to that, to all the ills of poverty, illness and untimely death, just like all the other animals on earth, and will always remain thus until one wide grave engulfs them all together (whether honest or dishonest, it makes no difference here) and flings them, who were capable of having believed themselves to be the final end of creation, back into the abyss of the purposeless chaos of matter from which they were drawn. – The end, therefore, which this well-intentioned person had and should have had before his eyes in his conformity to the moral law, he would have to give up as impossible… (KU 5: 452, 317-318)

According to Beiser, Kant's "ultimate worry is…*existential*: the despair that comes from believing that all our moral efforts and strivings in the world are in vain…[for] if we believe…that all our efforts will come to nothing–then we will have no motivation to act at all." (Beiser 2006, 616) Wood argues similarly that the doctrine of the highest good emerges from Kant's meditations of "man's situation as such", and involves "a profound conception of the human condition as a whole." (Wood 1970, 1) The reason why commentators have not grasped the significance of the highest good, Wood thinks, is due to a failure in the context of Kant's philosophy writ-large. He goes on to write that this doctrine "guides man in his rational pursuit of his unconditioned final end, showing him how he may view the world of his moral action so as not to be lead astray by the illusion of moral despair which threatens his pursuit of his lofty practical destination." (Wood 1970, 8) The alternative to belief in the possibility of achieving the highest good through our efforts is a descent into "moral despair."

This line of defense goes some way to account for Kant's statement that if it is not possible for an agent to believe in the highest good, then the moral law "must therefore in itself be false." (KpV 5: 114, 95) In the "Analytic" of the *Critique of Practical Reason*, Kant argues that the moral law is unconditionally valid; the designation of an imperative as *categorical* means that it is not suspended by any other considerations. But this seems inconsistent with the "Dialectic" where the prospect of its "falsehood" is raised. Both Wood and Beck put this statement down to a quixotic attempt by Kant to produce a contradiction that mirrors the nature of the antinomies of the first *Critique*. However, if we review the entire sentence, noting that *falsch* has an extremely wide range of possible equivalents in English, many of which do not support the sense of contradiction, we can reinterpret the issue as the futility of pursuing a fantastic and imaginary goal, rather than on the "falsity" of the law:

> If, therefore, the highest good is impossible in accordance with practical rules, then the moral law, which commands us to promote it, must be fantastic and directed to empty imaginary ends and must therefore in itself be false (*falsch*)… (KpV 5: 114, 95)

This is in evidence in Cassirer's rendering of the passage:

> In other words, since it is impossible that the *summum bonum* should be brought into being, by way of acting in conformity with practical rules, the moral law which commands that the *summum bonum* is to be promoted must be one which is in pursuit of fantasies and of vain and imaginary purposes–being, in fact, a law which has an inherently spurious character. (Ibid., tr. Cassirer, 143)

According to Kant, the moral law, as the determining ground of the will, is responsible for prompting the agent to adopt the object of promoting the highest good. Kant is then merely making the point that an agent needs to be able to believe in the possibility of an objective before they will be motivated to embark upon its pursuit. A theory of practical disposition is "false" or spurious if it does not take this consideration into account.

Beck looks to the imperfect parallel between practical and theoretical reason in order to deflate the importance of the practical antinomy, but when we consider the different objects that theoretical and practical reason are concerned with we should assume some difference in the way these antinomies appear. Kant constantly stresses not only these differences but also the primacy of practical reason over its theoretical employment (KpV 5: 3, 3; 5: 6, 5-6; 5: 50-58, 44-50; 5: 119-122, 100-102). In addition, Beck thinks that Kant is merely trying to force his material to fit a somewhat arbitrary architectonic conception. The dialectic of practical reason does not concern judgments regarding an object given in intuition, rather it involves two mutually incompatible positions in regards to the relationship between the morality and happiness in the determination of the practical disposition. We should remember that Kant thinks dialectic is an unavoidable illusion of reason, that arises from the tendency not only to seek the unconditioned condition, but to make of this hypothesis a *fait accompli*. In theoretical reason this means implicitly using the unconditioned condition as if it is a fact that an object corresponds to the idea of it. In practical reason it is to think there is a simple identity between morality and happiness making the highest good merely a matter of will or prudence. Kant, who takes a somewhat dark and pessimistic view of the state of human affairs, thinks appearances are otherwise, and therefore, that we can only hope for the highest good if we postulate the conditions (the immortality of the soul and the existence of god) that make it possible.

II- The Object/Determining Ground Distinction

The argument so far is that the highest good is not meant to add content to an otherwise purely formal conception of the moral law, rather it is an element in a formal conception of practical reason. Yet the doctrine of the highest good necessitates a fragile hope in the face of a world where morality and happiness are not necessarily reconciled. However, the world in question is the world of appearances, and Kant is able to leverage the doctrine of transcendental idealism to argue that we should not presume that experience exhausts all possibilities, making room for faith in the possibility that morality and happiness may be ultimately reconciled. For motivational reasons we need to believe in the possibility of the highest good, and its rationality is not foreclosed by theoretical considerations; however, we have yet to consider whether this doctrine smuggles a degree of heteronomy into the moral disposition that effectively sullies the purity of the moral will. To do this we must turn to the determining ground/object distinction, and evaluate Kant's, and his apologist's, defense against the inconsistency charge.

Introducing the theme of the highest good in the "Dialectic" section of the second *Critique*, Kant insists that the pursuit of the highest good is necessary for moral willing but is "not on that account to be taken as its *determining ground*." (KpV 5: 109, 92) As we have seen, Allen Wood takes it that the determining ground of an action is its motivation, and therefore he understands Kant to be saying that, "human action, from a practical point of view is both motivated and purposive." (Wood 1970, 41) As we can do the same thing from different motives, there is some initial plausibility to this distinction. For example, I can make a purchase in a store because I want to possess a certain item or because I want to meet the cashier. But is the object of the will, the intention to purchase, the act of purchasing, the purpose we intend through this act, or a combination of all three? Kant writes that:

> ...[practical] reason is concerned with the determining grounds of the will, which is a faculty either of producing objects corresponding to representations or of determining itself to effect such objects (whether the physical power is sufficient or not) [that is, of determining its causality]. (KpV 5: 15, 12)

As the object of practical reason is something that is produced, and that is independent of any physical limitations, it seems that Kant must be referring to intentions. If we were to substitute "purpose" for "object" in the foregoing passage, Kant would look to be saying that practical reason determines the will to "effect" purposes regardless of whether there is sufficient physical power to do so, but this would not seem to be rational. Taking it then that "object of the will" refers to intentions, there are two senses of intention here: the formation of an intention in relation to a representation and to act for the sake of some intention. We can see that these two senses of intention are distinct when we reflect on the fact that we can form and express an intention with all sincerity and never act upon it.

If I form an intention to make a purchase, then the object of the will is an action I intend to execute. However this action serves a purpose that I intend that is not limited to the confines of the particular action. We can therefore make a distinction between the *immediate* object of the will–the intention to engage in a specific act—and the *mediate* object of the will–the intention one has when engaging in a particular act, or more simply, the purpose of the act. In this case, making a purchase is the immediate object of the will and either meeting the cashier or possessing the item is the mediate object of the will. According to Wood the object of the will is its purpose in acting, but what we make as our purpose is what we intend in acting. If someone were to question why I made the purchase, they could ask what was my intention or purpose in so doing. If we take the object or intention to be to purchase the item, then we can say that the motivation is either to meet the cashier or to possess the item; but if the intention can also be the mediate object of the will, then we cannot distinguish between mediate intention and motivation, for in both cases it is either to possess the item or meet the cashier. Therefore, if the object of the will is taken to be anything other than the immediate intention to engage in a specific action, that is, if the object of the will also encompasses our purpose in acting, then the distinction between the object and determining ground of the will disappears.

To avoid this problem we can elect to restrict the meaning of "object" to the immediate object of the will, which, in this case, is the making of a purchase. But if, when moving towards the cashier with some item in my hand, a friend were to ask me what I am doing, and I were to answer that I am going to make a purchase, then I would be obtuse. My friend can see that I am going to make a purchase; the question is what is my purpose, my *objective* in so doing. Perhaps the decisive consideration, however, is that if we restrict the meaning of "object" to refer only to the immediate object of the will, then the highest good cannot be the object of the will, because that would leave empty conceptual space for some mediate object that is intended through the highest good, which is absurd.

In the following passage, it is tempting to speculate that Kant sees this problem. He certainly recognizes that the two concepts cannot be easily held apart and in fact seem to come together. He writes:

> …if the moral law is already included as supreme condition in the concept of the highest good, the highest good is then not merely *object*: the concept of it and the representation of its existence as possible by our practical reason are at the same time the *determining ground* of the pure will because in that case the moral law, already included and thought in this

> concept, and no other object, in fact determines the will in accordance with the principle of autonomy. (KpV 5: 109-110, 92)

A preliminary observation about this passage is that Kant seems to be referring to the moral law as an object, for he says "the moral law…and no *other* object…determines the will." This implies that the moral law and the highest good can both be considered as either the determining grounds or the object of the will. This does not help maintain the integrity of the distinction. To defend the distinction we could say that the moral law is an object only insofar as it is part of the highest good; the moral law is the supreme good side of the synthesis that generates the Kantian highest good; but the distinction is meant to distinguish determining grounds from object. Furthermore, to say that the moral law is an object must be equivalent to saying that it is one's intention to be dutiful, and if that is why the will is determined "in accordance with the principle of autonomy," then we have said that object of the will is its determining ground.

Willing is, for Kant, a matter of adopting maxims. The maxim for an action is its determining grounds. More prosaically, a maxim is a reason for action. Any maxim has an end or purpose, which is the object of the will. Circumstances are also part of reasons for action, so any reason for action can be more than just the purpose of the action; therefore, there is more to maxims than the end or object of the will. In this way we have a formal distinction between determining grounds and object; the question is whether this formal distinction is enough to maintain the motivational distinction between determining grounds and object.

We have seen from the discussion of the practical antinomy that Kant thinks that the object and determining grounds of the will are not identical, so we must consider in what sense they both are "at the same time the determining ground of the pure will." Kant has made this distinction precisely to hold the two principles separate in their motivational influence on the will; but if, as Wood suggests, the determining grounds of the will is just Kantianese for motivation, then Kant is now saying that the highest good is also part of the pure will's motivation.

As we have seen, Beiser thinks that Kant introduces the idea of the highest good in order to ward off the pessimistic beliefs that are likely to undermine our motivation to maintain a moral disposition. The atheist, according to Kant, does not believe that there is some ultimate moral order prevailing over the universe; it may well be that the just suffer and unjust prosper, and when each dies there is no reckoning. But in the light of this, to what end does one strive to make the world a better place? As Beiser points out, the atheist is at any moment in danger of seeing the arduous task of moral dutifulness as ultimately futile. Now, when we say that an action is futile, we are usually expressing the fact, or explaining why, we are no longer motivated to its pursuit. It is also possible to have an all-encompassing "sense" of futility at the level of the beliefs that inform our outlook on life; an "existential crisis" precipitated by the thought that nothing is worthwhile, life is pointless, and there is no reason to go on; like the "arrest of life" described by Tolstoy (1996 [1889]). With either the judgment that an act is futile, or the sense of the futility of things, our motivations are undermined; futility is a problem because it demotivates. According to Beiser, Kant thinks that we must believe in the possibility of achieving the highest good through our efforts if we are to continue making the effort of being a virtuous person, and the consequence of the absence of this belief is the undermining of our motivations. But if we need to believe in the possibility of the highest good because otherwise moral striving is futile, we are saying that the highest good is a motivational influence.

The same problem crops up in Wood's discussion of Kant's conception of finite rational volition. Wood presents us with an example of someone whose actions, he thinks, must be seen in a positive moral light. He asks us to imagine someone who agitates for the institution of legal codes that mandate a certain basic minimum standard for public housing (Wood 1970, 46-50). This person is motivated by a certain moral indignation at the present situation. Now, it is of course true that this person may well benefit from this agitation, but given the nature of social policy, this benefit is far off in years and probably somewhat modest. Indeed, it could be argued that this person would be better served, from a selfish point of view, by focusing on getting rich. In any case, Wood presents us with a recognizable picture of someone acting for the common good from motives that seem about as noble as we can imagine inhering in the "real" world. The problem is that despite his best efforts, Wood cannot give a knockdown argument against the motive-mongering tendency to always find a selfish motive behind any action. Even if we agree with the example as Wood presents it, we can still attribute some personal and selfish reward that keeps the social activist going along the long road to reform. Perhaps it is that this project gives meaning to a life that would otherwise seem empty and banal. To engage in a moral struggle affirms our life, and gives us something to live for; it helps ward off the spiritual lassitude to which we are sometimes prone. The motivation behind the housing reformer's project may simply be that it makes her happier.

The problem with the defense mounted by Kant's apologists is now clear: by interpreting the doctrine of the highest good as the factor in practical reason that saves the moral agent from a sense of futility and despair, both Wood and Beiser blur the very distinction they hold out as the solution to the inconsistency charge, and end up validating Schopenhauer's sardonic observation that there is always "a voluntary gift for which virtue, after which work has been done stealthily holds its hand open." Once again, if we agree with Wood and Beiser that the "determining ground" of the will is its motivation, then the highest good is part of moral motivation. Kant repudiates the idea that the highest good provides "support and stability" (TP 8: 279) to the moral will, but if there is any plausibility to the suggestions of Wood and Beiser, which it seems there are in some respects, then it is dogmatic to insist that the highest good provides no added incentive to a moral command that is otherwise "spurious."

It is clear what Kant's intentions are in regard to his discussion of the highest good, and the determining ground/object distinction. He wants to say that the moral law alone is the supreme determining ground of the will, and the highest good only provides a will so disposed to virtue with a project in which it may crystallize it intentions. If the highest good is part of the will's determining ground, it is so only in a subordinate manner. All this saves the purity of the moral will. The problem is that the distinction between ground and object is constantly blurred. Very often it does appear that Kant wants to be able to describe both the moral law and the highest good as either a determining ground or an object when it suits him to do so. But in so doing the argument designed to save the purity of the will is undermined. There is a wider philosophical issue here to do with how we conceive of motivation. Not only are the terms used in describing motivation–intention, purpose, motive, reason, and so forth–vague, but they overlap each other in a variety of ways. This means that we can redescribe the issue we are trying to get at in a variety of ways, leading to considerable confusion. The confusing way that Kant draws and deploys the distinction at hand in his philosophy, seems to be a result of this kind of problem.

Motive mongering

Kant has two objectives in the *Critique of Practical Reason*: to establish that "pure reason is practical" (KpV 5: 3, 3) and to argue against "empirically conditioned reason from presuming that it, alone and exclusively, furnishes the determining ground of the will." (KpV 5: 16, 12) These two theses are related, but the first establishes more than the second as it paves the way for the categorical imperative. If the determining ground/object distinction does not maintain a motivational distinction between the moral law and the highest good, or remove the suspicion that some incentive other than respect is operative in our motivations, then the first thesis and major claim is undermined. However it is still possible for Kant to succeed in the more modest goal of arguing that "empirically conditioned reason" is not the sole determining ground of the will.

The position that Kant wishes to oppose here is one that claims certainty about motivations, namely the motive mongering tendency to seek the true explanation for any act in self-interest. Kant only needs to undermine this certainty. The problem is that, while it is clear that people are selfish and that self-interest has a firm basis in the needs of organic life, it has yet to be shown that anyone has ever acted from truly moral motives. The motive monger rejects the distinction between morality and prudence as no more than a fiction and calls Kant to account at the tribunal of reality: Kant says that if pure reason is practical "it proves its reality and that of its concepts by what it does" (KpV 5: 3, 3) the skeptical response is: "Show us the deed." Yet, there are times when Kant also says that no one can ever be sure if they or anyone else has ever acted on the basis of the categorical imperative. In some ways this is an astonishing admission. By casting doubt on the reality of the central claim of his morality, it seems to threaten and undermine his entire moral project. But given his basic philosophical position, it is impossible for him to say otherwise. The determining grounds of an act are not appearances and we cannot verify the existence of anything that is not an appearance in the empirical world. We can claim some knowledge in trivial cases (hunger is a motive to eat) but we have no such knowledge at the level where these inquiries become important. Any statement that purports to explain why some people grow up virtuously where others in the same circumstances do not, goes beyond the limits of experience.

The motive monger can argue that the philosophy of prudence has a firm basis in the reality, whereas Kantian rational motivation traces its roots back to determining grounds in an unknowable noumenal realm, in which we are asked to believe. This, it may be objected, stretches our credulity. However the certainty of the motive monger might also be overstated. We cannot look into the hearts of other people, and psychoanalysis suggests that we are even opaque to ourselves. It may be more or less likely whether or not a given action is selfishly motivated or not, but there must nevertheless remain a degree of uncertainty in any attribution of motive. Furthermore, the inability to discern the determining grounds of actions, or to establish that there can be an instance where the object of an action is not its determining grounds, does not mean that the promise of some future happiness must necessarily be taken as the incentive for all seemingly moral behavior. The argument that the ground of motivation is indeterminate establishes the weaker conclusion that it is always in principle undecidable whether or not there is a pure moral will. This uncertainty cuts both ways. It prevents Kant from ever giving an entirely convincing and knockdown argument for the reality of the categorical imperative, but it also undermines the certainty of the motive monger's belief that there is never a selfless act.

Works Cited

Allison, H. *Kant's Theory of Freedom* (Cambridge University Press, 1990).

Beck, L. W. *A Commentary to Kant's Critique of Practical Reason* (University of Chicago Press, 1960).

Beiser, F. "Moral Faith and the Highest Good," in *The Cambridge Companion to Kant and Modern Philosophy* (Cambridge University Press, 2006).

Greene, T. M. "The Historical Context and Religious Significance of Kant's Religion," in *Religion Within the Limits of Reason Alone*, tr. Greene and Hudson (Harper & Row, 1960).

Kant, Immanuel *Critique of Judgment*, tr. Paul Guyer and Eric Matthews (Cambridge University Press, 2000).

—. *Critique of Practical Reason*, tr. Mary Gregor (Cambridge University Press, 1996).

—. *Critique of Practical Reason*, tr. H.W. Cassirer (Marquette University Press, 1998).

—. *Groundwork of the Metaphysics of Morals*, tr. Mary Gregor (Cambridge University Press, 1996).

—. *Lectures on Ethics*, tr. Peter Heath (Cambridge University Press, 1997).

—. *Metaphysics of Morals*, tr. Mary Gregor (Cambridge University Press, 1997).

—. *Religion Within the Boundaries of Mere Reason*, tr. Allen Wood (Cambridge University Press, 1998).

Schopenhauer, A. *The World as Will and Representation*, vol. I, tr. E.J.F. Payne (Dover, 1959).

Silber, J. "The Importance of the Highest Good in Kant's Ethics," *Ethics*, 73 (1963).

—. "Kant's Conception of the Highest Good as Immanent and Transcendent," *The Philosophical Review*, 68, 4 (1959).

Tolstoy, L. *Confession*, tr. David Patterson (Norton, 1996).
Wood, A. *Kant's Moral Religion* (Cornell University Press, 1970).
Yovel, Y. *Kant and the Philosophy of History* (Princeton University Press, 1980).

CHAPTER SEVEN

THE END OF THE *CRITIQUES*: KANT'S MORAL "CREATIONISM"

KARL AMERIKS

Kant's major works are best known for their beginning rather than concluding sections, and the *Critique of the Power of Judgment* seems to be no exception to this pattern.[1] Its §§ 90-91 are the last numbered sections of the book as a whole, and also of the final main part of the book, which is called a mere "appendix" on methodology (§§ 79-91). These sections review the significance of the moral proof of God's existence, an argument that Kant treats in several other places, and they are followed by a kind of appendix of their own, an unnumbered "General Comment" that at first can look like a redundant afterthought. Nonetheless, the concluding portion of KU is worth close consideration as a whole, for it contains some of Kant's most remarkable claims, claims whose complex and radical

[1] This work, *Die Kritik der Urteilskraft* (1790) will be cited as KU, with references to it, and other works by Kant, using the standard citation of the Academy edition volume and page number. Quotations from KU (adjusted for terms discussed in the text, such as "holding true") are from *Critique of Judgment*, translated by Werner Pluhar (Indianapolis: Hackett, 1987). See also the recent Cambridge edition, which deserves credit for being the first to use the most accurate English translation of the title: *Critique of the Power of Judgment*, edited by Paul Guyer, translated by Paul Guyer and Eric Matthews (Cambridge: Cambridge University Press, 2000). References to the *Critique of Pure Reason* will use the standard "A" and "B" references to the first (1781) and second (1787) editions, translated by Norman Kemp Smith (London: Macmillan, 1929). To keep my textual analysis within a manageable length here, I focus only on KU § 90ff., but it should be kept in mind that the theme of creation is treated in many other places by Kant, perhaps most notably in § 84, which is entitled, "On the Final Purpose of the Existence of a World, i.e., of Creation Itself," and concludes: "the moral principle…alone qualifies man, the subject of morality, to be the final purpose of creation, to which all of nature is subordinated." (KU 5: 436n)

nature still tends to be overlooked or misunderstood. At the end of a book devoted precisely to the topic of teleology, it is only natural to expect a significant confirmation of what Kant's whole system has been primarily aiming at all along. Once one makes one's way through a maze of terminological complications, the final conclusion of Kant's *Critiques* can be understood as confirming what I believe most of us would now call a more objectivist than subjectivist attitude toward the conclusion that persons have been created for a purpose.

There are two striking features of the title of § 90, "On the Kind of Holding to be True Involved in a Teleological Proof of God." First, this title introduces the general attitude of *Fürwahrhalten*, a useful Kantian term for which there is no common English equivalent. Here it is rendered as "holding to be true," or simply "holding true." It has also been translated as "assent" or "affirmation," but these terms mask the crucial reference to "holding" and "truth," and they do not make clear enough that what is involved is not an entirely arbitrary and merely speculative attitude. Second, the title places this task within the general context of what it calls the issue of "teleological proof" rather than immediately in relation to the particular moral argument for the existence of God that is the major topic throughout the final sections of KU.[2] The use of the term "teleological" prepares the reader for the fact that Kant's procedure in this section will involve not directly expounding his own moral argument but instead indirectly moving toward its appreciation by first discussing the argumentative value and basic structure of proofs in general, and especially of proofs of a theoretical teleological kind, which are much more familiar than the innovative species of argument that Kant calls "moral" or "practical." (I will use these terms, and "ethical" also, interchangeably because in this context it is clear that by "practical" Kant means the kind of "pure practical" considerations that he identifies with his notion of what is moral.) This whole last portion of the text thus itself takes on a kind of purposive circular form: after § 90 treats, in a very critical way, the general notion of theoretical arguments for knowledge of a purposive original being, § 91 discusses, in a very positive way, the specific moral-teleological kind of holding true called "practical faith," and then the concluding General Comment explicitly returns to the book's overall concern with teleology by explaining how moral faith alone fully satisfies this concern, and that of theology as well, in a way that is still consistent with the restrictions of Critical philosophy.

---

[2] This feature can be missed when using the Cambridge translation, which follows a later variant reading that puts the term "moral" here in the section title instead of the original "teleological."

I- "The Various Kinds of Holding to be True Involved in a Teleological Proof of God"

The title of § 90 links four topics: (A) holding true, (B) teleology, (C) proof, and (D) God. The mention here of "holding true" is largely a forward reference to the book's concluding emphasis on faith; the other three topics are treated in earlier sections but without an exploration of their relation to this specific attitude. The "various kinds" of "holding true" are not directly explored until § 91; § 90.1 (i.e., the first paragraph of § 90) concentrates instead on the topic of proof in general, and on the distinction between "convincing" or "objective" argument, and "persuasive"[3] or merely "subjective" argument. The latter notion is characterized as "pseudo-proof," *Scheinbeweis*, and the term *Schein* is used explicitly as a reminder of the whole "aesthetic" realm of appearance as such. In a broad sense, this realm concerns both of the book's two main parts, which concern judgments about taste (§§ 1-60) and organisms (§§ 61-78) and turn out to have the mixed result that even though their claims to validity are not ungrounded, they are "merely reflective" and do not result in determinative judgment. This general kind of mixed result, although at a higher level of "holding true," will turn out to characterize even the best kind of argument linking teleology and God, the other two main terms in the section's title. Kant believes a much lower level of argument, however, is exhibited by the most common attempt to link these two terms, namely "natural theology" (KU 5: 461), which is the immediate example that Kant offers of *Scheinbeweis*. This is a reminder that, as critique, KU's entire appendix can be read primarily as an attack on the whole tradition of natural theology insofar as this discipline purports to be both truly about God and able to succeed independently of moral theology.

In § 90.1 Kant picks up on his earlier discussion of physicoteleological and ethicoteleological arguments (§§ 85, 86) by claiming that insofar as the first kind of teleological argument appears to reach God and become truly theological, it relies on "mingling" (KU 5: 462; cf. KU 5: 477) unnoticed with the convincing force of the second kind of argument, and thus it obtains persuasiveness and popularity only due to an illusion that philosophy needs to unmask. Insofar as the physicoteleological argument aims specifically at reaching the conclusion that God exists in what Kant calls the "adequate" sense of a supreme moral being, it turns out to be

[3] The German term here for "persuade" is "*überreden*," and this has a negative connotation that tends to be lost in English, for it suggests that someone has been merely "talked into" something.

merely subjective. In contrast, the ethicoteleological argument for God has a higher standing, and the remainder of the section is devoted to preparing for an appreciation of exactly what this standing can be, given its assumed validity at this point in the text, and the fact that Kant has already indicated that nonetheless it is to be characterized as "subjective" (KU 5: 446, 450, 453, 457) in some respect.

In § 90.2, Kant continues with the task of giving a preliminary clarification of proof in general, and he now distinguishes, within the class of objective arguments, between those that are fully convincing (presumably a priori ones) and those that can "contribute" to convincing (presumably empirical ones). This distinction cuts across another basic distinction that Kant makes here, one between what he calls determinative judging of what an object is *in itself* and reflective judging of what it is like only *for us* (Kant's italics, KU 5: 462), that is, as human beings in general limited in very specific epistemic ways, for example, in not being able to see how the organic unities that constantly appear purposive to us might nonetheless have an ultimately mechanical ground. Presumably, *this* particular "for us/in itself" distinction in judgment types is *not* meant to map directly onto Kant's basic metaphysical phenomenal/noumenal distinction, because Kant does allow determinative judging of phenomena (and even without speaking of what an object is like "in itself"), and yet his transcendental idealism also implies that in a sense *all* our phenomenal judgments are about objects "only for us" (so this restriction does not make them "merely reflective" and has to do solely with their basic dependence on space and time as mere forms of sensibility). Kant does not elaborate this point here, but simply announces that theoretical *reflective* judging "cannot ever" even "tend to convince," whereas *practical* reflective judging can "indeed claim to convince sufficiently from a practical point of view." (KU 5: 463) Clarifying what this last kind of judging means is extremely important because it is the only kind that Kant says can allow us to make proper claims about God. Before directly engaging in that positive task, however, Kant devotes the remainder of § 90 to distinguishing four types of *theoretical* argument and explaining why none of them has a chance to be convincing with respect to the existence of God "in the full sense" (KU 5: 463) that he takes to be relevant, namely, as a moral creator of the world.

The main points in Kant's discussion of the these four types of argument—syllogistic, analogical, probable, and hypothetical—do not break new ground, and the most interesting consideration in this subsection is almost buried in a long footnote. The weakness of syllogistic reasoning is that it is wholly unclear how (without recourse to mystical intuition) it alone can lead us, as is needed here, to know something synthetic about anything transcending the sensory realm that Kant takes to provide the only cognitive basis available for our premises. Similar difficulties infect probabilistic theoretical reasoning. Kant's claim about its limitation is basically the Humean point that the only probabilities we can reason from, that is, "bottom up," are relative to an empirical base, and it is not clear how such a base can show anything even merely probable about something non-empirical such as God. Hypothetical, or "top down" reasoning, is said to be in even more trouble here. Whereas probabilistic reasoning at least has some kind of actual evidence base to argue from (even if it is insufficient), Kant contends that a theoretical hypothesis cannot be properly put forth until it can be understood as a "real possibility" (and it is especially difficult to see how we can do this for something non-sensible) and not merely an idea that does not seem inherently contradictory. This is presented as a surprisingly strict requirement, for Kant says that this kind of possibility cannot be merely a matter of "chimerical" conceivability but "must not be open to any doubt." (KU 5: 466; cf. KU 5: 394) One might well wonder whether his own philosophical notions can satisfy such strictures, for even after the *Critiques* it would seem that a theological fatalist or extremely cautious epistemologist might understandably doubt, for example, that human beings actually have any of the specific kinds of spontaneity that the Critical philosophy invokes. Kant did not generally think of his philosophy in terms of hypotheses in this sense (KrV A xxv; cf. B xxii n., and A 772/ B 800f.), however, and his Critical philosophy appears to begin with various very basic "matters of fact," and to move forward from these by appealing, first, to necessities of transcendental argumentation, and then to a new metaphysical model that supposedly has a unique capacity to make such necessities "intelligible." (KrV B 41)[4] His familiarity with hypotheses in the context of natural science appears to have led him to prefer that the term be used only for notions that involve at least a plausible exhibition of *concrete* structures that can lead to a genuine "explanation" of discernible effects, as, for example, with the hypothesis of invisible corpuscles or forces, and that do not involve what he took to be absurdities such as a *generatio aequivoca* (KU 5: 419), a production of life from "lifeless" matter.[5] It is striking in any case that, when Kant raises his fundamental

---

[4] See Karl Ameriks, *Interpreting Kant's Critiques* (Oxford: Clarendon Press, 2003), Introduction.

[5] See *Understanding Purpose: Kant and the Philosophy of Biology*, edited by Philippe Huneman (Rochester, N.Y.: Rochester University Press, 2007), vol. 8 North American Kant Studies in Philosophy.

objection to natural theology later (KU 5: 470), what he stresses is the gap between any merely theoretical hypothesis and the specific need to identify a genuinely moral (and, therefore, possibly divine) cause, and in that context he takes it that what is most relevant are normative considerations rather than any issue of quasi-mechanical explanatory laws.

I have left to the last what is the most complicated form of theoretical inference that Kant allows and criticizes here, namely analogical reasoning. The weakness that he stresses with mere analogical reasoning is that, although it can allow us to *think* of a being that transcends the sensory realm, it cannot allow *us* to *determine* what this being is like "in itself." (KU 5: 465n) If, for example, we think that the cause of the world operates through understanding (KU 5: 465), we still cannot see exactly what it is that constitutes this transcendent understanding. Such an understanding is fundamentally independent of sensibility, whereas the only understanding that we can in fact comprehend (and that licenses the original analogical consideration), namely our own, is always fundamentally connected with sensibility.

This criticism introduces a complicated metaphysical problem that reoccurs often in this text. Several times Kant criticizes a way of arguing insofar as it aims to determine what something is like "in itself," and then he characterizes it as "restricted" insofar as it cannot succeed in this determination. One might at first suppose that this restriction simply expresses Kant's phenomenal/noumenal distinction, but, for reasons suggested above, such a relatively simple supposition cannot be made here. One could still consider, for example, that there might be some kind of very significant judgments about something that is in some sense *noumenal* even though these judgments do *not* go so far as directly to provide "insight" into its nature "in itself" in contrast to its relational features. Human freedom for example, or the mere causal power of God, seem to be very substantive notions, but they are not themselves being treated as "in itself" features, and yet, on Kant's view, they clearly also cannot be treated as phenomenal. So, although at first one might understandably suppose that Kant's line between the phenomenal (and empirical) and the noumenal corresponds precisely to the line between the relational and the intrinsic,[6] it certainly seems that some central *relational* Kantian features, precisely as they are discussed in this text, such as our freedom, or non-empirical causality in general (whether or not these

---

[6] See Ameriks, *Interpreting Kant's Critiques*, ch. 5; and cf. Rae Langton, *Kantian Humility: Our Ignorance of Things in Themselves* (Oxford: Clarendon Press, 1998).

features can be theoretically proved to exist), cannot be characterized in mere empirical terms--and so the presumed correspondence fails.

An additional complication that arises here is that, even when Kant himself repeatedly characterizes the feature of human freedom as attaching to us as "supersensible" and "noumenal," (KU 5: 435) he at the same time says it concerns what happens "*in this world*," and thus, in that broad sense, within the realm of "nature."[7] Here again another tempting and relatively simple way of thinking of basic Kantian distinctions must give way. Although at first it might seem that the phenomenal/noumenal distinction corresponds precisely to the "worldly"/transcendent distinction, this is also not in every sense correct. For Kant the notion of the "world" or cosmos is explicitly defined in terms of the largest sphere of *mutually* interacting things,[8] and hence, no matter how much a transcendent entity such as God may act upon our world, that entity's independence from being acted upon by other entities keeps it from being literally part of the world. Similarly, although Kant strongly encourages us to think (i.e., keep on thinking) about ourselves in specific ways that cannot be a matter of mere empirical and sensory (space/time) properties, he also holds that when we do think of ourselves even in this way, these thoughts clearly must apply to us as beings who do not *altogether* transcend "the world." This is because, unlike what can be true about God, nothing about us can be literally "beyond the world" altogether, although in a *loose* sense one might (and Kant often does) speak of anything that involves our possible non-sensory side (such as absolute freedom, or an intelligence or "immortality" that goes beyond any "now" accessible experience) as taking us into "another," "intelligible" world. That is, it takes us beyond *merely* sensory features to another, very different set of "higher" features, but these features remain nonetheless within the whole realm that God can transcend and create.

All this introduces at least four (or five) levels of possible metaphysical complexity: first, the merely empirical and sensory features of empirical beings; second, the non-sensory features—some relational, such as freedom, and some presumably non-relational—of empirical beings (notably us); third, the non-empirical but (external) relational

---

[7] On Kant's implicit "twofold concept of nature" here, see KrV A 811/B 839, and KpV 5: 124; and see the helpful analysis by Friedo Ricken, "Die Postulate der reinen praktischen Vernunft (122-128)," in *Kritik der praktischen Vernunft*, edited by Otfried Höffe (Berlin: Akademie Verlag, 2002), pp. 193-7.

[8] See e.g., Metaphysik Herder 28:39, in *Lectures on Metaphysics/ Immanuel Kant*, edited and translated by Karl Ameriks and Steve Naragon (Cambridge: Cambridge University Press, 1997).

features of whatever is beyond being part of the sensible domain (e. g., God's understanding or will directed to the world, or perhaps—to add a fifth level—non-empirical affection by other beings); and fourth, the intrinsic or "in itself" features of transcendent being. Note that only knowledge of the first level is clearly phenomenal, whereas thought or knowledge about *all* the other levels, and not only the last and highest one, would amount to something that Kant himself calls noumenal.

This implies that if Kant were to say that our reflective judging is fundamentally restricted *simply* insofar as it can say nothing about the highest level, then this still would not clearly mean that its claims are not highly significant in some metaphysical sense. This point is closely related to the issue of how much is really lost when Kant says, for example, that the claims of the moral argument hold "merely subjectively"; if this restriction is simply relative to not providing theoretical determination of the highest level, then this still leaves a lot to say that is not otherwise restricted. These distinctions imply that we should not be surprised to find that crucial Kantian notions, such as "final purpose" and "highest good," can involve a complex mixing of levels. No wonder, then, that there have been discussions[9] about whether Kant thinks of these notions as applying to "this" *or* rather "another" world; properly understood (given the preceding distinctions), *both* answers can be correct, and even the first in a noumenal sense. Insofar as the highest good must involve human freedom, it is already in part beyond the whole sensible world (and as involving a "world to come," it is even further beyond what we can know at any time), and yet it is still part, a noumenal part, of the entire world "below" God. The highest good is thus in a sense both beyond and within the world: it is, we presume, beyond what the natural world can disclose or arrange of itself as such, and yet if the highest good is actualized it will be actualized entirely within the states of beings who are mundane and not transcendent.

Another complication arises from the fact that in his criticisms here Kant focuses specifically on the notion of the understanding. In a sense, this focus is only to be expected, because it is precisely this faculty that Kant connects with what he sees as the most promising, but still futile, characterizations available to theoretical teleology, namely, those restricted to the notion of a mere architectonic organizer of the world. If

---

[9] See Fricken, "Die Postulate," pp. 187-202; Eckart Förster, "Die Dialektik der reinen praktischen Vernunft (107-121)," in *Kritik der praktischen Vernunft*, edited by Otfried Höffe (Berlin: Akademie Verlag, 2002), pp. 173-86; and Frederick Beiser, "Moral Faith and the Highest Good," in *The Cambridge Companion to Kant and Modern Philosophy*, edited by Paul Guyer (Cambridge: Cambridge University Press, 2006), pp. 588-629.

one were instead to focus on the faculty of reason, however, one might hope to find (as e.g., Hegel would contend) much more abundant material for a positive analogical argument about God. In fact, Kant eventually explores precisely this option but only through an emphasis on practical reason. He leaves no room for theoretical reason to suffice on its own here, presumably because he takes his criticism of syllogistic (which he develops more elsewhere, KrV A 300/B 357) and hypothetical inference to dispose of whatever might be claimed possible for theoretical reason as such in its attempt to be a substantive theology.

A last related complication, one that reveals the admirable subtlety of Kant's reasoning, concerns a long footnote that he adds to his discussion of analogy. This note points out that even though animals such as beavers construct complex products that in many ways resemble our artifacts, this does not prove that their efforts are due specifically to reason as opposed to instinct (KU 5: 464n). Instead, we can say that since they, like us, certainly seem to belong to the genus of living beings, their constructions can and should be considered to be due to mere instinct, for we do not have an adequate ground to suppose that they are due to the faculty of reason that appears to be what distinguishes (because of significant difference in other effects) our species from their own. Similarly, Kant stresses that even if we posit a superior being as a cause of the world as a whole, and of an effect that reflectively must appear to us to be an artifact (a product of rational intentions), we still cannot say that its productive activity definitely involves the same kind of higher faculty as our own, because our understanding is sensible, and that of the superior being is precisely not thought to be sensible.

Kant's note breaks off at this point, but there two significant further options worth noting. First, for all we know theoretically, even a transcendent superior being might operate through a power that is actually more like instinctive and mechanical necessity than purposive intelligence (KU 5: 441-2). Hence, our picture of it as purposive is a merely subjective and reflective judging on our part; although we could never explain exactly how it could accomplish its effects through such crude means, we cannot say that we can determine that this is not happening.

There is also another option, and a theologically more encouraging one, that Kant does not immediately consider. All he says here is that the idea of a world cause by itself has "no generic concept in common" with the kind of causing we are familiar with except "that of a thing as such." (KU 5: 464n) This seems too restrictive, for once again one might contend, and precisely on Kantian grounds, that we are, through our own intelligence, familiar with operations of *reason* as well as mere understanding, and so there might be some appropriate way for us to think of a superior being as not merely causing the world but as doing so through a faculty of reason that in an important sense could be the same as our own –precisely because we know our own reason, as opposed to mere understanding, as a faculty that is not immediately characterized in terms of a relation to sensibility. Nonetheless, if one is allowed simply to accept as given the entire argument of the *Critique of Pure Reason*, then it would follow that even our pure theoretical reason as such still has fundamental restrictions (it is not an intuitive intellect and must always use discursive understanding) and has by itself no determining power. What this implies, of course, is not that we should give up exploring analogies between our reason and a superior source of the world, but simply that we should move on, as Kant himself does, to consider what this implies for the potential of the other form of our reason, namely pure practical reason and its implications.

II- "On the Kind of Holding to be True from Practical Faith"

The main argument of § 91 has a three-part structure that largely mirrors, in a positive inversion, the structure of the preceding section's critique of theoretical approaches. The first paragraph reasserts the section's general focus on distinguishing diverse cognitive attitudes, and the second paragraph in effect lists, in what turns out to be a new order of importance, the specific options of opinion, knowledge (*Wissen*), and faith (*Glaube*). After devoting a paragraph to explaining each of these attitudes, Kant's discussion highlights the conclusion that faith, rooted simply in the moral-teleological argument, constitutes the most satisfying kind of holding to be true, for it alone provides a rational confirmation of the ideas of the highest good, immortality, and God as conditions essential to fulfilling our required commitment to morality and freedom. In a final set of paragraphs, separated by a dividing line, Kant then repeats his standard diagnosis of why all theoretical attempts to justify each of these supersensible ideas have had to fail.

Kant starts the section with a typical distinction between the metaphysical issue of directly investigating "the possibilities of things themselves" (KU 5: 467) and the methodological or epistemological issue of simply comparing different kinds of "cognizable things" (KU 5: 467): matters of mere opinion (*opinabilia*), matters of fact (*scibilia*), and matters of faith alone (*mere credibilia*). This order is a significant shift from Kant's discussions in the *Critique of Pure Reason* (KrV A 822/B 850) and the *Logic* (VL 9: 65),[10] where the context is primarily theoretical ("logical perfection" of cognition in regard to "modality") and *Glaube* is listed at first as preceding knowledge, as if it were simply inferior to it.[11] In these discussions, "opinion" designates a holding true that is merely theoretical, with grounds that are subjectively as well as objectively insufficient; *Glaube* is treated at first simply as a practical attitude with grounds that are said to be subjectively sufficient but objectively insufficient; and "knowing" is understood in a rigorous sense that requires grounds that are both subjectively and objectively sufficient and is illustrated solely by theoretical reason.

An awkward feature of the taxonomies in the first *Critique* and the *Logic* is that they do not clear out an explicit place for a very important fourth kind of holding true: the basic practical cognition of the moral law and its *immediate* implications. This kind of cognition is too immediate to fall under the heading of what Kant calls faith. The *Logic* (VL 9: 69-70) recognizes that this level of "practical cognition in morality" is too certain to be called "mere belief," but it is still not explicitly placed under the heading of knowledge ("practical conviction" is discussed briefly at VL 9: 72, but it is said to be "entirely certain" and "often firmer than any knowing"—which implies a sharp contrast). In the *Critique of Pure Reason* Kant may have skipped over this kind of cognition because, being so preoccupied there with drawing attention to morality in terms of its ends so that he could highlight the ultimate positive conclusion of his whole system, he left the more basic doctrine of the moral law to be exposited in the *Critique of Practical Reason*. Unfortunately, by not insisting on placing basic practical cognition clearly within the general sphere of knowledge, perhaps because it obviously cannot fall under heading of the theoretical knowing (*Wissen*, and not merely "cognition," *Erkenntnis*), Kant encouraged the tendency to treat even our most fundamental practical kind of holding true as only "subjective"—even though in his system it actually has a firmness and universal scope (because it applies in principle to all rational beings, and not only agents in

[10] See also "What Does it Mean to Orient Oneself in Thought?" 8:140; *Religion within the Boundaries of Mere Reason*, 6: 153; and "On the Dignified Tone Recently Adopted in Philosophy," 8: 395. "*Logic*" refers to the "Jäsche Logic" (VL 9: 1-150), the only version of Kant's lectures on the topic that were published in his lifetime (1800); in *Lectures on Logic/ Immanuel Kant*, edited and translated by J. Michael Young (Cambridge: Cambridge University Press, 1992).

[11] No wonder that the issue of the proper ordering of the attitudes of *Glauben* and *Wissen* is a major point of dispute in the post-Kantian era, especially for Jacobi, Fichte, Hegel, and Kierkegaard.

the natural world) that arguably makes it even more, rather than less, objective than theoretical knowing.

III- "Cognizable Matters" Reconsidered

Of the three kinds of "cognizable matters" discussed in § 91, Kant's treatment of "opinion" has the least news to offer. It resembles the earlier discussion of probability and hypothesis in § 90: opinion is appropriate only for empirical matters for which there can be some prior sensory basis or in principle later confirmation (KU 5: 467), but which are not yet proved. The major portion of the discussion concerns items that are excluded from this sphere, such as "ideas of reason." These ideas by definition go beyond the reach of possible experience and thus are not at all even in the field of what Kant calls opinion--although he surely must have understood that, in a casual ordinary language sense, people constantly say that they have "opinions" on such matters. Even though they cannot count as "matters of opinion," Kant thinks it important to note already here that, whereas some "mere" ideas (KU 5: 468) are directly absurd (e.g., a "spiritual body," which is supposed to be something beyond the sensible while also somehow having sensible features), others are such that, although they could never have any theoretical warrant, they could have an "objective reality" given by practical reason. Thus, even without having been named as such, the notion of the priority of faith has entered the discussion.

Under the heading of "matters of fact," Kant lists matters that can be exhibited by theoretical intuition, either empirical or pure (e.g., geometrical features), but then he adds what he himself calls the "remarkable" claim—not expressed in parallel sections of the *Critique of Pure Reason* or the *Logic* (but see KpV 5: 93) —that the "objective reality" of human freedom, in its absolute and theoretical meaning (as uncaused causing in general) as a "rational idea," "can be established through practical laws, and (if we act in conformity with these) in actual acts, and hence in experience." (KU 5: 468) Although he does not mention it, this is obviously a reference to the new doctrine of the "fact of reason" presented in the *Critique of Practical Reason* (KpV 5: 42). Kant's strong positive claim here might at first seem to be a clearly dogmatic violation of his general Critical restriction that through "experience" (in either its empirical or pure aspects) we cannot determine the truth of any nonsensory and unconditioned matters, and hence cannot prove, or even make probable, our absolute freedom. What can keep Kant's strong claim in § 91 at least consistent with his Critical system is the fact that he makes clear that he is basing it only on practical reason, and the earlier restriction on cognizing the supersensible should therefore be understood as concerning "experience" simply in a theoretical sense. Although at § 91 Kant certainly had the opportunity to say something stronger if he wanted to, it is striking that KU, just like the second *Critique*, is consistent enough not even to suggest in any way that we might have access to the actuality of our absolute freedom through any purely theoretical base.[12]

In addition, Kant understands that even these most basic claims of practical reason, the moral law and freedom, do not provide a ground that is meant to defeat a radical skeptic (KU 5: 450n; cf. "the most stubborn skepticism," KrV A 829/B 857). They simply expresses the point that *if* one "accepts" morality in the fundamental Kantian sense, which involves the categorical imperative, then (especially since the first *Critique* supposedly shows that there is no known theoretical impossibility in the absolute freedom that this imperative demands) it follows that one "in fact" can and should hold that one is free, and can take one's "actual acts" to exhibit that freedom. The presumed fundamental truth underlying this fact does not require, however, that one actually act morally (i.e., for duty), or even ever intend to accept morality's priority, for Kant holds that, while all human agents can see that there is the moral demand, and thus implicitly that they are free to respond to it, most of them choose not to affirm it (KrV A 830/B 858n, "morality… is not practically preponderant"). In this way, the idea of the moral law, with its implication of the fact of freedom, does not require a special pro-moral attitude and can still be claimed to be a unique concrete metaphysical truth that is universally accessible. It takes the form of what even Kant's *Logic* calls a "certain cognition," (VL 9: 68n) and so it should not be surprising if it is listed in KU as a "matter of fact" rather than faith. But although Kant uses terms such as "*scibilia*", "proved," and "established," he strikingly does not use *Wissen* or list "knowing" explicitly, despite what would be expected as a heading for his discussion here.

Kant should also not be misunderstood to be saying that our freedom itself is something literally given, in the sense of any kind of direct vision of uncaused causing as such, even in basic moral experience. What is given is the moral law and the sense of its demanding "presence," and then, within and solely on the basis of at least some appreciation of that law, one can realize that one must be (supposedly) taking oneself thereby to be free—"immediately," that is, in this very consciousness and its

[12] See Karl Ameriks, *Kant's Theory of Mind* (Oxford: Clarendon Press, 1982; 2nd ed. 2000), ch. 6.

supposed results, and yet "noumenally," that is, in a way that can never be warranted by sensory evidence. (This is how I read KU 5: 474, "freedom is a supersensible concept…that proves in nature that it has objective reality.") The proper assertion of an absolute "can" thus follows only upon the recognition, however dim, of an "ought. "

It is significant that, despite all these qualifications, Kant still does bring the actuality of our freedom (and its *ratio cognoscendi*) here under the heading of "fact" rather than "opinion" or "faith." And, as a "fact," it would seem to involve an objective grounding, a grounding that according to Kant's *Logic* is found only in knowledge in contrast to faith. But § 91 does not explicitly go so far, and although the *Logic* grants that there is certain moral "cognition," it, like the first *Critique*, moves on very quickly to discussing the different topic of rational moral "faith" (*des moralischen Vernunftglaubens*) in the postulates, which it describes as a holding true that is subjectively rather than objectively grounded, even though here the subjective grounds are "equivalent to objective grounds" (albeit in a way that is "not logical but practical" VL 9: 72). As in other parts of Kant's philosophy, this contrast between the subjective and the objective has several overlapping layers of meaning and can easily be misunderstood.

It should not be forgotten that even the paradigmatic judgments of Kant's theoretical philosophy are themselves sometimes called "subjective" rather than "objective," simply in the sense that they have to do with matters of experience that are transcendentally ideal. Moreover, even though Kant at times stresses the special first person character of faith, and can seem to be ascribing this character to moral cognition as such, because of the essential involvement of the subject's free commitment ("only I myself can be certain of the validity and unalterability of my practical belief," VL 9: 70; cf. KrV A 829/B 857, "I must not even say 'it is morally certain' but 'I am morally certain…'"), it remains true that he is strongly committed to the notion that all rational agents as such necessarily can share an appreciation of the moral law, and even of the truths of faith, and therefore these matters are by no means subjective in a merely individual or purely optional sense. In the *Critique of Pure Reason* Kant also suggests that there is a subjective character in faith that has to do with the fact that there is something about practical knowledge that "cannot be communicated" because it involves what he calls "moral sentiment." (KrV A 829/B 857) And yet, by the time of the *Critique of Practical Reason* at the latest, Kant makes clear that however private the sentiment and free decisions of the moral agent may be, the genuine cognition of the law of morality is their fundamental ground, and this is not merely a "natural interest" (cf. KrV A 830/B 858n) but a truth whose universal validity can extend even beyond the sphere of all natural beings. Hence, it can be argued that Kant should have gone so far as explicitly to call at least the most basic cognitions of practical reason (the moral law and our freedom) nothing less than "objective" forms of holding true, and perhaps even "knowledge" in the strictest sense. Instead, he seems originally to have allowed the special complexity and apparent subjectivity of the *non-immediate* practical cognitions of the "two articles of faith," "God and a future life," (KrV A 829/B 857f) to obscure the objective status of morality as such. Once this questionable terminological tendency is exposed, it may be possible to argue further that not only our most basic practical cognitions, but even the non-immediate ones can be understood as much more objective and "knowledge-like" than Kant's language often suggests.

Kant is definitely very aware of a difference between the basic and the non-immediate levels of practical reason, because § 91 clearly limits the "matter of fact" status to the idea of freedom as such and does not extend it to the postulates of God and immortality, which are placed in the realm of faith. This at first can seem odd because he also calls freedom a postulate (KU 5: 238), which might suggest that they are all on a level. But not all postulates are alike: "A postulate is a practical, immediately certain proposition, or [NB] a principle that determines a possible action." (*Logic*, VL 9:112; cf. KpV 5: 22n.) The "or" marks a significant difference. Because our freedom is so "immediately" tied to the moral law all by itself, it is, Kant realizes, on a very different level than the indirectly inferred notions of God and immortality, which have to do with reflective conditions of our realizing the ends of morality in action, and not simply intending to accept the law. One might even argue that these two notions, together with that of the highest good rather than freedom, are really the three prime "postulates of pure practical reason," since they are designated the only matters of faith, and as such they alone call for *special philosophical* support. It may be largely an architectonic accident, having to do with Kant's interest in having postulates for three ideas of reason that match the traditional disciplines of rational psychology, cosmology, and theology, that led him often to list the trio immortality/freedom/God, rather than the much more closely related trio highest good/immortality/God.

The main distinction between freedom and the other ideas is that Kant supposes that the experience of freedom, and it alone, can be understood as fundamentally occurring entirely *with oneself*, for all it requires is having an intention as a moral agent at all: "This formal character of my acts [in intending to follow the moral law], in which alone their intrinsic moral value consists, is wholly in my power," (KU 5: 471n) but the "attainment of the final purpose [the highest good] it enjoins on us is not wholly in our power…so that our attainment of that final purpose is not practically necessary as [i.e., in the same way] duty itself is" (KU 5: 470; cf. the distinction at VL 9: 68n and 16: 513 between an action itself, in the sense of an intention, and our "extending" ourselves to the "possession" of the end).

This distinction has enormous significance for Kantian morality in general. Although Kant holds that human action inevitably involves an end in the sense of a distinct product that goes beyond the act of intention itself, he also assumes that we can never have full control of such products and their effects on us. Thus, even though we are, as rational, always looking for consequences that would make us happy, no such consequence by itself can have a direct and necessary connection to our willing, or, therefore, a necessary value. The fundamental metaphysical distinction between intention and product is thus what leads Kant to dismiss any claim that happiness has an unconditional value.[13] Since in fact we can never know if and how we will obtain it, seeking it in any particular way makes us a hostage of contingent fortune—whereas a good intention has an unconditional value because it is something that we know we can always immediately bring into being without concern for reward. The distinction between intention and product also leads Kant to argue that, since, as finite agents, we inevitably and properly are interested in the products of our efforts, we need to seek whatever could nonetheless indirectly guarantee that our actions somehow do get the necessarily right consequences, and lead to happiness proportionate to proper intentions.

This need to arrange a possible "guarantee" is precisely what defines Kant's third and highest type of holding true, moral faith. Faith involves a multistage development, first, from the cognition of the basic moral law to the acceptance of the highest good as a necessary ideal, then to the recognition of and commitment to the necessary conditions of its possible realization (which, aside from the freedom that is in our own control, involve the postulates of God and immortality), and, finally, to the approximating and steadfast realization of the highest good itself, which becomes more and more an actuality and not a mere ideal. Because the relation between all three matters of faith and our original moral intentions is metaphysically external rather than internal, our confidence in their existence or realization has to be highly qualified, and hence it involves

---

[13] See Rae Langton, "Objective and Unconditioned Value," *The Philosophical Review* 116 (2007), 157-185.

grounds that are not merely, like the grounds of our assertion of freedom, in some general sense "subjective," simply because practical and free at all, but can now be said to be subjective in an *extra* and reflective sense simply because they involve a non-immediate and "risky" relation, a relation about which we must always lack determinative certainty.

This riskiness is, I believe, the main reason why faith can understandably remain short of being what Kant *calls* a matter of knowledge, even it is also distinguished by being more than opinion and having grounds binding on all human agents. In the *Logic*, Kant says that belief in general goes beyond mere opinion because of its "relation to action": "Thus, for example, the merchant, in order to make a deal, not only needs to have the opinion that something is to be gained thereby, but also needs to believe it (i.e., that his opinion is sufficient for an undertaking freighted with uncertainty)." (VL 9: 68n, 16: 513)[14] By "belief" in this very general sense, Kant obviously means a practical *rational* attitude that is not a mere matter of individual subjectivity but has a basis in appreciating external factors relevant to one's "undertaking." Because of such "external factors," there is an inescapable riskiness in all kinds of belief, and not only the moral faith that is Kant's focus in § 91. In the first *Critique*, unlike KU, Kant devoted space to also discussing "pragmatic" and "doctrinal" belief (KrV A 824-6/B 852-4). The former kind of belief resembles the merchant example; the latter is Kant's term for the attitude accompanying the physicoteleological argument, which he classifies as a form of theoretical rather than practical reason. What these two kinds of holding true have in common is that they involve taking risks with respect to causal connections in a way that goes beyond ordinary scientific reasoning and is closely bound to our concerns with action, although in very different ways: in the first case with a "payoff" that has immediate practical interest for us, in the second case with finding a perspective that would allow us to understand the whole natural world around us as itself literally a scene of action, as the artifact of an intentional cause, and not merely a blind mechanism.

It is admittedly tempting to consider Kant's notion of moral faith, and its relation to action, as sharing some of the worst characteristics of these two contexts: the crude instrumentality of the better, and illegitimate projection of the theoretical teleologist. Moreover, when one reads that faith is rational but "merely an assumption…to make in a practical respect," (KU 5: 470) it can seem as if faith does not imply literally taking

[14] Cf. Leslie Stevenson, "Opinion, Belief or Faith, and Knowledge," *Kantian Review* 7 (2003), p. 92; and Andrew Chignell, "Belief in Kant," *The Philosophical Review* 116 (2007), p. 345.

it to be true that its objects are actual but is just a convenient fiction that one plays with, simply to move on more smoothly, like the thought that others are not really knaves. These reactions are understandable but, I believe, unnecessarily dismissive, for Kant can also be read as meaning something fairly realistic and defensible in saying that faith is an attitude which is valid "only" "in a practical respect." We could again take his main point here to be that faith in general has at its topic external action (KU 5: 447: "moral teleology [unlike geometry] does deal with us as beings in the world and hence as connected with other things in the world"), that is, a real separation of inner intentions and particular natural effects. It can therefore never have the kind of internality and hence demonstrative certainty that Kant reserves for knowing in the strict sense, whether it be of theoretical or moral reason's own basic laws. On this reading, faith is still understood as a taking to be true of what actually is; it just happens to be a taking that must face the special risks of going beyond whatever is simply within our own mind. This is compatible with its involving various types of rationality and necessity, even if it must go beyond the certainties of determinative judgment.

The several different kinds of necessity (listed below as [A]-[F]) involved in faith and its preconditions need to be distinguished. The understanding of the original mere idea of the highest good, that is, [A] seeing its *necessity as part* of practical reason's defining *ideal*, does not itself already require faith but can be called a direct "practical cognition" (KU 5: 470) that is a precondition for faith. The highest good in this sense turns out, however, to be not merely one ideal among others but something whose *pursuit* is in fact [B] *practically necessary* in a pure, and not merely prudential or hypothetical sense. It supplies the only goal for us as moral agents that is indispensable and of unqualified value, and so its pursuit is fundamentally free but normatively "non-optional." Kant calls this goal the only "unconditional" "need" that we have, and hence it reveals the "primacy of the practical"[15] in contrast to all the ultimately optional projects of accumulating theoretical information, or even of trying to infer that the theoretical complexity of the natural world requires an even more complex external and intentional cause. This doctrine of primacy does not mean that claims of practical reason are primary in every way, however, for like any other claims that can responsibly be held to be true, they too must respect the general theoretical, that is, metaphysical and epistemological, constraint of meeting conditions of real possibility. Hence

[15] Cf. Sebastian Gardner, "The Primacy of Practical Reason," in *A Companion to Kant*, edited by Graham Bird (Malden/ Oxford: Blackwell, 2006), pp. 259-74.

the knowledge obtained in more basic forms of holding to be true, for example, the truths of science and their transcendentally ideal explanation, also turns out to be a necessary precondition of faith.

While it is practically necessary, no matter what they are doing, that rational agents have an interest in some externally realized end of their actions, the only particular normatively necessary goal among these ends is defined by the highest good. Hence it is a "commanded effect," (KU 5: 469) and [C], as such a *necessary effect,* its final state, as opposed to its mere original pursuit, also calls for faith: "this commanded effect, together with [D] *the sole conditions* conceivable by us under which that effect is possible [namely belief in God and immortality] are the only objects whatsoever that can be called matters of faith." (KU 5: 469) The "sole conditions conceivable by us" phrase is a significant restriction and signals that these matters of faith, unlike the acceptance of the bare moral law and its ideal goal, are "only reflectively" necessary (KU 5: 455). We are led to postulate them within the context of facing the imponderables of real action, and with the full realization that we cannot make the determining judgment that there is no other way in which the intended results could arise. In this respect, the postulates carry the same basic risk as any hypotheses (cf. KU 5: 450-51); there might be some other key factors than what we understand as the "sole condition," but these factors are simply not on the horizon of our reflective judgment. In the moral case, however, our reflective judgment is brought into action inevitably rather than optionally, so if in fact no other way of rationally proceeding is in view for us, we must endorse the postulates. In the *Logic* Kant says, "in order to advance, we must first reflect, that is, see to what power a cognition belongs." (VL 9: 73) In this context, reflection can reveal that although there are no theoretical ways of "knowing" how the necessarily "commanded effect" of the highest good is really possible, it is open to us to have faith and, in effect, to use our metaphysical imagination, within the bounds of conceptual possibilities that the rational idea of theoretical reason in general has opened up, to assume what is needed in order not to have to give up reason's own practical demands in our actions.

Kant's whole argument for the postulates clearly presumes some very substantive but largely implicit empirical premises, for example, that the world tomorrow will not all on its own, either in the ordinary course of events or through some bizarre cosmic realignment or worldwide revolution, suddenly "fall into place," with agents and nature cooperating perfectly so that proper moral intentions and just rewards are brought about everywhere (KU 5: 471n indicates that any such expectation is "baseless and idle"). Hence Kant is presuming not only the basic necessities implied by the bare practical "fact of reason," that is, the core experience of the presence of the moral law, but also [E] *additional reflective necessities* implied by the common "experience" that the world open to our sensible cognitive powers is not, on its own, anything even approximating a scene of self-rewarding morality. He is presuming that his reflection has not, and will not, come to disclose any unappreciated "powers of cognition" that might reveal how we could relate to the idea of the highest good independently of faith (for example, by somehow learning that the idea comes simply from evolutionary or ideological pressures). It is in this situation then, that we are "forced" to go along with what seems to be the only imaginably viable, and therefore necessary, way to save the coherence of our reason as a whole, by postulating the theoretical fact of the existence of non-natural entities that will make the ends that our practical reason demands not illusory after all.

When Kant calls faith the "mind's steadfast principle to hold as true what we must necessarily presuppose [for the actualization of the highest good] (KU 5: 471), and adds that "without faith the moral way of thinking lacks firm steadfastness," (KU 5:472; cf. KU 5: 446, 452) he is also clearly making it a form of "holding true" in the most fundamental sense. It must literally involve a "holding," or (F) *necessary persistence*, and not a mere casual saying or guessing, because it has to do with finding a way constantly to maintain a project of continuing to act toward a certain goal in the face of no positive theoretical evidence at all of reaching it. And it has to do so with a literal commitment to truth, because, according to one's own reflective judgment nothing short of the actuality of the entities that are posited can imaginably result in the goal that is commanded.

Kant realizes that his notion of faith is original and stipulative, and it is in no way equivalent to what one might call the "historical" notion of "faith" expressed in trust in the veracity of testimony and biblical accounts of extraordinary events (KU 5: 469; cf. VL 9:73n). Kant's kind of faith goes beyond empirical evidence altogether, whereas he takes it that the claims of traditional faith concern facts within the sensible world and need in principle to be measured by empirical evidence, and thus involve what are merely theoretical and contingent claims, rather than practical and necessary ones. In the end, however, Kant's faith endorses the core audacious claim of his religious tradition: that we should think, and take it to be necessarily rational to continue to hold, that all natural existence is due to a creator who satisfies the "determinate concept…of a moral author of the world," and who has as his final purpose nothing less than the very same final purpose that we are also the essential co-operating co-producers of, namely, the highest good of the world. All this is conceivable because practical reason turns out after all to provide a common determinate law, a formula of reason, for ourselves and this moral author (KU 5: 474). The analogical reasoning that was totally unsuccessful in theoretical teleology turns out to be central to the success of moral theology, and Kant's whole system ends in nothing less than a vindication of this theology's basically rationalist conclusions.

IV- Final Comment on Teleology

At the start of his concluding Comment, Kant rehearses his standard objections to the ontological and cosmological arguments, and then stresses again that the physicoteleological argument, no matter how generously it is interpreted, cannot begin to prove a being with powers that are determinate enough to validate the notion of God as a supreme being (KU 5: 477). No amount of intricate fine arrangements in nature proves the presence of an all-powerful or perfect being (KU 5: 480). Kant also stresses that this kind of argument cannot explain why nature exists in the first place; it can only point to an understanding that may have arranged the shape that nature takes on, as an extraordinarily complex organic whole. This point is supposed to contrast with the richer conclusions of moral faith, but one might well ask whether one has to conceive of a moral "author," as Kant repeatedly does here, as a literal creator of nature's existence and not merely a "wise architect" of it with respect to a proper moral as well as natural complexity.[16] And one could also argue that a moral designer, just like a mere architect of natural complexity, need not be literally all-powerful, -good, and -wise. A lesser being, or group of beings, that is still adequate to bring about a highest good situation, even in the context of an enormous amount of given and not created material, could be all that the moral argument needs (whether or not this validates a supreme being in what Kant would recognize as a "full sense").

In addition to repeating some earlier critical themes, Kant reinforces the overriding positive importance of his relatively brief excursion into the exposition of faith. Although most of KU is devoted to the phenomenon of natural teleology, which he grants has the merit of "leading" us to the moral argument by drawing our attention to the striking apparent purposiveness of organic forms (KU 5: 478), in fact the phenomenon of these forms is not crucial. Even with a world that was judged to be merely

---

[16] See Robert M. Adams, "Moral Arguments for Theistic Belief," in *Rationality and Religious Belief*, edited by C. F. Delaney (Notre Dame: University of Notre Dame Press, 1979), pp. 116-40.

mechanically arranged and did not impress us aesthetically, one could still make the moral argument (KU 5: 479), and so it is no mere "supplement" for physicotheology but a self-sufficient substitute. Kant also goes so far as to push his moral argument closer to traditional theology than mere physicotheology by claiming that his moral faith involves religion "as the recognition of our duties as divine commands." (KU 5: 481) This is a theme he takes up further in later work.[17] Here he seems to be concerned primarily with making clear that he is still saying that God is not to be pictured as an arbitrary creator of moral values. On the contrary, precisely because our knowledge of God is mediated by our prior knowledge of morality, we can say that the commands of God will have to turn out be in agreement with the normative standards that we already know from a pre-theological "recognition of our duties."

Finally, after having devoted most of his extensive Comment to a repetition of themes quite familiar from earlier sections of KU, Kant suddenly shifts, in the penultimate paragraph of the book, to facing a serious "alleged contradiction" between the claims of his moral theology and "what the critique of speculative reason said about the categories" (KU 5: 482). The final three-page paragraph then tries to put to rest the "misgivings" that Kant anticipates from those who note that he does insist on "using the categories for a cognition of God." (KU 5: 482) The solution is to say that this use does not violate the bounds set to our knowledge by the *Critique* because the use is "solely from a practical and not a theoretical view." (KU 5: 482) The final challenge in understanding Kant's system is to find a reading of this feature of his moral theology that would neither turn it back into an objectionable dogmatism nor emasculate it of any of the "objective" and "truth" claiming force that, on our earlier analysis, it appears to allow. (Kant’s own discussion of the moral argument seems to shift in different works, but to simplify matters I will focus on KU on its own.)

There are two directly opposing ways to try to read Kant's "solely from a practical view" phrase, one quite objective, the other quite subjective. On the strong objective reading, all that is required is a distinction between premises and their epistemic strength, and conclusions and their ontological meaning. To say that something is "practical" in this sense is simply to say that part of its justification has to do with considerations that are not entirely theoretical and certain. This would in no way undermine the claim that the conclusions can themselves still stand as meant as

[17] See John E. Hare, *God's Call: Moral Realism, Divine Commands, and Human Autonomy* (Grand Rapids, MI: Eerdmanns, 2001).

literally true (Kant does call the postulates "theoretical propositions," KpV 5: 122); it would just mean that they are based in part on normative and reflective rather than merely descriptive and determinative judgments. In contrast, a strong subjective reading would say that the postulates are not claimed to be literally objective; they are simply formulae that are invoked for the mere psychological effect of making an agent's practical commitment less likely to weaken.[18]

It is impossible to accept both of these strong readings at once, but each of them evidently has some backing. Subjectivist interpreters would no doubt be struck by Kant's statement that "I am in no way entitled to flatter myself that I can attribute an understanding to this being [the God posited in the moral argument] and cognize this being through a property" (KU 5: 484; cf. KU 5: 457, "our aim is not to determine that being's nature that is inaccessible to us, but to determine ourselves and our will"). Objectivist interpreters would stress Kant's going on to say, "from a different point of view [practical], I certainly can, indeed must use the analogy with an understanding to think even a supersensible being yet without trying to cognize it through this theoretically…for then we can have, through properties and attributes of God's causality that we think in him merely by analogy, a cognition of God and his existence (a theology) that has all the reality required from a practical point of view" (KU 5: 485). What is taken away with one hand almost seems to be given back by the other. That is, the objectivist might say, Kant is simply warning us that the attribution is not claimed to be *based* on mere theoretical evidence, and is not said to be a certain determination "from the theoretical point of view (as to what the nature of God, which is inscrutable for us, is in itself)" (KU 5: 482). On this reading, moral theology is still not limited to making mere psychological statements about human subjects but is a proper holding true of claims about a transcendent entity, although only in a non-theoretically grounded way and only with respect to various relations that it has to us. In other words, the moral argument can still involve what I designated earlier as the second and third levels of noumenal significance, even if it cannot rise to the fourth and highest level, the determination of what a transcendent being is like entirely within itself.

One's reaction to this dispute will depend a lot on one's general understanding of Kant's view on matters such as meaning, determination, and determinative judging. Kant sometimes suggests that merely "thinking" a nonsensible being through the categories is an entirely

[18] See e.g., Paul Guyer, "From a Practical Point of View: Kant's Conception of a Postulate of Pure Practical Reason," in *Kant on Freedom, Law and Happiness* (Cambridge: Cambridge University Press, 2000), pp. 333-71.

meaningless exercise, a mere playing with words; but usually he indicates that all he is getting at is that such thought is insufficient for making *warranted* cognitive claims, and that statements that make well-formed grammatical use of the categories are in some sense "empty" unless they can at least be backed by an understanding of the “real possibility” of the entity or feature being discussed (see e.g., *Prolegomena*, 4: 313). This might be called the requirement of “objective reality,” which concerns *cognitive* possibility, and is usually determined not by the pure meaning of the categories alone but by their combination with the epistemic rules for sensible intuition. Meeting these rules provides something less than a proof of objective actuality and something more than a mere claim of a lack of logical possibility. What complicates matters here is that in places such as § 91, Kant makes clear that he also allows practical cognition to provide us “objective reality” in some cases, even in the absence of any theoretical evidence regarding sensory intuition.

Kant illustrates some of these complexities by noting that although I may “think a supersensible being as the first mover, and hence think it by means of the category of causality,” “this does not in the least allow me to cognize this being itself (as first mover).” (KU 5: 483) However, “if I start from the order in the world,” and in particular from its similarity to effects of my own understanding, which I do cognize (KU 5: 484), it might seem that some rational and true claims about something transcendent and objective could still be made. Kant’s critique of the physicotheological argument implies that nonmoral considerations would not be an adequate basis for such claims, but this still leaves open a practical rational approach: “an ethicotheology is indeed possible. For although morality with its rule [the basic moral law] can subsist without theology, morality with the final aim [the highest good and its conditions, e.g., a being with the power of a wise and good God] that this same rule enjoins on us cannot subsist without theology, but reason would in that case be at a loss concerning that aim.” (KU 5: 485)

In other words, we are rationally encouraged to assert what practical cognition requires for its commanded effects. Here it sounds as if Kant’s theological conclusions, even though reached by a very roundabout route, are entirely objective after all. And yet, right before he begins treating this whole problem, Kant emphasizes that we need theology “solely for a subjective aim: for religion, i.e., for the practical—specifically the moral use of reason.” (KU 5: 482) Here one can still wonder why the reference to subjectivity is needed; why is a practical argument concerned any more with subjectivity than a theoretical argument, since both must in any case still refer to a mind? The best answer, I believe, is that Kant’s *refrain* about subjectivity, even here, depends not on the mere fact that a mind is involved, or that morality (as opposed to logic or science) is involved at all (since the moral law has an especially strong objectivity), but hinges on the point that a "final aim" is involved, and this involves separate and contingent effects, effects tied up with our concern for happiness through fulfillment in a world that is precisely not under our own control. The clearest ground for this reading occurs in a note in a section before the Comment itself. Here Kant explains that when he calls the moral argument "sufficient subjectively" rather than "meant to provide an objectively valid proof," (KU 5: 450n) this is because it has to do not with what is "necessary for morality" itself, namely the moral law, but rather with an assumption "necessary for us" about the "happiness of all rational beings in the world." In other words, what gives this argument the special mark of "subjectivity" is just our distinctive and ultimately contingent need to be satisfied by something real and separate from us in this world—and therefore not to be able to know how that satisfaction will take place through any of our capacities of determinative judgment. As long as one understands in this way what the basis is of Kant's designation of the moral argument and faith as distinctively and inescapably involving "subjectivity," it should not matter what general term one uses to characterize his position, for even an "objectivist" should not be surprised that, insofar as faith is intertwined in this way with happiness, it can involve a special "subjective" character in a Kantian philosophy.

Works Cited

Adams, R.M. "Moral Arguments for Theistic Belief" in C.F. Delaney (ed.) *Rationality and Religious Belief* (Notre Dame: University of Notre Dame Press, 1979).

Ameriks, K. *Kant and the Historical Turn: Philosophy as Critical Interpretation* (Oxford: Clarendon Press, 2006).

—. "Introduction" in *Interpreting Kant's Critiques* (Oxford: Clarendon Press, 2003).

Beiser, F. "Moral Faith and the Highest Good" in P. Guyer (ed.) *The Cambridge Companion to Kant and Modern Philosophy* (Cambridge: Cambridge University Press, 2006).

Chignell, A. "Belief in Kant," *The Philosophical Review*, 116 (2007).

Förster, E. "Die Dialektik der reinen praktischen Vernunft," in O. Höffe (ed.) *Kritik der prakischen Vernunft* (Berlin, Akademie Verlag, 2002).

—. "Die Wandlungen in Kants Gotteslehre," in *Zeitschrift für philosophische Forschung* (1998).

Gardner, S. "The Primacy of Practical Reason," in G. Bird (ed.) *A Companion to Kant* (Malden/Oxford: Blackwell, 2006).

Guyer, P. "From a Practical Point of View: Kant's Conception of a Postulate of Pure Practical Reason," in P. Guyer *Kant on Freedom, Law and Happiness* (Cambridge: Cambridge University Press, 2000).

Hare, J.E. *God's Call: Moral Realism, Divine Commands, and Human Autonomy* (Grand Rapids, MI: Eerdmanns, 2001).

Huneman, P. *Understanding Purpose: Kant and the Philosophy of Biology,* North American Kant Studies in Philosophy, 8 (Rochester, NY: Rochester University Press, 2007).

Kant, I. *Critique of the Power of Judgment*, P. Guyer (ed.) and P. Guyer and E. Matthews (trans.) (Cambridge: Cambridge University Press, 2000).

__. "Metaphysik Herder," in K. Ameriks and S. Naragon (eds. and trans.) *Lectures on Metaphysics/Immanuel Kant* (Cambridge: Cambridge University Press, 1997).

__. "Jäsche Logic," in J.M. Young (ed.) *Lectures on Logic/Immanuel Kant* (Cambridge: Cambridge University Press, 1992).

—. *Critique of Judgment*, trans. W. Pluhar (Indianapolis: Hackett, 1987).

—. *Critique of Pure Reason*, trans. N.K. Smith (London: Macmillan, 1929).

Langton, R. "Objective and Unconditioned Value," *The Philosophical Review*, 116 (2007).

—. *Kantian Humility: Our Ignorance of Things in Themselves* (Oxford: Clarendon Press, 1998).

Ricken, F. "Die Postulate der reinen praktischen Vernunft" in O. Höffe (ed.) *Kritik der praktischen Vernunft* (Berlin: Akademie Verlag, 2002).

Stevenson, L. "Opinion, Belief or Faith, and Knowledge," *Kantian Review*, 7 (2003).

Wood, A.W. *Kant's Moral Religion* (Ithaca: Cornell University Press, 1970).

CHAPTER EIGHT

HOW TO BE EVIL: THE MORAL PSYCHOLOGY OF IMMORALITY

ROBERT GRESSIS

Kant is one of the few major philosophers to deal at length with evil. Unfortunately, his theory of evil, as presented in *Religion within the Boundaries of Mere Reason*, seems to be unbelievable. Rather than enumerate all the problems scholars have found in that work, I will instead defend Kant against one particular claim, made most recently by Claudia Card:

> On Kant's view, the same evil is present in all wrongs –serious and trivial ones alike– that are committed by anyone who subordinates morality to self interest. The deliberate choices of both murderer and subway free rider are wrong in exactly the same way. The fact that no one suffers in one case and someone dies in the other is, for Kant, morally irrelevant. It affects neither his judgment of the act nor his judgment of the agent. Yet, on any ordinary understanding of evil, one act (murder) is evil, and the other, although wrong, is not.[1]

In other words, Kant oversimplifies evil. By seeing every instance of evil as having the same common element –the inordinate pursuit of self-interest— Kant deforms what he is trying to explain.

While Kant indeed claims that people are evil because they subordinate the moral law to the "law of self-love," this is an abstract way of putting things. In fact, Kant has much of substance to say, both about what evil people are like and their reasons for acting, that is not only nuanced, but illuminating for contemporary philosophers.

[1] See C. Card, *The Atrocity Paradigm: A Theory of Evil* (Oxford: Oxford University Press, 2002), p. 82.

I- Self-deception

Though Kant thinks an overweening desire for happiness is the root of all evil, self-deception plays an equally important role, for without self-deception no one would be capable of acting immorally, much less evilly (I take immoral action stemming from *akrasia* to be merely immoral, at least sometimes, whereas immoral action stemming from willful disobedience to the moral law is always evil). This follows from two assumptions: (1) no one can be determined to action by any of her desires; (2) the moral law is admitted by everyone to be overridingly authoritative.

If people could be determined to action by their desires, then evildoers could merely be people unlucky enough to have powerful desires for causing harm, ignoring others, etc. Kant denies this, though, asserting what is nowadays called the "Incorporation Thesis": "freedom of the power of choice has the characteristic, entirely peculiar to it, that it cannot be determined to action through any incentive *except so far as the human being has incorporated it into his maxim* (has made it into a universal rule for himself, according to which he wills to conduct himself)" (R 6: 23-4; italics in any quotation from Kant are Kant's own).[2] Kant's point is that our desires (or "incentives") never *make* us do anything; rather, we do not act on desires unless we first treat them as giving us reasons for action.

Kant is well-known for claiming that our moral obligations provide us with overriding reasons for action. In other words, if an agent has to choose between satisfying a sensible desire and fulfilling a duty, she always has more reason to carry out her duty, no matter how great the cost to her (or anyone else's) well-being.[3]

Not only does carrying out one's duty always have more going for it, normatively speaking, than satisfying sensible desires, but Kant thinks everyone accepts this. Common moral cognition has the categorical imperative "always before its eyes and uses [it] as the norm for its appraisals" (G 4: 403-4).

The conjunction of the Incorporation Thesis and the universally accepted overriding authority of the moral law makes it difficult to explain evil action. It seems that when acting evilly people would have to reason, "I know that I should not do x, and my desire for x cannot force me to do x, but I still choose to do x for a reason even I recognize to have no *ultima*

---

[2] See H. Allison, *Kant's Theory of Freedom* (Cambridge University Press, 1990), p. 5.

[3] The "necessity of my action from *pure* respect for the practical law is what constitutes duty, to which every other motive must give way because it is the condition of a will good *in itself*, the worth of which surpasses all else" (G 4: 403).

facie authority." If these were the facts of the case, then evil action would be unintelligible.

It is here that Kant invokes self-deception: people can act evilly only if they convince themselves that what they are doing is not evil. If it were not for self-deception, people would be unable to engage in evil at all. This is why Kant writes: "[t]he **greatest** violation of a human being's duty to himself regarded merely as a moral being … is the contrary of truthfulness, *lying*" (MS 6: 429; unless otherwise indicated, all boldfacing in quotations from Kant is my own). That is, self-deception is the greatest violation of duty because it is the moral transgression from which all others spring.[4]

Self-deception allows a person to convince herself that an evil action is really morally licit. We have to be careful, though; if self-deception is *too* successful, then a person would not be culpable for her wrongdoing –after all, if you truly did not know that some act were immoral, then you would be ignorant of its moral status, and you could not sensibly be blamed for it (unless you knowingly brought about your ignorance).[5]

Kant models self-deception on interpersonal deception. "It is easy to show that the human being is actually guilty of many **inner** lies, but it seems more difficult to explain how they are possible; for a lie requires a second person whom one intends to deceive, whereas to deceive oneself on purpose seems to contain a contradiction" (MS 6: 430, boldfacing Kant's). We can deceive ourselves because we can "divide" our minds into two "parts" (though we do not know how this is possible), one part that accepts x but says $\sim x$, and another part that believes $\sim x$ because it was told to by the other part. Thus, even though an evil person on some level does not believe her evil actions to be evil, on a deeper level she knows what her moral obligations are, and knows them to have priority over her illicit desires. As Kant memorably puts it in the *Groundwork of the Metaphysics of Morals*:

> There is no one–not even the most hardened scoundrel, if only he is otherwise accustomed to use reason–who, when one sets before him examples of honesty of purpose, of steadfastness in following good maxims, of sympathy and general benevolence (even combined with great

---

[4] Admittedly, Kant says that self-deception is the greatest violation only of *self-regarding* duties, not of duties in general. Given the thesis of this chapter, though, one can, at least in a certain sense, call it the greatest violation of one's duties (full stop) because of its status as a necessary precondition for any immorality.

[5] This is a contentious claim, but it is one Kant would have endorsed (see VE 27: 614), and one that many people endorse even now.

> sacrifices of advantage and comfort), does not wish that he might also be so disposed. (G 4: 454)[6]

I.1. Maxims and *Gesinnungen*

To appreciate Kant's account of evil people, one has to familiarize oneself with his doctrine of the *Gesinnung* (disposition). Unfortunately, since the *Gesinnung* is itself a maxim, to understand it requires an understanding of Kant's doctrine of maxims. However, what a maxim precisely is remains highly disputed in the secondary literature; thus, any substantive explication of a *Gesinnung*, including of course mine, will be controversial. However, because maxims are not my focus in this essay, I will provide not provide much textual support for my take on maxims.[7]

Maxims

Maxims can be thought of as responses to imperatives and desires (in Kant's terminology, "incentives"). Imperatives are principles according to which certain kinds of action count as good as obligatory in certain kinds of circumstances.[8] Thus, "if you want to poison someone, you ought to use cyanide" and "if you want to advance your self-interest, do not lie" are both imperatives.

Imperatives can be "live" or "idle" depending on whether an agent has a relevant desire. For example, I accept that cyanide is good for poisoning (that is, I accept the imperative of poisoning), but because I do not desire to poison anyone the imperative of poisoning is idle for me; I do not see poisoning as good.[9] If I did desire to poison someone, and I accepted the imperative of poisoning, then the imperative of poisoning would be live for me, and I would see poisoning as good. That is, accepting the

---

[6] See also VE 27: 465.

[7] I take elements from Allison, *Kant's Theory of Freedom*, ch. 5; Patricia Kitcher, "What is a Maxim?", *Philosophical Topics* 31 (2003), pp. 215-43; and Richard McCarty, "Maxims in Kant's Practical Philosophy," *Journal of the History of Philosophy*, 44 (2006), pp. 65-83.

[8] "All imperatives are expressed by an *ought* and indicate by this the relation of an objective law of reason to a will that by its subjective constitution is not necessarily determined by it (a necessitation). They say that to do or omit something would be good" (G 4: 413).

[9] Throughout this section, I talk about "accepting" imperatives and maxims; I do not mean to imply that these acts of acceptance are ever conscious acts of decision-making (though they could be). Rather, I mean only to suggest that the agent who accepts a maxim can be held responsible for doing so. I thank Timothy Rosenkoetter for suggesting this locution.

imperative of poisoning and having a desire for poisoning someone results in my accepting the maxim, "if you want to poison someone, you ought to use cyanide." Maxims are thus motivating judgments –more specifically, whenever someone accepts a maxim, she both accepts a principle according to which some action is to be done and wants to perform that action.[10]

Whenever an agent acts, there is some maxim on which she acts.[11] In other words, an agent cannot act without seeing her action as good, either because it is morally required or because it conduces to a state of affairs whose reality she desires.[12] In addition, maxims function as the major premises of practical syllogisms.[13] For example, before I can act to eat a sandwich, I (subconsciously) work through the following practical syllogism:

> In circumstances where I am hungry, it is good to eat something that will satisfy my hunger; (maxim)[14]

---

[10] The locution, "motivating judgment" is a bit misleading. I do not mean to say that with all maxims, it is the judgment that brings about the motivation (though with morally worthy maxims this is the case); I mean only to say that they are not *just* judgments that some action is to be done, but are judgments that are accompanied by a motivating pull.

[11] "[A]s a freely acting being, a human being actually cannot do anything without the will – he acts always according to maxims even if not universally" (VM 28: 678).

[12] The Scholastic formula, *we desire nothing except under the form of the good; nothing is avoided except under the form of the bad* "may mean: we represent to ourselves something as good when and *because we desire* (will) *it*, or also: we desire something *because we represent it to ourselves as good*, so that either desire is the determining ground of the concept of the object as a good, or the concept of the good is the determining ground of desire (of the will)." (KpV 5: 59n)

[13] One will note that the maxim in this example is the major premise of a practical syllogism. I believe this is Kant's view as well: "Voluntary action insofar as it comes about according to maxims (maxims, principles practically subjective because they would be the major premise in practical syllogisms)." (VM 28: 678) Cf. KpV 5: 90. For more on reading maxims as the major premises of practical syllogisms, see Lewis White Beck, *A Commentary to Kant's Critique of Practical Reason* (Chicago: Chicago University Press, 1960), 81 and 128-29; Kitcher, "What Is a Maxim?", pp. 215-43; and McCarty, "Maxims in Kant's Philosophy," pp. 65-83.

[14] The form of a maxim is thus, "in circumstances *C*, I ought to do action *A*" or, interchangeably (for Kant), "in *C*, doing *A* is good." Most contemporary philosophers do not see such a connection between an action's goodness and its bindingness –we think that one could perfectly well see the execution of some

> I am hungry, and eating this sandwich will satisfy my hunger; (minor premise)
> Therefore, eating this sandwich is good. (conclusion that could eventuate in action)

I would like to note three consequences of this understanding of maxims before going on to *Gesinnungen*. First, agents can know something about the maxims on which they act, even if they do not consciously carry out a practical syllogism before acting; this is because they know what they see as good, and so can figure out, if they are honest with themselves, how best to describe the actions they undertake. However, because (1) agents can see an action as good for two kinds of reason –either because it is intrinsically good or because it will realize a desirable state of affairs– and because (2), when they face a morally significant decision, they always have reason to want to see themselves as acting out of respect for the moral law, it follows that (3) when someone makes a morally significant decision, she can never be sure whether she does so just because she wants to realize a desirable state of affairs or just because the action is commanded by the moral law or both.[15]

Second, because people desire many different kinds of things, and because the moral law requires many different kinds of action, people at all times accept many different maxims according to which many different kinds of things count as good. For example, someone who wants to diet but who also wants to eat a doughnut accepts two maxims: "when one is overweight, it is good to diet" and "when one is hungry, it is good to eat fattening food." Which one she acts on is up to her. To elaborate: because the maxims a person accepts determine what sort of things she sees as good (and only her accepted maxims determine what she sees as good), it follows that you can many discover the range of maxims a person holds by figuring out which kinds of outcomes she sees as good to promote or actions she sees as good to carry out.

Third, maxims are hierarchically arranged.[16] For example, if I see exercising as good, I can give an explanation for why it is good. If asked, I would say exercising is good because it improves one's health. If asked

---

action as good, and yet not see it as in any way, prudentially or morally, obligatory. If I am right, Kant denies this intuition of ours; he thinks that if we genuinely both want to do something and see it as good to do, either because it advances our self-interest, or because it is morally good, then it will also feel (to some degree) binding.

[15] Hence Kant's claim that "we cannot observe maxims, we cannot do so *unproblematically* even within ourselves" (R 6: 20).

[16] See R 6: 21n and 25.

why I think health is good, I can answer that it extends one's life-span, allows one to undertake the rest of one's projects more easily, etc. If asked why those results are good, I can give another explanation (and note that each different explanation shows my commitment to a different maxim). Kant thinks, though, that all such explanations terminate in two kinds of goodness that do not admit of any explanation that shows why they are good: *x* is good because it makes me happier, or *x* is good because it is morally right.[17] In other words, Kant thinks everyone accepts two quite general maxims, which I shall call the "Prudential Maxim" ("in any circumstances, happiness is good" or "in all circumstances, I ought to make myself happier"; Kant calls this maxim the "law/principle of self-love") and the "Moral Maxim" ("in any circumstances, following the moral law is good" or "in all circumstances, I ought to obey the moral law").[18]

Gesinnungen

The *Gesinnung* one has depends on whether one makes the Prudential or the Moral Maxim supreme. A person who makes the Moral Maxim supreme has a good *Gesinnung*, and so is a good person, and one who makes the Prudential Maxim supreme has an evil *Gesinnung*, and so is an evil person:

> the difference, whether the human being is good or evil, must not lie in the difference between the incentives that he incorporates into his maxim (not in the material of the maxim) but in their *subordination* (in the form of the maxim): *which of the two he makes the condition of the other*. It follows that the human being (even the best) is evil only because he reverses the moral order of his incentives in incorporating them into his maxims. (R 6: 36)

Given that the *Gesinnung* is itself a maxim, and given that what characterizes an evil *Gesinnung* is that in it the Moral Maxim is subordinated to the Prudential Maxim, it stands to reason that an evil person is someone who happily follows the Moral Maxim *except when doing so would force her to act against the Prudential Maxim*. In other

---

[17] "Men are actuated by two motives; one is drawn from within them, and that is the motive of self-love; the other is the moral motive, drawn from others, and that is the motive of the general love of mankind." (VE 27: 422)

[18] For the "Principle of self-love," see KpV 5: 22; for the "law of self-love," see VE 27: 422 and R 6: 36. For the claim that Kant thinks people accept both the Prudential and the Moral Maxims, see R 6: 36: "[the human being] indeed incorporates the moral law into [his] maxims, together with the law of self-love."

words, someone with an evil *Gesinnung* should have as her "supreme" [*oberste*] maxim, "in all circumstances where there is a conflict between promoting happiness and acting morally, it is good to promote happiness."

Because an agent's maxims determine what she perceives to be good or worth undertaking, it follows that someone with an evil *Gesinnung* sees morally required actions as worth doing only when they do not conflict with her pursuit of happiness. When morality and happiness do conflict, though, an evil person will see the moral action as less worth doing than the prudential one.

One might think having an evil *Gesinnung* is quite rare. After all, someone who *always* perceived the moral option to be less worthwhile than the prudential one looks like someone who would never perform even a single good act.[19] However, Kant thinks evil is quite widespread.[20] Indeed, as I shall show in section 3, Kant thinks each of us starts with an evil *Gesinnung* (though through God's grace we can each overcome it and become good).[21] Does Kant therefore hold the implausible view that most people never perform even one morally good act?[22]

I do not think Kant holds this view, for he writes, "the statement, 'The human being is *evil*,' cannot mean anything else than that he is conscious of the moral law and yet has incorporated into his maxim **the (occasional)**

---

[19] It is important to note an asymmetry between happiness and morality on this score. What makes morally required actions better than prudentially recommended actions is their universalizability; to oversimplify, they help everyone, not just oneself. So, if I see my moral obligations as better, all things considered, than prudential actions, this is because I see helping the world to be more important than helping myself. Still, even if I see helping the world to be more valuable than helping myself, it is still sometimes the case that prudential actions may involve reaping great benefits or avoiding great costs *just for me*. And even a good agent can find it difficult to ignore great personal benefits or costs, because of her natural concern for her own happiness. By contrast, someone who is evil already sees her own happiness as more important than helping the world. Given this, it is hard to imagine why such an agent would *ever* sacrifice even a little of her own happiness for even a great benefit to the world (except for prudential reasons, such as the fear of her deplorable choice being discovered).

[20] See R 6: 32-33.

[21] See R 6: 44-45.

[22] Some might think so based on this remark: "[f]rom love of humankind I am willing to admit that even most of our actions are in conformity with duty; but if we look more closely at the intentions and aspirations in them we everywhere come upon the dear self, which is always turning up; and it is on this that their purpose is based" (G 4: 407). I take this, though, to an expression of pessimism rather than Kant's considered position.

deviation from it" (R 6: 32). Obviously, if an evil person may include only the *occasional* deviation from the Moral Maxim, then the implication is that she may occasionally follow it as well.

Still, even though Kant does not hold this view, the question remains of how can he legitimately avoid it, given that an evil person makes obedience to the Moral Maxim conditional on her obedience to the Prudential Maxim. To see how, one must attend briefly to two facets of his conception of happiness. First, the understanding of happiness that recurs most in Kant's corpus is well-represented by this one: "a rational being's consciousness of the agreeableness of life uninterruptedly accompanying his whole existence is *happiness*." (KpV 5: 22)[23] Most interpreters of Kant's theory of happiness emphasize both the "agreeableness of life" and the "whole existence" mentioned in the definition, and so conclude that happiness within Kant's system amounts to the maximal set of satisfied desires, where the subjective feeling of pleasure is the indicator of the level of satisfaction.[24] While these elements are surely important, I want to stress as well the fact that "**consciousness** of the agreeableness of life" is crucial as well, for central to Kant's notion of happiness is the feeling that one's life is going well overall. That is, when one reflects on "his whole existence" he judges that there is an "agreeableness of life" accompanying it.[25]

How do you know whether your life is going well, though? That is, against what standard can you measure the goodness of your life to determine how well you are doing in terms of satisfying your desires? Kant thinks the standard against which people compare their own lives is the lives of others, more specifically the lives of the people most salient to them: "[t]he greatest source of happiness or unhappiness, of faring well or ill, of content or discontent, lies in the relationship to other people." (VE 27: 366-67) Or as Kant memorably puts the point: "if everyone alike in the town is eating rotten cheese, I eat it too, with satisfaction and a cheerful

[23] He uses it in this sense at G 4: 399, 405, and 418; KpV 5: 25, 61, and 73; KU 5: 208 and 434n; R 6: 58 and 67; TP 8: 282, 283, and 290; VE 27: 366-67, 499, and 598; and VM 28: 446, 593, and 899.

[24] See p. 189 of Daniel O'Connor, "Kant's Conception of Happiness," *Journal of Value Inquiry* 16 (1982), pp. 189-205.

[25] This is not to say that a person needs to reflect on how his life is going to be happy; it could be that he would assent to this if asked (and he has reason to be honest, etc.), or he might have a subconscious sense or tacit belief that this is the case.

mind, whereas if everyone else were well-fed, and I alone in sorry circumstances, I would deem it a misfortune." (VE 27: 367)[26]

So, to be happy one has to think one's life overall is going well, and to think that, a person must think at least that her life is going well relative to others. Thus, to say that someone, owing to her evil *Gesinnung*, judges her happiness to be more important than morality is the same as saying that she is willing to flout her moral obligations whenever doing so allows her to think that her life is going as well or better than others.[27]

Because different people have different conclusions about what makes a life go well, some people are perfectly willing to sacrifice, say, base sensuous pleasures in order to live up to their moral obligations. An Olympic athlete with an evil *Gesinnung* may have no problem refraining from stealing someone's car, even if it would give her lots of pleasure, because having a nice car is not what she thinks makes her life go well; however, she may be willing to take performance-enhancing drugs.[28] In

---

[26] See also R 6: 27.

[27] There is an alternative reading on which one should understand Kant's claim that the evil person makes the Prudential Maxim the condition of her allegiance to the Moral Maxim differently from how I do. On this reading, the evil person makes advancing her own happiness the condition of her obedience to morality only in the sense that she subordinates morality to her happiness *by and large*. Thus, on any given occasion she may subordinate her happiness to her morality; the only thing is, she usually does not (see p. 39 of Allen Wood, "The Good Without Limitation (GMS I, 393-394)," in C. Horn and D. Schönecker (eds.), *Groundwork for the Metaphysics of Morals* (Berlin: Walter de Gruyter, 2006), pp. 25-44 for an example of this interpretation). While this reading doubtlessly seems more realistic than the one I have advanced, I think it is a worse fit with the text, for two reasons. First, it seems to entail the claim that a good person is simply someone who does not, by and large, subordinate her happiness to morality; this is because Kant is a rigorist (R 6: 22) – he thinks that there are only two kinds of people, good and evil ones – so if an evil person is someone who generally advances her happiness over morality, then it follows that a good person is someone of whom this is not true. However, Kant thinks being a good person is much more demanding than this; indeed, committing even a single evil act can be enough, on Kant's view, for a person to count as evil (see R 6: 20). Second, Kant thinks it is inconceivable how an evil person can make herself into a good person (see R 6: 44-45). But if an evil person were simply someone who generally subordinated morality to happiness, then why it should be inconceivable to change from evil to good would be hard to fathom.

[28] Why only "*may* be willing"–why not "would definitely be willing"? This is because acting morally also brings certain pleasures, and allows a person to think her life is going well. Kant notes that even for the evil person "actions can still turn out to be as much in conformity to the law as if they had originated from true

other words, not all people with evil *Gesinnungen* see the same kinds of immoral actions as permissible. Regardless of what they find happiness in, what evil people have in common is that they do not see certain actions as morally obligatory that they should see as morally obligatory.

In addition to the different judgments people may come to about what makes them happy, Kant has an account of the different attitudes people with evil *Gesinnungen* can have to morality, an account he does not offer in the *Religion*. These different ways of manifesting an evil *Gesinnung* amount to significantly different ways of looking at the "practical world," and so of being evil.[29] In what follows, I articulate both these different ways of being evil, and the routes agents typically take in order to end up as these different kinds of people.

II- Evil People: Variations on a Theme

One might wonder how a person can become evil in the first place. After all, it is in everyone's nature to assent to the moral law.[30] Moreover, each of us has a conscience that involuntarily arises to warn us whenever we are about to do something wrong, and that harshly judges us after we engage in wrongdoing. "Every human being has a conscience and finds himself observed, threatened, and, in general, kept in awe (respect coupled with fear) by an internal judge … It follows him like his shadow when he plans to escape." (MS 6: 438)[31]

One must first of all note that each of us begins with an evil *Gesinnung* (or at least, we should assume this). "We cannot start out in the ethical training of our connatural moral predisposition to the good with an innocence which is natural to us but must rather begin from the

---

principles –as when reason uses the unity of the maxims in general, which is characteristic of the moral law, merely to introduce into the incentives of inclination, under the name of *happiness*, a unity of maxims which they cannot otherwise have." (R 6: 36-37) Thus, the evil athlete may refrain from taking performance-enhancing drugs, even though they would make her a better athlete, but only because she thinks such a refraining will make her happier, and not because it is morally required.

[29] I find these different accounts mostly in the 1784 Collins manuscript of Kant's lectures on ethics, the *Critique of Practical Reason*, and the 1793-94 Vigilantius manuscript of Kant's lectures on ethics. Although Kant did not work out the doctrine of the *Gesinnung* until the 1793 *Religion*, there is evidence that Kant had the doctrine of the *Gesinnung* in mind in 1788 (see KpV 5: 140 and 143) and even in 1784 (see VE 27: 274).

[30] Kant calls this the "predisposition to personality" (R 6: 27-28).

[31] See also VE 27: 615-17.

supposition of a depravity in our power of choice in adopting maxims contrary to the original ethical predisposition." (R 6: 51)[32] Thus, even though we all assent to the moral law, we also start out having freely subordinated the Moral Maxim to the Prudential Maxim.[33] Still, even though upon the onset of rationality we each have an evil *Gesinnung*, the specific vices and immoral outlooks that will characterize as adults are not determined until after we employ certain strategies for dealing with our consciences.

The fact that we each start out with an evil *Gesinnung* partially explains how we can end up with more fully developed evil *Gesinnungen*. However, it is not the whole story; there is still something that needs to be said about how Kant understands the operations of the conscience.

Reading what Kant has to say about the conscience might leave one with the impression that the conscience is always active, functioning as a moral warning bell before an immoral act and as a disappointed parent afterwards. This is not Kant's view, though; instead, he thinks that we have an obligation to train ourselves to hear the voice of conscience, to obey its requirements, and to feel humiliated by its judgments. "The duty … is only to cultivate one's conscience, to sharpen one's attentiveness to the voice of the inner judge and to use every means to obtain a hearing for it." (MS 6: 401) The more attentive one is able to become to one's conscience, the more "conscientious" one becomes.[34]

If one does not properly train one's conscience, one ends up "unconscientious." Indeed, not only does the person who does not properly habituate his conscience become unconscientious, but he who is conscientious can become unconscientious through repeatedly ignoring his conscience or self-deceptively rationalizing his behavior to it when it rises up:[35]

> [t]he *conscientia concomitans*, or accompanying conscience, at length becomes weak through habituation, and in the end one becomes as

---

[32] This "depravity in the power of choice" is equivalent to having an evil *Gesinnung*; after describing the state of mind he labels "depravity," Kant writes that with depravity "the mind's attitude is … corrupted at its root (so far as the moral disposition is concerned), and hence the human being is designated as evil" (R 6: 30).

[33] We "cannot derive this disposition [*Gesinnung*], or rather its highest ground, from a first act of the power of choice in time, we call it a characteristic of the power of choice that pertains to it by nature (even though the disposition is in fact grounded in freedom)." (R 6: 25)

[34] See VE 27: 575.

[35] See KpV 5: 79-80 and 98 and VE 27: 317 and 359.

> accustomed to vice as to tobacco-smoke. Conscience eventually loses all respect, and then, too, the accusation ceases, having become superfluous, since nothing is any longer decided or carried out in the courtroom. (VE 27: 356)

Note that the unconscientious person is still aware (at least potentially) of what is truly right and wrong; he just does not care about it: when it is said that a certain human being *has* no conscience, what is meant is that he pays no heed to its verdict. For if he really had no conscience, he could not even conceive of the duty to have one, since he would neither impute anything to himself as conforming with duty nor reproach himself with anything as contrary to duty (MS 6: 400-1). This is the path, then, that people take to become the evil people they end up as: everyone starts with an evil *Gesinnung* (that is, everyone starts seeing her happiness as more important than being moral); because of their evil *Gesinnungen*, people will freely ignore their consciences with regard to certain vices (after all, it makes them happier to indulge those vices); finally, because people are capable of self-deception, they can create "moral fantasies" about their status vis-à-vis the moral law or other agents. I shall now explore these moral fantasies.

II. 1.The Adequacy Fantasy

Kant's most elaborate remark regarding moral fantasies runs:

> Moral fantasies may relate either to the moral law itself, or to our moral actions. The first such delusion is to fancy of the moral law that it is indulgent in regard to ourselves. But the other is to fancy of our moral perfections that they are in conformity with the moral law. The first is more harmful than the second, for if a man fancies that his perfections are compatible with the moral law, it is still easy to dissuade him of this, by pointing to the purity of the moral law. But if a man frames for himself the idea of an indulgent moral law, he has a false law, whereby he also creates maxims and principles such that even his actions can then have no moral goodness. (VE 27: 348)

Here Kant distinguishes two moral fantasies: the fantasy wherein one thinks "of the moral law that it is indulgent in regard to ourselves"; a person who entertains this fantasy "frames for himself the idea of an indulgent moral law, he has a false law, whereby he also creates maxims and principles such that even his actions can then have no moral goodness." I call this fantasy the "exceptionalist fantasy."

The second moral fantasy, which Kant finds less harmful than the exceptionalist fantasy, is the fantasy that "our moral perfections … are in conformity with the moral law." Because such a person thinks only "that his perfections are compatible with the moral law," rather than, say, the most that could possibly be demanded by the moral law, I call his fantasy the "adequacy fantasy," for he thinks only that he is morally adequate, rather than morally special or perfect (as the exceptionalist thinks).

I shall explore the adequacy fantasy first, not only because it is, I believe, more common than the exceptionalist fantasy, but also because the processes that yield the adequacy fantasy can also lead from it to the exceptionalist fantasy. As I shall show, the adequacy fantasy results from a surfeit of self-love, while the exceptionalist fantasy springs from self-conceit.

The adequacy fantasist thinks she is morally adequate; she is no saint, but she is no monster either. I believe most people have this view of themselves; and on Kant's view, not only is it mistaken, it is evil.

Why is it mistaken? Because the moral law is quite demanding; it asks of us not only to avoid violating perfect obligations, but to do as much as we can to carry out our imperfect obligations of perfecting ourselves and promoting others' happiness.[36] Thus, the adequacy fantasist, who thinks of herself as at least not a bad (and possibly as a good) person, is wrong. Unless she devotes herself utterly to following the moral law, she falls far short of being morally blameless. But on Kant's action theory, there are only two possible explanations for why someone falls short of doing what the moral law demands: weakness of will or adherence to an evil principle. Since it is implausible to think that someone perennially weak of will would nonetheless think of herself as not a bad (or as a good) person, the adequacy fantasist adheres to an evil principle.

What evil principle is that? Kant explicates it as follows:

> *Philautia*, or moral self-love, is to be contrasted with arrogance, or moral self-conceit. The difference between them is that the former is only an inclination to be content with one's perfections, whereas the latter makes an unwarranted pretension to merit. It lays claim to more moral perfections than are due to it; but self-love makes no demands, it is always merely content with itself and devoid of self-reproach. The one is proud of its moral perfections, the other is not, believing itself merely to be blameless and without fault. *Arrogantia* is thus a far more damaging defect. *Philautia* tests itself against the moral law, not as a guiding-principle but by way of

[36] It "is indeed impossible that in the sight of God, as the law of the highest morality, we can do more than is incumbent, since in regard to Him, everything is required; but in relation to other men, we can certainly have merits." (VE 27: 665)

> examples, and then one may well have cause to be self-satisfied. The examples of moral men are standards drawn from experience; the moral law, however, is a standard set by reason; if the first of these is used, the result is either *philautia* or *arrogantia*. The latter arises if the moral law is thought of in a narrow and indulgent fashion, or if the moral judge within us is partisan. (VE 27: 357)

The adequacy fantasist "is always merely content with [herself] and devoid of self-reproach," and she believes herself "to be blameless and without fault," because she tests her conduct against that required by the moral law "not as a guiding-principle but by way of examples."

Kant calls the attitude characteristic of the adequacy fantasy "*philautia*" or "moral self-love." By understanding what *philautia*/moral self-love is, we can figure out what Kant means by saying that the adequacy fantasist tests herself against the moral via examples, rather than through direct comparison to it.

"All love is either love that wishes well, or love that likes well. Well-wishing love consists in the wish and inclination to promote the happiness of others. The love that likes well is the pleasure we take in showing approval of another's perfections." (VE 27: 417) This passage teaches that there are two kinds of love: well-wishing love [*Wohlwollen*], which is a desire to promote others' happiness, and well-liking love [*Wohlgefallen*], which is the approval of another's perfections (or more likely, the approval of another *because* of her perfections). Consequently, there are two genera of self-love: well-wishing self-love, which is the desire to promote one's own happiness,[37] and well-liking self-love, which is the approval of one's own perfections, or of oneself on the basis of one's own perfections.[38] Finally, within the genus of well-liking self-love, there are two species: well-liking non-moral self-love, which is the approval of oneself on the basis of one's non-moral perfections, and well-liking moral self-love, which is the approval of oneself on the basis of one's moral perfections – these include one's humanity, which is the ability to set oneself ends and act from pure respect for the law,[39] and one's moral worth, which is the worth one has corresponding to the degree to which one properly uses

[37] There "is in all men without restriction a love of well-wishing towards themselves," (VE 27: 620) or, to put it in terms more typical of Kant, "all people have already, of themselves, the strongest and deepest inclination to happiness." (G 4: 399)

[38] The "love that takes pleasure in oneself, a self-love, is an inclination to be well-content with oneself in judging of one's perfection." (VE 27: 357)

[39] See G 4: 436; MS 6: 434-35; and VE 27: 407.

one's humanity (i.e., one's moral worth depends on how much one follows the moral law out of respect).[40]

When Kant connects the adequacy fantasy to moral self-love, he has well-liking moral self-love in mind. Now, well-liking moral self-love is not always illicit; for instance, someone who delights in herself because of her humanity does precisely what she is supposed to do. Similarly, someone who feels self-esteem because she carries out a duty that cuts strongly against her self-interest does nothing wrong.[41] What Kant must be associating with the adequacy fantasy, then, is *undeserved* well-liking moral self-love.

One way of exemplifying undeserved well-liking moral self-love is claiming moral perfections for yourself that you not deserve (someone who thinks herself saintly but acts wickedly –as I shall show, this is how an exceptionalist fantasist operates), for example because you judge yourself according to a false moral law. Another way, though, is to incorrectly attribute moral perfections to yourself, not because you judge yourself by the wrong moral law, but rather because you incorrectly apply the right moral law.[42] This is the route the adequacy fantasist takes.

Note that the adequacy fantasist judges that she is morally blameless, not morally perfect. This is surprising; if you are going to apply the moral law to yourself incorrectly, why not do so in a way that results in your coming out truly exceptional? To answer this question, one must investigate the etiology of the adequacy fantasy.

Since people grow up in a corrupt society –and given what Kant thinks it takes for a society to count as morally good, we can assume all societies (except for the one exemplifying the highest good) are corrupt–[43] they are educated into thinking of morality in the wrong way; children receive their moral education through examples of morally meritorious conduct rather than principles.[44] These examples, though, usually involve highly difficult exploits; consequently, instead of admiring the dedication to duty the examples (hopefully) display, children become confused and value the

---

[40] See KpV 5: 157 and 161; VE 349, 609, 610, 621, 622, 675, and 703; and MS 6: 435.

[41] See MS 6: 435.

[42] Of course, if you judge yourself by the wrong standard, then you may account to yourself more (or fewer) perfections than you in fact deserve. But this is importantly different from judging yourself wrongly according to the proper standard.

[43] See R 6: 94-95.

[44] "Everything in education depends on establishing the right principles throughout and making them comprehensible and acceptable to children." (VP 9: 492-93)

non-moral merit (roughly, how hard it is to do) in the action instead.[45] This, combined with the natural disposition to value happiness over morality, results in adults who value honor (the normal response to merit)[46] over moral worth.

In addition to these factors, though, the demandingness of the moral law itself pushes people away from it. Even though everyone both begins with an evil *Gesinnung* and must train herself to become conscientious, no one is entirely deaf to morality. Most of us strive to be morally good people, at least during some periods of our lives. Trying to be moral, though, is a permanently unsuccessful enterprise; however morally worthy one makes oneself, one always falls short of what the law exhorts. "True humility follows **unavoidably** from our sincere and exact comparison of ourselves with the moral law (its holiness and strictness)." (MS 6: 436)[47] Falling short of being moral, though, brings with it humiliation by the moral law, a humiliation which pains us and shows us up for what we are. "The consciousness and feeling of the insignificance of one's moral worth *in comparison with the* **law** is *humility* (*humilitas moralis*)." (MS 6: 435, boldface Kant's)

So, we start out seeing the pursuit of happiness as better than the satisfaction of moral obligations, we get educated into valuing merit over moral worth, and when we do try to live up to the moral law, we cannot help but to fail. No matter how we may want to stop caring about morality altogether though, most of us cannot help but to see following the moral law as obligatory, and to desire its validation.

The way we square our desire for happiness with our desire for moral worth is not by making a new moral law for ourselves but by changing some of the rules of the game. We still admit the same moral demands, but reduce the penalties for failures in compliance: a failure to live up to the moral law in some way *x* is penalized with humiliation only if we think

---

[45] Kant thinks that merit–which is a measure of the degree of difficulty of an action, such that the more difficult the action, the more meritorious it is–properly attaches only to wide duties or actions performed out of respect for the moral law (see Robert Johnson, "Kant's Conception of Merit," *Pacific Philosophical Quarterly* 77 (1996), pp. 313-37). Of course, just because these are the only actions that actually have merit, people can regard many other kinds of action–and even external goods–as being meritorious.

[46] "We can value a thing for what it is worth, but high esteem and honor we can give only to that which has merit." (VE 27: 409)

[47] "Now man, when he judges himself, in whatever situation he may be, finds that he is never without faults, and always has grounds for self-improvement." (VE 27: 571)

that other members of our peer group commonly live up to *x*, or easily could have lived up to *x* had they been in our situation. In other words, because we never fully satisfy the moral law, we admit we are not saints, but because we do about as well as those around us, we convince ourselves we are not bad people either. This is the sense in which the adequacy fantasist "tests [herself] against the moral law, not as a guiding-principle but by way of examples."

In thinking of the moral law in this fashion, adequacy fantasists show themselves to think about moral worth in the same way they think about merit. Actions are meritorious only if they are both valuable and relatively difficult to do; if an action is *relatively* difficult to do, though, it is because it is difficult relative to a certain class of people. Throwing an eighty mile per hour fastball is extremely difficult to do for someone who is not a major league baseball player, and so is meritorious relative to the class of people who are not major league ballplayers and who value speedy fastballs, but it is of little worth to a major league pitcher. Similarly, relative to a community of well-off professionals in the USA, stealing a trinket from a convenience store is considered immoral, but giving 20% of one's income to the poor is morally quite good –supererogatory, even. "People are very much inclined to take others as the measure of their own moral worth." (VE 27: 349)

It is possible for an adequacy fantasist to act from respect for the law. Even if she wants to steal, the well-off professional will think it is immoral, and so should not be done. However, she is also likely to think that members of her class just do not do that sort of thing; what would people think, after all, should she be discovered? Thus, even when it seems the adequacy fantasist acts from respect, she may in fact act from baser motives, motives having to do with maintaining her self-conception as a member of the right group. The reason she wants to maintain this self-conception, though, is that it makes her happier –should she disgrace herself to her fellow lawyers, academics, businesspeople, etc., she will feel her life is going much less well than she wants.

One of the moral failings the adequacy fantasy leads to, then, is the failure to live up to those moral obligations that members of one's peer group do not think important. Indeed, adequacy fantasists may even think of some moral obligation as positively *bad* to live up (the citizen of evil states like the Soviet Union or Nazi Germany might see helping the Cossacks or the Jews as immoral, rather than mandatory or optional). As Kant writes:

> Men like, in general, to have examples, and if one exists they are happy to excuse themselves, on the ground that everybody lives that way. But if

> examples are available, to which appeal can be made, then it encourages people to emulate them. A bad example, however, is a stumbling-block and gives occasion for two evils; for imitation as a pattern, and for excuse. (VE 27: 334)

Not only do adequacy fantasists fail to live up to those obligations that their community thinks unimportant, they also fail to take steps to improve themselves: Men are happy … to cling to the belief of their forefathers, for in that case they think, even though it be false, that they are absolved from blame; it was their ancestors who impelled them to it and if a man can only shift the blame to others, he is content, and things thereby to shield himself from responsibility (VE 27: 334). Adequacy fantasists neglect the project of moral reform for the same reason they become adequacy fantasists in the first place: because it makes them happier. They will feel pressure to morally improve themselves only if their peers morally improve themselves (and if *that* is their reason for moral improvement it is not obviously real moral improvement). But if their peers are also adequacy fantasists, then moral improvement will look less appealing than other ways of getting honor from their peers, for not only does moral improvement often require a sacrifice of happiness, but it always brings with it the danger that the moral law itself will humiliate them for not doing even more improvement. Thus, in a community of adequacy fantasists, there is little incentive for focusing on moral reform when there are other, easier ways of reaping honor.

II.2.The Exceptionalist Fantasy

There are two important differences between the adequacy fantasy and the exceptionalist fantasy. First, whereas the adequacy fantasist accepts the moral law but thinks she is blameless before it, the exceptionalist fantasist accepts an "indulgent" moral law, one that allows her freedoms that it does not allow others. Second, whereas the adequacy fantasist is happy enough to think herself the equal of her peers in moral worth, the exceptionalist fantasist wants to think herself her peers' better.

In his remarks on the adequacy and exceptionalist fantasies from VE 27: 357, Kant equates the adequacy fantasy with undeserved moral self-love (i.e., feeling content with oneself upon contemplating one's moral perfections), but the exceptionalist fantasy with "arrogance" or "moral self-conceit." The exceptionalist fantasist "makes an unwarranted pretension to merit," "lays claim to more moral perfections than are due to" her, and "is proud of [her] moral perfections." As with the adequacy fantasy, we can get a better understanding of the exceptionalist fantasy if we appreciate the route one must take to end up entertaining it.

Interestingly, Kant claims that *either* the adequacy fantasy (*philautia*) or the exceptionalist fantasy (*arrogantia*) can result if one tests oneself against "the examples of moral men" or "standards drawn from experience." The same process can thus produce either an adequacy or an exceptionalist fantasist. However, I believe the adequacy fantasy is a way station to the exceptionalist fantasy: pressures within the adequacy fantasy can produce the exceptionalist fantasy.

The adequacy fantasist gets a sense of her moral worth not by comparing her conduct to what the moral law demands of her, but instead to those she regards as her peers. There are two ways to surpass one's peers in moral worth if one is an adequacy fantasist. First, one can perform tasks of great moral merit, thereby earning honor from one's fellows. Alternatively, one can denigrate the performances of one's fellows:

> There are … two ways … of getting even with the other's perfections. Either I seek to acquire those perfections of his for myself as well, or I try to diminish them. Whether I enlarge my own perfection, or lessen his, I always come out the better man. Now since the latter comes easiest, men will sooner diminish the other's perfections than enhance their own. (VE 27: 436-7)

If an adequacy fantasist's peer gives a large portion of his income to charity, and this is considered morally meritorious by his peer-group, the adequacy fantasist will feel diminished by this. After all, she wants to be happy, and to be happy she has to think her life is going as well as those of her peers. But if her peer achieves great moral accomplishments, she will see her life as going less well than her peer's, and so will feel less happy. Because she has an evil *Gesinnung*, she will seek to restore the balance. However, since it can be quite difficult to perform a feat of great moral merit, she would rather do something easier –after all, she is an adequacy fantasist in the first place partly because it is much easier to be an adequacy fantasist than someone who tries but fails to live up to the moral law directly. This easier task is disparaging her peer's accomplishment; for example, she could tell herself that he gave away his money merely to make himself feel good, to increase his reputation, etc.

An adequacy fantasist can make himself seem comparatively better off not only by disparaging others but also by puffing himself up. However, he need not puff himself up by doing anything of great difficulty, but rather by adverting to his good intentions:

> Moral *philautia*, where a man has a high opinion of himself in regard to his moral perfections, is contemptible. It arises when a man holds his dispositions to be good ones, and thinks by empty wishes and romantic ideas to promote the welfare of the world; he loves the Tartar, and would like to practice kindness towards him, but gives no thought to his closest neighbors. That whereby the heart only becomes flabby, is the *philautia* that consists in mere wishes, and is otherwise inactive. (VE 27: 358-59)

The problem with convincing yourself of your moral worth by pointing to your good wishes is that, if you repeat this lie to yourself often enough, you can come to believe it so strongly that you become self-conceited. That is, you can come to believe not only that you are morally blameless, but that you are positively morally great (you make an "unwarranted pretension to merit").[48]

An adequacy fantasist who comes to believe she is morally great is halfway to being an exceptionalist fantasist;[49] however, she is not a full-blooded exceptionalist until she accepts an indulgent moral law. She ends up endorsing such a law as follows: first, she holds to the moral law, but determines her moral worth by comparing herself to her peers; second, she thinks she is morally worthier than her peers; third, if she is conceited enough, she will think that she has some "moral leeway" –that is, she can engage in some immorality, which will reduce her moral worth accordingly, but if she has enough moral worth, she will still end up better than her peers. If she engages in such immorality often enough, though, she will habituate herself to it, and will come to see it as morally permissible, at least for people of her moral worth. At this point, she is fully an exceptionalist: she adheres to a moral law according to which all have the same obligations, except for people as morally worthy as she.

---

[48] Note that "merit" can come in both non-moral and moral forms (where moral merit would be a property of moral obligations that are particularly difficult to discharge). Since Kant says the exceptionalist has "moral self-conceit," we can assume that the merit she attributes to herself is moral merit.

[49] The adequacy fantasist who thinks herself morally great will most likely think herself morally superior to her peers, which is morally self-conceited: "People are very much inclined to take others as the measure of their own moral worth, and if they then believe themselves superior to some, it would be self-conceit to think thus." (VE 27: 349) However, when self-conceit is defined in this way, almost every adequacy fantasist has some measure of it, for even if she thinks herself the moral equal of her peers, she is likely to think herself morally worthier than members of some "lower" group. So, moral self-conceit alone is not enough to qualify as an exceptionalist fantasist.

Thus, she ends up as someone who regularly flouts the moral law but also thinks herself morally wonderful.

The adequacy fantasy, then, is dangerous not only because it leads people to ignore some of their moral obligations and induces moral torpor, but also because it can turn into the even more dangerous exceptionalist fantasy. This is why Kant, in the *Critique of Practical Reason*, describes self-love (*philautia*) as the propensity to self-conceit (*arrogantia*).[50]

III. Responding to Card's Critique

We are now positioned to respond to Card's claim that Kant's moral psychology of immorality is too simple. I believe I have already shown that, even if Kant's psychology of individual evil actions is over-simplistic, there is still much to be learned from Kant's account of evil people. However, while I think that Kant's empirical hedonism (the doctrine that whenever we act for non-moral reasons, we act to increase our pleasure) is implausible in significant ways, even it is unfazed by Card's particular critique.

Card's critique, remember, is that Kant sees all evil actions as stemming from the desire to make oneself happier. This is supposed to be problematic, though, because there are manifold motivations behind evil actions; one might violate a moral obligation just to make oneself happier, but one might also act evilly because one identifies with a cause greater than oneself, or even (perhaps) simply because it is morally prohibited to act wickedly.

In response, we should recall Kant's conception of happiness. To say that people seek their own happiness at the expense of morality allows for a wide variety of evil action. If one's happiness depends on entertaining a certain self-conception –say, of oneself as a great academic or public servant—then one can act so as to maintain this self-conception even when it requires sacrifices of pleasure.

---

[50] He defines self-love as the "propensity to make oneself as having subjective determining grounds of choice into the objective determining ground of the will in general" and says that a self-love that realizes its propensity is self-conceit ("if self-love makes itself lawgiving and the unconditional practical principle, it can be called *self-conceit*." (KpV 5: 74)) Unfortunately, a full account of Kant's remarks on self-love and self-conceit in the second *Critique* would take me beyond the scope of this paper.

This response takes us only so far, for we should remember that Kant is a hedonist about non-moral action.[51] That is, he thinks that people desire particular states of affairs only because they expect to experience pleasure upon the realization of those states of affairs: "we desire merely that which pleases us, pleasure is the cause of our desiring." (VM 29: 900)[52] Indeed, not only do people desire things merely because they expect pleasure from them, but they choose what to pursue depending on *how much* pleasure they expect from them: "[t]he only thing that concerns [man], in order to decide upon a choice, is how intense, how long, how easily acquired, and how often repeated this agreeableness is." (KpV 5: 23) How do we square this simple, seemingly mechanistic account of pleasure-seeking with the account I presented above?

There are two ways, one rooted in the text and one a speculative extension of it. The first way, from the text, requires first of all a proper understanding of the relationship between pleasure and happiness. As it turns out, the desire for pleasure can conflict with the desire for happiness. After all, the desire for happiness is a desire that one's life go relatively well, whereas the desire for pleasure is the desire for a certain feeling; but what if, in order for one's life to go relatively well, one has to endure pain? Or alternatively, what if, in order to experience a highly pleasing state of affairs, one has to sacrifice something that would make one's life go well?

Kant addresses this problem in the *Groundwork*:

> the precept of happiness is often so constituted that it greatly infringes upon some inclinations, and yet one can form no determinate and sure concept of the sum of the satisfaction of all inclinations under the name of happiness. Hence it is not to be wondered at that a single inclination, determinate both as to what it promises and as to the time within which it can be satisfied, can often outweigh a fluctuating idea, and that a man–for example, one suffering from gout–can choose to enjoy what he likes and put up with what he can since, according to his calculations, on this occasion at least he has not sacrificed the enjoyment of the present moment to the perhaps groundless expectation of a happiness that is supposed to lie in health. (G 4: 399)

---

[51] Here I disagree with Andrew Reath, "Hedonism, Heteronomy, and Kant's Principle of Happiness," in *Agency and Autonomy in Kant's Moral Theory: Selected Essays* (Oxford: Clarendon Press, 2006), ch. 2, and side with Barbara Herman, "Rethinking Kant's Hedonism," in *Moral Literacy* (Cambridge, MA: Harvard University Press, 2007), ch. 8.

[52] See KpV 5: 23; VM 28: 587-88, and 29: 878 and 1024; and VpR 28: 1060.

The idea of happiness is vague; no one exactly knows what will make her life go as well as possible–she can only make educated guesses, especially when experiencing pleasure is part of what (she thinks) makes her life go comparatively well. Given happiness's vagueness, though, it follows that she can confuse herself about what will make her happier. She may muse, "the nearer pleasure is more definite, whereas the farther pleasure, although greater, is less likely. Overall, then, perhaps the nearer pleasure *will* make me happier!" Thus, when tempted, she can use happiness's indeterminacy to deceive herself into thinking that the course of action she soberly believes would make her less happy will in fact make her happier, because it is likelier to come to pass ("a single inclination, determinate both as to what it promises and as to the time within which it can be satisfied, can often outweigh a fluctuating idea").

Thus, although Kant is an empirical hedonist, he thinks that the desire for happiness should take precedence over the desire for pleasure. So, an exceptionalist fantasist can sacrifice much of her well-being because doing so allows her to confirm her exceptional moral status, which makes her happier.

The second, more speculative possibility holds that evil people can act both selflessly and evilly by acting from a kind of false respect. This can be most clearly seen in the case of the exceptionalist fantasist. The exceptionalist fantasist holds to an indulgent moral law, one that permits actions to her that it denies to others. However, the principle to which she adheres still has a law-like form. Thus, she could do something immoral and painful, because she thinks it is her moral obligation.

Take the example of a slave-holder. He believes it morally permissible for him to enslave others; but if he were enslaved, he would think it monstrous. Nonetheless, he might hold that he has moral obligations to his slaves –perhaps he must Christianize them, and part of this duty requires teaching them obedience. He might not like using the whip, but he might persist anyway, because he thinks it his sacred duty.

Now, he thinks Christianizing is his duty because attributing such a duty to himself allows him to maintain the illusion that he is a moral paragon while also permitting him the use of slave-labor, which makes his life easier. Both maintaining the illusion of moral diligence and making his life easier contribute to his happiness. Nonetheless, it could be the case that discharging his horrendous "duties" pains him; if so, he might very well be motivated into it by respect for his indulgent moral law.

Timorousness and Other Fantasies

The adequacy fantasist accepts the moral law but deceives herself into thinking that her moral worth depends on how she compares to others in moral attainment rather than how she compares to the law. The exceptionalist fantasist does not even accept the moral law but instead replaces it with an indulgent simulacrum. There is a third possibility that Kant broaches, though he does not describe it as a moral fantasy; instead he calls it "timorousness": "humility can … have injurious consequences, if it is wrongly understood. For it brings timorousness and not courage with it, if a man believes that owing to the defectiveness of his actions they never comply with the moral law, from which inertia arises thereafter, in that he ventures to do nothing at all." (VE 27: 350)[53]

The timorous person accepts the moral law and understands how to determine one's true moral worth. However, because she so often fails at living up to the moral law, she deceives herself into thinking that it makes impossible demands on her. Consequently, she gets out of the morality game—after all, if it is impossible to live up to your moral duties, why even try?

Timorousness is a kind of evil if for no other reason than that the timorous person is likely to be morally inactive. However, the timorous person can undercut others' moral efforts by discouraging them from trying to morally improve themselves, and so can be seen as evil because of his propensity to corrupt others:

> Moral unbelief … is when one does not believe in the reality of virtue. It is a misanthropic attitude to suppose it an Idea. It is a conceit to satisfy one's inclination; a man can go far in it, and actually carry it so far that he is not even considered a righteous man, and then he will also never even try to become one. It is not good to cast suspicion on virtue and the seeds of belief in man, which many learned men have done, in order the better to demonstrate to man his corrupted state, and to take away from him the idea that he is virtuous. (VE 27: 316-17)

Notice that timorousness is "a conceit to satisfy one's inclination"; that is, the reason one becomes timorous is that it is easier to be timorous than to try but fail to live up to the moral law. Timorousness, like the adequacy and exceptionalist fantasies, is initiated in order to make oneself happier, and is achieved through self-deception.

---

[53] See VE 27: 610-11.

One can imagine other moral fantasies, although Kant does not mention them. For instance, one could believe that one's moral worth is not a function at all of adherence to the law but instead depends on one's talents, wealth, natural gifts, etc. Similarly, one could believe that only some people have dignity, or that dignity comes in degrees. There are, more than likely, other possibilities too. But exploring them will have to be left for later. In the meantime, I hope to have shown that Kant's moral psychology of immorality is not only more nuanced than critics like Card would have us believe, but also that it has something to offer contemporary philosophers thinking about evil.[54]

Works Cited

Allison, H. *Kant's Theory of Freedom* (Cambridge: Cambridge University Press, 1990).

Beck, L. W. *A Commentary to Kant's Critique of Practical Reason.* (Chicago: Chicago University Press, 1960).

Card, C. *The Atrocity Paradigm: A Theory of Evil* (Oxford: Oxford University Press, 2002).

Herman, B. "Rethinking Kant's Hedonism," in *Moral Literacy* (Cambridge, MA: Harvard University Press, 2007).

Johnson, R. "Kant's Conception of Merit," *Pacific Philosophical Quarterly* 77 (1996).

Kitcher, P. "What is a Maxim?" *Philosophical Topics* 31 (2003).

McCarty, R. "Maxims in Kant's Practical Philosophy," *Journal of the History of Philosophy* 44 (2006).

O'Connor, D. "Kant's Conception of Happiness," *Journal of Value Inquiry* 16 (1982).

Reath, A. "Hedonism, Heteronomy, and Kant's Principle of Happiness," in *Agency and Autonomy in Kant's Moral Theory: Selected Essays* (Oxford: Clarendon Press, 2006).

Scanlon, T.M. *What We Owe to Each Other* (Cambridge, MA: The Belknap Press of Harvard University Press, 1998).

Wood, A.W. "The Good Without Limitation (GMS I, 393-394)," in C. Horn and D. Schönecker (eds.) *Groundwork for the Metaphysics of Morals* (Berlin: Walter de Gruyter, 2006).

[54] For helpful comments on earlier drafts of this paper, I would like to thank Stephen Darwall, Michelle Kosch, Ian Proops, and the members of the Fourth Annual Meeting of the Eastern Study Group of the North American Kant Society. A special thanks goes to Pablo Muchnik and Cambridge Scholars Press for their work in putting this collection together.

CHAPTER NINE

JUSTICE AND REVOLUTION IN KANT'S POLITICAL PHILOSOPHY

DAVID CUMMISKEY

Kant was a forceful defender of representative government, political freedom, and the inherent dignity of all persons. Kant thus sympathized with the progressive forces in the Glorious Revolution of 1688, the American Revolution, the French Revolution, and the Irish attempt to achieve independence. Indeed, Kant maintained that the enthusiasm experienced by the spectators of the French Revolution constituted evidence of the fundamental moral disposition in human nature. Nonetheless, an absolute prohibition on revolution is at the very heart of Kant's *Doctrine of Right* in his *The Metaphysics of Morals* (MS).[1] Kant's opposition to even progressive revolutions is clearly puzzling. In defending the Rights of Man against violent tyrants and despotic power, the counter use of force and violence is widely recognized as a legitimate

---

[1] Immanuel Kant (1797), *The Metaphysics of Morals*, abbreviation (MS), translated by Mary Gregor (Cambridge, 1991) and included in *Practical Philosophy* (Cambridge Edition of the works of Immanuel Kant, 1996)). Parenthetical references will be provided for this work as well as Kant's *Groundwork of the Metaphysics of Morals*, abbreviation (G), trans. H. J. Paton (Harper & Row, 1964/1785), *The Critique of Practical Reason*, abbreviation (KpV), trans. by Lewis White Beck (Bobbs-Merill, 1965), and Kant's *Perpetual Peace and Other Essays*, trans. Ted Humphrey (Hackett, 1983), abbreviation (EF) for the essay "To Perpetual Peace: A Philosophical Sketch" (1795) and (TP) "On The Old Proverb: That May Be True In Theory but is of No Practical Use" (1793). Page numbers refer to the Prussian Academy edition, which are also provided in the above translations (*Kant's gesammelte Schriften* [Berlin: Preussische Academie der Wissenschaften, 1900-1942]). In addition to Mary Gregor's translation of *The Metaphysics of Morals*, I also rely on John Ladd's earlier translation.,*The Metaphysical Elements of Justice* (Bobbs-Merrill, 1965 & 2nd edition Hackett, 1999).

means of last resort. When Nelson Mandela refused to renounce revolutionary actions as a means to ending South African apartheid, the "enthusiasm" and support from distant people from around the world testified once again to the "moral disposition" in humanity. But was Mandela in fact wrong to hold that he, and all people, may legitimately use force to resist violent and repressive state power, and thereby defend their basic human rights? Surely, it is at least morally permissible to defend oneself and others too, when basic rights are threatened. Why then did Kant, despite applauding the sentiments of sympathy for progressive revolutions, condemn the actions of the revolutionaries?

Kant's stringent and seemingly reactionary conclusion has surprised Kant's readers for generations. According to Kant, the people must endure even "the most unbearable abuse of supreme authority" (MS 320). It does not matter how unjust or repressive a government may be, there is no right on the part of the subjects to revolt. Furthermore, his opposition to the right of revolution was no mere passing opinion. It appears in all of his major discussions of justice and Kant sticks to his position even in responding to a critic challenging the consistency of his position. One would thus expect Kant to have good, if not sound, grounds for his conclusion.

Given the wide ranging influence of Kant's moral and political theory, we should discover the deeper basis for Kant's surprising conclusion. In particular, the apparent conflict between Kant's commitment to individual rights and his doctrine of obedience to thoroughly despotic states calls for a detailed explanation and a clear resolution. Most essays, on Kant's theory of revolution, focus on the tension between Kant's sympathetic discussion of the French Revolution and his prohibition on revolution. Although this tension is of interest, I shall focus on the apparent conflict within Kant's theory of justice itself: Given Kant's spirited defense of representative democracy, of the constitutional division of powers, of the political freedom and equality of persons, and of moral autonomy (that is, the imperative to rationally self-legislate the maxims of one's action) what are we to make of Kant's explicit and repeated insistence that civil rebellion is never justified? Since Kant agrees that actual states are often not only imperfect but also corrupt or despotic, this seems to imply that we have a duty to obey, or at least endure, illegitimate civil laws. Indeed, the actual executor of supreme coercive power may act in ways that are directly contrary to the ends of justice. Are we really morally obliged to tolerate state power when it is used to enforce systematic injustice?

In the first and second parts of this chapter, I reconstruct Kant's position. We see how Kant's justification of property and civil society entails a specific interpretation of his absolute prohibition on revolution. In particular, we see that the prohibition on revolution is part of a general prohibition on the individual use of coercive means to promote individual ends.[2] In the third part, I turn to a critical analysis of Kant's absolute prohibition on rebellion. In the end, I defend Kant's conclusion that one may never rebel against a civil state but, nonetheless, I argue that Kant is mistaken in taking this to imply that we must endure the powers that be. We should not use violence to reform imperfect civil societies but awesome power alone does not transform a mafia into a legitimate government. Indeed, when state power is systematically used to exclude some for the benefit of others then it is simply Lawless organized power. In such a case, morally speaking, we are confronted with an unjust state of war, not a civil society. I argue that there is an unconditional duty, which is based on the basic principles of Kantian justice, to resist the Lawless powers that be, and to strive to bring forth, even by violent means, a true civil society.[3]

---

[2] In addition to his main argument for the prohibition on revolution, Kant raises other objections to revolution. Most prominent is Kant's claim that the principle of publicity "solves with utter ease" the question of the legitimacy of rebellion (see EF 382). The explanation that follows this bold claim is complex, overly compressed, and not very convincing. I leave this argument aside and I also do not assess Kant's more pragmatic arguments against violent revolution.

[3] Kant's prohibition on revolution has inspired many responses. In one of my favorite responses, Beck claims that Kant believed that the duty to fight injustice is an imperfect duty and he thus argues that Kant's views on revolution are simply one more example of Kant incapacity to deal with conflicting duties (see L.W. Beck in "Kant and the Right of Revolution" in *Essays on Kant and Hume*; Yale, 1978). On the view here defended, Beck is mistaken in treating the Kantian duty to rebel as merely an imperfect duty. Leaving aside the difficulties with the perfect/imperfect distinction, the Kantian right of rebellion is based on considerations of justice. For Kant, justice involves duties which can be coercively enforced and (allegedly) all such duties are perfect duties. It has also been argued that Kant's positive statements about particular revolutions are part of his natural anthropology (and not part of his practical philosophy). I am sympathetic to Thomas Seebohm's use of the distinction between anthropology and justice to resolve the conflict between Kant's theory of justice and his sympathies for the French revolution (see Thomas Seebohm "Kant's Theory of Revolution" *Social Research* 48:557-587, 1981). I argue, however, that, in addition to being significant for natural anthropology, progressive revolutions are also required by considerations of justice. H. S. Reiss recognizes that Kant's theory of justice itself provides a justification for revolution (see "Kant on the Right of Rebellion," *Journal of the History of Ideas* 17: 179- 192, 1956). In particular, Reiss focuses on Kant's optimism about historical progress, and he objects to Kant's position on the

I- Kant's Theory of Justice

Kant's prohibition on revolution is based on his theory of justice. Although I cannot here reconstruct Kant's elaborate theory of justice, four central points are necessary for understanding Kant's conclusion: first, the theory of justified coercion; second, the duty to make property possible; third, the duty to enter into a civil society; and fourth, the right to use violent means to bring about a civil society.

First, under what conditions can one legitimately use force or threats of force to control the conduct of others? According to Kant, we may legitimately use coercion only in response to the unlawful conduct of others. We cannot, of course, force people to be good but we can force them to act as they ought to act; that is, even though we cannot coerce internal motives, we can coerce external actions. The actions which are done under the threat of coercion are described by Kant as externally legislated. In contrast, actions which are done because of our inner motives are internally legislated. For Kant, principles of justice are simply the body of external laws, that is, the laws that can be externally legislated (MS 229).

Since the principle of all legitimacy is the categorical imperative (that is, "act only on that maxims through which you can at the same time will that it should become a universal law") external laws governing actions must be possible universal laws. Justice (Right) thus involves "the sum of the conditions under which the choice of one can be united with the choice of another in accordance with a universal law of freedom." (MS 230) The universal law of justice, the categorical imperative of justice, is thus: "so act externally that the free use of your choice can coexist with the freedom of everyone in accordance with a universal law." (MS 230-31)

If an action is permissible, that is, compatible with universal lawful freedom of action, then it is also legitimate to use coercion against anyone preventing the permissible action. As Kant explains,

---

inevitable progressive force of free discussion. Reiss does not address what I take to be the central issue of the relationship between state power and political exclusion. The author that comes closest to the view here defended is Sarah Williams Holt in "Revolution, Contradiction, and Kantian Citizenship" in *Kant's Metaphysics of Morals: Interpretive Essays* edited by Mark Timmons (Oxford 2002). Holt contrasts Kant's position with Hobbes' prohibition on rebellion and emphasizes the different conceptions of citizenship and equality in the two approaches. From this different starting point, she also concludes that Kantian justice may sometimes justify violent revolutions.

> if a certain use of freedom is itself a hindrance to freedom in accordance with universal laws (i.e. wrong), coercion that is opposed to this (as a hindering of a hindering to freedom) is consistent with freedom in accordance with universal laws, that is, it is right. Hence there is connected with Right by the principle of contradiction an authorization to coerce someone who infringes it … one can locate the concept of Right directly in the possibility of connecting universal reciprocal coercion with the freedom of everyone. (MS 231-32)

Justice involves the authorization to use coercion to promote lawful freedom.

The next obvious question involves the nature of lawful freedom. Kant apparently takes it to be obvious that intrinsic violence, violence for its own sake, is a violation of lawful freedom. Even in a state of nature, maxims of self-defense are permissible (MS 307 and 312). Similarly, if you wrestle an unowned apple from my hand you attack my lawful freedom simply by attacking my hand (MS 250). Thus, even if there was no right of private ownership, acts of violence and of physical force would be impermissible. Although Kant does not explicitly say so, we may conclude that these actions are direct violations of justice and do not depend on civil society for their legitimate external enforcement. In this context, we too shall assume that murder and mayhem directly violate the constraints of justice.[4]

The controversial questions of justice, however, do not involve the illegitimacy of murder and violence. The core of legal justice involves property claims and contracts. Kant maintains that property and contracts both involve the agent's legitimate authority over something external; namely, either the possession of external things or the performance of actions by others (MS 247-248).[5] In order to simplify matters, I will focus on property rights in particular. We have just seen that justice involves the enforcement of lawful freedom. Since property rights extend the agent's authority to external things, we need to uncover the relationship between legitimate property claims and lawful freedom.

Specifically, how can it be permissible for one person to claim a previously unowned object as his or her own? In claiming an object as

[4] Kant says very little about murder and violence and it is not at all obvious how the universalizability test should handle such cases. For an excellent discussion of this problem see Barbara Herman, "Murder and Mayhem: Violence and Kantian Casuistry" (in *The Monist* vol. 72 no. 2, 1989; pp. 411-431 and reprinted in *The Practice of Moral Judgment*, Harvard 1996).

[5] Kant includes women and servants as a type of property but it can be shown that this claim is inconsistent with his theory of property and his larger moral theory.

mine, since all others can no longer use the object, I thereby restrict their freedom. Furthermore, since it is impossible to secure the consent of all other rational beings, private acquisition restricts the freedom of others without their consent. If private ownership is legitimate, then it places all others under an obligation to respect my claim. It follows that my act of acquisition creates an obligation for all others without their consent. In general, however, one cannot incur an obligation without doing something. The acquisition of property and the resulting restriction of others' freedom thus must be justified. How can a unilateral act of my will generate an obligation for all others?

This brings us to the second and third points listed above: For Kant the justification of property rights and of civil society is one and the same: it is a duty to act so that private ownership of things is possible and this entails a duty to enter into a civil society. Briefly, Kant argues, I believe successfully, that it is necessary (that is, a demand of practical reason) that it be possible for external objects to be used and possessed by finite rational beings (MS 246-252). The juridical postulate of practical reason states "it is a duty of Right [of justice] to act toward others so that what is external (usable) can also become someone's [property]." (MS 252) But, as we have just seen, the acquisition of property restricts the freedom of others without their consent and a unilateral restriction of others' freedom is generally prohibited by the universal principle of justice.

Kant is thus led to explain that the juridical postulate of practical reason is a "permissive law" which "confers on us an authorization that we cannot derive from the mere concept of justice in general, namely, the authorization to impose an obligation on all others –an obligation that they otherwise would not have had– to refrain from using objects of our will because we were the first to take possession of them." (MS 247, Ladd) Kant's notion of a permissive law is thus crucial to his deduction of property rights and, as we shall see, civil society. Most simply, a permissive law involves a permission to do or allow something which is generally prohibited in order to bring about the state of affairs which is the goal, or intention of the general prohibition (EF 347-348).

In particular, in claiming possession of an object, one may restrict others' negative freedom, by imposing an obligation on all others without their consent, because the permission to do so results in a greater degree of negative freedom for all than otherwise would be possible. If there were no right to acquire property, then all objects would be unusable. All others would still have no legitimate claim to the object which, in accordance with the permissive law, I acquire by first possession. The permissive law is thus consistent with the intention of the general prohibition on non-consensual restrictions of negative freedom; that is, the permission increases the freedom of each without interfering with the universal lawful freedom of all.

In evaluating Kant's prohibition on rebellion, we must ask whether, contra-Kant, the concept of a permissive law can also play a significant role in justifying some revolutionary activity. In principle, revolutionary activity may bring about the state of affairs which is the point or goal of the general prohibition on rebellious activity. Of course, we are not yet able to evaluate this suggestion. We will return to this issue after setting out the rest of Kant's argument for his conclusion.

The second point entails the third important point: According to the Universal Principle of Right (or Justice), "Any action is *right* if it can coexist with everyone's freedom in accordance with a universal law." (MS 230) Since the permissive law, which legitimizes my right of first possession, applies to all rational beings, it also imposes a reciprocal duty to respect the proprietary claims of others (MS 255). Nonetheless, unilateral coercion cannot provide a legitimate basis for the enforcement of rights. As Kant explains,

> Now a unilateral will cannot serve as a coercive law for everyone with regard to possession that is external and therefore contingent, since that would infringe upon freedom in accordance with universal laws. So it is only a will putting everyone under obligation, hence only a collective general (common) and powerful will, that can provide everyone with this assurance. But the condition of being under a general external (i.e. public) lawgiving accompanied with power is the civil condition. So only in a civil condition can something external be mine or yours. (MS 256)

Since a civil society is simply a society governed by such a general will, Kant concludes that reciprocal duties are only legitimately enforced in a civil society. In evaluating Kant's position, we shall repeatedly return to Kant's conceptions of unilateral and non-unilateral coercion. First, however, we need to appreciate the important conclusion which follows from the conjunction of this claim and the duty to make property possible. Since it is a duty of justice to make property rights possible and since property rights are only possible in a civil society, all persons are required to enter into a civil society.

The third point leads to the fourth and final preliminary point: As we saw above, lawful freedom is consistent with the coercive enforcement of rights. Since we must make use of and take possession of external objects, and since duties of justice are coercible duties, "the subject must be also be permitted to constrain [or, to compel] everyone else with whom he comes into conflict about whether an external object is his or another's to enter along with him into a civil constitution." (MS 256) His reasons for this last point are fairly straightforward.

Despite the moral disposition in human nature, Kant recognizes that all human beings are subject to unconscious partiality (MS 312) and conscious self-interest. "Man feels in himself a powerful counterweight to all the commands of duty... the counterweight of his needs and inclinations." (G 405) Indeed, Kant recognizes a Hobbesean or Nietzschean element in human nature: We are all aware of "the inclination of men generally to lord it over others as their master (not to respect the superiority of the rights of others when they feel superior to them in strength or cunning)." (MS 307) As a consequence of this aspect of human nature, anyone who refuses to enter a civil society is a threat to all others. Since I may legitimately coerce coercers (that is, remove hindrances to lawful freedom), if someone is threatening me, I do not have to wait to protect myself until after I have "suffered a loss" from someone who refuses to enter into a civil society with me. It follows that "one is authorized to use coercion against someone who already, by his nature, threatens him with coercion." (MS 307) Against those who embrace lawless freedom, preemptive strikes are sometimes justified. It is thus permissible to use unilateral coercion, and to "impel the other by force" to leave the state of nature and enter a civil society (MS 312). In the Ladd translation of the same passage, the point is made even more forcefully, "everyone may use violent means to compel another to enter into a juridical state of society." (MS 312, Ladd)

The point, however, of a civil society is to restrict the authorization to use coercion to the united general will of the people. For coercion to have the force of a law, it must be governed by a common general will. Conversely, a primary basis of the general will of a people is their common interest in having public laws which enforce property claims. As Hobbes argued and Kant agreed, even "a people comprised of devils" and thus with no moral disposition have an interest in avoiding the destructive Hobbesean or Lockean anarchy of a state of nature (EF 366 and MS 311). In short, the use of unilateral coercion is permissible only in a state of nature and the ultimate goal of permissible unilateral coercion is the creation of a shared civil society.

When I claim an object as mine, based on my first empirical possession of the object, the exclusionary nature of my claim, places others under a duty to refrain from the use of the object. For this initial claim to have the juridical validity of a coercive right, I must enter into a civil society with anyone contesting my claim.[6] If I refuse to enter into a civil society then my claim, however initially valid, does not meet the conditions of a coercively enforceable right. Conversely, if the individual contesting my right refuses to enter into a shared civil society, when I am willing to do so, then I may resist his competing claim with force and I am additionally justified in using violent means, if necessary, to force him or her to enter into a shared civil society. Legitimate claims become coercive rights in a civil society but, nonetheless, the duty to enter into a civil society may be unilaterally and violently enforced (MS 256-257 and 313). Once one understands the logical structure of Kant's argument, one recognizes that these two claims are consistent and mutually entailed by the argument.

We start with the permissive law which allows the acquisition of unowned property. The initial acquisition of property generates a duty on all others to refrain from using the newly acquired object and a reciprocal duty on the part of the possessor to enter into a civil society with all others. So, if I claim any object, I become duty bound to enter a civil society governed by a general will. *The exercise of the permission leads to an unconditional obligation*. But, because of the necessity of need, all finite rational beings must make use of external objects. It follows that every

---

[6] Since rights are publicly enforceable claims, prior to the formation of a civil society all property claims are only provisional. The civil society makes possible the legitimate coercive enforcement of property and thereby transforms the essentially provisional ownership of the state of nature into lawful property rights (MS 256-257).The reason for this is clear: Since the legitimacy of my property claim depends on my reciprocal duty to respect the legitimate claims of others (MS 255), and since my unilateral will can no more bind the other than the other's unilateral will can bind me (MS 256), in acquiring a thing I also fall under an obligation to enter into a civil society governed by a shared general will with anyone contesting my claim. Thus, only the general will of a civil society can legitimately adjudicate conflicting claims and enforce one of the claims. If I refuse to enter into a civil society with the other or if the civil judgment opposes my claim, then I do not have an enforceable right to the thing. In this sense, my initial claim is provisional on the impartial judgment of the civil society. Thus, in the state of nature, all ownership is only provisional. Nonetheless, there is legitimate first possession in the state of nature because the point of civil society is to secure and guarantee what is yours and what is mine. The civil society, however, provides the only legitimate condition for the coercive enforcement of competing claims. As Kant explains, civil society presupposes prior legitimate possession of things but the coercively enforceable right to a thing presupposes a civil society (MS 256-257 and 313). For a more thorough discussion of this issue, see Kenneth R Westphal "A Kantian Theory of Possession" *Kant's Metaphysics of Morals: Interpretive Essays* edited by Mark Timmons (Oxford 2002).

finite rational being, given the possibility of conflicts over rights, *is unconditionally bound to enter into a shared civil society.*

II. Revolution and the Idea of the State

The argument so far establishes the unilaterally enforceable duty to enter into a shared civil society. This argument rules out all forceful resistance to any united civil society which strives to protect individual rights. But Kant has not yet established the illegitimacy of all revolutionary activity. In particular, he has not established that it is illegitimate to use coercive means to end a situation in which "state" coercion does not express the general will of the people. If we have a duty of justice to secure the enjoyment of property by bringing about a shared civil society, then why do we not also have a duty to resist or overthrow a civil society that threatens the equitable enjoyment of property?

Indeed, why assume that any actual state is the product of the united general will of the people? It would seem that Kant has only demonstrated that revolutionary activity is impermissible if state power is actually a reflection of the general will. This clearly is not Kant's position. Kant emphasizes that "the presently existing legislative authority ought to be obeyed, whatever its origin" (MS 319) and that the "people [have] a duty to put up with what is held to be an unbearable abuse of supreme authority." (MS 320) It thus seems that political obligation is not conditioned by the legitimacy of the government or the reasonableness of its commands.

In response to a reviewer of his work, Kant explains his controversial conclusion:

> No object of experience can be given that adequately corresponds to an Idea. A perfect juridical [just] constitution among men would be an example of such an Idea. When a people are united through laws under a suzerain [or, an authority], then the people are given as an object of experience conforming to the *Idea in general* of the unity of the people under a supreme powerful Will. Admittedly, this is only an appearance ... Although the [actual] constitution may contain grave defects and gross errors and may need to be gradually improved in important respects, still, as such, it is absolutely unpermitted and culpable to oppose it. If the people were to hold that they were justified in using violence against a constitution, however, defective it might be, and against the supreme authority, they would be supposing that they had a right to put violence as the supreme prescriptive act of legislation in the place of every right and Law. (MS 371-372, Ladd)

There is much in Kant's response which we need to explicate. The key points are (i) Kant's distinction between the Idea of the state and actual states and (ii) Kant's claim that popular opposition to the supreme authority replaces Law with violence.

Prior to clarifying his response, however, let me note the problematic assumption Kant seems to be making. Kant claims that all instances of de facto state power present at least an appearance of the Idea of a juridical state. I take it that this implies that whenever one has a territorial coercive monopoly one has coercion regulated by the rule of Law, and an imperfect but sufficiently just civil society is therefore instantiated. As a result, Kant is led to his claim that, no matter how defective and abusive it may be, we must endure the rule of the supreme power. This is thus a surprising assumption which leads to a very unattractive conclusion.

Let us pause and consider the grounds for attributing this assumption to Kant: Is he really committed to such a Hobbesian account of sovereign power? In order to avoid the extreme interpretation of Kant's prohibition on rebellion, one might argue that Kant does not actually endorse the controversial assumption which leads to this unattractive conclusion. It is tempting to credit Kant with a more subtle, *unstated* position which distinguishes between a "current viable, though perhaps quite imperfect project of protecting people in morally important freedoms that are threatened in the state of nature" and "a successful mafia take-over of Nevada." Only the former, it might be claimed, is an example of sovereign power. Kant's prohibition on rebellion would then apply only to imperfect projects of protecting important rights. It would not apply to any successful exercise of organized, territorial, coercive power.

Clearly, if Kant supported violent revolution, then he had reason to fear the Prussian censors. Furthermore, in responding to the above mentioned reviewer, Kant grants the paradox in his views of rebellion but insists that he cannot be convicted of heterodoxy (MS 371). The basic preconditions for a dissimulation interpretation are thus in place: fear of the censors and a paradoxical conclusion. We are thus to believe that Kant hid his true views behind statements crafted to mislead the powers that be; for he knew the "astute and careful" reader would recognize his subtle and coyly stated position. In principle, I have nothing against this type of textual interpretation. It seems a fitting approach to some difficult, perhaps inconsistent, passages in Rousseau and Hume, for example. On the other hand, I am less sympathetic with its use in discovering Plato's secret doctrines. In interpreting Kant's stand on revolution, however, I believe it should be a method of last resort.[7]

First, in general, Kant was opposed to the use of violence as a means. I believe that he was genuinely horrified by the death and destruction of a violent revolution. Indeed, his level of passion in discussing the horror of the formal execution of a monarch (MS 32On) is matched only by his emotion in his ode to "Duty!" in the *Critique of Practical Reason* (KpV 86-87). In addition, Kant was as a firm believer in the inevitable moral progress of the human race. By a process of slow and gradual enlightenment, republican constitutions and perpetual peace will prevail throughout the world (MS 352-355 and EF). Thus, on the one hand, Kant repeatedly and forcefully insisted that all active rebellion violates an unconditional duty of justice. On the other hand, he also assures us that, in due time, peace and justice will indeed prevail. Kant simply believed that rebellion is both wrong and unnecessary. Kant advocated peaceful progressive evolution rather than violent revolution. This is such a plausible interpretation of Kant's overall view that a dissimulation hypothesis is just not called for.

Second, Kant's views about the unconditional demands of honesty are notorious: We cannot lie to a murderer in order to save a life. In addition, in his only published discussion of civil disobedience (which will be discussed below), Kant insists that, even under royal command and threat

---

[7] For a different perspective on this question, see Kenneth Westphal "Kant's Qualified Principle of Obedience to Authority in the *Metaphysical Elements of Justice*." (in G. Funke, ed., *Akten des 7. internationalen Kant-Kongress* (Bonn: Bouvier, 1991), II.2:353-66) and "Kant on the State, Law, and Obedience to Authority in the Alleged 'Anti-revolutionary' Writings" (*Journal of Philosophical Research* 17 (1991-92):383-426). Kant's reaction to the censors, in presenting his religious views, seems to add some support to the dissimulation interpretation of Kant's views on revolution. When he was ordered not to publicly express his views on Christianity, he obeyed. Still, the religious case is, to my mind, utterly distinct in kind and degree from the alleged deception in this case. Even if silence is a legitimate response to state censorship, Kant was far from silent on this issue. On the contrary, in the appendix to MS which addressed a reviewer's criticism, he insisted on his conclusion (MS 371-372). Of course, Kant may have been winking all along but I find this quite implausible. In addition, Kant's obedient silence actually supports the interpretation offered below. After all, Kant did do what he was told to do. Nonetheless, if Kant recognized that it is a *duty of justice* to struggle against institutional exclusion, as I argue in section III, then Kant would still be wrong to "silently" mislead his readers about the true nature of their duties. One can legitimately obey or keep silent (as we shall see below) only if one does not thereby offend against duty by doing something that is wrong in itself.

of death, it is not permissible to bear false witness. According to Kant, it is better to die then to lie. Yet, we are expected to believe that Kant deceptively hides, and perhaps even denies, his true conclusions? I suggest, instead, that we take Kant at his word and we search for his best justification for his prohibition on violent revolution.

Recall Kant's stated position: He insists that the people are obliged to obey the powers that be irrespective of their origin (MS 319), of their intolerable abuses of authority (MS 320), of the grave defects and gross errors in their constitutions (MS 372). Kant emphasizes that "the unconditional submission of the popular Will (which is in itself not united and hence is lawless) to the sovereign Will (uniting everyone through one single law) is a deed that can begin only with the seizure of the supreme authority and in this way provides a foundation for a public Law in the first place." (MS 372, Ladd)

How then can Kant, given his stated view, distinguish between a successful mafia takeover of Nevada and the problematic origins and gross imperfections of other imperfect but adequate exercises of state power? Given the assumption that the take-over has been successful, the origin is irrelevant. Any distinction between the two must appeal to the nature of the abuses, defects, and errors. Kant, however, maintains that any successful grasp of supreme executive and legislative authority presents us with at least an *appearance* of the Idea of the state and of a people united under Law. He concludes that to act against even a mere appearance of the Idea of the state is unconditionally forbidden.

If, however, one is convinced that Kant's true view is indeed the more subtle unstated view, then the argument for his true view still must be constructed for him –for, by hypothesis, he could not present it for fear of the censors. In the next section, we shall see the more limited prohibition which actually follows from Kant's theory of justice. If Kant was coy, then, perhaps, this is also his real view. Since ultimately we are concerned with what *follows* from Kant's argument, we may set aside questions about Kant's hidden intentions. For simplicity, however, I will focus on Kant's stated view and its adequacy.

I shall argue, first, that Kant's prohibition on rebellion is plausible in a state which is imperfectly committed to the free and equal treatment of all persons under the law but, second, that it simply does not apply to a state of affairs in which a privileged group of individuals use centralized coercive power to perpetuate a state of inequality and injustice. Kant must acknowledge that there are conditions coercive power must meet before it can constitute legitimate government power; and, thus, before we are faced with even an imperfect civil society. In section III, I will develop and defend this objection. For the moment, we shall set aside this objection and strive to more fully understand Kant's position. We shall see that, in an imperfect (but inclusive) civil society, Kant provides a plausible account of the basis and extent of our political obligations.

The concept of a society governed by a united general will, according to Kant, is an Idea of reason. An Idea of reason is as an ideal which is used as a guide to proper conduct; it is a practical concept expressed by a normative principle. Kant insists that, even though our imperfect society clearly does not satisfy the Idea of the state, we still owe political obedience to the ruler. In order to understand Kant's position, we must discover the regulative, normative, role of the Idea of the state.[8]

First, let us consider the perspective of the ruler. For Kant, the Idea of the state is a moral standard which the ruler, the *de facto* supreme authority of the state, morally ought to use in ruling the state. Thus, the ruler, as legislator, ought to legislate so as to reflect "the general and united will of the people," that is, "the concurring and united will of all, insofar as each decides the same thing for all." (MS 314) The ruler, as executive authority, ought to enforce only such laws. If the ruler uses the supreme coercive authority for private or partial ends, then the ruler acts wrongly and the state is corrupted.

The subjects, on the other hand, *should not* use the Idea of the state to judge the legitimacy of their state. Since the general will of the people must be *represented*, that is, some procedure for determining the general will is necessary, and since the government claims authority to determine the general will, Kant maintains that we (the subjects) should adopt the procedure of treating *de facto* supreme power as the only source of legitimate coercive power.[9] In this way, the subjects are united under a

---

[8] For our purposes, we do not need to determine the practical social and legislative results of the regulative and guiding idea of the general will. There is promise, however, in Harry van der Linden's suggestion that "the moral society [is] a society of autonomous or co-legislative institutions, aiming at universal happiness" (*Kantian Ethics and Socialism*, Hackett 1988; p.192). I would argue, however, for a more explicitly distribution-sensitive interpretation. In addition, Kantian value theory requires that the realization of the conditions necessary for the development and exercise of our rational capacities take priority over the maximization of happiness. With these two modifications, Kant's theory of justice would be a distinctly Kantian form of indirect (or rule) consequentialism (see Cummiskey *Kantian Consequentialism*, Oxford 1996).

[9] Christine Korsgaard has emphasized the importance of the public representation of the general will in "Taking the Law into our own Hands: Kant on the Right to Revolution" in A. Reath, B. Herman, and C. Korsgaard, eds., *Reclaiming the History of Ethics: Essays for John Rawls* (Cambridge University Press, 1997).

system of law and an appearance of the Idea of the state is realized; that is, the coercive enforcement of claims takes on at least an appearance of the Idea of coercion regulated by a shared general will. All revolutionary activity involves the unilateral coercion of some citizens (namely, the members of the government) by other citizens (namely, the rebellious subjects) and it thus violates the fundamental condition of civil society: the transfer of the coercive enforcement of justice to the general will as manifest in a public constitution.

Of course, the government may be mistaken in its judgment of the demands of the general will but so too may the rebellious subjects. If some faction of the subjects replace their will with the government's will, there is no reason to think that there has been any gain in determining the true general will of the people. As Rousseau, Mill, and others have emphasized, even if a majority of the subjects rebel, they may represent only a tyranny of the majority. Indeed, Kant argues that "the head of the nation can as easily justify his harsh treatment of the subjects by appeal to their rebelliousness as they can justify their unrest by adducing complaints about unwarranted suffering at his hands" (TP 300). Thus, by enduring the actual government's authority, one at least maintains an appearance of justice that would be lost by any and all acts of factional rebellion.

The government's pronouncements on the general will may or may not accurately represent the true general will. The subjects are thus free to dissent from the government's judgment even after it has been duly pronounced. Such actions do not involve coercive violence and they are thus consistent with the required state monopoly on coercive power. This is why the subjects retain, and why the ruler should promote, the right of dissent and "the freedom of the pen." (TP 304) Indeed, in the interest of discovering the demands of justice, the ruler should encourage the people to use the "freedom of the pen" to offer advice and even to criticize the ruler (but not, of course, to incite rebellion) (TP 304).

Similarly, the subjects do not have a duty to obey all of the sovereign's commands. Specifically, Kant writes: "*Obey the authority who has power over you* (in whatever does not conflict with inner morality)." (MS 371) [Ladd translation: "Obey the suzerain (in everything that does not conflict with internal morality) who has authority over you!"] Kant's writings provide some explicit examples of what Kant had in mind by "internal morality." In *The Critique of Practical Reason*, Kant states that one should refuse to lie even under royal command (KpV 155-56). As I mentioned above, this is Kant's only published example of permissible civil disobedience. There is, however, Kant's unpublished note which tells us that we may rebel in cases that involve "the enforcement of a religion, compulsion to unnatural sins, assassination, etc."[10] Lastly, in *Religion within the Limits of Reason Alone*, Kant writes that "when men command anything which in itself is evil (directly opposed to the law of morality) we dare not, and ought not, obey them."[11] Kant goes on to explain that we are to obey all other statutory laws, even if they do not appear to us to reflect the true general will of the people.

Kant clearly permits conscientious refusal. I believe that one can stretch a bit and claim that Kant also leaves room for Gandian style "passive" resistance to particular commands and laws. His position is thus more palatable then it may at first appear. But, Kant never sanctions violent revolution. The subjects should speak their minds but, provided the commanded act is not wrong in itself, do as they are told.

A right of rebellion would entail that the subjects have the right to coerce the sovereign ruler.[12] But the sovereign power of the civil society is to provide the public, non-unilateral, enforcement of property rights. According to the Idea of civil society, state coercion is guided by the general will and it is the only type of justified coercion. The general will, however, is not simply the will of the majority. It thus must be interpreted by a supreme, authoritative, representative of the united people. This is a chief role of a supreme court in constitutional democracies. When it comes to the final interpretation and enforcement of the law, the subjects must set aside their particular judgments, even when it reflects the popular will of the majority, and defer to the rule of law. In this way the subjects fulfill their political obligations, as required by the Idea of the state. The actual supreme ruler of the state (or supreme court) has the responsibility and final authority to interpret the general will. Of course, my obedience as a subject does not guarantee that the ruler will correctly discern the general will or do his or her duty. According to Kant, when I disagree with the de facto ruler, my duty is to express my dissent; not to enforce my opinion.

---

[10] L.W. Beck in "Kant and the Right of Revolution" in *Essays on Kant and Hume* (Yale, 1978) p.173 (AK 594-595).

[11] Kant *Religion* Ak. VI, 99n; translated by Greene and Hudson (Harper, 1960) p. 90.

[12] Kant also argues that if the people could coerce the ruler then the people and not the ruler would be sovereign. There is thus a contradiction in the claim that the people (who are the subjects not the sovereign) have the right to coerce the sovereign ruler (for then the ruler would be the subject and the people the sovereign). Since this is an uninteresting legalistic point, I do not pursue it (see Beck pp. 175-176). From our perspective, the relevant point here is that if both the ruler and the subjects have the right to coerce each other, then there is no final public procedure for adjudicating conflicting rights.

According to Kant, the prohibition on rebellion is essentially a corollary of the unconditional duty to enter into a civil society. This is an important point. It is not the ruler whom we wrong by rebellion but the rule of Law itself and thus the very foundation of the commonwealth (EF 382, TP 299, MS 319-320).[13] Kant's position here is not an aberration; in fact it coheres nicely with his account of the practical significance of the Idea of the kingdom of ends. Recall that a kingdom of ends would be the result of each rational being treating all others, never simply as a means, but always at the same time as an end in itself. It is "a systematic union of rational beings under common objective laws" (G 433). Of course, as Kant explains, even if I strictly follow the categorical imperative, I cannot count on all others to do so as well and thus my legitimate purposes may not be realized as they would be in a kingdom of ends. "But in spite of this the law' Act on the maxims of a member who makes universal law for a merely possible kingdom of ends' remains in full force since its command is categorical" (G 439). Similarly, even though I cannot count on the ruler of my state to be faithful to duty, the Idea of the state nonetheless categorically obliges me as a subject to obey the ruler. Indeed, the ruler's moral failures may undermine my expectations of happiness, but personal happiness is not the Kantian ground of duty. "And precisely here we encounter the paradox that without any further end or advantage to be attained the mere dignity of humanity, that is, rational nature in man –and consequently reverence for a mere Idea– should function as an inflexible

[13] Kant's prohibition on rebellion is analogous to his uncompromising prohibition on lying to murderers. In addition to the obvious similarities, in both cases Kant does not base the prohibition on the rights of the sovereign or of the murderer. The murderer at the door does not have a right to the truth, Kant explains, because "truth is not a possession the right to which can be granted to one and refused to another; and next and chiefly, because the duty of veracity (of which alone we are speaking here) makes no distinction between persons towards whom we have this duty, and towards whom we may be free from it ... although by a certain lie I in fact do no wrong to any person, yet I infringe the principle of justice in regard to all indispensable statements in general ... and this is much worse than to commit an injustice to any individual." We are not here concerned with the soundness of Kant's position on lying to murders, but the similarity in the structure of Kant's arguments is instructive. If we are to understand Kant's reasoning we must focus on the justification of state power in general rather than on the legitimacy of the acts of a particular ruler. For a discussion of the similarities between Kant's prohibitions on lying and on rebellion, see Peter Nicholson "Kant on the Duty Never to Resist the Sovereign" (*Ethics* 1976: 214-230) but also see Wolfgang Schwarz "The Ambiguities of Resistance: A Reply to Nicholson" (*Ethics* 1977:255-259).

precept for the will." (G 439) Reverence for the mere Idea of the state is the determining ground of my political obligations; these obligations are not erased by the ruler's failure to be faithful to duty.

As I stated above, Kant's position is defensible in a society with a government which is committed to legislating in accordance with the united general will of all its subjects. When such a state fails in the fulfillment of its commitments, the appropriate reaction is one of political dialogue, expressive conduct, and perhaps even passive resistance. Violent revolution is not justified. Of course, the duty to endure imperfect governments does not justify complicity in a government's evil deeds. In short, we should not blindly obey but we may never actively revolt. Passive resistance may be necessary but coercive resistance is always unjustified.

Historically, however, few governments have been committed in any way to the Idea of the state. The history of governments is a history of exclusion and privilege without even a pretense of republican spirit. I may be obligated to obey an imperfect regime when it is generally committed to the Idea of the people united by a supreme and powerful general will, but Kant's argument simply does not apply to a state with no republican virtue.

III- Political Exclusion and Juridical Revolution

Kant's conception of a civil society adopts and extends Rousseau's notion of the general will as the basis of political obligation. Rousseau, however, recognized that the idea of the general will naturally limits the class of persons that are obligated by state power. Since Kant has little to say about the concept of the general will, it is useful to look back to Rousseau's account. The general will represents the unifying and common interest which transforms an aggregate of individuals into a body politic. Despite their diverse and perhaps competing private interests, the members of a civil society also have shared and common interests as citizens. The laws of a civil society are binding on a subject only if that subject's interests as a free and equal citizen are included in the determination of the general will.

As Rousseau points out in *The Social Contract,* laws may reflect the general will of some of its subjects and yet treat others as no more than slaves. In such a case, only the citizens of the slavery-dependent body politic are *obligated* to obey the (imperfect) procedures which determine the shared general will. The slaves may be forced into submission but they are not obligated to obey. Slavery is of course an extreme case but the same principle applies to more commonplace cases. Rousseau, for example, emphasizes the ever present danger of corruption of a society by the magistrates. Just as citizens share a general will so too do the magistrates and thus the laws may reflect the interests of the governors rather than the governed. In a similar fashion, the laws may reflect the common interest of one class or gender or race of a society and not include the interests of the others.[14] In all such cases, the excluded may find that it is *prudent* to obey the statutory laws, which constitute and perpetuate their oppression, but they have *no obligation* to obey a general will that is not theirs. The reason for this claim is familiar: we are obligated only to laws that we (can) give ourselves and one logically cannot consent to be a slave.[15] We are thus only obligated by a general will which includes our interests in determining the common interests of all.

The error in Kant's argument for an absolute prohibition on revolution should now be clear. Kant is assuming that even in imperfect societies, everyone subject to the sovereign power is also included in the juridical or lawful condition of the society. Clearly, however, an individual may be subject to the coercive power of a society without being a free and equal citizen of the society. It is a minimal condition of political inclusion, or citizenship, that one's interests, as both a finite and a rational being, count in the determination of the general will. The mere fact that I am faced with awesome organized coercive power cannot entail that this power in any way reflects a general will which is mine.

Indeed, state power often does not even purport to reflect a united general will of all of its subjects. The apartheid laws of South Africa, for example, clearly asserted the privileged interests of some citizens, and these laws served to enforce the systematic oppression of other subjects. In such a case, part of the society, the included, are refusing to enter into an inclusive civil society with the excluded individual(s). Provided that the excluded are willing to enter into a more just civil society with the included, we have a "state of nature" where the included are using superior power to oppress and exploit the excluded. Resistance is essentially a form of self defense in response to an unjust aggression. Given Kant's argument, the excluded can use violent means to force the included to enter into a more fully inclusive civil society.

What are the duties of the included to the excluded? All persons are to strive, in so far as they are able, to promote a condition in which all those

---

[14] See Rousseau, *On the Social Contract*, Bk. I ch. v-vi, Bk. II ch. i-vi, Bk. III ch. ii, x, and especially Bk. III xv, & Bk. IV ch. ii.

[15] See Rousseau, *On the Social Contract,* Bk. I ch ii-v; and Arthur Kuflick "The Inalienability of Autonomy" (in *Philosophy and Public Affairs* 13, 1984:271-298).

worthy of happiness are able to achieve happiness, a condition Kant refers to as the highest good (KpV 106-20). The doctrine of virtue clearly requires that we make the happiness of others our end and that we thus strive to eliminate, by legitimate means, oppressive and unjust restrictions on the freedom of the excluded. A united civil society is an end in itself, an end that each person *ought* to have. In addition, however, I believe that it is also an unconditional duty of justice to bring about a fully inclusive juridical condition.

First of all, in deriving property rights and in his "articles for perpetual peace among nations," Kant's argument depends upon his notion of a permissive law. A permissive law involves a permission to do or allow something which is generally prohibited in order to bring about the state of affairs which is the goal, or intention of the general prohibition (EF 347-348). In cases of systematic institutional injustice there must also be a permissive law which allows one to set aside the general prohibition on unilateral coercion in order to bring about (at least an appearance of) the juridical condition, that is, the just or lawful civil society, which is the point of the general prohibition. The permissive conclusion is inescapable: as a matter of principle, revolutionary activity is permissible. The fundamental duty of justice, however, requires an even stronger conclusion.

When the law systematically excludes some people from its equal protection, when the government functions as a tool of oppression rather than a guarantor of individual rights, then it is an unconditional duty of justice to resist or to transform the unlawful state in the most effective manner available. As we saw above, Kant clearly argues that whenever there is a potential conflict over mutual rights, there is a duty to enter into a shared civil society (MS 256 and 306-308). Kant is quite explicit on this point, it is "an unconditioned and primary duty with respect to every external relation in general among men, who cannot help but influence one another" (TP 289). It follows that, if the included are situated such that they unavoidably influence the excluded, the included have an unconditioned and primary duty to enter into a juridical condition with the excluded. We have also seen that "everyone may use violent means to compel another to enter into a juridical state of society." (MS 312, Ladd) It thus also follows that everyone, the included and the excluded, have a coercively enforceable duty to enter into a fully inclusive civil society.

Although Kant rejects happiness based principles of justice, his theory of justice has a clear consequentialist element. The juridical postulate of practical reason (the duty to make property possible) entails a duty to *bring about a state of affairs* where reciprocal property rights are determined by and enforced by a united general will. We are to do *whatever is necessary*, including using violent means, to bring about this juridical state of affairs. Given these consequentialist aspects of Kant's theory of justice, in principle, it must be permissible to use coercive or violent means to undermine, reform, or remove a regime using coercive power to perpetuate a non-juridical state of affairs. Whether, in any particular circumstance, violent revolutionary activity is also advisable must be determined by difficult, pragmatic, consequentialist considerations. Caution should, of course, rule such decisions. Still, there are unfortunate cases where the calculus is clear and action is called for. Revolution is not only permissible, it is also, regrettably, sometimes required.

Have we not, however, reintroduced the problem which civil society was supposed to solve; that is, the problem of the unbridled exercise of unilateral coercion? Was Kant wrong to conclude that the legitimate coercive enforcement of rights must be determined from a universal, general perspective not from a partial, individual perspective? Let us return to Kant's derivation of civil society.

As we have seen, Kant's concerns are the adjudication of conflicting property claims and the pernicious effects of partiality. It is clearly not legitimate for any person's unilateral will to determine legitimate property rights in cases of conflicting claims, for this would violate the reciprocal rights of others. It simply cannot be a universal law that each person unilaterally has authority to determine legitimate ownership, for then two or more persons could each own, that is, have exclusive authority over, one and the same object (a contradiction in conception). When it comes to "external and contingent possessions," no matter how erroneous one believes the decision to be, there is a duty of justice to abide by the decision of an impartial procedure (MS 256). It follows that some impartial decision procedure should have final authority in determining legitimate claims.

It does not follow, however, that one must also simply obey when fundamental rights are being systematically undermined by the existing political procedures. This is both a moral point and a logical point. It is a moral point, first, because the dangers of partiality simply cannot justify allowing the systematic institutional exclusion, oppression, and even extermination of persons. The point of a civil society is that it promotes the rights of humanity (MS 240). The complete abandonment of moral judgment, however, is morally more dangerous than the partial distortion of moral judgment could ever be.

Second, the duty to enter a juridical condition is based on the necessity of justifying property acquisition under the constraint of the universal principle of justice: Justice (Right) is “the sum of the conditions under which the choice of one can be united with the choice of another in accordance with a universal law of freedom.” (MS 230) We are all duty bound to enter into or bring about a civil society because otherwise property claims and negative freedom would conflict. But, the successful organization of overwhelming force, also known as state power, does not necessarily transform a state of nature into the requisite juridical condition. The structure of Kant’s argument simply cannot generate a duty to obey a supreme coercive power that systematically violates the negative freedom and basic rights of some of its subjects. A commitment to basic civil rights for all is thus a limiting condition on the duty to obey the powers that be.

The duty to enter into a civil society also logically entails a duty to judge the legitimacy of coercive power. Justice obliges us to abandon the state of nature and enter into a civil society. But, we simply cannot fulfill such a duty without assessing whether we are in a state of nature or a civil society. The duty to defer to impartial procedures logically presupposes a judgment that a procedure is indeed sufficiently impartial. Indeed, the basic starting point of Kantian ethics is the perspective of an agent acting on principle. Thus for a Kantian, the decision of an impartial procedure is final but the individual simply must be the final judge of the procedure itself. When the law is a tool of systematic oppression, a conscientious moral agent must take *justice* into her own hands. In such a case, one acts without *legal* justification. But, nonetheless, for the sake of justice, one must act.

Conclusion

Kant’s prohibition on revolution is as extreme as it appears to be and it is entailed by his theory of coercion and his deduction of property rights. Nonetheless, the juridical requirement to enter a civil society justifies an unconditional duty to combat, by the most effective means available, all instances of systematic institutional injustice. Such rebellious activity is a hindrance to a hindrance to freedom and thus consistent with universal lawful freedom. There is no right to resist a civil society. There is, however, a right to determine whether the coercive power which confronts one presents even the *appearance* of the Idea of a civil society. In order to represent the general will, one must do more than simply present awesome force. Each individual who is subjected to the coercive power of an aspiring ruler must determine for him or her self whether obedience is consistent with the demands of justice. If one is to satisfy the unconditional juridical duty to bring about an inclusive civil society, then the society one shares with others must be sufficiently committed to civil rights for all. Surely such a limited degree of autonomous judgment about one's obligation is consistent with the practical necessity of sovereign authority. Additionally, such a limited coercive right (against illegitimate coercers) is not contradictory, for it is a right which is prior to all other civil duties.

There are circumstances which require a Kantian to be a revolutionary. Whether Kant likes it or not, this is indeed the conclusion which actually follows from his arguments. Individual judgment must sometimes override organized power. The Kantian principle of autonomy is the ground under, but should not be buried under, the principle of political obedience.

Works Cited

Beck, L.W. "Kant and the Right of Revolution," in *Essays on Kant and Hume*. Yale University Press, 1978.

Cummiskey, David. *Kantian Consequentialism.* Oxford University Press, 1996.

Herman, Barbara. "Murder and Mayhem: Violence and Kantian Casuistry," in *The Monist* 72.2 (1989): 411-431; and reprinted in *The Practice of Moral Judgment*. Harvard University Press, 1996.

Holt, Sarah Williams. "Revolution, Contradiction, and Kantian Citizenship," in *Kant's Metaphysics of Morals: Interpretive Essays* edited by Mark Timmons. Oxford University Press, 2002.

Kant, Immanuel. *Kant's gesammelte Schriften.* Berlin: Preussische Academie der Wissenschaften, 1900-1942.

—. *The Metaphysics of Morals* (MS), translated by Mary Gregor. Cambridge University Press, 1991.

—. *Practical Philosophy*, translated by Mary Gregor. Cambridge Edition of the Works of Immanuel Kant, 1996.

—. (*Groundwork of the Metaphysics of Morals* (G), translated H. J. Paton. Harper & Row, 1964.

—. "To Perpetual Peace: A Philosophical Sketch" (EF) and "On The Old Proverb: That May Be True In Theory but is of No Practical Use" (TP) in *Perpetual Peace and Other Essays*, translated by Ted Humphrey. Hackett Publishers, 1983.

—. *The Metaphysical Elements of Justice* (MS), translated by John Ladd. Bobbs-Merrill, 1965. Second edition, Hackett Publishers, 1999.

—. *The Critique of Practical Reason* (KpV), translated by Lewis White Beck. Bobbs Merill, 1965.

—. *Religion within the Limits of Reason Alone* (R), translated by Greene and Hudson. Harper & Row, 1960.

Korsgaard, Christine. "Taking the Law into our own Hands: Kant on the Right to Revolution" in *Reclaiming the History of Ethics: Essays for John Rawls*, edited by Reath, Herman, and C. Korsgaard. Cambridge University Press, 1997.

Kuflick, Arthur. "The Inalienability of Autonomy," in *Philosophy and Public Affairs* 13, (1984):271-298.

Nicholson, Peter. "Kant on the Duty Never to Resist the Sovereign" in *Ethics* (1976): 214-230.

Reiss, H. S. "Kant on the Right of Rebellion," in *Journal of the History of Ideas* 17 (1956): 179- 192.

Rousseau, *On the Social Contract,* translated by Donald A. Cress. Hackett Publishing, 1988.

Schwarz, Wolfgang. "The Ambiguities of Resistance: A Reply to Nicholson," in *Ethics* (1977): 255-259.

Seebohm, Thomas. "Kant's Theory of Revolution," in *Social Research* 48 (1981): 557-587.

van der Linden, Harry. *Kantian Ethics and Socialism.* Hackett Publishers, 1988.

Westphal, Kenneth. "Kant's Qualified Principle of Obedience to Authority in the *Metaphysical Elements of Justice*," in G. Funke, ed., *Akten des 7. internationalen Kant-Kongress* (Bonn: Bouvier, 1991): II.2:353-66.

—. "Kant on the State, Law, and Obedience to Authority in the Alleged 'Anti-revolutionary' Writings," in *Journal of Philosophical Research* 17 (1991-92):383-426.

—. "A Kantian Theory of Possession" in *Kant's Metaphysics of Morals: Interpretive Essays* edited by Mark Timmons. Oxford University Press, 2002.

CHAPTER TEN

THE PRINCIPLE OF DETERMINABILITY AND THE POSSIBILITY OF SYNTHETIC *A PRIORI* JUDGMENTS IN KANT AND MAIMON

SEUNG-KEE LEE

A number of articles and books have been published of late in which the role of Salomon Maimon's philosophy is emphasized in the development of German idealism from Kant to Fichte.[1] Central to Maimon's philosophy is his celebrated "principle of determinability" (*Satz der Bestimmbarkeit*), which he called "the principle of philosophy as a whole."[2] Although scholars have readily acknowledged the importance of

[1] Peter Baumanns, *Fichtes Wissenschaftslehre: Problem ihres Anfangs. Mit einem Kommentar zu § 1 der "Grundlage der gesammten Wissenschaftslehre"* (Bonn: Bouvier, 1974), pp. 55-56; Achim Engstler, *Untersuchungen zum Idealismus Salomon Maimons* (Stuttgart: Fromann-Holzboog, 1990), pp. 243-59; Peter Thielke, "Getting Maimon's Goad: Discursivity, Skepticism, and Fichte's Idealism," *Journal of the History of Philosophy* 39 (2001), pp.101-34; Frederick. C. Beiser, *The Fate of Reason: German Philosophy from Kant to Fichte* (Cambridge, Mass: Harvard University Press, 1987), pp. 283-323, and "Maimon and Fichte," in Gideon Freudenthal, ed. *Salomon Maimon: Rational Dogmatist, Empirical Skeptic: Critical Assessments* (Dordrecht: Springer, 2003), pp. 233-48; Daniel Breazeale, "*Der Satz der Bestimmbarkeit*: Fichte's Reception and Transformation of Maimon's Principle of Synthetic Thinking," *Internationales Jahrbuch des Deutschen Idealismus* 1 (2003), pp. 115-40; Yitzhak Melamed, "Salomon Maimon and the Rise of Spinozism in German Idealism," *The Journal of the History of Philosophy* 42 (2004), pp. 67-96.

[2] Salomon Maimon, "Letters of Philaletes to Aenesidemus," in *Between Kant and Hegel: Texts in the Development of Post-Kantian Idealism*, trans. George Di Giovanni and H. Harris (Indianapolis: Hackett, 2000), p. 165; *GW*, 5: 310. All quotations from "Letters of Philaletes to Aenesidemus" are from this edition.

the principle for Maimon's philosophy in general, surprisingly little has been written that is helpful for understanding the principle's origin, nature, and function.[3] Those who actually discuss the principle in their writings have noted Spinoza, Leibniz, or even Maimonides as its possible origin.[4] Those who mention Kant as a possible origin, recognizing that he himself introduces a principle of determinability in the *Critique of Pure Reason* (A 572 ff./B 600 ff.), do so, however, only to conclude that the connection between Kant's and Maimon's principle is at best tenuous.[5]

References to Maimon's writings are to the pagination of *Gesammelte Werke*, ed. V. Verra (Hildesheim: Olms, 1965), cited as "*GW*," followed by volume and page number.

[3] In his "Getting Maimon's Goad," Thielke does not discuss Maimon's principle of determinability, which he mentions once in a footnote, remarking that "the details of this principle remain rather murky" (p. 114, n. 43). Breazeale, in his "*Satz der Bestimmbarkeit*," says that "many scholars" would "agree with Thielke that 'the details of this principle remain rather murky'" (p. 118, n. 4). Engstler, in his *Untersuchungen*, says "…glaube Ich es rechtfertigen zu können, dass in meinen Untersuchungen Maimons Ausführungen über das 'Bestimmbare und die Bestimmung' ausgespart bleiben. Diese Ausführungen, die den später 'Satz der Bestimmbarkeit' genannten Grundsatz antizipieren, betreffen im 'Versuch' nämlich die Definition und die Anwendung der *Substanz*kategorie …" (pp. 21-22, n. 32). As I shall demonstrate, however, the principle of determinability applies to all the logical forms of judgment, and therefore, to all the categories (not only to that of substance), in Kant as well as in Maimon's philosophy. Thielke, in his "Discursivity and Causality," like Engstler, does not seem to see that what he calls "the condition of irreversibility" (p. 446, p. 462) that he sees at work in Kant's Second Analogy is none other than the principle of determinability as it is applied to that form of judgment (hypothetical) which unites "a succession of perceptions" (see KrV B 233-34, and my discussion of this passage below). Maimon's criticism of the Second Analogy, then, is not that Kant's account is without a principle of determinability (pp. 457-58), but rather that Kant's *own* version of the principle is insufficient to achieve what it is designed to accomplish, namely, to show how the concepts in a judgment can stand in a relation of determinacy.

[4] Melamed, "Salomon Maimon," pp. 67-96; Elhanan Yakira, "From Kant to Leibniz? Salomon Maimon and the Question of Predication," in Gideon Freudenthal, ed. *Salomon Maimon: Rational Dogmatist,* pp. 54-79, and see also Friedrich Kuntze, *Die Philosophie Salomon Maimons* (Heidelberg: Winters, 1912), pp. 276-308; Samuel Atlas, *From Critical to Speculative Idealism: The Philosophy of Salomon Maimon* (The Hague: Martinus Nijhoff, 1964), pp. 161-67.

[5] Two passages from the *Critique of Pure Reason* are commonly cited as the possible origin of Maimon's principle. The first is the Appendix to the Amphiboly of the Concepts of Reflection (KrV A 261 ff./B 316 ff.), in which Kant correlates the form-matter distinction with the determinable-determination distinction.

Such conclusion is derived, however, from a cursory rather than a thorough examination of the function of the principle in the *Critique of Pure Reason*. In fact, a careful reader will discover that Maimon's principle is a rehabilitated version of Kant's determinate-indeterminate distinction, which underlies Kant's theory of judgment. More important, the principle of determinability is introduced by Kant and Maimon to explain how synthetic *a priori* judgments are possible.[6] What Maimon

---

Yakira, in his "From Kant to Leibniz?," mentions this passage only to show how Kant "radicalizes" Leibniz's theory of predication. He does not explain whether the passage influences Maimon (p. 62). Günter Zöller, in his *Fichte's Transcendental Philosophy: The Original Duplicity of Intelligence and Will* (Cambridge: Cambridge University Press, 1998), also mentions the passage and speaks of "Kant's distinction between matter as the determinable and form as its determination ...and the subsequent employment of the distinction in Salomon Maimon's *Versuch über die Transcendentalphilosophie*..." (p. 141 n. 27) Zöller does not develop this point further in his book. Another passage in the *Critique of Pure Reason* that is commonly cited as the possible origin of Maimon's principle is in the section on the Transcendental Ideal of the Transcendental Dialectic (KrV A 572 ff./B 600 ff.), where "the principle of determinability" is explicitly mentioned by Kant. Melamed, in his "Salomon Maimon," briefly discusses this passage, but only to conclude that "despite the similar name and the common aim of providing a principle for synthetic thinking, Maimon's law and Kant's principle are significantly different, both with regard to their content, as well as in their realms of applicability" (p. 88). Unfortunately, Melamed does not discuss Kant's determinate-indeterminate distinction as it is elaborated in the passages in the *Critique of Pure Reason* that I shall discuss below. Moreover, surprisingly, Melamed does not mention Spinoza's principle that "all determination is negation" (*omnis determinatio est negatio*), which seems to have influenced not only Maimon but Kant as well. Breazeale, in his "*Satz der Bestimmbarkeit*," in referring to the Transcendental Ideal passage, says that the principle of determinability, as Kant understands it, is "a purely formal principle, based directly upon the principle of contradiction" (p. 117). According to Breazeale, Maimon, however, "has something altogether different in view," namely, "*a principle of real thinking*" (pp. 117-18).

[6] Here one might object that it is misleading to suggest that there is any resemblance between Kant and Maimon's principle of determinability. I answer that there are reasons to think that one could justifiably speak of there being the same principle of determinability at work in both Kant and Maimon's philosophy. For one thing, the way in which the principle *actually* functions is the same in both Maimon and Kant's philosophy, as I shall demonstrate below. What is more, in his "What Should Kantians Learn from Maimon's Skepticism?" (in Gideon Freudenthal, ed. *Salomon Maimon: Rational Dogmatist*), Paul Franks says, "The suggestion that Kant's Principle of Determinability, given in the Transcendental

thinks his own principle succeeds in doing is precisely what he believed Kant's determinate-indeterminate distinction was supposed to, but failed to show, namely, how the subject and predicate concepts in a judgment can stand in a *determinate* (as opposed to merely indeterminate) relation; for, to show how such a relation is possible is tantamount to showing how synthetic *a priori* judgments are possible.

One reason why few, if any, have recognized this function of the principle is that Kant's analytic-synthetic distinction has hitherto been construed mainly in terms of the question of whether or not the predicate is contained in (or can be derived from) the concept of the subject. Few, if any, have observed that Kant has another formulation of the distinction, a formulation that is based on the determinate-indeterminate distinction. Understanding this formulation reveals to us another dimension to Kant's analytic-synthetic distinction and thus enables us to gain a fresh perspective on the meaning of Kant's question, How are synthetic *a priori* judgments possible? But more important for the purpose of this paper, it is this formulation that will influence and shape the development of post-Kantian German idealism.

In a letter written in 1795 Fichte says that Kant's question, "how are synthetic *a priori* judgments possible?" is the same as the question, "If the I originally posits *only itself*, how then does it come to posit something else as well, something posited as opposed to the I? How does it happen

---

Ideal, plays a central role throughout the critical corpus opens the possibility for detailed comparison with Maimon's Principle of Determinability and its role in the derivation of the categories." Franks says that this derivation or deduction was something that "Kant never carried out" (p. 211 n.36). If Franks is right, it is plausible to assume that the role that the determinate-indeterminate distinction plays in the Analytic of Concepts of the *Critique of Pure Reason* is ultimately a function of the Principle of Determinability, which Kant introduces in the chapter on the Transcendental Ideal in the Transcendental Dialectic. Whether the Principle of Determinability and the Principle of Thoroughgoing Determination in the Transcendental Ideal have a role to play in the Transcendental Analytic has been debated by Beatrice Longuenesse, "The Transcendental Ideal and the Unity of the Critical System," in *Kant on the Human Standpoint* (Cambridge: Cambridge University Press, 2005), pp. 211-35, and Michelle Grier, *Kant's Doctrine of Transcendental Illusion* (Cambridge: Cambridge University Press, 2001), pp. 237-51. The argument of the present paper, according to which the principle of determinability is the principle of synthetic *a priori* judgments in Maimon as well as in Kant, appears to support Longuenesse's position. This cannot be developed here.

that the I goes outside of itself?"[7] The young Schelling, in one of his early writings published in the same year, remarks that Kant's question "is none other than: How is it possible for the absolute I to step out of itself and oppose to itself a not-I?"[8] In order to understand how Kant's question could be rephrased by Fichte and Schelling in such different terms, it will not help if the question is understood as merely asking how the predicate, which is not contained in the subject concept, can nevertheless be conjoined with it *a priori*, that is, independently of experience. One comes closer to grasping the meaning and the significance of Fichte and Schelling's rephrasing of Kant' question if the latter is understood as asking instead how it is possible for the logical forms of judgment to be employed *determinately* (as opposed to indeterminately), that is, in such a way that the predicate and the subject concepts are connected not merely in thought, but also in the object. In fact, both Fichte and Schelling will employ the principle of determinability in order to answer Kant's question. But it is impossible to comprehend adequately why and how Fichte and Schelling employ the principle without first understanding how Maimon used his *Satz der Bestimmbarkeit* in order to answer Kant's question. Fichte, who was "an avid reader of Maimon,"[9] will transform Maimon's *Satz der Bestimmbarkeit* into his own *Satz der Wechselbestimmung* ("principle of reciprocal determination").

My aim in this paper is, first, to show how Kant's analytic-synthetic distinction is grounded on the determinate-indeterminate distinction,[10] then, to examine Maimon's interpretation of the problem of the synthetic *a priori*, as well as his solution to the problem on the basis of the principle

---

[7] J. G. Fichte, *Fichte: Early Philosophical Writings*, trans. and ed. Daniel Breazeale (Ithaca: Cornell University Press, 1988), p. 399; *GA*, 3, n. 294. References to Fichte's writings are to the pagination of *J. G. Fichte – Gesamtausgabe der Bayerischen Akademie der Wissenschaften*, ed. Reinhard Lauth, Hans Jacob, and Hans Gliwitsky (Stuttgart-Bad Cannsatt: Frommann-Holtzboog, 1962–), cited by "*GA*," followed by volume, part, and page number.

[8] F. W. J. Schelling, *Of the I as Principle of Philosophy*, in *The Unconditional in Human Knowledge: Four Early Essays (1794-1796)*, trans. Fritz Marti (Lewisburg: Bucknell University Press, 1980), p. 81; *SW*, 1, 175. References to Schelling's writings are to the pagination of *Sämmtliche Werke*, ed. K.F.A. Schelling (Stuttgart and Augsburg: J. G. Cotta, 1856-61), cited as "*SW*," followed by volume and page number.

[9] Breazeale, "*Satz der Bestimmbarkeit*," p. 124.

[10] The first section is a summary of the first two parts of my paper, "The Determinate-Indeterminate Distinction and Kant's Theory of Judgment," *Kant-Studien* 95 (2004), pp. 204-25.

of determinability. Space limitations make it impossible for me to develop the accounts of Fichte and Schelling in this paper. Nevertheless, I would like to conclude by providing a sketch of the relation between Maimon and Fichte with regard to the problem of the synthetic *a priori* and the way this relation will shape the course of post-Kantian German idealism.

I- Kant

In the *Critique of Pure Reason* Kant distinguishes between general and transcendental logic. While general logic "concerns the use of the understanding without regard to the difference of objects," transcendental logic concerns "the laws of the understanding and reason, but only insofar as they are related to objects *a priori*" (KrV A 57/B 82).[11] In accordance with this formulation, Kant points out in the following passage that the same categorical form of judgment ('S is P') can be employed in two different ways, namely, determinately and indeterminately:

> [The categories] are concepts of an object in general, by means of which its intuition is regarded as *determined* with regard to one of the *logical functions* for judgments. Thus the function of the *categorical* judgment was that of the relationship of the subject to the predicate, e.g., "All bodies are divisible." Yet in regard to the merely logical use of the understanding, it would remain undetermined which of these two concepts will be given the function of the subject and which will be given that of the predicate. For one can also say: "Something divisible is a body." Through the category of substance, however, if I bring the concept of a body under it, it is determined that its empirical intuition in experience must always be considered as subject, never as mere predicate; and likewise with all the other categories (KrV B 128-29).

In this passage Kant distinguishes between the two ways in which the

---

[11] Kant, *Critique of Pure Reason*, trans. and ed. Paul Guyer and Allen Wood (Cambridge: Cambridge University Press, 1997), pp. 196-97. All quotations from the *Critique of Pure Reason* are from this edition. References to Kant's writings are to the pagination of *Kants Gesammelte Schriften, herausgegeben von der Deutschen Akademie der Wissenschaften*, 29 vols. (Berlin: de Gruyter, 1902–), cited as "*Ak*," followed by volume and page number. For citations to the *Critique of Pure Reason* (KrV) I follow the standard practice of citing the pagination of the first (1781) or 'A' and second (1787) or 'B' editions.

same logical form of judgment can be employed in the act of judging, namely, determinately and indeterminately. It is important to emphasize that in this passage Kant identifies what he calls "the logical use" of the categorical form of judgment with the *indeterminate* nature of its function in judging. In the second edition version of the Paralogisms of Pure Reason, Kant explains in reference to a proposition involving the concept of substance that "the concept of a subject is here taken merely logically, and it remains undetermined whether or not substance is to be understood by it." (KrV B 419)[12] These passages indicate that while general logic deals with the indeterminate use, transcendental logic deals with the determinate use of the logical forms of judgment.[13]

Another piece of textual evidence for the foregoing interpretation is found in a footnote in the Preface to the *Metaphysical Foundations of Natural Science*. Kant writes:

> The table of the categories completely contains all the pure concepts of the understanding as well as the formal actions of the understanding in judgments, from which such pure concepts are derived and from which they also differ in nothing except that in the concept of the understanding, an object is thought as *determined* in regard to one or the other function of judgments. (E.g., in the categorical judgment "the stone is hard," the "stone" is employed as subject and "hard" as predicate, so that *it remains permissible for the understanding to interchange the logical function of these concepts and say "something hard is a stone"* [italics mine]. On the other hand, when I represent to myself as *determined in the object* that the stone in every possible determination of an object, and not of the mere concept, must be thought only as subject and the hardness only as predicate, the same logical functions now become pure concepts of the understanding for cognizing objects, namely, substance and accident).[14]

Thus Kant explains that there are two ways in which the same logical form of judgment can be employed in the act of judging, viz., in a

---

[12] Cf. P 4: 324.

[13] It is true that Kant also speaks of "determination" in general logic, as, for example, when a concept is determined by another concept in a genus/species relationship (See VL 9: 146). But what is thus determined by or "contained under" a concept is yet another *concept*. From the standpoint of *transcendental* logic, in others words, logical determination still leaves undetermined whether the concept relates to an *object*.

[14] Kant, *Metaphysical Foundations of Natural Science*, in *Philosophy of Material Nature*, trans. James W. Ellington (Indianapolis: Hackett, 1985), p. 13; *Ak*, 4: 475n.

determinate way (for "cognizing objects") and an indeterminate way (for relating concepts in mere "thought"). In other words, whether or not the logical form of judgment applies to an object (i.e., is used as a *category*) depends on whether or not it is *determined* which of the two concepts is given the function of the subject and which is given the function of the predicate.The logical use of the understanding leaves it *undetermined* which concept will be given which function.

Kant also explains how the hypothetical form of judgment ('If P then Q') can be employed determinately and indeterminately. In section 29 of the *Prolegomena*, Kant says, "in perception we may meet with a rule of relation which runs thus: that a certain appearance is constantly followed by another (though not vice versa); and this is a case for me to use the hypothetical judgment …"[15] In the chapter on the Second Analogy of the Analytic of Principles in the *Critique of Pure Reason*, Kant specifies what gets determined and what remains undetermined when the hypothetical form of judgment is employed:

> Now connection is not the work of mere sense and intuition, but is here rather the product of a synthetic faculty of the imagination, which determines inner sense with regard to temporal relations. This, however, can combine the two states in question in two different ways, so that either one or the other precedes in time; for time cannot be perceived in itself, nor can what precedes and what follows in objects be as it were empirically determined in relation to it. I am therefore only conscious that my imagination places one state before and the other after, not that the one state precedes the other in the object; or, in other words, through the mere perception the *objective relation* of the appearances that are succeeding one another remains undetermined. Now in order for this to be cognized as determined, the relation between the two states must be thought in such a way that it is thereby necessarily determined which of them must be placed before and which after, and not vice versa. The concept, however, that carries a necessity of synthetic unity with it can only be a pure concept of the understanding, which does not lie in the perception, and that is here the concept of the *relation of cause and effect...* (KrV B 233-34)

Thus, just as the *categorical* form of judgment can be employed in two ways, that is, in such a way as to leave "undetermined which of [the] two concepts will be given the function of the subject and which will be given that of the predicate," or in such a way that "it is determined that its

[15] Kant, *Prolegomena to Any Future Metaphysics,* trans. Paul Carus and ed. Lewis White Beck (Indianapolis: Hackett, 1950), p. 59; *Ak*, 4: 311-12.

empirical intuition in experience must always be considered as subject, never as mere predicate," (KrV B 128-29) so the *hypothetical* form of judgment can be employed in two ways, that is, in such a way as to leave "undetermined" which of the two states is to "precede" and which is to "follow" the other, or in such a way as to determine "which [state] must be placed before and which after, and not vice versa," or which "state preceded the other in the object." (KrV B 233-34)

Given that there exists in Kant's theoretical philosophy a distinction between an indeterminate and a determinate employment of the logical form of judgment, it may now be asked, On what basis does Kant make this distinction? Kant contrasts the expression, "the logical use of the understanding," (KrV B 128) which, as was already noted, involves the *indeterminate* employment of the logical forms of thought, with "the transcendental use of the power of judgment," (KrV B 167) which, Kant tells us, involves "the sensible condition under which alone pure concepts of the understanding can be employed, i.e., …the schematism of the pure understanding." (KrV A 136/B 175) This remark makes it clear that it is the provision of the *schema* or "the transcendental time-determination," that makes possible a *determinate* (as opposed to an indeterminate) employment of the logical forms of judgment. Kant says:

> Hence an application of the category to appearances becomes possible by means of the transcendental time-determination which, as the schema of the concept of the understanding, mediates the subsumption of the latter under the former (KrV A 139/B 178).

Moreover, in the Analytic of Concepts in the *Critique of Pure Reason*, Kant says "we can… trace all actions of the understanding back to judgments." (KrV A 69/B 94) In the Appendix to the Transcendental Dialectic, Kant writes: "the actions of the understanding … apart from the schema of sensibility, are *undetermined*." (KrV A 664/B 692) Thus, what allows an indeterminate judgment to turn into a determinate judgment is the transcendental schema.[16]

It may be inferred from the foregoing analysis that the logical forms of thought are always employed in an indeterminate manner in all *analytic* judgments. Since analytic judgments require no intuition, they relate concepts in mere "thought" (not "in the object").[17] In the example referred

---

[16] Cf. KrV A 245-46.

[17] Beatrice Longuenesse, *Kant and the Capacity to Judge* (Princeton: Princeton University Press, 1998), says that in an analytic judgment, which has "no relation

to above, for instance, "all bodies are divisible" involves the "logical use of the understanding," for "it remains *undetermined* to which of the two concepts the function of the subject, and to which the function of predicate, is to be assigned. For we can also say, "Something divisible is a body" [italics mine] (KrV B 128-9). In a letter written in 1789, Kant says that the judgment, "every body is divisible," is an analytic judgment, for the predicate concept of divisibility is contained in the subject concept of body.[18] It is clear from the passage in question, therefore, that for Kant analytic judgments are indeterminate; all such judgments are based on "the logical use of the understanding," which involves the indeterminate employment of the logical function of thought. Kant makes the same point in his theory of practical propositions, as I will show below. What emerges from this analysis is that the distinction between analytic and synthetic judgments is grounded on the distinction between the indeterminate and the determinate employment of the logical forms, i.e., between the mere connection of concepts in thought and the connection of representations in an object.[19]

I would now like to examine how the set of distinctions made above play themselves out in Kant's *practical* philosophy. Such examination will thus strengthen the thesis that Kant's analytic-synthetic distinction is based on the determinate-indeterminate distinction.

As we have already seen, in the *Critique of Pure Reason* Kant says that general logic "concerns the use of the understanding without regard to the difference of objects," whereas transcendental logic concerns "the laws of the understanding and reason, but only insofar as they are related to objects *a priori*." (KrV A 57/B 82) In the *Groundwork of the Metaphysics of Morals* (1785), Kant tells us that while what he calls general practical philosophy[20] "consider[s] motives without regard to the

---

to a sensible intuition… no category is involved" (p. 79).

[18] Kant, *Philosophical Correspondence 1759-99*, trans. and ed. Arnulf Zweig (Chicago: University of Chicago Press, 1967), p. 138; *Ak*, 11: 35.

[19] As the quoted passage from the *Metaphysical Foundations* makes clear, one species of synthetic *a posteriori* judgment, which Kant calls "judgments of perception" in the *Prolegomena*, are also indeterminate; the concepts united in such judgments, as "subjectively valid," hold only in thought. Objectively valid synthetic *a posteriori* judgments or "judgments of experience" and synthetic *a priori* judgments are species of determinate judgments. I develop this more fully in "The Determinate-Indeterminate Distinction and Kant's Theory of Judgment," pp. 207-12.

[20] Or *Allgemeinen praktischen Weltweishiet*. See "Introduction" in *Lectures on Ethics*, trans. Peter Heath and ed. J. B. Schneewind and Peter Heath (Cambridge:

difference in their source," the metaphysics of morals considers a "will of a particular kind, such as one determined without any empirical motives by *a priori* principles; in a word, ...a pure will."[21]

In fact, general practical philosophy "differs from a metaphysics of morals in the same way that general logic is distinguished from transcendental philosophy."[22] Just as general logic considers "the actions and rules of thinking in general," while transcendental philosophy presents "the particular actions and rules of pure thinking," general practical philosophy considers "only volition in general," while the metaphysics of morals investigates the "principles" of a "will of a particular kind," viz., "of a possible pure will."[23]

In the *Ethik Mrongovius*[24] Kant says "General practical philosophy is related to morals as logic is to metaphysics." Kant continues:

> in general practical philosophy it is undetermined, whether we have motivating grounds or not. Logic abstracts from our cognitions. General practical philosophy [abstracts] from the grounds of motivation.[25]

It should be noted that, as this passage from the lectures on ethics indicates, for Kant, to say that a judgment leaves something "undetermined" is equivalent to saying that it "abstracts from" something. As a matter of fact, other phrases besides "leave undetermined [*unbestimmt*]" and "abstract from [*abstrahirt von*]" that Kant uses to express that mode of considering which has no reference to any particular thing include "without regard to [*ohne Rücksicht auf*]," "indifferent to [*gleichgültig*]," and "leave undecided [*unausgemacht*]." Besides the term "*unbestimmt*," there are thus at least four different ways in which Kant expresses the same notion about the indeterminacy of judgments.[26]

To what precisely does the distinction between the determinate and indeterminate functions of willing refer? In the second chapter of the *Critique of Practical Reason*, immediately prior to introducing "the table of the categories of freedom," Kant writes:

Cambridge University Press, 1997), pp. xix-xxvii.

[21] Kant, *Foundations of the Metaphysics of Morals,* trans. Lewis White Beck (New York: Macmillan, 1990), pp. 6-7; *Ak*, 4: 390-91.

[22] Ibid., p. 6; *Ak*, 4: 390.

[23] Ibid.

[24] See "Introduction" in *Lectures on Ethics*, p. xvii.

[25] *Ak*, 29: 597-98.

[26] See, e.g., *Ak*, 29: 598; KrV A 290/B 346; KpV 5: 105; P 4: 324.

> these categories concern only practical reason in general and so proceed in their order from those which are *as yet morally undetermined and sensibly conditioned* to those which, *being sensibly unconditioned, are determined only by the moral law* [italics mine].[27]

As this passage indicates, the determinate-indeterminate distinction in Kant's practical philosophy mirrors the non-moral and moral forms of willing, or, as Kant puts it in the Second Introduction to the *Critique of the Power of Judgment*, between "technically" and "morally" practical propositions[28], or, still, that between hypothetical and categorical imperatives. In the *Ethik Mrongovius*, Kant says: "general practical philosophy exhibits the rules whereby the will is determined *a posteriori*."[29] As the passage from the *Critique of Practical Reason* cited above indicates, for Kant, those forms of willing which are "determined *a posteriori*" (or based on "empirical motives") are "morally undetermined." In other words, general practical philosophy considers those forms of willing which are "morally undetermined and sensibly conditioned," i.e., hypothetical imperatives. On the other hand, those forms of willing which are "sensibly unconditioned [and] determined only by the moral law," or in a word, the categorical imperatives, are considered by the metaphysics of morals.[30]

It should be evident by now why Kant regards hypothetical and categorical imperatives as analytic and synthetic *a priori* practical propositions respectively. Namely, for Kant, all analytic propositions, whether theoretical *or* practical, *leave something undetermined*. In chapter 3 of the Analytic of Principles in the *Critique of Pure Reason*, for example, Kant says the following about "an analytic assertion":

> since ["an analytic assertion"] is occupied only with that which is already thought in the concept, it leaves it *undecided* whether the concept even has any relation to objects, or only signifies the unity of thinking in general (which entirely *abstracts from* the way in which an object might be given); it is enough for him to know what lies in its concept; what the concept might pertain to is *indifferent* to him [italics mine] (KrV A 258-59/B 314-15).

---

[27] Kant, *Critique of Practical Reason* (KpV), trans. Lewis White Beck (New York: Macmillan, 1956), p. 68; *Ak*, 5: 66

[28] *Ak*, 20: 201. Cf. KU 5: 173, and VL 9: 87.

[29] *Ak*, 29: 597.

[30] G 4: 390.

Hence, analytic judgments are those judgments which "abstract from," "leave undecided," are "indifferent to," or leave *undetermined* whether there is any relation to objects. Indeed, we have already seen that Kant uses all these expressions interchangeably. In the *Logic*, moreover, Kant, in distinguishing between what he calls "analytically" and "synthetically universal rules," says that while analytically universal rules "abstract from differences," synthetically universal rules "attend to distinctions and consequently determine in regard to them too."[31]

In sum, just as all theoretical propositions, which leave undetermined the question about the relation to an object, are analytic, so also are all practical propositions that leave undetermined the question of whether there is a motivating ground of the will. In other words, hypothetical imperatives are regarded as *analytic* practical propositions because they leave undetermined whether there is a motivating ground. On the other hand, categorical imperatives are regarded as *synthetic a priori* practical propositions because they involve a determination of the will "only by the moral law."

II- Maimon

As it is well known, both Kant and Fichte thought very highly of Maimon as an interpreter and critic of Kant's transcendental philosophy. In a letter written to Marcus Herz in 1789, Kant, referring to a manuscript of Maimon's first important work, *Versuch über die Transcendentalphilosophie* or *Essay in Transcendental Philosophy* (1790), said, "one glance at the work made me realize its excellence and that not only had none of my critics understood me and the main questions as well as Herr Maimon does but also very few men possess so much acumen for such deep investigations as he…"[32] In 1795, Fichte wrote in a letter, "My respect for Maimon's talent knows no bounds. I firmly believe that he has completely overturned the entire Kantian philosophy as it has been understood by everyone until now, *…and I am prepared to prove it.* No one noticed what he had done; they looked down on him from their heights. I believe that future centuries will mock us bitterly."[33]

---

[31] Kant, *Lectures on Logic*, trans. and ed. J. Michael Young (Cambridge: Cambridge University Press, 1992), p. 599; *Ak*, 9: 102-3.

[32] Kant, *Correspondence*, trans. and ed. Arnulf Zweig (Cambridge: Cambridge University Press, 1999), pp. 311-12; *Ak*, 11: 49.

[33] *Fichte: Early Philosophical Writings*, pp. 383-84; *GA*, 3, n. 272.

The significance of Maimon's writings, especially his *Essay in Transcendental Philosophy*, which was both a critique of and an attempt to revise Kant's transcendental philosophy, for understanding post-Kantian German idealism is conveyed by Frederick Beiser's remark that "To study Fichte, Schelling, or Hegel without having read Maimon's *Versuch* is like studying Kant without having read Hume's *Treatise*."[34] Indeed, Maimon's influence on post-Kantian idealists is considerable.[35] For the purposes of this paper, I shall restrict my examination of Maimon's philosophy to his critique of Kant's solution to the problem of the synthetic *a priori* and to Maimon's *Satz der Bestimmbarkeit* which he introduces as his own solution to the same problem, a solution that he believed was superior to Kant's. What is crucial for the purpose of this paper is to see that Maimon understood that, for Kant, the very possibility of the analytic-synthetic distinction depends on the capacity of the human mind to determine or leave undetermined a particular content of thought. Maimon's principle of determinability is introduced as an attempt on his part to rehabilitate Kant's determinate-indeterminate distinction in order to render this distinction truly capable of solving the problem of showing how synthetic *a priori* judgments are possible.

George di Giovanni says: "unlike the criticisms of Reinhold or Aenesidemus [i.e., Schulze], Maimon has the virtue of respecting the terms of Kant's own statement of the critical problem."[36] In fact, Beiser says that "Maimon's aim is not to criticize Kant's philosophy, but to transform it from within..."[37] In examining the validity of Kant's critical philosophy, Maimon goes right to the heart of this philosophy, the transcendental deduction of the categories. But Maimon believed that the central question that lies behind the transcendental deduction is how synthetic *a priori* judgments can apply to experience.[38] It is important to note that Maimon understands Kant's analytic-synthetic distinction, and therefore also the notion of synthetic *a priori* judgment, in terms of the determinate-indeterminate distinction. In his *Essay in Transcendental Philosophy*, Maimon explains "the meaning [*Bedeutung*]" of Kant's question, How are synthetic *a priori* judgments possible?, as follows:

---

[34] Beiser, *The Fate of Reason*, p. 286.
[35] See ibid., pp. 285-323.
[36] George Di Giovanni, "The Facts of Consciousness," in *Between Kant and Hegel*, p. 33.
[37] Beiser, *The Fate of Reason*, p. 303.
[38] Ibid., p. 286. Cf. Maimon, "Letters of Philaletes," pp. 184-88; *GW*, 5, 403-12.

> One can well conceive that analytical propositions are possible *a priori*, for they namely rest on the principle of contradiction, which does not refer to a determinate object and refers instead to an object in general, so that they [analytical propositions] must be found in the understanding even before the representation of determinate objects; synthetic propositions refer on the contrary to a determinate object; how can they then precede the representation of the object itself, i.e., [how can they] be *a priori*?[39]

Most of the recent scholars who have examined Maimon's analysis of Kant's analytic-synthetic distinction have emphasized the fact that Maimon rejects the distinction as Kant formulated it and that he re-defines it according to his own principles.[40] It is true that in some passages Maimon introduces his own account of the distinction that seems to differ from Kant's. But what the scholars have failed to notice is that Maimon's analysis of Kant's distinction in his *Essay in Transcendental Philosophy* is based on an accurate understanding of the distinction, as the passage cited above makes evident. Maimon, that is to say, understands that Kant's distinction is grounded on the determinate-indeterminate distinction. In fact, in his essay titled "Letters of Philaletes to Aenesidemus," written six years after his *Essay in Transcendental Philosophy*, Maimon begins his critical analysis by noting that Kant's "distinction between analytic and synthetic judgments" is a distinction "against which I have nothing to object."[41] He then proceeds to explain Kant's distinction in terms of the determinate-indeterminate distinction, just as he had done in his *Essay in Transcendental Philosophy*. So, for example, Maimon says that Kant was right to maintain that the principle of all analytic judgments is the principle of contradiction, which "refers to an indeterminate object in general."[42] Accordingly, for Maimon, the question, "How are analytical judgments possible?," means "How can we predicate *a priori* something

---

[39] "dass analytische Sätze a priori möglich sind, ist wohl begreiflich, weil sie nämlich auf dem Satz des Widerspruchs beruhen, der auf keinen bestimmen, sondern auf einen Gegenstand überhaupt sich bezieht, folglich müssen sie auch vor der Vorstellung des bestimmten Gegenstandes im Verstande anzutreffen seyn; die synthetische Sätze hingegen beziehen sich auf einen bestimmten gegenstand, wie können sie also der Vorstellung vom Gegenstande selbst vorausgehen, d.h., a priori seyn?" *GW*, 2, 172. The translation is my own.

[40] See Oded Schechter, "The Logic of Speculative Philosophy and Skepticism in Maimon's Philosophy: *Satz der Bestimmbarkeit* and the role of Synthesis," in Gideon Freudenthal, ed. *Salomon Maimon: Rational Dogmatist,* pp. 37-8.

[41] Maimon, "Letters of Philaletes," p. 188; *GW*, 5, 412.

[42] Ibid., p. 196; *GW*, 5, 430-31.

necessary of any determinate object, *prior* to the knowledge of its particular determinations?"[43] On the other hand, the question, "How are *a priori* synthetic judgments possible in mathematics?"[44] means "How can we predicate of *determinate objects*, with *necessity*, as being first determined not through these *determinate objects* but through the *form of cognition* with respect to an *object in general*, predicates that are only given through *those very objects*?"[45]

Maimon recognizes that Kant answers the question, How are synthetic *a priori* judgments possible?, by appealing to the schema. Maimon (as will be shown below) does agree with Kant that, if it is to be shown how synthetic *a priori* judgments are possible, it must be explained how the concepts in a judgment can stand in a determinate relation, that is, in such a way that they refer to an object. But Maimon argues that Kant's explanation as to how this determinate relation is effected is insufficient. As we recall, Kant had argued that it is the schema (or "the transcendental time-determination") that allows the logical forms of judgment to be employed determinately (as opposed to indeterminately). Maimon argues, however, that the appeal to schema fails to explain specifically why, for example, the hypothetical form of judgment ('If P then Q') must be applicable to certain objects. Maimon asks, Does Kant's schema explain why one particular object must necessarily precede the other, and why the latter must necessarily follow the first and not vice-versa? Maimon's answer is no. For example, does Kant's schema, which is supposed to transform the merely hypothetical form of judgment to the category of cause and effect, explain why, for example, 'fire' must always precede 'warmth' as its cause, and why 'warmth' must always follow 'fire' as its effect, and not vice-versa? Maimon thinks it does not. As he explains:

> There still remains the further question, since these [i.e., *a priori*] *concepts* and *propositions* have their reality simply as conditions of the *possibility of* experience in general, how can they refer to *determinate* objects of experience? From the fact that *objects* must be thought *in general* in the relationship, for instance, of cause and effect if an *experience* is to be

---

[43] Ibid., p. 189; *GW*, 5, 415.

[44] As it is well known, Maimon argues that synthetic *a priori* judgments are impossible in physics or "pure natural science." Therein lies part of Maimon's skepticism. See Gideon Freudenthal, "Maimon's Subversion of Kant's *Critique of Pure Reason*: There are no Synthetic *a priori* Judgments in Physics," in Gideon Freudenthal, ed. *Salomon Maimon: Rational Dogmatist*, pp. 144-75, and Paul Franks, "What Should Kantians Learn from Maimon's Skepticism?," pp. 200-32.

[45] Maimon, "Letters of Philaletes," p. 189; *GW*, 5, 415.

possible at all, it still cannot be explained why (e.g.) 'fire' and 'warmth' in particular must stand in this relationship.[46]

As Maimon sees it, Kant merely *asserts* that the schema makes this application possible; but he fails to explain precisely *how* it establishes the particular relationship in question.[47]

It is at this point in his analysis that Maimon introduces "the principle of determinability" (*Satz der Bestimmbarkeit*). In Maimon's view, while Kant was right to say that the principle of all analytic judgments is the law of contradiction, he was wrong to think that the schema could serve as a sufficient principle of all synthetic *a priori* judgments. What Kant failed to show in particular is how the determinate-indeterminate distinction, which he developed in connection with the employment of the logical forms of judgment, could *specify* the precise relation that must obtain between the two concepts in a judgment in such a way that it would be demonstrated how this relation could hold not only in thought but also in the object. Maimon's principle of determinability is supposed to show just this.

Maimon says that the principle of determinability is "a principle of all *objectively real* thought, and consequently of *philosophy* as a whole, too."[48] He contrasts "real thoughts" with "arbitrary thoughts" and with "formal thoughts." The principle of determinability explains how there can be real thoughts. According to Maimon, "no proposition can refer to real objects if its subject and predicate are not in the relationship of determinability."[49] So, for Maimon, what determines whether a thought is real, or merely arbitrary, or formal, is the nature of the relation that obtains between the subject and the predicate concepts in a judgment. As we saw, for Kant, there were two ways in which the subject and predicate concepts can be related, that is, either determinately or indeterminately. Maimon agrees with Kant that when the subject and predicate concepts are in the relation of determinability, they constitute a real thought. Maimon also agrees with Kant in maintaining that one can distinguish between two

---

[46] Ibid., p. 191; *GW*, 5, 419.

[47] Although Maimon does not explicitly mention the term "schema" in the passage from the "Letters of Philaletes," the fact that he proceeds to discuss the role of *Urteilskraft* and the example, "the plate is round," both of which are mentioned by Kant in the schematism chapter, shows that Maimon is referring to schema in the passage. Cf. *Versuch einer neuen Logik oder Theorie des Denkens*, in *GW*, 5, 191-92.

[48] Maimon, "Letters of Philaletes," p. 165; *GW*, 5, 310.

[49] Ibid., p. 166; *GW*, 5, 312.

ways in which the subject and predicate concepts can be related *indeterminately*: "arbitrarily" and "formally." Maimon's example of an arbitrary thought is the judgment "a line can be black." This thought is arbitrary because "'line' and 'black' are not in the *relation of determinacy*."[50] To say that two concepts are held together in the "relation of determinacy" means that "one of its components is cognized as *subject* and the other as *predicate*, and not vice versa… Without this *criterion* [i.e., the principle of determinability], thought can only be *formal* or quite *arbitrary*."[51] As regards another example of an arbitrary thought, "a line is sweet," Maimon says that the concept of line and the concept of sweet "being thought together in the relation of *subject* and *predicate* is merely arbitrary…"[52] Maimon then asks:

> … how can we employ these pure concepts and principles, even in respect to *objects given a priori, absolutely a priori*? For since they refer quite generally to *indeterminate objects of cognition* simply as a possibility, we have no *ground* for actually employing them in respect to determinate objects. What right do we have, for instance, in the case of 'straight line', to think that the concept of line in general is the *subject*, and that of *straightness* is the predicate, and not vice versa? Indeed, what right do we have to think that these concepts stand at all in the relation of (real) *subject* and *predicate*, and thereby to determine '*straight line*' as a *real object*? Why not also think 'line' and 'sweetness' in the same relation, and thus determine the concept 'sweet line' as a *real* object? The answer is that the right is given to us by the *principle of determinability*.[53]

The first two sentences of this passage make it clear that, for Maimon (and Kant), the general problem to be solved is, How can the pure, logical forms of judgment be employed determinately (and not merely indeterminately), that is, in such a way that, in the case of the categorical form of judgment, it is determined which of the two concepts is given the function of the subject and which will be given the function of the predicate, and not vice versa? The principle of determinability is described more specifically as follows:

> … a *real* object is possible only because the *manifold* held together in it is cognized in the *relation of determinability*, i.e., one of its components is

[50] Ibid.
[51] Ibid., p. 173; *GW*, 5, 327.
[52] Ibid., p. 174; *GW*, 5, 330.
[53] Ibid., p. 174; *GW*, 5, 329.

> cognized as *subject* and the other as *predicate*, and not vice versa. The first component is the one which is *determinable*, and can be object of consciousness by itself; the other is the *determination* of the first, and can be object of consciousness only in combination with it, not by itself. Without this *criterion*, thought can only be *formal* or quite *arbitrary*, not *real*."[54]

The principle is also stated as follows: "The given manifold must be internally so related that the subject can also be an object of consciousness in general by itself, without the predicate, but not the predicate without the subject."[55] Maimon's example is "straight line": "'Line' is determined in thought as the *subject* and 'being straight' as the *predicate* because 'line' can be an *object of consciousness* even *by itself*, whereas 'rectilinearity' can be so as the *determination* of 'line', not *by itself*."[56] On the other hand, such thoughts as 'sweet line' or 'a stone that attracts gold' are "arbitrary" because "subject and predicate can each occur in consciousness without the other."[57] Some thoughts are neither "arbitrary" nor "real," but "formal." The example Maimon gives is that of the concept of decahedron, "a corporeal figure of ten planes."[58] This thought is not arbitrary "for 'planes' do indeed stand to 'space' as *determination* to *determinable*, and apart from 'space' they cannot occur in consciousness."[59] However, "the object being thought through it is *impossible*"; thus "it cannot refer to any *real* object."[60] Such a thought is called "formal," and "it expresses a possible relation between objects, themselves indeterminate."[61]

III. From Maimon to German Idealism

As Daniel Breazeale tells us, "It is widely known that Fichte was an avid reader of Maimon during the period when he was working out the first full-scale presentation of the foundations of his new system."[62] In fact, Breazeale correctly points out that Fichte transforms Maimon's

---

[54] Ibid., p. 173; *GW*, 5, 327.
[55] Ibid., p. 198; *GW*, 5, 435.
[56] Ibid., p. 174; *GW*, 5, 329-30.
[57] Ibid., p. 198; *GW*, 5, 434.
[58] Ibid., p. 166; *GW*, 5, 312.
[59] Ibid.
[60] Ibid., p. 166; *GW*, 5, 312-13.
[61] Ibid., p. 198; *GW*, 5, 434.
[62] Breazeale, "*Satz der Bestimmbarkeit*," p. 124.

"Principle of Determinability" (*Satz der Bestimmbarkeit*) into his own "Principle of Reciprocal Determination" (*Satz der Wechselbestimmung*).[63] What Breazeale does not point out, however, is that Fichte uses his own revised version of Maimon's principle in order to answer Kant's question, How are synthetic *a priori* judgments possible?

In the Second Introduction to the so-called *Wissenschaftslehre nova methodo* of 1796/99, Fichte remarks that Kant "reduced the task of philosophy to answering the question, 'How are synthetic judgments *a priori* possible?'" Fichte immediately adds that he will "phrase the same question as follows: 'How do we come to assume that something external to us corresponds to the representations within us?' These two questions are the same."[64] In a letter written to Reinhold in July 1795, moreover, Fichte says that "the principal question with which the *Wissenschaftslehre* continues to occupy itself… is the following: If the I originally posits *only itself*, how then does it come to posit something else as well, something posited as opposed to the I? How does it happen that the I goes outside of itself? (The question 'How are synthetic *a priori* propositions possible?" is only a part of this principal question. …)"[65] In order to answer this question, Fichte employs not only Maimon's principle of determinability but also Kant's determinate-indeterminate distinction. For Fichte, every moment of consciousness involves what he calls "a movement of transition from determinability [or indeterminacy] to determinacy." In section 10 of the *Wissenschaftslehre nova methodo*, Fichte regards it as a "general principle" that "all consciousness arises from a movement of transition from what is determinable to what is determinate."[66]; in section 9, moreover, Fichte says that "to observe the freedom of the I in the act of comprehending an object," one must "do so in terms of a movement of transition from what is determinable to what is determinate."[67] According to Hegel, Fichte's I "is the true synthetic *a priori* judgment, in accord with the expression of Kant."[68]

---

[63] Ibid., p. 127, p. 128.

[64] *Fichte: Foundations of Transcendental Philosophy: Wissenschaftslehre Nova Methodo* (1796/99), trans. and ed. Daniel Breazeale (Ithaca: Cornell University Press, 1992), p. 87; *GA*, 4, 2, 17-18.

[65] *Fichte: Early Philosophical Writings*, p. 399; *GA*, 3, n. 294.

[66] *Fichte: Foundations of Transcendental Philosophy*, pp. 237-38; *GA*, 4, 2, 100

[67] Ibid., p. 232; *GA*, 4, 2, 98.

[68] *Hegel's Lectures on the History of Philosophy*, trans. E. S. Haldane and Frances H. Simson, 3 vols. (Atlantic Highlands: Humanities Press, 1983), vol. 3: p. 389; *Werke*, 20: 388.

Kant's question, How are synthetic *a priori* judgments possible? is raised and dealt with also by Schelling in his *Of the I as Principle of Philosophy* and the *Philosophical Letters on Dogmatism and Criticism*, both published in 1795. According to Schelling, Kant's question "in its highest abstraction is none other than: How is it possible for the absolute I to step out of itself and oppose to itself a not-I?"[69] In the *Philosophical Letters*, moreover, Schelling says that Kant's question is the same as the question, "*How do I ever come to egress [herausgehen] from the absolute, and to progress toward an opposite?*"[70] In fact, Schelling says that to answer this question is "the main task of all philosophy"[71] or "the problem of *all* philosophy, not only of one particular system."[72] Schelling does not make any explicit reference to a "principle of determinability" in his discussion of how the I comes to oppose to itself a not-I, but a close examination of Schelling's arguments in the texts in question indicates that the principle of determination does play an important role in his solution to this problem.[73]

Space limitations prevent me from developing the accounts of Fichte and Schelling in this paper.[74] I would like to conclude with the remark that Kant, Maimon, Fichte, Schelling, and Hegel, *as transcendental philosophers,* saw as their main task answering the question, How are synthetic *a priori* judgments possible? But it is impossible to understand adequately *what* this question *meant* to them as well as *how* they answered it apart from an understanding of Kant's determinate-indeterminate distinction and the ways in which this distinction was taken up and applied in their own thought by the post-Kantian German idealists.

---

[69] Schelling, *Of the I as Principle of Philosophy*, p. 81; *SW*, 1, 175.

[70] Schelling, *Philosophical Letters on Dogmatism and Idealism*, in *The Unconditional in Human Knowledge*, p. 164; *SW*, 1, 294.

[71] Ibid., p. 177; *SW*, 1, 313.

[72] Ibid., p. 177; *SW*, 1, 313-14.

[73] See, for example, *Philosophical Letters*, pp. 181-82 nt; *SW*, 1, 320 nt., and *Of the I as Principle of Philosophy*, p. 115; *SW*, 1, 223.

[74] I have provided a sketch of such accounts (including the account of Hegel) in my paper, "How Are Synthetic Judgments Possible *A Priori*? From Kant to Hegel," delivered at the XXII World Congress of Philosophy, July 30-August 5, 2008, Seoul, Korea.

Works Cited

Works by Kant

Kants Gesammelte Schriften, herausgegeben von der Deutschen Akademie der Wissenschaften. 29 vols. Berlin: de Gruyter, 1902–

Kant, Immanuel. *Correspondence*. Trans. and ed. Arnulf Zweig. Cambridge: Cambridge University Press, 1999.

—. *Critique of Practical Reason*. Trans. Lewis White Beck. New York: Macmillan, 1956.

—. *Critique of Pure Reason*. Trans. and ed. Paul Guyer and Allen Wood. Cambridge: Cambridge University Press, 1997.

—. *Foundations of the Metaphysics of Morals*. Trans. Lewis White Beck. New York: Macmillan, 1990.

—. *Lectures on Ethics*. Trans. Peter Heath and ed. J. B. Schneewind and Peter Heath. Cambridge: Cambridge University Press, 1997.

—. *Lectures on Logic*. Trans. and ed. J. Michael Young. Cambridge: Cambridge University Press, 1992.

—. *Metaphysical Foundations of Natural Science*. In *Philosophy of Material Nature*. Trans. James W. Ellington. Indianapolis: Hackett, 1985.

—. *Philosophical Correspondence, 1759-99*. Trans. and ed. Arnulf Zweig. Chicago: University of Chicago Press, 1967.

—. *Prolegomena to Any Future Metaphysics*. Trans. Paul Carus and ed. Lewis White Beck. Indianapolis: Hackett, 1950.

Works by Maimon

Gesammelte Werke. Ed. V. Verra. Hildesheim: Olms, 1965.

Maimon, Salomon. "Letters of Philaletes to Aenesidemus." In *Between Kant and Hegel: Texts in the Development of Post-Kantian Idealism*. Trans. George Di Giovanni and H. Harris. Indianapolis: Hackett, 2000: 159-203.

Works by Fichte

J. G. Fichte – Gesamtausgabe der Bayerischen Akademie der Wissenschaften. Ed. Reinhard Lauth, Hans Jacob, and Hans Gliwitsky. Stuttgart-Bad Cannsatt: Frommann-Holtzboog, 1962–

Fichte, J. G. *Fichte: Early Philosophical Writings*. Trans. and ed. Daniel Breazeale. Ithaca: Cornell University Press, 1988.

—. *Fichte: Foundations of Transcendental Philosophy: Wissenschaftslehre Nova Methodo* (1796/99). Trans. and ed. Daniel Breazeale. Ithaca: Cornell University Press, 1992.

Works by Schelling

Sämmtliche Werke. Ed. K.F.A. Schelling. Stuttgart and Augsburg: J. G. Cotta, 1856-61.

Schelling, F. W. J. *On the possibility of a Form of All Philosophy*, *Of the I as Principle of Philosophy*, and *Philosophical Letters on Dogmatism and Idealism*. In *The Unconditional in Human Knowledge: Four Early Essays (1794-1796)*. Trans. Fritz Marti. Lewisburg: Bucknell University Press, 1980: 35-218.

Works by Others

Atlas, Samuel. *From Critical to Speculative Idealism: The Philosophy of Salomon Maimon*. The Hague: Martinus Nijhoff, 1964.

Baumanns, Peter. *Fichtes Wissenschaftslehre: Problem ihres Anfangs. Mit einem Kommentar zu § 1 der "Grundlage der gesammten Wissenschaftslehre*." Bonn: Bouvier Verlag H. Grundmann, 1974.

Beiser, Frederick. C. *The Fate of Reason: German Philosophy from Kant to Fichte*. Cambridge, Mass: Harvard University press, 1987.

—. "Maimon and Fichte." In Gideon Freudenthal, ed. *Salomon Maimon: Rational Dogmatist,* 233-48.

Bergmann, Samuel H. *The Philosophy of Solomon Maimon*. Trans. Noah J. Jacobs. Jerusalem: Magnes Press, 1967.

Breazeale, Daniel. "*Der Satz der Bestimmbarkeit*: Fichte's Reception and Transformation of Maimon's Principle of Synthetic Thinking." In *Internationales Jahrbuch des Deutschen Idealismus* 1 (2003): 115-40.

Di Giovanni, George. "The Facts of Consciousness." In *Between Kant and Hegel,* 3-50.

Engstler, Achim. *Untersuchungen zum Idealismus Salomon Maimons*. Stuttgart: Fromann-Holzboog, 1990.

Franks, Paul. "What Should Kantians Learn from Maimon's Skepticism?" In Gideon Freudenthal, ed. *Salomon Maimon: Rational Dogmatist,*

200-32.

Freudenthal, Gideon. "Maimon's Subversion of Kant's *Critique of Pure Reason*: There are no Synthetic *a priori* Judgments in Physics." In Gideon Freudenthal, ed. *Salomon Maimon: Rational Dogmatist*, 144-75.

—. Ed. *Salomon Maimon: Rational Dogmatist,Empirical Skeptic: Critical Assessments*. Ed. Gideon Freudenthal, Dordrecht: Springer, 2003: 233-48.

Grier, Michelle. *Kant's Doctrine of Transcendental Illusion*. Cambridge: Cambridge University Press, 2001.

Hegel, G. W. F. *Hegel's Lectures on the History of Philosophy*. Trans. E. S. Haldane and Frances H. Simson. 3 vols. Atlantic Highlands: Humanities Press, 1983.

Kuntze, Friedrich. *Die Philosophie Salomon Maimons*. Heidelberg: Winters, 1912.

Lee, Seung-Kee. "The Determinate-Indeterminate Distinction and Kant's Theory of Judgment." *Kant-Studien* 95 (2004): 204-25.

Longuenesse, Beatrice. *Kant and the Capacity to Judge*. Princeton: Princeton University Press, 1998.

—. "The Transcendental Ideal and the Unity of the Critical System." In *Kant on the Human Standpoint*. Cambridge: Cambridge University Press, 2005: 211-35.

Melamed, Yitzhak. "Salomon Maimon and the Rise of Spinozism in German Idealism." *The Journal of the History of Philosophy* 42 (2004): 67-96.

Schechter, Oded. "The Logic of Speculative Philosophy and Skepticism in Maimon's Philosophy: *Satz der Bestimmbarkeit* and the role of Synthesis." In Gideon Freudenthal, ed. *Salomon Maimon: Rational Dogmatist,* 18-53.

Thielke, Peter. "Getting Maimon's Goad: Discursivity, Skepticism, and Fichte's Idealism." *Journal of the History of Philosophy* 39 (2001): 101-34.

—. "Discursivity and Causality: Maimon's Challenge to the Second Analogy." *Kant-Studien* 92 (2001): 440-63.

Yakira, Elhanan. "From Kant to Leibniz? Salomon Maimon and the Question of Predication." In Gideon Freudenthal, ed. *Salomon Maimon: Rational Dogmatist,* 54-79.

Zöller, Günter. *Fichte's Transcendental Philosophy: The Original Duplicity of Intelligence and Will*. Cambridge: Cambridge University Press, 1998.

CHAPTER ELEVEN

THE THIRD DOGMA OF RATIONALISM

MARK OKRENT

Self Apprehension

John Haugeland has recently suggested that traditional rationalism falls prey to two unfounded 'dogmas', positivism and cognitivism.[1] According to Haugeland, positivism is the metaphysical view that 'reality is exhausted by the facts', while cognivitism is the assumption that 'reason is to be understood in terms of cognitive operations on cognitive states', where a cognitive state is a propositional attitude towards a propositional content and a cognitive operation is a rational inference. Although I am far more sanguine than Haugeland is that, properly qualified and understood, the language of cognitivism, with its talk of beliefs and desires, can be both benign and useful, I agree with his general claim that both of these assumptions, however widespread, are mere unwarranted dogmas. In particular, I think that the doctrine that explicit rational inference is necessary for an agent to act for reasons, engage in purposeful action and possess intentionality is an unwarranted dogma based solely on a misleading view of the nature of purposeful action.

Quine's diagnosis of the first two dogmas of empiricism led to Davidson's diagnosis of a third dogma of empiricism, the dogma that there are conceptual schemes. I have located a third dogma of rationalism that has roughly the same relation to Haugeland's first two dogmas that Davidson's third dogma has to Quine's. The third dogma of rationalism is the view that in order for an agent to have any intentions directed towards the world, that agent must have intentions that are directed towards its own intentions as its own intentions. That is, the third dogma of rationalism is

---

[1] John Haugeland, "Two Dogmas of Rationalism", unpublished paper, delivered at The Sixth Annual Meeting of The International Society for Phenomenological Studies, Pacific Grove, CA, July 16, 2004.

that the abilities to have second order intentions, to intend one's own intentions as intentions and to apprehend oneself as an intentional agent, are necessary conditions on being an intentional agent at all.

As with any self-respecting dogma, the first clear and precise statement of this dogma appears in Kant, most clearly in Section 16 of the B Deduction. "It must be possible for the 'I think' to accompany all my representations; for otherwise something would be represented in me which could not be thought at all, and that is equivalent to saying that the representation would be impossible, or at least would be nothing to me."[2]

But the view also shows up repeatedly in the work of many prominent twentieth century philosophers, including Davidson, Sellars, Korsgaard, and Brandom, many of whom explicitly mention their debt to Kant. Davidson, for example, frequently expresses the view in the traditional language of cognitivism. To cite one instance, in "Rational Animals" he says "…in order to have any propositional attitude at all, it is necessary to have the concept of a belief, to have a belief about some belief."[3] Given this way of putting the point, one might be tempted to say that for Davidson (and one might as well add, Brandom, Sellars, and Korsgaard) only a being that is capable of self consciousness is capable of true, real, original intentionality. But this way of stating the content of the dogma is accurate only if one is clear that for these thinkers 'self-consciousness' is given a certain definite analysis. What Davidson really suggests in the above quote is that what is necessary for an agent to have any intentional states is that that agent have states that reflexively intend some of their own states *as* intentional states, that the agent have some states that have the content that some other states of theirs are intentional. This is the import of the Kantian 'I think' and I will take this to be the canonical form of the third dogma of rationalism.

In this paper I develop four related themes. In the first part of the paper I offer an interpretation of Kant's statement of the Third Dogma in the B Deduction that is sensitive to its context in Kant's critical philosophy In the second section I argue that the third dogma of rationalism, in its twentieth century guise, is motivated by a certain definite way of understanding the importance, role, and nature of what John Haugeland calls cognitive operations, that is, rational inference. Third, I argue that, perhaps surprisingly, this view of the role and importance of rational inference is motivated by the Kantian analysis of *practical* reason, in

---

[2] Immanuel Kant, *Critique of Pure Reason* (KrV), trans. Norman Kemp Smith (London: Macmillan, 1968), KrV B. 131.

[3] Donald Davidson, "Rational Animals" in *Subjective, Intersubjective, Objective*((Oxford: Oxford University Press, 2001), p. 104.

particular by Kant's analysis of what it is to act for or because of a reason. Fourth, I argue that this analysis of acting for a reason is fundamentally misguided and for that reason the third dogma of rationalism is unwarranted.

Kant on Judgment and the 'I Think'

For Kant, "It must be possible for the 'I think' to accompany all my representations; for otherwise something would be represented in me which could not be thought at all, and that is equivalent to saying that the representation would be impossible, or at least would be nothing to me."[4] This assertion, while pithy and memorable, is also unfortunately written in such a way that it is easy to misinterpret. Kant clearly is committed by this statement to the view that the possibility of the 'I think' accompanying some representation is necessary for the possibility of that representation being thought as the representation of something. This is what the crucial second clause asserts. It is possible to think of some representation as representing some thing only if it is possible for the 'I think' to accompany this representation. But does this imply that for x to be a representation of some thing it must be possible for the 'I think' to accompany it? That of course depends upon whether or not the possibility of x being thought as a representation of z is essential to x being a representation of z. And this *seems* to be the import of Kant's third clause, where he says that 'something represented in me could not be thought' is equivalent to saying that 'the representation is impossible'. But then he apparently takes this equivalence back in the final, parenthetical, clause. According to this final parenthesis, the assertion "representation x can not be thought by me as representing z, because I can not affix the 'I think' to it", is *not equivalent* to 'x representing z is impossible, because I can not affix the 'I think' to it." Rather, it is equivalent to 'representation x would be nothing to me if I can not affix the 'I think' to it". And this is clearly a different claim than the stronger claim, apparently asserted in the second clause, that no object can be represented without the possibility of the 'I think'. But which of these is Kant's considered opinion on the status and role of the 'I think'?

There is excellent reason to believe that the final parenthetical clause governs the whole and that Kant does not equate x being a representation of z with the possibility of x being 'thought' by me as a representation of z. Indeed, Kant is quite clear, both in the *Critique* and elsewhere, that he believes that it is possible for there to be a representation in y of which y is

---

[4] Ibid.

not even conscious, let alone capable of thinking. In the division of types of representations in the Dialectic, for example, Kant distinguishes between the genus 'representation' and its' species *perceptio*, or 'representation with consciousness'.[5] More importantly, in the Jasche *Logic* Kant continues the division by distinguishing between two forms of *perceptio*: to be acquainted (*kennen*) with something, "or to represent something in comparison with other things, both as to sameness and as to difference" and being acquainted with something with *consciousness*, or *cognition* (*erkennen*). Both of these, Kant tells us, involve intentions directed towards objects, but animals are only acquainted with objects, they do not cognize them. "Animals are acquainted with objects too, but they do not *cognize* them.[6] It is only in the next division that Kant reaches understanding, "to cognize something through the understanding by means of concepts, or to conceive." So, for Kant in 1800 (the date of the Jasche *Logic*), it is possible for an agent to have a representation of something, be conscious of that representation, and even represent that representation in relation to others in respect to sameness and difference, and thus be acquainted with objects, without that agent using concepts or being conscious *that* they are acquainted with objects. And, since in the Jasche *Logic* Kant uses 'to think' as equivalent with 'to cognize with concepts',[7] it is obvious that when he says in the B Deduction that if it were impossible for the 'I think' to accompany a representation x, then x could not be thought by me, this can't be equivalent to saying that if it were impossible for the 'I think' to accompany x, it would be impossible for x to be a representation of z.

What, then, *is* the 'I think' necessary for? For Kant, it is primarily necessary for two things, both of which are mentioned in the famous quote above: 'thinking' a representation as a representation of an object; and a representation, and the object represented by that representation, being something 'to me'. But how are we to interpret these?

What does Kant mean when he speaks about 'something represented in me which is thought'? One of the keys to interpreting this is given in Kant's division of representations in the Lectures on Logic. He tells us there that animals, who are incapable of having the 'I think' accompany their representations, can be acquainted with objects perceptually, and even represent similarities and differences, but they can't cognize objects. To be acquainted with something is to "represent something with other

[5] Ibid., A320/B376.

[6] Kant, *Lectures on Logic* (VL), ed. J.M. Young (Cambridge: Cambridge University Press, 1992), pp. 569-70.

[7] Cf. ibid., p. 564.

things, both as to sameness and as to difference". Cognition, on the other hand, Kant says, is being acquainted with something with *consciousness*. The acquaintance side of this division is clear enough. When one is acquainted with an object one represents that object as similar to and different from other objects. When my dog Sammie sees other dogs he reacts in similar fashion to all of them but differently in each of those cases than he does when he sees a squirrel. And this gives us reason to believe not only that his representations of the dogs are similar to one another and different from his representations of squirrels, but also that in some sense Sam synthesizes these representations and compares them in regard to their similarities and differences. In Kant's terms, Sammie represents the dogs in comparison with the squirrels in respect to sameness and difference. But what, then, does cognition, which Sam is incapable of, add? Kant says that cognition is acquaintance with consciousness. And at first sight this is odd, because an act in which one is acquainted with an object, such as my dog perceiving the difference between a dog and a squirrel, is already itself a conscious representation for Kant. So what can he mean when he says that cognition is acquaintance with something with consciousness?

In the division of kinds of representation in the Jasche *Logic* Kant says that the division is "in regard to the objective content'. That is, acquaintance is different from cognition, and simple perceptual cognition is different from a conceptual cognitive understanding, in respect to *what is represented* in these various types of state. From this perspective, when Kant speaks of cognition as acquaintance *with consciousness* (his emphasis), *what* is differentially conscious in cognitive states is not the state itself, but rather the *content* of those states. That is, Kant is suggesting that the differentia of cognitive acts is that the acts of acquaintance in which the sameness and difference of objects is represented are *themselves* consciously represented in cognitive acts. So, to return to my dog, he represents dogs and squirrels differently, and he can even distinguish between them when instances of both are present. He can represent something in comparison with other things, both as to sameness and to difference. But he does not represent that sameness and difference itself *as such*. That is, Sam is incapable of intending *that* he represents dogs and squirrels differently, and that these representations differ from one another in such and such respects. It is for this reason that Sam is incapable of using concepts. To have the concept 'dog' is at least to be potentially conscious of those respects in which representations of all dogs are similar and the respects in which the representations of all dogs are different from the representations of non-dogs.[8]

The distinguishing feature of human representation is not introduced in the Transcendental Deduction through a contrast with animal representation, as it is in the Lectures on Logic. Nevertheless, the same differentia are suggested there as in the Logic. The Deduction in B begins with the suggestion that the distinguishing 'act of spontaneity' of the faculty of the understanding, an act which has "the general title 'synthesis'", is "the combination of a manifold in general".[9] This way of putting the matter makes it sounds as if what is at issue is the act of putting together representations itself. Fortunately, Kant immediately corrects this misleading impression. For he tells us, first, that it is not mere combination of representations which is the act of understanding, but the *representation* of the combination, and, second, that what is contained in combination is not merely a manifold and its synthesis, but also *the representation* of the *unity* of the combination or synthesis of a manifold: "...of all *representations* combination is the only one which cannot be given through objects." "But the concept of combination includes, besides the concept of the manifold and of its synthesis, also the concept of the unity of the manifold. Combination is the representation of the *synthetic* unity of the manifold. The representation of this unity cannot, therefore, arise out of the combination. On the contrary, it is what, by adding itself to the representation of the manifold, first makes possible the concept of the combination."[10] That is, the understanding combines a manifold in the sense that it represents the manifold as unified in a single representation – it represents the unity of what is manifold. Each of our representations of dogs is itself a synthesis or combination of a manifold of different representations. My dog, insofar as he is acquainted with objects, can have such synthetic representations. Indeed, he can represent two dogs together and note their similarity. But he can not represent that similarity of representation in a single representation by recognizing that both of these synthetic representations have been synthesized in the same way and that they are both instances of the same type of representation, 'dog'. The representation in which we recognize that Sam is similar to Fido and all other dogs in respect of being a dog, is, of course, the judgment that

---

[8] I discuss these passages in the Jasche *Logic*, and the crucial issues they raise for Kant interpretation, far more fully than I can do here in my paper "Acquaintance and Cognition" in *Aesthetics and Cognition in Kant's Critical Philosophy*, ed, Rebecca Kukla (Cambridge: Cambridge University Press, 2006), pp. 85-108.

[9] Kant, KrV B130.

[10] Ibid., KrV B130-131.

Sammie is a dog. It is for this reason that in the *Logic* Kant explicitly asserts that the distinguishing mark of human cognition is that is it discursive. Only we can form judgments, and, as we will see, according to Kant we can form judgments only if it is possible for the 'I think' to accompany our representations. This is the, relatively modest and circumscribed, Kantian form of the third dogma of rationalism.

In both the A and B Deductions Kant immediately follows his discussions of the consciousness of the unity of synthesis with the first introduction of the necessity of the unity of apperception. This 'I think', which must be capable of accompanying all of my cognitive representations, is itself, for Kant, a representation which embodies a consciousness of the unity of the synthesis of all that is manifold in my experience. "The synthetic proposition, that all the variety of empirical consciousness must be combined in one single self-consciousness, is the absolutely first and synthetic principle of our thought in general. But it must not be forgotten that the bare representation 'I' in relation to all other representations (the collective unity of which it makes possible) is transcendental consciousness."[11] Indeed, this 'I think' is a specific kind of representation, a 'thought'. "On the other hand, in the transcendental synthesis of the manifold of representations in general, and therefore in the synthetic original unity of apperception, I am conscious of myself, not as I appear to myself, nor as I am in myself, but only that I am. This representation is a *thought*, not an *intuition*."[12] *What* I am conscious of in this thought, this "bare representation 'I'", is the 'unity of synthesis', or combination, of my various representations. Putting this all together, the 'I' which must be capable of accompanying all of my representations is the representation of the unitary act of thinking which relates all of my various representations into a single consciousness or experience.

Kant's line of argument here seems to be as follows. What is distinctive about human cognition is the ability to represent or be conscious of the unifying or combining character of our own mental activity in a single unifying representation. Typically, such a representation itself ultimately involves a concept applied in a judgment to a synthesized manifold; e.g., 'That is a dog'. When one represents in this way, what is represented is the type of synthesizing character of one's own activity. As such, every such representing act, no matter what concept is applied, is also an act of self representing, an act in which one conceptually represents one's own combining activity. Since it is the

[11] Ibid., KrV A117n.
[12] Ibid., KrV B157.

synthetic representation of that dog which is conceptually characterized as 'dog', and that representation has that character in part in virtue of the character of the synthesizing activity that constituted that complex representation, it is one's own activity that one types when one types a representation as one of a dog. So to be capable of conceptually cognizing something as a dog, one must be capable of conceptually cognizing one's dog representations as one's own representations, in the sense that they are recognized as the product of a certain sort of combining activity on my part. What I have which my dog Sam lacks is precisely this ability to be acquainted with objects with consciousness, that is, the reflective capacity to cognize and type my own acts. That which *all* such acts of combination share in common is just that they are all my acts. But insofar as I can cognize conceptually I have the reflective capacity to type my own acts, so I have the ability to conceptually represent, to think, my own acts *as* my own acts. That is, I can conceptually cognize, or think, an object only if the thought 'I think' can accompany the act in which I think the object. For Kant, what the 'I think' is necessary for is the capacity to judge and to conceptually represent objects by forming discursive judgments about them.

At the same time the possibility of the 'I think' is also required if any representation or object is to be anything 'to me'. Something is something 'to me' only if it is recognizable by me as something which *I* am cognizing. That is, for a dog to be something to me I must be able to represent *that* the dog is being thought by me as a dog. But this possibility just *is* the possibility of representing the act in which I intend the dog as my act, that is, the possibility of the 'I think' accompanying the cognition of the dog as dog. It is thus analytically true that some thing can be something to me only if I am capable of affixing the 'I think' to its representation.

We can thus see that for Kant the ability to self-consciously represent oneself as thinking, or judging, is a necessary condition on the possibility of thinking, or judging, at all. What needs to be added to the Kantian position to generate a full-blown statement of the third dogma of rationalism is an additional commitment, the claim that no creature who is incapable of forming judgments is capable of intending objects as objects. I have argued elsewhere the Kant himself waffles on just this point. At times he speaks as if he is committed to the view that only agents who are capable of asserting judgments are capable of intending objects as objects. In other moods Kant seems to admit the possibility that non-judging creatures are indeed capable of intending objects.[13] Regardless of whether or not the historical Kant believed that there is no intentionality without the possibility of judgment, however, there is no question that many of his twentieth century successors committed themselves to just this view. And with this commitment they arrived at the complete third dogma position that self-conscious second order intentionality is a necessary condition on *all* intentionality. In the remainder of this paper I consider the structure of the arguments that twentieth century Kantians have used to support this conclusion.[14]

Necessary Conditions on Intentionality

In the next section of this paper I will take Davidson's discussion of the necessary conditions on an agent having intentions as representative of the twentieth century version of the 'third dogma' tradition. There are three reasons for doing so. First, Davidson's discussions of this issue are clear. Second, as opposed to similar discussions in Sellars and Brandom, his discussions are brief. And third, the most distinguished contemporary Sellarsian, Robert Brandom, has explicitly endorsed Davidson's views, (though, as we will see, he adds to them), so we might with confidence abstract from whatever differences remain between Davidson's fundamentally Quinean approach and the Sellarsian version of the story. As Brandom has developed the tradition beyond the point at which Davidson stops, the following part of my discussion will focus on his views.

Davidson's argument proceeds in two steps, and each step is clearly transcendental in form. First he argues that the intentional attitude of believing plays a central role in intentional life. For Davidson, an agent has any intentions at all only if among those intentions some are beliefs. Second, he argues that having some other kind of intentional state is a necessary condition on an agent having any beliefs. As will become clear in the following, Davidson takes the class of agents that have beliefs to be coextensive with the class of agents that can form judgments, and all of his arguments for the second stage in his argument, and thus for the third dogma of rationalism, turn on that identification.

Davidson offers a variety of intentional attitudes as necessary for

[13] Cf. my "Acquaintance and Cognition" cited above.

[14] An earlier version of much of the material in this section has appeared in my "The 'I Think' and the For-the-Sake-of-Which" in "*Transcendental Heidegger*, S. Crowell and J. Malpas, eds. (Stanford: Stanford University Press, 2007) pp. 151-168.

belief. The canonical candidate for this role is the concept of belief: "… I argue that in order to have a belief, it is necessary to have the concept of belief."[15] This condition provides the focus for all of Davidson's other formulations of the conditions on belief. Because one can't have a concept of belief unless at the minimum one can group beliefs together as distinct from non-beliefs in virtue of being beliefs, in order to have a concept of belief one must be able at a minimum to believe of some beliefs that they are beliefs. That is, one must be capable of having some beliefs about beliefs if one is to have a concept of belief. "…in order to have any propositional attitude at all, it is necessary to have the concept of a belief, to have a belief about some belief." But, for Davidson, that which distinguishes beliefs as beliefs is that they are intentional states of an agent that, in virtue of their content, could be true or false. Since this is what a belief *is* no agent could have a concept of belief or recognize a belief as a belief unless she also could intend the possibility of error and understand being true and being false, and their contrast. "Someone cannot have a belief unless he understands the possibility of being mistaken, and this requires grasping the contrast between truth and error – true belief and false belief."[16] But the contrast between truth and error is grounded in the distinction between the way the world is and the way an agent takes the world to be. So no agent who lacks a concept of an objective world or of objective truth can have a concept of belief. And, finally, Davidson holds that the capacity to be surprised trades on an agent's ability to recognize that her previous beliefs were false, and so he concludes that this capacity for surprise is an infallible marker of a concept of falsity and thus of the presence of the concept of belief. So, if an agent has intentional states at all only if she has a concept of belief, then an agent has intentional states only if she is capable of surprise.

But why does Davidson hold that only agents who possess the concept of belief can have beliefs? Ordinarily one needn't have the concept of X in order to have or be X, even for intentional states. The clue to Davidson's adherence to this version of the third dogma is contained in the quote from "Thought and Talk" that I just cited. The mediating term relating having a belief and having the concept of belief is the ability to understand the possibility of being mistaken. For Davidson, it is not only the case that if an agent has the concept of belief, she also has the capacity to understand that she is mistaken. It is also the case, for Davidson, that if an agent has the ability to understand that she is mistaken, then she has the concept of

---

[15] D. Davidson, "Rational Animals", p. 102.

[16] Donald Davidson, "Thought and Talk" in *Inquiries into Truth and Interpretation* (Oxford: Clarendon Press, 1984), p. 170.

belief. And, Davidson argues, since only an agent who 'understands the possibility of being mistaken' counts as having beliefs, and only agents who have the concept of belief can understand the possibility of being mistaken, having the concept of belief is a necessary condition on having beliefs.

So Davidson's argument turns on two distinct claims. First, he holds that the ability of an agent to understand being mistaken is necessary for that agent to have beliefs. And second, he holds that having a concept of belief, and thus second order beliefs, is necessary for grasping the possibility of being mistaken. From these premises Davidson infers his version of the Third Dogma: Having beliefs about beliefs, beliefs of the second-order, is necessary for having any beliefs at all. But what supports these premises? In one sense of 'understanding being mistaken', it is easy enough to see why someone might think that having a concept of belief is necessary for understanding being mistaken. If 'understanding being mistaken' consists in forming the *judgment* that one has committed an error or has had a false belief, then an agent can understand that they are mistaken only if that agent has a concept of belief. To judge of some state that it is false I must at least take that item to be a candidate for truth and falsity, that is, I must judge that the item satisfies the concept of belief. But, then, having a concept of belief is necessary for one to judge of a belief that it is a mistake. But why do Davidson and other adherents of the third dogma think that the ability to understand the possibility of making a mistake, in this *judgmental* sense, is necessary for having beliefs? On its face, the concept of belief demands that to be a belief a state must be a candidate for truth or falsity, and this requires that the state has some 'content', specify some way the world might be, and that the state is true if the world is that way and false if it is not. The belief B that some belief A is mistaken, then, is a state that has the 'content', that specifies the possibility, that the content of A not line up with the way the world actually is. So to claim, as Davidson does and the third dogma demands, that an agent can't have beliefs without being capable of judging that some belief is mistaken, is to claim that an agent can't have beliefs about the world unless that agent has some beliefs about beliefs that specify that her beliefs about the world might be mistaken. But what is it about belief that, for the adherents of the third dogma, motivates *this* claim?

In order to answer this question, and thus to see why the adherents of the Third Dogma tradition think that second order belief is necessary for belief *tout court*, it is necessary to understand what adherents to this tradition think that beliefs *are*. I think that Haugeland points the direction to the answer to this question when he points out that for Davidson (and

Dennett, Sellars, Brandom, etc.) "…cognitive states and processes are determinate only relative to the interpretability of manifest behavior". This is the case for these thinkers (and, I might as well admit, for me as well) because for them, and for me, what a state with intentional content *is* is a state that potentially plays a certain definite role in a certain kind of interpretation and understanding of the behavior of an agent. The kind of interpretation in which such states figure is the kind of interpretation that sees what the agent does as having a *point*, as occurring *in order to* reach a goal. On this view, intentional states in general, that is, states with content, and beliefs in particular, that is, states that are to be evaluated in terms of truth and falsity, have the intentional content that they have in virtue of their roles in 'fleshing out' this kind of interpretation. So to understand why the adherents of the third dogma think that understanding the possibility of error, in the sense of being capable of judging that some belief is false, is necessary for having intentionality, we must understand how they interpret the interpretation of the purposeful activity of agents.

Action and Reasons

According to the interpretationalist view of intentional states that stands behind the twentieth century version of the Third Dogma position, only agents whose actions have a point, who attempt to achieve goals, have intentionality. This is a traditional Aristotelian view. But not all things that react differentially to their environment do so in order to achieve some end. An iron bar reacts differentially to the presence or absence of water vapor in its neighborhood (by rusting or not), but its behavior has no point. The behavior of my 13 year old, on the other hand, clearly marks her as acting so as to achieve ends of her own. There must, then, be features of the behavior of an entity that mark that behavior as having a goal and it is the presence of such features that alert us to the possibility that the entity is an agent who has intentionality and beliefs.

The features in the behavior of an agent that marks that behavior as action that has a point are holistic in the sense that they have to do with the overall structure of the behavior of the agent. We are only justified in suggesting that an agent is attempting to achieve goals by acting for reasons related to those goals when we can discern a certain pattern in the agent's behavior. At a minimum, the behavior must be generally 'successful' at resulting in certain definite states of affairs in varying situations, and what the agent does must itself vary flexibly in accordance with variations in the environment so as to result in those preferred outcomes. Take my dog Sammie, for example, which periodically picks up a chewy toy and drops it at my feet. *Partially* on the basis of this act I am inclined to attribute to him the desire to play fetch, together with the belief that cuing me in this way will get me to play the game with him. After all, this behavior on Sammie's part frequently results in my picking up the toy and throwing it, and if this were the point of Sammie's behavior, this would be an *appropriate* thing for him to do. Now, of course, I don't always play fetch with Sam when he cues me in this fashion. Sometimes, as we say, Sam has the false belief that I will play with him if he cues me in this way. But unless what the agent, Sammie, does is *in general* flexibly suitable for bringing about certain preferred 'ends' or goals in changing circumstances we would not even consider the possibility that what that agent does has the goal of bringing about those ends.

But, as the example of the iron bar always producing iron oxide in the presence of water reminds us, not every response to a given environment that generally results in a certain outcome counts as an act that has that outcome as a goal. Acting for a goal is a phenomenon that essentially occurs over time. To count as having a point most of what the agent does must keep changing in response to variations in the environment so as to keep honing in on the goal. At the most fundamental level it is this consistent appropriateness of behavior for bringing about preferred results in shifting circumstances, even though the physically described behavior keeps changing, that marks the difference between the iron bar and my dog.

The fact that activity with a goal involves a holistically suitable response to a changing environment has enormous implications for what it is for an agent to act in order to achieve an end. For every time the agent does something what it does alters its environment. So every time the agent acts it changes how it should act in the future so as to achieve its goals. And, since an agent acts for a goal only if in general it acts suitably for bringing about that goal in changing circumstances, an agent acts for a goal only if it can in general string together various acts in such a way that the entire string of acts fits together so as to achieve that goal.

It is this fact, that to interpret an agent as acting in order to achieve an end one must interpret the agent as doing a variety of things that together serve to progressively realize that end, that provides the anchor for the interpretationist view of intentionality. As opposed to iron bars, agents don't do the same things in the same circumstances at different times. Rather, what they do at a time in a given environment varies as a function of the overall point of the agent's activity at that time. A given leopard in a given physical environment might, or might not, head for a tree full of monkeys depending on whether its goal is to eat or not. But if its goal is to eat, what it does at each successive stage of its quest must vary in response to the way in which its own activity changes the situation, or might change the situation. Going towards the tree, for example, might alert the monkeys to its presence, and the monkeys might then take appropriate countermeasures that would make it difficult for the leopard to achieve its goal, to eat. So the leopard attempts to hide. That is, achieving the ultimate goal of eating involves the leopard in acting with a more proximate goal, to hide. But, the interpretationist argues, when the agent, the leopard in this case, acts in order to hide, there must be some fact about the agent that disposes it to act in order to hide, that is, act in ways that have the goal of hiding from the monkeys. Any agent that has *that* kind of state, that is, a state that disposes it to act in order to hide from the monkeys, can be said to have the *desire* to hide from the monkeys. The 'content' of the desire is just the 'in order to' of the acts that the desire would motivate if it motivated behavior. And, since the attempt to hide counts as having that goal only as part of a larger pattern of purposeful action in which the ends of each bit of behavior fit together into a generally effective instrumental chain, no agent can count as having a single 'desire' unless most of her desires fit together in a way that 'makes sense', that is, fit together in a generally consistent instrumental pattern.

The role of beliefs on the interpretationist model is just to pick up the slack between the 'in order to' of acts and what the acts actually achieve. There is variability in response by agents in identical situations that is not captured by differences in ends. Two leopards might be identically situated relative to a tree full of monkeys, and both might want to eat them, but they still might act differently. One might go to the left of the tree, the other might go right, and the first might be successful in catching and eating a monkey and the other fail in its attempt, perhaps because the left side of the tree is downwind. For the interpretationist there must be something about the two leopards that explains this difference in action, but by hypothesis it can't be that they have different desires or goals. For the interpretationist, what is different is the 'beliefs' of the two agents. It is possible for agents with the same goals to act differently in identical situations because not everything an agent does to achieve an end need be successful for that agent to be acting so as to achieve that goal. That is, an agent can be acting for some end without reaching it. All that is necessary for an agent's behavior to have a point is that most of what it does is successful at achieving its goals. But then much of what it does can fail, that is, result in states that it does not desire. Now, when an agent is successful its acts mesh with the actual environment so as to bring about the agent's preferred end. But this is not the case with failed acts. On the other hand, had the initial state of the world at the time that the agent acted been different in some definite way, what the agent did *would* have resulted in success. So, in our example, what is common to the actions of the successful and unsuccessful leopard is that both of those behaviors would result in the leopard eating a monkey under some definite wind conditions. That is, the leopards' actions share a goal and the leopards share the desire to eat monkeys. What is different is that those conditions under which the behavior would be successful are different and only one of those set of conditions is actual. That is, the first leopard has true beliefs regarding its environment and the second has false beliefs, but both act in ways that would be successful were their respective beliefs true. So beliefs are states of agents that interact with desires to help to interpret the variations in the behavior of an agent in a given environment. The 'content' of a belief is the possible state of the world in which, if actual, the agent's act would be successful at achieving its goal.

The fact that agents who act in order to achieve ends generally act in interconnected ways that over time are flexibly suitable to achieve those ends in changing environments has a further, crucial consequence. Such agents must be good at 'figuring out' the potential consequences of their acts. Otherwise they could not perform in a manner appropriate for achieving their ends as conditions vary in response to their own activity. But to do this amounts to coming to have new beliefs about the world that are themselves *appropriate*, or *justified* by the agent's prior beliefs and the sensory information concerning its environment that is available to it. For example, over time I find that Sammie drops toys at my feet far more frequently than he drops them at the feet of my son, and this makes sense if Sammie believes that I am more likely to play with him than my son is. But that he believes this in turn makes sense in light of the fact that in Sam's past experience I have been far more likely to play with him than my son has. That is, if Sammie had been rational he would have inferred, from his prior beliefs and sensory experience, just this belief, that I, but not my son, would respond to this cue on this occasion. Generalizing, we can see that to interpret an agent as acting for goals we must be able to assign beliefs and desires to that agent that fit together into a pattern that reflects proper inferential connections, If what an agent does has some point, then that agent's intentional states must be related to each other in inferentially appropriate ways.

We can thus see that according to the interpretationist model for understanding intentionality an agent acts in order to accomplish goals only if it is possible to interpret that agent as having beliefs and desires the contents of which are both capable of explaining the overall activity of the agent and are interrelated to each other in inferentially appropriate ways. As Haugeland says, for the interpretationist, "cognitive states and processes are determinate only relative to the interpretability of manifest behavior'. This is because on this model the content of intentional states just is the peculiar role of those states in the interpretation of the agent's behavior as goal directed. But why, then, is the paradigmatic interpretationist, Donald Davidson, committed to the view that an agent cannot have intentional states without understanding the possibility of being mistaken? Nothing in the story we have been telling seems to require that some of the intentional states that are assigned to an agent in the course of teleologically interpreting her behavior must intend other states as intentional, and thus intend them as potentially mistaken.

But the story we have been telling is incomplete. A list of necessary conditions is not a sufficient condition. If an agent acts for a goal then it must be possible to interpret that agent as acting as if it had intentional states that are linked in inferentially appropriate patterns, but it doesn't follow from it being possible to so interpret an agent that that agent is acting in order to accomplish goals. In addition, the agent must be acting as she does *because* she has those intentional states. In fact, Davidson, Sellars, and Brandom implicitly appeal to an additional requirement on intentionality that they assert that non-self-conscious agents cannot satisfy: Any agent that acts for reasons, and thus possesses beliefs and other intentions, must act *because* of her reasons.

Consider a case that is strictly analogous with Sammie's fetch inducing behavior. I often ask my son to play catch with me, but I less frequently ask my daughter to do so. I *think* that I do this because I have evidence that my son is a better bet for this cuing behavior then my daughter is. After all, when asked, he has played with me in the past more frequently than my daughter has, or so I believe. And that justifies my current belief that my son is a better bet. But even if it is true that in the past Nick has played catch with me more frequently than Valerie it doesn't follow that this is the correct explanation for my behavior on this occasion. In fact, the correct explanation might be simply that I am sexist, and have a stereotypical and false view of women, and this view *causes* me to act as I do. That is, it doesn't follow from the fact that my beliefs line up in inferentially appropriate patterns, that they do so *because* those beliefs are appropriately inferentially connected. And it doesn't follow from the fact that what I do is what I would do if I were acting rationally, that what I do I do because I am acting rationally. And, finally, it doesn't appear to follow from the fact that I can assign beliefs and desires to Sam in an appropriate inferential pattern so as to explain his actions, as if he has reasons for what he does, that he in fact does what he does because of his reasons.

The moral of this little story is that an agent acts for reasons, and thus is a candidate for having beliefs, only if she does what she does because of her reasons. And it does not seem to follow simply from the fact that an agent acts *as if* it acted for reasons that it acts *because* of those reasons. It is this condition, that rational agents must act because of their reasons, Davidson (and Sellars, and Brandom) think non-self-conscious agents can't possibly meet. To see why they think this we must look briefly at Kant's analysis of what it is to act because of a reason.

Self-Correction And The Conception Of Law

Because agents whose behavior has a point must generally act appropriately to achieve their ends in changing circumstances, and circumstances change in response to their own ongoing behavior, such agents must act differently when they succeed from how they act when they fail. The leopard that walks west in order to reach a hole that contained water last week for the sake of drinking acts differently if the hole still contains water from how she acts if it is empty: in the first case she laps with her tongue, in the second she moves with her legs. For any successful teleological agent, such differential behavior must correlate pretty well with the correctness or the mistakenness of its prior action, where success is measured by the agent's goals, and mistakes are responded to appropriately so as to achieve those goals. But an agent can be self-correcting in this way to a fairly great extent and still not be acting *because* what it does is a response to its own mistakes as mistakes. And it is only agents who vary their behavior because, or *for the reason that*, they have made a mistake (or not), that are candidates for intentional ascription. Consider the Sphex wasp that was made philosophically famous by Dennett:

> When the time comes for egg laying, the wasp Sphex builds a burrow for the purpose and seeks out a cricket which she stings in such a way as to paralyze but not kill it. She drags the cricket into the burrow, lays her eggs alongside, closes the burrow, then flies away, never to return. In due course, the eggs hatch and the wasp grubs feed off the paralyzed cricket, which has not decayed, having been kept in the wasp equivalent of deep freeze. To the human mind, such an elaborately organized and seemingly purposeful routine conveys a convincing flavor of logic and thoughtfulness - until more details are examined. For example, the Wasp's routine is to bring the paralyzed cricket to the burrow, leave it on the threshold, go

> inside to see that all is well, emerge, and then drag the cricket in. If the cricket is moved a few inches away while the wasp is inside making her preliminary inspection, the wasp, on emerging from the burrow, will bring the cricket back to the threshold, but not inside, and then will repeat the preparatory procedure of entering the burrow to see that everything is all right.[17]

The punch line of the story, of course, is that if the biologist is sufficiently persistent she can induce the wasp to repeat the pattern without end so that she never lays her eggs. Now, although I have used this story for other purposes at other times,[18] in this context the moral of the story is just the moral that Dennett wishes to draw. An agent can act as if she is acting for reasons without in fact acting because of her reasons. We know that the wasp is not acting because of reasons, even though it seems that she might be, because she is entirely unresponsive to the singular fact that what she does when she moves the cricket back to the doorstep is completely unsuccessful in furthering her ends. That is, she does not treat the *failure* of her acts to achieve her proximate ends as a *reason* to alter her behavior. If this failure gives us reason to believe that the wasp is not acting because of reasons, as it does, then we have reason to think that only an agent who corrects her mistakes because they are mistakes can act because of her reasons. But only an agent that acts because of reasons can have beliefs. So it is a necessary condition on an agent having beliefs that she act to correct her mistakes because they are mistakes. That is, the ability to respond to the mistakenness of actions as reasons for self-correction must be implicit in the practical behavior of an agent for that agent to be a candidate for rationality or intentionality. But the wasp's repeated routine in the face of recurrent failure indicates that she is not responsive to the *mistakenness* of her own behavior. So it follows that she has no beliefs.

We have now reached the bedrock intuition that stands behind the third dogma of rationalism. And the intuition itself is not an error. The intentionality of an agent demands a differential responsiveness to error as error on the part of the agent. But the implications of this intuition are not quite as clear as they might seem. For this assertion is not quite equivalent to the premise for Davidson's version of the third dogma that we have found in "Thought and Talk".

---

[17] Dean E. Wooldridge, *The Machinery of the Brain* (New York: McGraw-Hill, 1963), 82.

[18] Mark Okrent, *Rational Animals: The Teleological Roots of Intentionality* (Athens: Ohio University Press, 2007).

That premise was specified as follows: "Someone cannot have a belief unless he understands the possibility of being mistaken, and this requires grasping the contrast between truth and error…" The requirement on belief that we have uncovered, on the other hand, is that someone cannot have a belief unless the ability to respond to mistakes as mistakes, that is, as reasons for self-correction, is implicit in her activity. These are equivalent conditions only if an agent can implicitly respond in her practical activity to her mistakes as mistakes just in case she *understands the possibility of being mistaken*, and that this is impossible unless the agent *grasps the contrast between truth and error*. Now, understanding the possibility of being mistaken is a reflexive, second order intention that does indeed require grasping the contrast of truth and error, that is, intending an intention specifically as correct or incorrect. So if the capacity to respond to mistakes as mistakes can be implicit in behavior only if the agent understands the possibility of being mistaken, then the capacity for such second order intentions is indeed a necessary condition for intentionality. But why would one think this?

For an agent to respond to a mistake as a mistake is for the agent to take the fact that the mistake is a mistake as a *reason* to alter its behavior accordingly. We know that the wasp does not take the fact that the replacement of the cricket in its original position does not permanently alter the situation to be grounds for her to change her pattern because she does not change her pattern in the face of her failures. She does not treat her failure as a reason to change. So if we could discover what it is for an agent to treat a situation as a reason to act in a certain way we could also discover what it is for an agent to respond to a mistake as a mistake, and thereby discover what it is for an agent to satisfy the behavioral conditions on intentionality. Perhaps the clearest and best worked out suggestion regarding what it is to treat a situation as a reason is found in Kant's analysis of practical reason, and it is this analysis that leads to the third dogma of rationalism, by way of the implications of this analysis for the issue of what it is for an agent to treat a mistake as a mistake.

In summary, here is Kant's suggestion. "Everything in nature works according to law. Only a rational being has the capacity of acting according to the conception of laws, i.e., according to principles. This capacity is will. Since reason is required for the derivation of actions from laws, will is nothing else than practical reason."[19]

"Everything in nature works according to law." But according to Kant,

---

[19] I. Kant, *Foundations of the Metaphysics of Morals* (G), trans. L.W. Beck (Indianapolis: Bobbs-Merrill, 1959), p. 29.

the rational actions of rational beings, as rational acts, satisfy a different condition, although the condition also has to do with a relation to a rule or law. When rational agents act rationally what they do is according to a *conception* of law. That is, the rational acts of agents are mediated by the agent's conception of or grasp on a law. For example, I find myself to be angry with my daughter, but I recognize the principle that parents love, support, and do not hurt their children. I understand myself to be a parent. So I support my daughter, rather than hurting her, as I would if I were caused to act by my anger. I act as I do *because* I accept that I am a parent and I acknowledge the law that parents support their children. As Robert Brandom puts Kant's point, "What makes us act as we do is not the rule itself but our *acknowledgement* of it."[20]

It is crucial to note that on this analysis the normative force of the principle, what makes it a reason for the agent to act, is wrapped up with the agent's acknowledgement of the law as a law for him. Since it is the acknowledgement of the law that accounts for the action, if the agent is acting because of his reasons, it is the fact that the agent accepts the principle as applying to him that is the rational motive for the act. This fact is displayed in the distinctive status of the law that I acknowledge, and the equally distinctive status of my acknowledgement of that law. The law I accept is not descriptively true, and, what is more, I know it to be descriptively false. Nevertheless, what it is to be a parent entails that anyone who is a parent ought to act according to this principle, and my self-understanding as a parent, together with my acknowledgment of the law, *is* an acceptance of the obligation, as a parent, to act according to the law. The concept of a parent, which conditions must be satisfied for someone to count as a parent of someone else, combines in exceedingly complex ways certain factual biological relations, which are neither necessary nor sufficient for someone to be a parent, with certain social roles and functions that parents ought to fulfill, (a fact that is especially obvious to me, as one of my children is adopted). To even understand oneself to be a parent one must understand that one stands under these defining obligations, even if one need not fulfill them, and even if one can be a parent without understanding oneself as a parent. The fact that I am a parent has normative force, provides me with a reason to act, only insofar as I acknowledge myself to be a parent and understand what it is to be a parent in terms of a set of principles of parental action.

But as Kant makes clear in the continuation of the famous passage

---

[20] R. Brandom, *Making It Explicit* (Cambridge: Harvard University Press, 1994), p. 31.

from the *Groundwork* that I have been discussing, on his analysis, while such a conceptual understanding is necessary for the possibility of rational action, it is not sufficient. Rational action occurs *because* of the agent's reasons. And in Kant, this 'because' is understood in a distinctive fashion. For an action to be rationally motivated by the agent's reasons, for the action to occur because of the reasons, it is not enough that those reasons *cause* the action, or *explain* the action. Rather, the action must be *derived* from the reasons. Kant's name for this ability of rational agents to derive actions from laws and reasons is 'will', and will is essentially the rational capacity to infer a mode of action from a law. "Since reason is required for the derivation of actions from laws, will is nothing else than practical reason." That is, on Kant's analysis, no agent is capable of acting for reasons unless she is also capable of inferring that she ought to act in a certain way from a set of propositions that include a law and an acknowledgment that she stands under that law.

Now, if what it is for an agent to act for a reason is for that agent to rationally infer from her beliefs regarding a situation and some law that one ought to act in a certain definite fashion, as Kant holds, and one acts for a reason just in case one treats the mistakenness of mistakes as a reason to act, then Kant also offers us a theory regarding what it is to treat the mistakenness of mistakes as a reason to act. On this Kantian view to treat a mistake as a mistake and to alter one's behavior accordingly is just to explicitly *infer* some mode of action from one's acknowledgment of the fact that one has made a mistake together with one's acceptance of some law. That is, the paradigm case of correcting a mistake is the inference from the judgment that some belief is false to the assertion of that belief's negation, via the law of the excluded middle. On this rationalist view to act because of one's reasons, and thus to have intentionality, an agent must be capable of recognizing a mistake as a mistake so that the mistakenness of the mistake can serve as a *premise* in an argument. But an agent can be capable of such recognition only if she has a concept of belief and beliefs about beliefs. So Davidson's form of the third dogma of rationalism follows directly from the interpretationist understanding of intentionality combined with the Kantian account of what it is to act for reasons. Roughly, the argument goes as follows. From the first Critique one gets the premise that no agent is capable of forming judgments without being capable of second order intentions, of affixing the 'I think' to its own representations. From the *Groundwork* one gets the premise that no agent can act for reasons unless it is capable of forming judgments. And from a certain development of the interpretationist analysis of belief, one gets the premises that no agent can have beliefs unless it is capable of responding to its mistakes as mistakes, and no agent can respond to its mistakes as mistakes without being capable of acting for reasons. From all of this the third dogma of rationalism validly follows: No agent can have intentional states if it is incapable of having second order intentional states that intend its own intentional states as its own intentional states.

Evaluating The Third Dogma

My immediate target here is the premise of this argument that has the Kantian analysis of acting because of a reason as its point of origin. On that account, to act because of a reason is essentially to derive a consequence from a law together with an appreciation of a situation. On the Kantian view, to act for a reason an agent must be capable of correcting her mistakes and to correct one's mistakes is to recognize that some situation, belief or act fails to satisfy some law or principle, and to infer some new belief or act from this failure. But to recognize that some belief fails to satisfy some principle is to form a judgment, and judgments essentially involve second order intentional attitudes, so only agents who can have such second order acts can correct mistakes, act because of reasons, or have any intentions at all.

Unfortunately for the proponents of the third dogma, as an analysis of what it is to act because of a reason this Kantian account is wrong. The late Wittgenstein has given us a strong reason to believe that deriving action from law can't be the only way in which an agent can be responsive to, or act because of, a reason. The argument is given in the context of Wittgenstein's discussion of language use, is familiar, and I won't belabor it here. Roughly, the problem has to do with a regress regarding the application of laws to situations, or what Kant calls our faculty of judgment. On Kant's view, when we act for reasons, that action is mediated by our understanding of a law or rule, that is, by our interpretation of the law. Given Kant's own understanding of concepts as rules for sorting, understanding a law amounts to knowing how to apply it to given situations. Such understanding necessarily involves knowing what one ought to do in different situations. One can rationally act in accordance with a rule only if one understands the rule, but there are correct and incorrect ways to understand the rule. Now, if all rational action, or action because of reasons or norms, demands that one act because one acknowledges a rule, then one can correctly adopt an interpretation or understanding of our first rule, from among alternative deviant ways of understanding the import of the rule, only if one has a reason to adopt that understanding, which, on the analysis, amounts to choosing this interpretation because one acknowledges some other rule that prescribes this choice. But, by symmetry of reasoning, our application of this further law demands a prior understanding of some third law, and off we go.

The moral of this little Wittgensteinian story is that acting because of reasons cannot be explicit inference all the way down. If anything we, or anyone else, does is done because of our reasons, then some of what we do must be done because of reasons that are not fully articulate, and we must be able to act because of reasons that we do not use as premises in explicit arguments. There must be a way to act because of reasons that does not demand explicit inference.

It would seem to follow from this conclusion, that since there must be a way to act because of reasons that does not demand explicit inference, that there must be a way to respond to mistakes as mistakes that also does not require explicit inference, as there is no acting for reasons without responsiveness to mistakes as mistakes. But from this it would seem to follow that it is also possible that there might be agents with beliefs who lack any beliefs about beliefs, as the only justification we have found for this dogma is the view, now seen to be false, that there is no possibility of responding to mistakes as mistakes without the kind of explicit inference that requires second order beliefs. Nevertheless, some of those who accept the Wittgensteinian argument we have been considering still deny that non-reflective agents are capable of having beliefs, or acting because of reasons. In particular, Robert Brandom emphasizes just this point derived from Wittgenstein. Nevertheless, he still uses a Kantian style analysis of acting because of reasons to deny beliefs and other intentional states to non-reflexive agents. The remainder of this paper is devoted to a consideration of the structure of his argument.

Brandom draws two conclusions from the above line of Wittgensteinian argument. First, in the terms of our own discussion here, there must be a way of acting because of a reason that is implicit in the practice of an agent, rather than demanding an explicit inference from premises by that agent. (Brandom's own way of putting the point has to do with the necessity that there be some way in which an agent is responsive to norms in their practice that does not require explicitly understanding propositional claims.) Second, he insists that such a practical grasp of reasons is best understood in terms of *assessments* of propriety. "…there is another move available for understanding what it is for norms to be implicit in practices. This is to look not just at what is done – the performances that might or might not accord with a norm (appropriate or inappropriate) – but also at *assessments* of propriety. These are attitudes of taking or treating performances *as* correct or incorrect."[21] That is, Brandom's suggestion is that the primary, non-explicitly inferential way in which an agent is acting because of a reason, or (in Brandom's terms) is acting because she is responsive to a norm, is by *assessing* an act as correct or incorrect. This amounts to the view that responsiveness to reasons can implicitly manifest itself in the practical behavior of an agent by the agent somehow directly assessing an action as mistaken, or, in Brandom's terms, incorrect, without that assessment being mediated by an explicit cognitive inference.

This is the linchpin of Brandom's discussion of these issues. From here he argues two successive points. First, he argues that the norms or reasons in light of which we assess the actions of others are only instituted as reasons or norms by the very attitudes of assessment we apply. For Brandom, what we ought to do is what we ought to do *only* in virtue of the fact that it is *acknowledged* as what we ought to do in the practices of assessment. This is Brandom's residual adherence to the Kantian analysis of acting because of a reason. Second, he infers from this that such assessment is primarily social in character: Assessment of correctness and incorrectness of performance is something we do to and for each other.

Here is how the argument goes. Since Brandom agrees with Kant that reasons only have normative force insofar as they are acknowledged, it follows that *any* behavior by a single agent that merely accords with a norm but does not include explicit acknowledgement of the reason fails to be an action performed because of the norm, precisely because the agent lacks such an acknowledgement of the reason. Nevertheless, according to the Wittgensteinian argument that we have been discussing, there *must* be some way that acknowledgement of norms can be merely implicit in the practice of an agent. So Brandom thinks that we are faced with an aporia.

Brandom thinks that the *only* way in which this aporia can be overcome is by appealing to a social context. Each of the agents in a community responds to the acts of others as if those acts were correct or incorrect according to some rule by approving and sanctioning those acts. So, for example, I might intervene and punish any member of my group that I observe crossing a street when a light is red, and other members of my community might intervene in a similar way. That we do so is a function of the kind of training that we have undergone in the past combined with the fact that we are the type of social creatures that we are. But, given that for Brandom reasons are reasons only by being

---

[21] R. Brandom, *Making It Explicit* (Cambridge, Harvard University Press, 1994), p. 63.

acknowledged, and none of us, my self or my peers, are capable of acknowledging the principle 'don't cross street when light is red', because none of us is capable of explicitly formulating the principle, none of this really counts as acting because of reasons. Nevertheless, each new member of the community is trained by the same sanctioning practices that trained us to act *as if* they were responsive to the reason for not crossing at a time that is partially embodied in the rule concerning red lights. Similarly, the same kind of sanctioning and rewarding practices could also be efficacious in training the members of a community of the right type of animal to engage in *vocal* activities, activities that were structured *as if* the members of the community were responding to one another's utterances for appropriate inferential reasons. So, to continue our example, at this stage the members of the community not only sanction individuals who cross when the light is red, and reward those who don't, (thereby training the individuals both to act as if they are following a rule and to get those individuals to train yet other individuals in the same way), but the members of the community now also train each other so as to *say* 'light is red' when it is red, and 'no cross the street', both when someone refrains from crossing and when the light is red. For Brandom, this still does not count as acting for a reason, for as yet there can be no explicit acknowledgement of any rule or reason. But once the members of the community have reached the stage at which their verbal practices amount to acting as if they were following the logical rules for the conditional, everything changes. At this point, those practices themselves allow the members of the community to make the practices they are following explicit. For at this stage, it becomes possible to *say* that 'If the light is red, don't cross the street', and, given all of the background training involved in reaching this point, this allows for the possibility of explicitly *acknowledging* this as a principle to be followed, by treating this statement as a premise in an argument that results in an action as a conclusion. At that point, the back of the aporia is broken, and it becomes possible for the members of the linguistic community to become truly rational, because they are now capable of really acting because of reasons by inferring correctness and incorrectness of performances from rules in the approved Kantian manner. What had been mere animal conditioning becomes acting for reasons by the very act of making explicit the rules that the agents have been conditioned to follow so that those rules can be acknowledged as norms.

The aporia that Brandom constructs turns on the incompatibility of two claims, the Kantian assertion that if an agent is acting for reasons then that agent must infer its action from the acknowledgement of a principle, and the Wittgensteinian observation that if *all* actions for reasons obeyed the Kantian dictum, we would be faced with an impossible regress of reasons. Brandom's solution is to posit a set of community practices that train members of the society to act as if they are acting for reasons, even though they do not act *because* of those reasons. That is, Brandom dissolves the aporia by keeping the Kantian notion of acting because of a reason in full force, but recognizing that all acting because of a reason has as its necessary condition that the agents who act for reasons have been trained, by other members of their animal communities, to act *as if* they had reasons for what they are doing, *even though, strictly speaking, they do not*.

Now, whatever one thinks about the prospects for this way of dissolving Brandom's dilemma, there is a prior issue about whether the aporia that this line of argument is meant to resolve is a real dilemma at all. There is, after all, a problem to be solved here only if Brandom is right in agreeing with Kant that a reason has normative force only if it is acknowledged as a reason. But there is good reason to think that this claim is implausible. First, consider the fact that in many of the paradigm cases in which we take ourselves to be acting for reasons we simply cannot even *formulate* the rule or norm the acknowledgement of which on this Kantian view constitutes an essential part of our reason for acting. If we could formulate these rules it would be much easier to pass the Turing test than it has turned out to be. But if in many paradigm cases, such as language use, we can't explicitly formulate the principles we are following in acting because of our reasons, how can it be the case that the explicit acknowledgement of those principles is necessary for an agent to act because of a reason?

Beyond this fact, there are familiar cases in which we respond to mistakes as mistakes, and *self-correct* our behavior, solely on the basis of our perceptual interaction with the world, short-circuiting the supposed necessity for acknowledgement of the reason as a reason, without interfering with the fact that we are acting because of reasons. Consider the following example taken from Michael Tye's discussion of Davidson's version of the third dogma of rationalism. "Suppose, for example, I believe that my car had been stolen upon finding it missing in the carpark. I start to walk to the security office on campus. As I do so, I see my car parked on the other side of the street, and I suddenly remember that I left it there on this occasion. No longer believing that my car has been stolen, I change direction and head directly to it. Here surely I revise my beliefs in light of my perceptual evidence and thereby my behavior. But I need not have any (explicit) belief about a belief. In this sense, I need not (explicitly) recognize my mistake: I need not consider my belief that my car has been stolen as such at all. I am certainly acting for reasons, however; and as my reasons change, by behavior changes too."[22]

Now what is it that makes it so obvious to Tye, and to us, that when he changes his behavior here in response to a perceptual encounter that he is 'certainly acting for reasons'? The answer, I think, is clear. The perception provides perceptual *information* about the world, and this information leads to a *self-assessment* of Tye's *own* behavior, and a correction of that behavior as wrong. Assessment begins at home. The primary form of assessment is the self assessment of an agent's own behavior as appropriate or inappropriate in light of the ends of the agent and the changing state of the world. The very pattern of action that provides the sine-qua-non for attribution of purposeful action at all, flexibly suitable behavior by the agent for achieving her goals, in changing circumstances, guarantees that the agent is self correcting, and in that sense, self assessing. It is of course true that any agent must be capable of responding appropriately to the mistakenness of mistakes. But any agent that acts as if it is responsive to reasons must also satisfy this condition as well, at least to the extent necessary in order to display suitably flexible behavior for achieving its minimal goals. The normativity of reasons is dependent upon the goals that direct purposeful action. It is a mere dogma of rationalism that reasons only become reasons if they are reflexively acknowledged as such. And failing this dogma, there is no reason to accept the further rationalist dogma that there is no intentionality without second order intentions.

As we have seen, the bedrock intuition behind the third dogma of rationalism is that only agents who can respond appropriately to mistakes as mistakes can have intentions. Traditional rationalism interprets this requirement as demanding that only agents that reflexively understand the concept of being mistaken can be responsive to mistakes as mistakes. But this is an overly intellectualized way of understanding the self-assessment and self-correction that is inherent in all purposeful action. One of the great lessons to be learned from Heidegger is that purposeful action, understanding, and self-correction are primarily practical and circumspectively perceptual, and that for that reason specific inference and reflexive self-awareness, self-assessment, and self-correction are late secondary growths.

[22] M. Tye, *Consciousness, Color, and Content*, (Cambridge: MIT Press, 2000), pp. 177-178.

Self-assessment and self-correction comes in many different degrees, of course. At one extreme lie adult, linguistically competent human beings who can explicitly formulate laws that specify correct behavior and can correct the actions (as well as assessing those laws themselves), of themselves and others in light of those principles. At the other extreme lie plants and simple, genetically programmed animals such as Dennett's sphex wasp who, while capable of achieving apparent ends in standard conditions, have little flexibility for change of behavior in light of differing circumstances. As such organisms fail to display much in the way of self-assessment and self-correction in light of sensory evidence, they certainly do not merit the honorific of 'rational', and there is little or no reason to attribute intentional states to them. But there is a wide range of intermediate cases. And any agent who is capable of self-assessment and correction in the light of changing evidence, that is, any agent capable of learning from its mistakes, is also capable of acting in response to reasons, and thus capable of intentionality.

Epilogue

Doesn't the suggestion that I have advanced, that any agent who is capable of flexibly altering her behavior in the light of changing circumstances so as to achieve her goals counts as assessing that behavior and thus counts as acting because of her reasons, fail to account for the difference between acting because of a reason and acting as if one had reasons for what one does? I don't think so. I think that here Kant and his rationalist successors have fallen into the same kind of scope fallacy that afflicted Descartes, a fallacy that Kant and these same successors have done a great deal to reveal. As I am sure that you recall, Descartes argued that since any given belief might be false, it follows that all beliefs might be false simultaneously. But, as Davidson in particular often pointed out, this inference doesn't go through. It is only against a background of massive truth that the possibility of error can emerge. Without that background there is neither truth nor error, because the agent neither has beliefs nor acts because of her reasons. It is rather ironic that Davidson himself seems to have fallen into the same fallacy. He implicitly argues that because any given act of a self correcting non-reflective agent might not be performed because of the agent's reasons, that all of those acts simultaneously might not be performed because of the agent's reasons. But the same charity considerations which preclude the possibility of massive error of belief also preclude the possibility that all of a successful agent's acts might be only 'as if' performed because of her reasons. The successful agent who learns from her mistakes, that continues to update her behavior so as to increase her success and correct her failures, just *is* acting in response to reasons, acting because of her reasons. For this is what it is to act because of reasons.

Works Cited

Brandom, Robert. *Making It Explicit*. Cambridge: Harvard University Press, 1994.

Davidson, Donald. "Rational Animals." In *Subjective, Intersubjective, Objective*, by Donald Davidson, pp. 95-105. Oxford: Oxford University Press, 2001.

—. "Thought and Talk." In *Inquiries into Truth and Interpretation*, by Donald Davidson, pp. 155-170. Oxford: Clarendon Press, 1984.

Haugeland, John. "Two Dogmas of Rationalism." Unpublished paper, delivered at The Sixth Annual Meeting of The International Society for Phenomenological Studies, Pacific Grove, CA, July 16, 2004.

Kant, Immanuel. *Critique of Pure Reason*. Trans. Norman Kemp Smith. London: Macmillan, 1968.

—. *Foundations of the Metaphysics of Morals*. Trans. L.W. Beck. Indianapolis: Bobbs-Merrill.

—. *Lectures on Logic*. Ed. J.M. Young. Cambridge: Cambridge University Press, 1992.

Okrent, Mark. *Rational Animals: The Teleological Roots of Intentionality.* Athens: Ohio University Press, 2007.

—. "Acquaintance and Cognition." In *Aesthetics and Cognition in Kant's Critical Philosophy*, ed., Rebecca Kukla, pp. 85-108. Cambridge: Cambridge University Press, 2006.

—. "The 'I Think' and the For-the-Sake-of-Which." In "*Transcendental Heidegger*, ed. S. Crowell and J. Malpas, pp. 151-168. Stanford: Stanford University Press, 2007.)

Tye, Michael. *Consciousness, Color, and Content*. Cambridge: MIT Press.

Wooldridge, Dean. *The Machinery of the Brain.* New York: McGraw-Hill, 1963.

CHAPTER TWELVE

COMPETING ENLIGHTENMENT NARRATIVES: A CASE STUDY OF RORTY'S ANTI-KANTIANISM[1]

PABLO MUCHNIK

Kantian ethics contains elements which, in Rorty's view, are utterly misguided and in need of revision. Take, for instance, Kant's insistence on the unconditional as the trademark of morality, his stark opposition to prudence, his overarching concern with obligation, his downplaying of feeling, his confidence about the capacity of reason to motivate and guide us, his commitment to impartiality at the expense of emotional attachments, and his idealization of universal consent. Rorty finds in all these Kantian themes either fault or danger, because they provide a picture of morality that hinders the progress of liberalism and, to the extent that they place the source of obligation in the demands of a putative rational self, they condemn individuals to feeling alienated from their actual motives and reasons for action. To avoid such problems, Rorty develops a version of pragmatism that disposes of the unconditional, blurs the difference between morality and prudence, puts trust in place of obligation, gives a preeminent role to feelings and emotional attachments, and distrusts reason's claims to universal validity and commensuration.

The attack Rorty mounts on Kantian ethics draws on a historical narrative of the coming to age of our culture that bears surprising similarities to Kant's account of the Enlightenment in his famous 1784 essay.[2] In Rorty's version of the story, however, Kant's philosophy is

---

[1] I would like to express special thanks to Lauren S. Barthold, Jennifer McErlean, and Sharon Anderson-Gold for their insightful comments on a prior version of this paper.

[2] John McDowell has indicated how this narrative underlies Rorty's campaign against epistemology. Here I want to spell out its political and ethical implications.

mistakenly assimilated to a form of "Platonism." What is transcendental for Kant, Rorty takes to be transcendent: the "a priori" structures necessary to account for the possibility of a common world of meanings, and valid only *within* that world, Rorty places in a metaphysical realm bereft of spatiotemporal contingencies. My goal is to develop an alternative, "de-Platonized" reading of Kant, in order to protect Rorty's politics against its own poetic excesses. Given Rorty's description of the historical situation of Western culture, his assimilation of freedom with unlimited possibilities for self-creation undermines the very goals of his liberal utopia. I will argue, then, that a more sophisticated interpretation of the normative constraints of Kantian ethics would have a sobering effect on Rorty and better serve his aims.[3]

My argument roughly falls into three parts: first, I reconstruct the historical narrative Rorty uses to support his radical philosophical conclusions (§§I-III); then, I interpret the view of politics that arises out of Kant's vision of the Enlightenment (§§IV-V); finally, I diagnose the reasons of Rorty's misreading of Kant as a symptom of a new form of empiricism (§§VI-VII).

I- God's Lingering Shadows

Rorty's political and ethical views are often seen as an offshoot of the thoroughgoing anti-foundationalism of his *Philosophy and the Mirror of Nature*.[4] In Rorty's later writings, the salutary critique of the quasi-

---

See John McDowell, "Towards Rehabilitating Objectivity," in *Rorty and His Critics,* Robert Brandom (ed.) (Malden/Oxford: Blackwell Publishers, 2000), pp. 109–122.

[3] This is the crux of Habermas' polemics with Rorty. Although I share many of Habermas' worries, I want to bypass the contemporary version of the debate by connecting Kant and Rorty directly, instead of describing the intricacies of Rorty's "pragmatic turn," as is often done in the literature. (See Rorty's "Universality and Truth," where he places his thought in contemporary context, and Jürgen Habermas' "Rorty's Pragmatic Turn," both in *Rorty and His Critics*, op. cit., pp. 1-56) A metaphysically deflationary reading of "*What is Enlightenment?*" shows that the key to understanding this debate among contemporary liberals lies in a feature usually overlooked by readers of Kant, namely, his redrawing of the boundaries of privacy. My goal here is to show how one may reconcile aspects of Rorty's ironism with his liberalism by appealing to the critical distance characteristic of Kant's public use of reason.

[4] Charles Guignon and David Hiley show, however, how Rorty's political and ethical views inform his critique of epistemology-centered philosophy from the

religious impulse of epistemology-centered philosophy expands to an overarching fight against the metaphysical drive still operative in our culture. Paradigmatic examples of such a drive are, in Rorty's view, a longing after the *philosophical* justification of liberalism and the attempt at grounding the "human rights culture" in a *philosophical* anthropology.[5] These foundational cravings are for Rorty signs of a persistent tendency towards superstition, which he characterizes, following Santayana, as "the identification of the ideal with power."[6] That is, "the belief that any legitimate ideal –any ideal worth achieving– must be somehow grounded in something already actual. It cannot be 'merely' an ideal. It must have its source in something that imposes an obligation upon us. There must be something that sets this ideal before us and insists that we achieve it."[7] Thus, when philosophers try to secure the historically contingent achievements of liberalism by deriving them from an ahistorical view of the self or from universally valid transcendental structures, or when they defend human rights by an appeal to the dignity and rationality of human nature, Rorty believes they are taking refuge in something transcendent, something larger and more powerful than their fallible imagination, in sum, something "metaphysical."

The recurrent message in Rorty's writings is that these attempts at escaping the contingency and groundlessness of our ideals are detrimental and outmoded. Foundationalist projects are the expression of a superstitious diffidence that undermines the key virtue of contemporary individuals (i.e., their creative self-reliance), and have turned out to be obsolete, for as a matter of trial and error we realized that our practices do

---

very beginning. See *Richard Rorty*, Charles Guignon and David Hiley (eds.) (Cambridge: Cambridge University Press, 2003), p. 22.

[5] The longing for justification is said to inform much of the work of the early Rawls and Habermas. See, for example, Richard Rorty's "The Priority of Democracy to Philosophy," in *Objectivity, Relativism, and Truth: Philosophical Papers, Volume I* (ORT), (Cambridge: Cambridge University Press, 1991), pp. 175-96. Also, see "The Contingency of a Liberal Community," in *Contingency Irony and Solidarity* (CIS) (Cambridge: Cambridge University Press, 1989), chapter 3, particularly pp. 65-69. For the most systematic critique against the foundational attempts of human rights, see "Human Rights, Rationality, and Sentimentality," in *Truth and Progress: Philosophical Papers, Volume III* (TP) (Cambridge: Cambridge University Press, 1998), ch. 9, p. 167.

[6] See Richard Rorty's unpublished paper "Ideals Without Obligations." In this text, Rorty engages in a polemic against Pope Benedict XVI. He relies on George Santayana, from whom he borrows this definition of "superstition," to oppose the Pope's use of the "structure of human existence" as a moral reference point.

[7] Ibid.

well without them. Like Nietzsche's madman, Rorty insists, to the astonishment of the incredulous crowd, that "god is dead; but given the way people are, there may still for millennia be caves in which they show his shadow."[8] Reverence for a "reality" independent of human purposes, for "objective" constraints beyond mere consensus, for "unconditional" duties, etc., are signs of an untimely and oppressive attitude –shadows of a dead god. Rorty's philosophical task consists in closing the gap between the actual irrelevance of grounds to justify our practices and the persistent psychological need we still have for them. We must face the consequences of a long process of secularization that has led to the demise of anything transcendent, lying outside our conventions and backing them up. Our culture is now ready to shed the illusions systematic philosophy has fabricated to protect it.[9]

The animating principle of Rorty's philosophizing is, then, *how to breed* an individual in tune with the times, i.e., an individual able to acknowledge "the relative validity of [her] convictions and yet stand for them unflinchingly."[10] Only such a character would contribute, along with other human beings of similar disposition, to the realization of the *best possible world* as yet envisioned: the utopia of a liberal society where the private pursuit of perfection harmonizes with the collective project of diminishing suffering and humiliation. This quasi-autobiographical ideal type receives various names in Rorty's writings: the "pragmatist," the "liberal ironist," the "cultural critic," the "intellectual," etc., all of which designate the kind of agent best adapted to the institutional demands of contemporary, wealthy, liberal societies. Such a type does not pretend to be an answer to the *ontological* question "What are we? because we have come to see that the main lesson of both history and anthropology is our extraordinary malleability."[11] Rather, it is presented as an answer to the

---

[8] Friedrich Nietzsche, *The Gay Science* (Cambridge: Cambridge University Press, 2001), §108, p.109.

[9] For Rorty, there is no tribunal of reason, no objective cultural arbiter who could settle the question "*quid juris*" and secure the validity of our practices. Such a tribunal is a delusion as insidious as is the search for a monotheistic deity to guarantee moral cohesion in contemporary democratic polities. Philosophy, therefore, must modify its self-conception. The most it can offer is an *articulation* of our values; the task of *justification* is part of a Kantian legacy that survived its use and must be finally abandoned. See, e.g., "The Priority of Democracy to Philosophy," in ORT, pp. 178 and 175.

[10] Rorty takes this formulation from Joseph Schumpeter. See Rorty, CIS, p. 46.

[11] See "Human Rights," TP.169–170.

political question: "What sort of world can we prepare for our grandchildren?"[12]

Unlike Nietzsche, who interprets the emergence of contemporary individuality in terms of the advance of nihilism, Rorty's attitude towards it is unflinchingly optimistic.[13] The triumph and expansion of liberalism, particularly in its American version, far from leading to the despicable "last man," is for Rorty adequate substitute for traditional theodicy. Without appealing to anything transcendent, the liberal *Weltanschaung* satisfies our deep-rooted need for meaning, justice, and purpose, by offering the promise of self-realization and humaneness at a collective level. One of Rorty's heroes, Walt Whitman, expresses this radical transference of hope from god to fellow human beings in the claim that "the United States themselves are essentially the greatest poem":

> Whitman thought that we Americans have the most poetical nature because we are the first thoroughgoing experiment in national self-creation: the first nation-state with nobody but itself to please –not even God. We are the greatest poem because we put ourselves in the place of God: our essence is our existence, and our existence is in the future. Other nations thought of themselves as hymns to the glory of God. We redefine God as our future selves.[14]

This prophetic strand interjects an unexpected "seriousness" into Rorty's post-modern insouciance and indicates a deep affinity between his thought and modern utopian projects like Kant's, which also give world-shaping and redeeming status to human praxis. The distinctive trait of Rorty's pragmatism (its fundamental "article of faith," as one might call it) is that it refers "all questions of ultimate justification to the future, to the substance of things hoped for."[15] Such a philosophy is tailored to break with the nostalgia of what Rorty calls "Platonism," whose Protean nature assumes different shapes in the history of philosophy, all of which allegedly produce the same pernicious effect of leading to a spectatorial fascination with *theoria* and the enfeeblement of human agency.

---

[12] Ibid., p. 175.

[13] This apologetic attitude also distinguishes Rorty from thinkers like Adorno, Heidegger, and Foucault, who are skeptical about Enlightenment narratives of liberation and see contemporary society as a technological wasteland pervaded by refined mechanisms of control and power.

[14] See Richard Rorty, *Achieving our Country: Leftist Thought in Twentieth-Century America* (AOC) (Cambridge, MA: Harvard University Press, 1998), p. 22.

[15] See Richard Rorty, "Truth without Correspondence to Reality," in *Philosophy and Social Hope* (PSH) (London: Penguin Books, 1999), ch. 2, p. 27.

> 'Platonism' in the sense in which I use the term does not denote the (very complex, shifting, dubiously consistent) thoughts of the genius who wrote the *Dialogues*. Instead, it refers to a set of philosophical distinctions (appearance–reality, matter–mind, made–found, sensible–intellectual, etc.): what Dewey called 'a brood and nest of dualisms'.[16]

Figures as disparate as Descartes, Kant, Peirce, (the early) Rawls, Habermas, Taylor, etc., are all "Platonic." They assume that there is a "way things really are," an "essential self," a "rationality" which must be first grasped in order to "cut reality at its joints."[17] In opposition to this glassy, backward-looking view, Rorty proposes a forward-looking philosophy meant to empower our imagination and incite us to work towards liberalism at a global level and a Whitmanesque/Deweyan democracy in America. These are open-ended tasks modeled neither on an existing metaphysical template nor bestowed by a transcendent authority. Such externalities are subterfuges we have used in the past to confirm the rectitude of our strivings. Our culture no longer needs them. We can now face the exhilarating thought that the future is made, not given or recollected –it is *poiesis* not *episteme*, and in its creation there is no one to please or disappoint but ourselves. For, like in all poetic endeavors, liberalism and democracy "create the taste by which [they] will be judged."[18]

II- Inside the Cave

This sketchy outline of Rorty's thought suffices to suggests that, in spite of all his efforts, he has not fully extricated himself from the Platonic "nest of dualisms" he repudiates: Rorty is still fighting the old battle between philosophers and poets. He inverts –and to that extent perpetuates– the picture that *held us captive*. This is best seen in "Philosophy As a Transitional Genre," in which Rorty argues that

---

[16]See Rorty, PSH, Preface, p. xii.

[17]This umbrella view of "Platonism" allows Rorty to divide the philosophical scene into two camps: "pragmatists" like himself and his few heroes, and everyone else. This division, Richard Bernstein notes, not only reintroduces the dualism and essentialism Rorty sets himself to combat, but also undermines the constructive theoretical contributions philosophy can make to political discourse and action. See Richard Bernstein, "One Step Forward, Two Steps Backwards: Richard Rorty on Liberal Democracy and Philosophy," in *Political Theory*, Vol. 15, No. 4 (1987), p. 545.

[18] Rorty, PSH, 29.

"intellectuals of the West have, since the Renaissance, progressed through three stages: they have hoped for redemption first from God, then from philosophy, and now from literature."[19] Religion offered redemption through a non-cognitive relation to a non-human person, philosophy through a cognitive relation to propositions about reality which all inquirers could share, and literature through human artifacts that allow us to make "acquaintance of as great a variety of human beings as possible."[20] This developmental pattern is meant to put into question the source of legitimacy of the traditional "ascetic figures": a literary culture is one that "drops a presupposition common to religion and philosophy –that redemption must come from one's relation to something that is not just one more human creation."[21]

Rorty calls the poets to occupy the cultural vacuum. For, in his view, they are the best equipped to put transcendent impulses to immanent use. Such a dichotomy, however, still operates under the assumptions of the Platonic divided line: it inverts its direction and places *eikaisia* (imagination) as the topmost faculty. The metaphysical drive to leave the polis behind and take refuge in the *noetic* and eternal, Rorty wants to replace by trust (*pistis*) in the existing values of the polis. These images (*eikones*), he insists, are not shadows of an original above, but artifacts connecting us with the needs of fellow human beings. The redemptive power Plato sought in the greatest studies, and Christians of yore in the incarnated Christ, we can now seek in expanding and proliferating the ways to express the poetic freedom liberalism has made possible. Any constraint to this process must be condemned as part of an unfortunate, authoritarian, metaphysical heritage we have to overcome. Liberalism promises the land where a thousand and one flowers bloom: instead of reason, it offers emotion; instead of truth, opinion; instead of objectivity, solidarity; instead of philosophy, literature –the old dualisms upside down.

This world-historical picture not only accounts for Rorty's coupling of justice and affection, but also for his identification of the ethical core of

---

[19] See Richard Rorty, *Philosophy as Cultural Politics: Philosophical Papers, Volume IV* (PCP), (Cambridge: Cambridge University Press, 2007), ch. 6, p. 91. This text is a reworking of a lecture called "The Decline of Redemptive Truth and the Rise of a Literary Culture," which Rorty delivered at the University of Chicago in 2000.

[20] Ibid,, p. 91.

[21] Ibid,, p. 93. The sequence Rorty presents in this paper curiously reverses the Kierkegaardian stages, giving the aesthetic domain the trump card over the ethical and the religious.

liberalism with the reduction of cruelty.[22] Both claims boil down to the judgment that "cruelty is the worst thing we do." This is meant to oppose the traditional understanding of immorality as a form of sin, i.e., as a kind of transgression against the objective metaphysical rules revealed by divine authority or discovered by grasping the a priori cosmic order.[23] Since there are neither metaphysically privileged moral concepts nor moral truths independent from our contingent needs and purposes, human conventions cannot appeal to anything transcendent to exact obedience. Cruelty is the worst vice for a liberal, for it is a wrong done entirely to a fellow being.[24] The obligation to reduce suffering is purely immanent; it acknowledges that there is nothing beyond the mutual recognition of our frailty that could keep us in check, no authority besides the agreements we strike in each cave. Redemption, therefore, is not going to come from "above" –it is not an act of grace or respect for the moral law, but of "self-enlargement," a matter of becoming acquainted with as many vocabularies and experiences as possible.

Literature is emblematic of this expansion and helps Rorty illustrate a frame of mind in which aesthetic receptivity functions as the ethical mainspring. Engaged in the project of self-enlargement, individuals in a "literary culture" will eventually recognize that the differences they used to consider crucial (gender, ethnic or religious affiliation, sexual orientation, etc.) make no difference –they wane in light of our common susceptibility to suffering and humiliation.[25] Rorty's liberalism thus leads to a *community of poets*, where there is no philosopher-king to wield metaphysical truths, but a multiplicity of cultural artifacts vying for expression.

---

[22] See, e.g., Richard Rorty, "Justice as a Larger Loyalty" (PCP), op. cit., pp. 42 ff, and CIS, ch. 9, pp. 189 ff.

[23] The idea that avoiding cruelty is the cornerstone of liberalism Rorty takes from Judith Shklar. See Judith Shklar, "Putting Cruelty First," in *Ordinary Vices* (Cambridge, MA: Harvard University Press, 1984, chapter I), ch. 1, pp. 7 ff, and "The Liberalism of Fear," in *Liberalism and the Moral Life*, N. Rosenblum (ed.) (Cambridge, MA: Harvard University Press, 1989), pp. 21–38.

[24] John Kekes complains about the lack of definition of cruelty in the works of those who consider it the worst vice (a list that includes Rorty, Shklar, and Baier). I find the complaint right but shortsighted: only things without history can be defined. See John Kekes, "Cruelty and Liberalism," *Ethics*, Vol. 107, No. 4 (1996), pp. 834-844.

[25] See Rorty, "Human Rights, Rationality and Sentimentality," TP, ch. 9, p. 181.

III- Unlimited Redescriptions

I've been trying to show some of the ways in which Rorty links the appeals to a transcendent authority and the "way things really are," characteristic of the discourse of objectivity, to a single psychological source, i.e., the metaphysical yearning for which his philosophy offers a therapy. Rorty's medicine involves extreme measures: since a "reality" (epistemic or moral) other than our interpretations has proven to be yet another Platonic fable, we must accept that there is no truth other than the consensus we can reach through our contingent justificatory practices.[26] Although as an individual I am constrained by the rules of the practices I engage in, such practices have nothing *external* to constrain them. Furthermore, in case of competing opposite views, there are no *common internal* constraints that could help us decide on their respective claims. Each view expresses its own vocabulary and creates its own criteria of legitimacy, its *own taste*. Thus, "anything can be made to look good or bad by being redescribed."[27] Lacking neutral standards of adjudication, all we have is tireless experimentation.

> For us ironists, nothing can serve as a criticism of a final vocabulary save another such vocabulary; there is no answer to a redescription save a re-re-redescription. Since there is nothing beyond vocabularies which serves as a criterion of choice between them, criticism is a matter of looking on this picture and on that, not of comparing both pictures with the original.[28]

Rorty's liberalism is designed to turn the question-begging character of vocabularies into a virtue, compensating the loss of objectivity (i.e., epistemic uncertainty and moral groundlessness) with individual freedom. In a liberal society, any limitation to our poetic imagination, any boundary to the playful succession of vocabularies and private attempts at self-creation, is oppressive and unwarranted. The only justifiable limit comes at the level of *expression*, if, and only if, our private vocabulary clashes with the collective project of reducing suffering and humiliation.

---

[26] See Bernard Williams, "Auto-da-Fé: Consequences of Pragmatism," in *Reading Rorty*, A. Malchowski (ed.) (Malden/Oxford: Blackwell Publishers, 1990), p. 27.
[27] Rorty, CIS, 73.
[28] Rorty, CIS, 80. He defines a "final vocabulary" as "the set of words [all human beings] employ to justify their actions, their beliefs, and their lives." (CIS, p. 73) This vocabulary is "final" "in the sense that if doubt is cast on the worth of these words, their user has no noncircular argumentative recourse." (Ibid.)

Otherwise, our idiosyncratic conception of the good must be left completely free.

Rorty endorses here the orthodoxy of Mill's harm principle: "the aim of a just and free society [is to let] its citizens be as privatistic, "irrationalist," and aestheticist as they please so long as they do it on their own time –causing no harm to others and using no resources needed by those less advantaged."[29] Despite the talk of contingency, therefore, Rorty's liberal utopia rests on the assumption that there is an overwhelmingly good fit between irony and liberalism, which will permit "ironism, in the relevant sense, [to become] universal." What turned out to be theoretically impossible for philosophers to do, namely, to hold together "private perfection and human solidarity … in a single vision,"[30] becomes feasible, in practice, in the metaphysically groundless best possible world of liberal utopia: "liberal ironists are people who include among these ungroundable desires their own hope that suffering will be diminished, that humiliation of human beings by other human beings may cease."[31] The goal now is to breed more individuals capable of doing this difficult psychological trick.

In the preceding sections, I teased out the liberation narrative Rorty develops to frame and justify his views: the long-standing battle against superstition in Western culture, and the self-reliance which gradually arises from it, demand a philosophy that unmasks any appeal to the transcendent as an illicit endeavor to seek alliance with a power larger than us and escape responsibility for our own creations. Liberalism provides the institutional framework most compatible with developing this kind of individuality. Rorty's politics has individual self-reliance writ large –a claim that paradoxically reverts to the Platonic isomorphism between the soul and the polis, which Rorty's strict separation between private perfection and public justice was meant to undermine.

I find myself in agreement with the thrust of Rorty's liberation narrative, but worry about the consequences of his infatuation with *poeisis*. Private self-enlargement seems too erratic and volatile a project to secure the ethical core of liberalism. My fear is that, without some normative guidance, the proliferation of final vocabularies may easily lead to non-liberal goals. Fostering the possibility of unlimited redescriptions, Rorty's literary culture unwittingly deprives itself of the means to preserve its own liberal values. To spell out this suspicion, let me now turn to Kant's essay,

---

[29] Richard Rorty, CIS, xiv.

[30] Ibid.

[31] CIS, p. xv.

"An Answer to the Question: 'What is Enlightenment?'" Here we also find a narrative of cultural progress, but one in which liberation is the outcome of *internal* constraints that rule out *some* redescriptions, even before they come to be expressed in the marketplace of opinions. The advantage I see to Kantian strictures is that, without forfeiting the value of pluralism, they preserve a sense of "objectivity" which keeps at arm's length the metaphysical urge Rorty so eloquently denounces as being superstitious.

IV- Redrawing the Boundaries of Privacy[32]

Kant characterizes the "Enlightenment" as "man's emergence (*Ausgang*) from his self-incurred immaturity."[33] Very much like Rorty, Kant wants to overcome the discrepancy between the potential for self-determination existing in our culture and the psychological development of its members, who lack "resolution and courage to use [their] own understanding (*Verstand*) without the guidance of another."[34] Enlightenment is the task of overcoming this gap between understanding and will, i.e., between the capacity for self-legislation and its actualization. Such a task is not optional; it appears as a duty, for the immaturity in question is self-incurred (*selbst verschuldet*) and can only be removed by a change in our volitional configuration. This change entails abandoning a comfortable heteronomy, in which we –like children– surrender our understanding to the authoritative guidance of another. Enlightenment is thus the exit (*Ausgang*) from this voluntary childhood –the plenary assumption of autonomy,

The authoritative figures Kant refers to in this context are significant: "the teacher," who monopolizes the interpretation of "a book," "the doctor," who holds the secret for our wellbeing, and "the priest," who takes care of our spiritual salvation.[35] These figures represent strongholds of superstition in the different spheres of our life. They provide "dogmas and formulas" with which to underwrite an answer to the most important questions that afflict our reason, namely, what we can know, what we

---

[32] I draw here on the analysis of this text in §3 of my "Kant y La Antinomia de la Razón Política Moderna," *Revista Latinoamericana de Filosofía* (forthcoming).

[33] See Immanuel Kant, "Bentwortung der Frage: Was ist Aufklárung?" (WA, AA 8: 35). Quotations from Kant are from the *Akademie-Edition* Vol. 1-29 of *Kant's Gesammelte Schriften*, Berlin/Leipzig, 1902—. I follow the English translation, "An Answer to the Question: 'What is Enlightenment?'" in *Kant: Political Writings*, edited by Hans Reiss (NY: Cambridge University Press, 1991).

[34] Ibid.

[35] Ibid.

ought to do, and what we should hope for.[36] By submitting the use of our understanding to theirs, our beliefs receive the support of their authority. But in so doing, they deprive themselves of legitimacy: the passive attitude we assume in adopting them transforms their claims into mere imposition.

It is no accident, then, that the Kantian metaphor of maturity (*Mündigkeit*) contains in it the root "Mund" (mouth), the very source of discourse.[37] Immaturity (*Unmündigkeit)* is for Kant a form of ventriloquism. The tutor (*Vormund*) is like a mouthpiece that stands in front of (the literal meaning of the prefix "*vor*") my own mouth, and hence I find in me meanings (beliefs and values) of which I do not recognize myself as the author.[38] What my lips utter, *I* do not say. To the extent that the meanings I pronounce have been set by another, I do not speak for myself when I speak. In the midst of culture, I *chose* to remain part of nature – "part of the machine" (*Teil der Maschine*), as Kant puts it, a cog that reproduces the irrationality of the social mechanism.[39] Kant describes this alienated intersubjective relation in reified terms, using the image of the shepherd and the herd, in which the dignity of a human being is debased to the status of mere thing:

> Having first infatuated (*dumm gemacht*) their domesticated animals (*Hausvieh*), and carefully prevented the docile creatures from daring to take a single step without the leading-strings (*Gängelwagen*) to which they are tied, they next show them the danger which threatens them if they try to walk unaided. Now this danger is not in fact so great, for they would certainly learn to walk eventually after a few falls.[40]

---

[36] See Immanuel Kant, *Critique of Pure Reason* (KrV), P. Guyer and A. Wood (eds. and trans.) (Cambridge: Cambridge University Press, 1998), KrV A 805/B 833. M. Foucault makes this point. See Michael Foucault, "What is Enlightenment?" in *Ethics, Subjectivity, and Truth*, Paul Rabinow (ed.) (NY: The New Press, 1994), p. 308.

[37] I am adopting here the interpretation of Garret Green "Modern Culture Comes of Age: Hamann versus Kant on the Root Metaphor of Enlightenment," in *What is Enlightenment? Eighteenth Century Answers and Twentieth-Century Questions* (WiE), James Schmidt (ed.) (Berkeley and Los Angeles: University of California Press, 1996), p. 292. For a different view on this passage, cf. Rüdiger Bittner, "What is Enlightenment?," WiE, pp. 347-8.

[38] Garret Green, WiE, p. 292.

[39] Kant, WA, 8: 35. The claim that the immature have *chosen* their condition should not be construed as a case of "blaming the victim," but as a corollary of transcendental freedom See e.g., G 4: 458. As Garret Green shows, Hamann took issue against Kant on this point (WiE, pp. 293 ff).

[40] WA, 8: 35-6.

Immaturity acquires thus the significance of a wrong we inflict against our own humanity, i.e., against our capacity to set our own aims. The duty to overcome it does not come from an external authority, but –like in Rorty– from an idealized version of our selves. To feel at home in culture, we must create institutional conditions that would allow us to recognize the world we received as one we *also* made. Like Rorty's liberal utopia, such a world is "the substance of things hoped for," an object of desire, not something we possess, for "if it is now asked whether at present we live in an *enlightened* (*aufgeklärten*) age, the answer is: No, but we live in an age of *enlightenment* (*Zeitalter der Aufklärung*)."[41] Institutional progress proceeds by *gradually* realizing the conditions, now incipiently present, which allow us to shape external constraints (the matter of the world, so to speak) with the form of our own judgment.[42] This project is motivated by the idea of self-legislation, according to which the legitimacy of a given law resides precisely in the fact that we can *at the same time* (*zugleich*) conceive ourselves as its legislator. "To test whether any particular measure can be agreed upon as a law for a people, we need only ask whether a people could well impose such a law upon itself."[43] This test is tailored to expand our imagination: before proposing a law, authorities must place themselves as subjects in order to gauge the acceptability of their proposals; and before accepting a law, subjects must place themselves as legislators in order to gauge its validity. The exchangeability of roles and the ability of agents to wear "two hats" capture the gist of the liberal principle of popular sovereignty: to be legitimate, relations of command and obedience must be based on consent.[44] For, consensual relations transform the paternalistic bond of tutorship into genuine political friendship, ventriloquism into democratic dialogue.

The ethical aspect of this political relation Kant calls a "kingdom of ends" in the *Groundwork*:

> By a *kingdom* I understand a systematic union of various rational beings through common laws. Now since laws determine ends in terms of their

---

[41] WA, 8: 40, 58.

[42] Kant's melioristic politics fit well with Rortyan/Deweyan reformism. Both believe that revolution perpetuates prejudice and oppression. See WA, 8: 36, and AOC, "The Eclipse of the Reformist Left," ch. 2, pp. 39 ff.

[43] WA, 8: 39, 57.

[44] I take the expression "two hats" from John Christian Laursen. See Laursen's "The Subversive Kant: The Vocabulary of 'Public' and 'Publicity,' in WiE, op. cit., p. 257.

> universal validity, if we abstract from the personal differences of rational beings as well as from the content of their private ends we shall be able to think of a whole of all ends in systematic connection (a whole both of rational beings as ends in themselves and of the ends of his own that each may set himself, that is, a kingdom of ends… (G 4: 433)[45]

In contrast with Rorty's *community of poets*, where the idiosyncratic expression and proliferation of vocabularies is of uttermost value, Kant's *kingdom of ends* is one in which final vocabularies have always already undergone mutual accommodation. The demands of justice, which for Rorty represent a public/external limit, are internalized in Kant. Since not all poetic creations promote liberal individuality, Rorty's abhorrence of cruelty puts a limit *too late* on our private conceptions of the good: our final vocabulary is formed independently of our collective commitments, and all it matters is to keep it at bay if it increases suffering and humiliation in intersubjective relations. Since, according to Rorty, in modern liberal societies justice and private perfection cannot be held together in a single vision, the overall compatibility between the demands for self-creation and the demands for human solidarity must be ultimately a matter of good luck. The trumping force of liberal justice over idiosyncratic private projects cannot itself be justified: "For liberal ironists, there is no answer to the question "Why not be cruel?" –no noncircular theoretical backup for the belief that cruelty is horrible. Nor is there an answer to the question "How do you decide when to struggle against injustice and when to devote yourself to private projects of self creation?"[46]

Kant avoids these vicissitudes by redefining the boundaries of privacy: in order to treat each other *also* as ends in themselves, the desires, beliefs, and values that make up our final vocabulary must have been shaped, from their very inception, by a reflection on their acceptability to others.[47] To *claim* these fundamental meanings to be *mine,* the "I will" of morality and the "I think" of the understanding must have been able to accompany them

---

[45] Immanuel Kant, *Groundwork of the Metaphysics of Morals* (G), Mary Gregor (ed. and trans.) (Cambridge: Cambridge University Press, 1997).

[46] Richard Rorty, CIS, xv.

[47] The gist of the Kantian position is what Rawls pithily called "the primacy of right over the good." See John Rawls, *A Theory of Justice*, Revised Edition (Cambridge, MA: Harvard University Press, 2001), §6, p. 27. The transcendental condition for the possibility of this primacy lies in what Henry Allison dubbed Kant's "Incorporation-Thesis." See Henry Allison, *Kant's Theory of Freedom* (Cambridge: Cambridge University Press, 1990), p. 40.

–otherwise, my final vocabulary would have meanings *I* did not set, contents of which I am not the author. Without the metaphysics of a philosopher-king, the *kingdom of ends* represents the universal forfeiture of poetic narcissism, the willingness to enter into a union where the "I" is always already a "we."

Kant's key contribution to liberal theory is to have introduced an inescapable public/normative dimension into the private conceptions of the good of mature modern individuals – the ends an autonomous self sets for herself are permeated by the perspective of others who are also ends in themselves.[48] It is this permeability that forestalls oppressive intersubjective relations, for "if we abstract from personal differences …as well as from the content of … private ends we shall be able to think of a whole of ends in systematic connection." (G 4: 433) Such a connection, however, is precluded by Rorty's liberal ironist, for whom "the demands of self-creation and of human solidarity [are] equally valid, yet forever incommensurable."[49] Her commitment to diminish suffering and humiliation is as idiosyncratic as her love for orchids or Shakespeare. Contingency of fit and upbringing substitute here the normativity of content. The Rortyan project of universalizing liberal irony requires the indefinite iteration of the good luck that made a Rorty possible.

This wariness about the reliability of chance explains why Kant subordinates the value of *expressing* a vocabulary to its *communicability*.[50] While in the *community of poets* the public success of a redescription depends on its sheer rhetorical force, in the *kingdom of ends* communicative restrictions are operative in the very process of forming a vocabulary. To avoid ventriloquism, i.e., the passivity of being told how to live (what to believe, what to do, and what to hope for), the communicative "I claim" must be able to accompany all the expressions of my final vocabulary. To will, to think, and to claim, are for Kant activities whose interlocking rules shape the given (desires, intuitions, assertions) in ways that are intelligible and acceptable to others.

---

[48] See Thomas Auxter, "Kant's Conception of the Private Sphere," *The Philosophical Forum*, Vol. 12, (1981), pp. 298 ff. Auxter's distinction between the "personal" and the "private" points at the same permeability I am trying to indicate here.

[49] Richard Rorty, CIS, xv.

[50] The contrast between communication and expression is prominent in Onora O'Neill's interpretation of Kant's 1784 essay. See Onora O'Neill, "The Public Use of Reason," in *Constructions of Reason: Explorations of Kant's Practical Philosophy* (Cambridge: Cambridge University Press, 1989), ch. 2, p. 31.

The internal duality Kant presupposes in mature/modern human beings, i.e., their double character as subjects and legislators, recipients and creators of the world they inhabit, is thus linked to his re-drawing of the traditional boundaries of privacy. While Rorty conceives of the private as a *space* of non-intervention, for Kant privacy designates a mode of thinking (*Denkungsart*) –not the locus of thought, but the nature of its meanings. This sense comes to focus in the contrast Kant draws between the public and private uses of reason:

> The *public* use of man's reason must always be free, and it alone can bring about enlightenment among men; the *private use* of reason may quite often be very narrowly restricted, however, without undue hindrance to the progress of enlightenment. But by the public use of one's reason I mean that use which anyone may make of it as a *man of learning* (*Geleherter*) addressing the entire *reading public*. What I term the private use of reason is that which a person may make of it in a particular *civil* post or office with which he is entrusted.[51]

Kant associates the sphere of obedience and passivity with "the private use of reason." This can be "narrowly restricted, without undue hindrance to the progress of enlightenment," for here our identity is disguised by the role we play in the social structure. Kant gives the examples of the officer, the tax-official, and the clergyman to illustrate his view. These characters, which in the topography of traditional liberalism squarely belong to the public sphere, illustrate privacy for Kant: they are the vehicles of forces they represent, employees (*Beamten*) of a local authority, not individuals in strict sense. For, they do not speak in their own *person*, but on behalf of someone else, heteronomously. In the presence of others, their utterances remain merely private, expression of the idiosyncratic point of view of an authority/authorship that subtracts itself from criticism, and thus forfeits "the unfeigned respect that reason grants only to that which has been able to withstand its free and public examination."[52] Their benighted audience is not a real public. Blind acceptance of their contentions resembles that of domestic animals, more a matter of imposition and compliance than of endorsement. In contrast, the *Gelehrter* expects consent from the public. His meanings are shaped to reach an unrestricted audience: they must be released from the grip of local authorities and offered to others *as if* they have produced them themselves. Thus, the claims of the *man of learning* command without imposing, for their authority does not depend on a local

---

[51] WA, 8: 37.

[52] KrV A xiii.

Prince, but on the sheer persuasiveness of his arguments –assent on our part bespeaks the freedom of the exchange.[53]

It is important to note that Kant sees nothing intrinsically wrong with the private use of reason. He is the first to admit that there is an unavoidable element of mechanical rule following in every human organization. The problem for him arises when this narrow mind-set colonizes all aspects of the individual's life, obfuscating her capacity to assess and criticize the circumstances she finds herself in. It is not so much being rooted, but having *no escape* that Kant finds unnerving. For, the public use of reason is the capacity to scrutinize the validity of our attachments –and without attachment the scrutiny is empty talk. Kant insists that this use "must always be free," for any kind of constraint at this level would undermine the possibility of reconciling ourselves with our situation, of consenting to a world we have not made.

As Kant puts it, in abiding by the expectations of their roles, "it would be very harmful (*verderblich*)" if the officer challenges a military order, the "citizen ... refuses to pay taxes," or the clergyman were not "to instruct his pupils and his congregation in accordance with the doctrines of the church he serves."[54] As pieces of the social mechanism, these roles necessitate obedience. Yet, none of these figures could "reasonably be banned from making observations as a *Gelehrter* on the errors in the military service," taxation policies, or religious orthodoxy. Kant expects them to be willing to sacrifice the social rewards of complacency to the demands of honesty, to step back from the pressures of circumstances and publicly criticize the practices they engage in.[55]

That is, to use a turn of phrase dear to Kant, the contentions of local authorities are *subjectively* necessary for us, but remain *objectively* contingent. Public examination allows us to make voluntary their initially involuntary nature, and to correct our practices if they press for indecency. This critical distance does not require us moving all the way to god's point of view –severing all worldly ties the *Gelehrter* would have *nothing* to communicate. Kant's idea of addressing "the entire reading public" is not a metaphysical evasion, but a counter against relativism: what a cosmopolitan (*weltbürgerlich*) audience *accepts* as true (epistemic or

---

[53] These are features of what Phillip Rossi calls "the social authority of reason" and which he identifies as being essential for Kant's critical project. See Phillip Rossi, *The Social Authority of Reason* (Albany: SUNY Press, 2005), particularly chap. 3, pp. 41-67. Although I agree with the core of this view, I tend to give more positive value to privacy than Rossi seems to allow.

[54] WA, 8: 37.

[55] WA, 8: 37-8.

moral) cannot be decided by the rhetorical strength of a local (*bürgerlich*) vocabulary. Redescriptions are not omnipotent; they cannot make the good look bad for *all* of us. Their currency –if any– is limited to a limited group for a limited time.

V- At The Cave's Threshold

The political distinction between *expression* and *communication* I am trying to draw is analogous to the epistemic distinction Kant draws, in the *Prolegomena*, between *judgments of perception* and *judgments of experience*: the former are subjectively valid, since they merely require "the logical connection of perceptions," which expresses mental operations valid for the subject alone; the latter are objectively valid, for they unify intuitions according to rules all subjects could follow.[56] Their objectivity is not taken from a pre-existent "reality" they are supposed to mirror, but is the result of on act of constitution through which a common world of meanings arises –*nature* as "the sum total of the objects of experience." It is the same subject that either expresses or communicates, perceives or experiences, depending on the social character of the rules with which she forms her judgments and unifies what is given to her, i.e., rules valid for her consciousness alone or for "consciousness in general."

A similar constellation of concepts can be found in Kant's moral philosophy. For, the redefinition of the liberal boundaries of privacy is linked to Kant's conception of the will as practical reason, according to which we have always the capacity to revise and reject any set of beliefs and desires according to the demands of universality. I take this to mean that the Kantian self is always already engaged in a virtual conversation with "the entire reading public," i.e., driven by the desire to justify itself on grounds others cannot possibly reject.[57] This desire for justification allows it to break loose from the snares of the village, and constitute a virtual community of fellow citizens, a *kingdom of ends*.

The connection between Kant's view of the Enlightenment and his critical philosophy should now be obvious. "Our age is the genuine age of

---

[56] See Immanuel Kant, *Prolegomena to Any Future Metaphysics: With Selections from the* Critique of Pure Reason (P), Gary Hatfield (ed. and trans.) (Cambridge: Cambridge University Press, 1997), 4: 298.

[57] This is Thomas Scanlon's language. See Scanlon, "Contractualism and Utilitarianism," Amartya Sen and Bernard Williams (eds.), *Utilitarianism and Beyond* (Cambridge: Cambridge University Press, 1982), p. 116.

criticism (*Zeitalter der Kritik*) to which everything must submit."[58] This entails a "revolution in the way of thinking" (*Revolution der Denkart*) about objectivity: "reason has insight only into what it itself produces according to its own design."[59] This is the Copernican turn we hinted at in the prior section: I must also be able to see myself as the author of the culturally given meanings in order to call my final vocabulary *mine*. While the rules of expression set us apart (they have the validity of "judgments of perception" or of the pursuit of "happiness"), communication (*Mitteilung*) creates community. It alone elevates us from our private idiosyncrasies and constitutes a world we can share (*mitteilt*). This is the world opened by the categories of the understanding, with which we form a common world of natural objects by organizing intuitions, and by the "categorical imperative" of practical reason, with which we form a common world of values by organizing desires. Indeed, this is the cosmopolitan world that animates the Enlightenment dream –maturity in every activity and in every aspect of human existence.

Kant calls these different epistemic, moral, and political communicative constraints "a priori," not because they lie in a mysterious metaphysical realm beyond our practices, but because we recursively discover them as we try to explain the exchanges with those who seem "other" to "us."[60] They are not *transcendent*, as Rorty interprets them, but *transcendental*, embedded in a (fallible) presumption of mutual comprehension. Yet, although their application is always *immanent*, they should not be confused with actuality (*Wircklichkeit*), as our multiple cognitive errors and evil actions all too often demonstrate. They occupy an intermediary space that leaves room to criticize current beliefs and values, without falling into what Rorty calls "superstition," the naïve and immature presumption of reason to be in immediate contact with *things themselves.*[61]

In sum, Kantian a priori structures lie at the cave's threshold: they make it possible for us to become lucid to each other when we speak in public, but are not identical with our actual utterances, which may remain private and narrowly ethnocentric.

---

[58] KrV A xi.

[59] KrV B xiii.

[60] I am following Onora O'Neill here. See "Reason and Politics in the Kantian Enterprise," *Constructions of Reason*, ch. 1, p. 21.

[61] This is the type of transcendence that animates Habermas' communicative action and that Rorty considers an "empty boast" (Richard Rorty, "Universality and Truth," *Rorty and His Critics*, p. 6).

VI- No Exit

Kant agrees with Rorty on a fundamental point: it is "impossible …to step outside our skins…and compare ourselves with something absolute."[62] Yet, to conclude, as Rorty does, that "the traditions linguistic and other with which we do our thinking" provide the only justificatory standard, is to promote a dangerous kind of empiricism. Needless to say, here "the given" is not the sense data of epistemology (whose "myth" Rorty did so much to denounce), but "our practices," "our agreements," "our tradition," etc.[63] Whereas Rorty's ethnocentric confidence surrenders to their grip, Kant accepts their authority *conditionally*, i.e., as a result of having reflected upon the compatibility of "our practices" with the communicative demands of the public use of reason. Such a use, although always situational and shot through with particularity, vindicates itself when it aspires to be cosmopolitan and universal. For the idea of an "entire reading public" puts pressure on every dialect with which we may try to communicate. For Rorty, on the other hand, the endorsement of "our practices" is glorified. From the fact that there is no non-question begging way to justify our basic tenets (for we always speak from a local place of value), Rorty wrongly concludes that "our values" offer a secure abode. And this gives him nowhere to go, no critical escape, no normative retreat if, in the rhetorical struggles, liberal values are obliterated or destroyed.

Rorty's overconfident attitude towards *our practices* has been often criticized because it hushes a discussion about *what exactly* those practices are and hides their essentially contested nature.[64] I think this is symptomatic of a deeper problem: the ideal of a literary culture rests on a dubious kind of *social foundationalism*, which leaves the continuity of its liberal values in the hands of good luck.[65] For in a community of poets,

---

[62] Richard Rorty, *Consequences of Pragmatism: Essays, 1972-1980* (CP) (Minneapolis: University of Minnesota Press, 1982), Introduction, xix.

[63] See Richard Bernstein, "One Step Forward, two Steps Backward," 551,

[64] See, e.g., Bernstein, p.554, Jean Behke Elshtain, "Don't Be Cruel: Reflections on Rortyan Liberalism," in *Richard Rorty*, Charles Guignon and David Hiley (eds.), p. 143, and Nancy Fraser, "Solidarity or Singularity? Richard Rorty between Romanticism and Technocracy," in *Reading Rorty*, (Alan Malachowski ed.), pp. 309 ff.

[65] This is part of James Conant's criticism of Rorty's reading of *1984*. Conant recoils at the thought of the similarity of O'Brien and disenchanted liberal ironists who put their energies at the service of the Inner Party, when reducing suffering stops being a viable cultural option. Rorty's disregard for "objectivity" and "truth," Conant argues, seem to leave him with a weak line of defense if the values and

truth is another opinion. Rortyan justificatory practices are always provincial and do not wear "desire to get things right" on their sleeves. Whereas Kant's Enlightenment narrative offers tools to avoid this relativism, Rorty's narrative of cultural progress leaves hardly any room for criticizing the rightness of whatever is successful. Given the tragedy-prone, contingency-ridden world of ours, I find Rorty's position dangerous, at best naïve. The liberal character of our practices is a tender flower that can at any time wither.

VII- Concluding Remarks

As I read Kant's 1784 essay, I find nothing blameworthy in fulfilling a role and accommodating to the demands of our time and place; however, Kant insists, we *ought to* break loose from misplaced solidarities when they fail the test of conscience. Such "liberation" takes, indeed, courage. Kant's motto for the Enlightenment is appropriately "*sapere aude*," dare to know" –dare to challenge the authority of prejudice when it proves illegitimate, dare to question the primacy of your affections when they ask for dishonesty, dare to envision a larger community if compliance with yours is immoral, in a nutshell, dare to make your village cosmopolitan.

Objectivity –understood not metaphysically, i.e., as a conscience-independent "reality," but politically, as the search for universal validity– provides the friction necessary for the Kantian dove to fly.[66] There are, it is true, undeniable dualisms in Kant's position (private/public, parochial/cosmopolitan, immature/mature, etc.), but they entail neither a rigid hierarchy nor invite us to an otherworldly flight. If this is Platonism, as Rorty suggests, it is one without transcendent underpinnings. Indeed, Kantian agents have one of the essential features of Rorty's ironist, i.e., "radical and continuous doubts about [their] final vocabulary." What they lack is the uncertainty on how to resolve those doubts and the skepticism about the objectivity of the solution.[67] For, having been restricted by communicative constraints, their final vocabulary is surely in "systematic connection" with the vocabulary of other agents similarly restricted. This is not metaphysics, but sobering self-doubt.[68] Even if Rorty's poets get the

---

promises of liberalism happen to become outmoded. See James Conant, "Freedom, Cruelty, and Truth: Rorty versus Orwell," in *Rorty and His Critics*, pp. 268–342.

[66] KrVA5/B9.

[67] Richard Rorty, CIS, p. 73.

[68] CIS, xv: "Anybody who thinks that there are well-grounded theoretical answers to this sort of question –algorithms for resolving moral dilemmas of this sort– is still, in his heart, a theologian or a metaphysician. He believes in an order beyond

idea that they "could do even better in airless space," they can offer nothing like this to ensure the continuity of liberalism.[69]

Works Cited

Allison, H. *Kant's Theory of Freedom* (Cambridge University Press, 1990).

Auxter, T. "Kant's Conception of the Private Sphere," *The Philosophical Forum*, Vol. 12, Summer 1981, pp. 295-310.

Bernstein, R. "One Step Forward, Two Steps Backwards: Richard Rorty on Liberal Democracy and Philosophy," *Political Theory*, 15, (1987).

Conant, J. "Freedom, Cruelty, and Truth: Rorty versus Orwell," in R. Brandom (ed.) *Rorty and His Critics* (Malden/Oxford: Blackwell Publishers, 2000).

Elshtain, J.B. "Don't Be Cruel: Reflections on Rortyan Liberalilsm," in C. Guignon and D. Hiley (eds.) *Richard Rorty* (Cambridge: Cambridge University Press, 2003).

Foucault, M. "What is Enlightenment?" in P. Rabinow (ed.) *Ethics, Subjectivity, and Truth* (NY: The New York Press, 1994).

Fraser, N. "Solidarity or Singularity? Richard Rorty between Romanticism and Technocracy" in Alan Malachowski, (ed.) *Reading Rorty: Critical Responses to* Philosophy and the Mirror of Nature *(and Beyond)* (Malden/Oxford: Basil Blackwell, 1990).

Green, G. "Modern Culture Comes of Age: Hamann versus Kant on the Root Metaphor of Enlightenment" in J. Schmidt (ed.) *What is Enlightenment? Eighteenth Century Answers and Twentieth-Century Questions* (Berkeley/Los Angeles: University of California Press, 1996).

Guignon, C. and D. Hiley (eds.). *Richard Rorty* (Cambridge: Cambridge University Press, 2003).

Habermas, J. "Rorty's Pragmatic Turn" in Robert Brandom (ed.) *Rorty and His Critics* (Oxford/Malden: Blackwell Publishers, 2000).

Kant, I. *Critique of Pure Reason*, P. Guyer and A. Wood (eds. and trans.) (Cambridge: Cambridge University Press, 1998).

—. *Groundwork of the Metaphysics of Morals,* M. Gregor (ed. and trans.) (Cambridge: Cambridge: Cambridge University Press, 1997).

---

time and change which both determines the point of human existence and establishes a hierarchy of responsibilities."

[69] KrVA5/B9.

—. *Prolegomena to Any Future Metaphysics That Will Be Able to Come Forward as Science: with Selections from the* Critique of Pure Reason, G. Hatfield (ed. and trans.) (Cambridge: Cambridge University Press, 1997).

—. "An Answer to the Question: 'What is Enlightenment?'" H. Reiss (ed.) *Kant: Political Writings* (Cambridge: Cambridge University Press, 1991).

Kekes, J. "Cruelty and Liberalism," *Ethics*, 1, (1996).

Laursen, J.C. "The Subversive Kant: The Vocabulary of 'Public' and 'Publicity,'" in J. Schmidt (ed.) *What is Enlightenment? Eighteenth Century Answers and Twentieth-Century Questions* (Berkeley/Los Angeles: University of California Press, 1996).

McDowell, J. "Towards Rehabilitating Objectivity" in R. Brandom (ed.) *Rorty and His Critics* (Oxford/Malden: Blackwell Publishers, 2000).

Nietzsche, F. *The Gay Science* (Cambridge: Cambridge University Press, 2001).

O'Neill, O. "The Public Use of Reason," in *Constructions of Reason: Explorations of Kant's Practical Philosophy* (Cambridge: Cambridge University Press, 1989).

Rawls, J. *A Theory of Justice*, Revised Edition, (Cambridge, MA: Harvard University Press, 2001).

Rorty, R. *Philosophy as Cultural Politics, Philosophical Papers, Volume IV* (Cambridge University Press, 2007).

—. "Truth Without Correspondence to Reality," in *Philosophy and Social Hope* (London: Penguin Books, 1999).

—. "Human Rights, Rationality, and Sentimentality," in *Truth and Progress: Philosophical Papers, Volume 3* (Cambridge: Cambridge University Press, 1998).

—. *Achieving our Country: Leftist Thought in Twentieth-Century America* (Cambridge, MA: Harvard University Press, 1998).

—. "Justice as a Larger Loyalty," *Centre for the Study of Democracy*, 5, 1 (1997).

—. "The Priority of Democracy to Philosophy," in *Objectivity, Relativism, and Truth: Philosophical Papers, Volume 1* (Cambridge: Cambridge University Press, 1991).

—. "The Contingency of Community," in *Contingency Irony and Solidarity* (Cambridge: Cambridge University Press, 1989).

—. *Consequences of Pragmatism* (Minneapolis: University of Minnesota Press, 1982).

—. "Ideals Without Obligations," unpublished paper.

Rossi, P. *The Social Authority of Reason*, (Albany: SUNY Press, 2005).

Scanlon, T. "Contractualism and Utilitarianism," in A. Sen and B. Williams (eds.) *Utilitarianism and Beyond* (Cambridge: Cambridge University Press, 1982).

Shklar, J. "The Liberalism of Fear," in N. Rosenblum (ed.) *Liberalism and the Moral Life* (Cambridge, MA: Harvard University Press, 1989).

—. "Putting Cruelty First," in *Ordinary Vices* (Cambridge, MA: Harvard University Press, 1984).

William, B. "Auto-da-Fé: Consequences of Pragmatism," in A. Malachowski (ed.) *Reading Rorty: Critical Responses to* Philosophy and the Mirror of Nature *(and Beyond)* (Malden/Oxford: Basil Blackwell, 1990).

CONTRIBUTORS

Participants In ENAKS Conference

Jason R. Fisette is a doctoral student in philosophy at the New School for Social Research, New York. His research interests center on feminism, nineteenth and twentieth century continental philosophy, and moral philosophy. His most recent writing has been on the moral implications of embodiment in Hegel and Foucault.

Eoin O'Connell is a doctoral candidate in Fordham University's department of Philosophy. His present area of research is on the role of faith in Kant's practical philosophy. He also serves as Administrative Director of Fordham University's Institute of Irish Studies.

Diane Williamson is currently writing her dissertation at Vanderbilt University on the relationship between emotional intelligence and moral theory. She argues that emotional intelligence is an essentially moral concept and ought to be a central concept for moral theory. Previously, she gained a M.A. in Philosophy from Miami University and a B.A. in Philosophy from Grinnell College. She was nominated as a candidate for the Herz Prize.

Ben Vilhauer is Assistant Professor at William Paterson University. He received his Ph.D. from the University of Chicago in 2002. He works primarily on modern and contemporary free will theory, and he has written a dissertation and several articles on Kant's theory of free will.

Seung-Kee Lee is Associate Professor of Philosophy at Drew University in Madison, New Jersey. His Ph. D. is from The Catholic University of America (2000). He has published papers on Kant's theory of judgment. He is a contributor to the *Kant-Lexikon* (forthcoming).

Oliver Thorndike received his Ph.D. from Johns Hopkins University, Baltimore (2009). He has published "*Ethica deceptrix*: The significance of Baumgarten's notion of a chimerical ethics for the development of Kant's moral philosophy" (2007). Currently he is working on his first book,

"Kant's Transition Project in Practical Philosophy: From Spontaneity to Perception." His academic research experience includes a study conducted for the Berlin Academy of the Sciences investigating the publication of the *Opus postumum* (2001).

Robert Gressis received his Ph.D. in philosophy in 2007 from the University of Michigan where he wrote his dissertation on Kant's theory of evil under the direction of Stephen Darwall. He is a 2007-2008 Postdoctoral Research Associate at the University of Notre Dame's Center for the Philosophy of Religion, where he is working on a project about the meaning of life. His research interests include Kant, ethics, the history of modern philosophy, the philosophy of religion, and the aesthetics of comedy.

Session Chairs

David Cummiskey is Professor of Philosophy at Bates College. His research interests focus on contemporary Kantian ethics, consequentialism, and medical ethics. He is the author of *Kantian Consequentialism* (Oxford, 1996), and is currently working on Asian ethics and international approaches to issues in medical ethics.

Mark Okrent is Professor of Philosophy at Bates College. He is the author of *Heidegger's Pragmatism* (Cornell university Press, 1988) and *Rational Animals: The Teleological Roots of Intentionality* (Ohio University Press, 2007) as well as numerous articles on various topics in metaphysics, the metaphysics of mind, and the history of philosophy. Okrent's work focuses on questions concerning the necessary conditions on intentionality, and especially on the relation between the teleological directedness of action and the intentionality of mental states. In working on these issues he tends to derive insights from two sources, the pragmatic tradition in American philosophy that culminates, (after assimilating the techniques of classical analytic philosophy), in the work of Donald Davidson, and the German transcendental tradition, that culminates in the early work of Martin Heidegger.

Pablo Muchnik is Assistant Professor at Siena College, where he founded the *Symposium on Living Philosophers*, a program dedicated to feature the work of some of the most important contemporary public intellectuals. He was educated in Argentina, received his Ph.D. from the New School for Social Research, NY (2002) and studied a few years in Germany. His areas of specialization include Kant, modern philosophy, and political philosophy. He just finished his first book on Kant's doctrine of radical evil (unpublished), and is co-editing an anthology on this topic with Sharon Anderson-Gold.

Host

Robert B. Louden is Professor of Philosophy at the University of Southern Maine. He is the author of *The World We Want: How and Why the Ideals of the Enlightenment Still Elude Us* (2007), *Kant's Impure Ethics: From Rational Beings to Human Beings* (2000), and *Morality and Moral Theory: A Reappraisal and Reaffirmation*" (1992); co-editor and translator of Kant's *Anthropology, History, and Education* (2007) and Kant's *Lectures on Anthropology* (2008), translator of Kant's *Anthropology from a Pragmatic Point of View* (2006), editor of Schleiermacher's *Lectures on Philosophical Ethics* (2002), and co-editor of *The Greeks and Us* (1996).

Keynote Speaker

Karl Ameriks is McMahon-Hank Professor of Philosophy at Notre Dame. He is the author of *Kant and the Historical Turn* (2006), *Interpreting Kant's Critiques* (2003), *Kant and the Fate of Autonomy* (2000), *Kant's Theory of Mind* (1982; 2nd ed., 2000), editor of *Karl Leonhard Reinhold, Letters on the Kantian Philosophy* (2005), and the *The Cambridge Companion to German Idealism* (2000), co-editor of *The Modern Subject* (1995) and *Kants Ethik.* (2004), and co-translator of Kant's *Lectures on Metaphysics* (1997). Ameriks was the president of the Central Division of the APA and the North American Kant Society, and is co-editor of the series *Cambridge Texts in the History of Philosophy* (1994-) (approx. 70 vols.), and was a founding co-editor of the *International Yearbook of German Idealism*. He is the author of dozens of very influential articles on Kant and German Idealism.